**The joy of cricket: a bat, a ball and an open space are all that
is required to enjoy this most traditional of games.**

First published in 2010
Second edition 2011
Third edition 2012
Fourth edition 2013
Fifth edition 2014

Copyright © Carlton Books Limited 2010, 2011, 2012, 2013, 2014

Carlton Books Limited
20 Mortimer Street
London W1T 3JW

A CIP catalogue record for this book is available from the British Library

10 9 8 7 6 5 4 3 2 1

ISBN: 978-1-78097-560-3

Editor: Martin Corteel
Project art editor: Luke Griffin
Picture research: Paul Langan
Production: Rachel Burgess

Printed in Dubai

WORLD CRICKET RECORDS

FIFTH EDITION

CHRIS HAWKES

CARLTON
BOOKS

CONTENTS

Top: Ragama Herath (Sri Lanka); middle right: Dale Steyn (South Africa); far left: Brad Haddin (Australia); middle: Virat Kohli (India); left: Ian Bell (England).

INTRODUCTION

WELCOME to the fifth edition of a new venture in international cricket publishing – **World Cricket Records**. Ranging across the length and breadth of world cricket and including the men's game, women's cricket and youth cricket, the intention of this book is to explore, explain and intrigue the reader with the people, places and competitions that have made the game of cricket one of the most popular and widespread sports on the planet.

One of the enduring fascinations of the game of cricket, in all its forms (timed matches, limited-overs matches and the new kid on the block, Twenty20 cricket) is that the game can be broken down into the minutest of details. Every ball of every match played in the professional game over the years has been recorded for posterity, meaning that fans from all over the world can dip in and out of the game's records and ascertain any number of facts. Few other sports can be scrutinized to such an extent as cricket.

First and foremost, **World Cricket Records** is not a history book. It is a celebration of both the best and the worst of performances in Test cricket, one-day international cricket, the Twenty20 game, first-class domestic cricket, women's cricket and youth international cricket. It is an exposition of benchmarks – those to which every player in the game would wish to aspire and surpass as well as those that players would want to avoid. For every one of the game's most wanted records, there is a plethora of unwanted ones.

Such a book, of course, would not be possible without the considerable efforts of others. Cricket is blessed with numerous and comprehensive archives, with scorecards and statistics dating back to the game's earliest days in the 19th century. And all are available to the general public at the touch of a button. It has been a privilege to spend months trawling through these archives to find the hidden gems dotted throughout this book, to bring performances that could have been lost in the mists of time back to life and to introduce readers to the feats of players whose achievements could, otherwise, have been consigned to unopened books on dusty shelves. A sport can only be as rich as its history and, in that regard, cricket is blessed with considerable treasures.

Because cricket has become a 12-month sport, there had to be a cut-off point. As such, all statistics in the book are correct as of 6 April 2014.

Particular thanks are also due to Martin Corteel, whose encouragement while putting a book of this type together is both morale-boosting and invaluable, to Jim Lockwood and Luke Griffin for their keen eye for design, to David Ballheimer for his assiduous attention to the minutest of cricketing details, to Paul Langan, for his painstaking search through cricket's photo archives and to Rachel Burgess for her huge efforts with the book's production. This project would not have come together without their considerable input.

Chris Hawkes, London, April 2014

Mitchell Johnson returned to the Australia fold in spectacular style in 2013–14, taking 59 wickets in eight Test matches.

PART I: *TEST CRICKET*

Cricket had been played in various countries around the world for decades, but when, on the morning of Thursday, 15 March 1877, England's Arthur Shaw bowled to Australia's Charles Bannerman in Melbourne, a new phenomenon was born: Test cricket. More than 130 years later, the game has spread around the world and has left an indelible mark wherever it has settled.

Nobody is quite sure how it got its name, but Test cricket is just that: a complete and total test of a player's technique, his mental surety and, particularly in the modern game, his physical prowess. Its enduring fascination to players and spectators, of course, is that it is many other things beyond that: it can be an epic battle between bat and ball; it is a game in which, at any point during the five days, the balance of power can shift in an instant – an awe-inspiring catch, an unplayable delivery, an ill-advised shot or a farcical, out-of-the-blue run-out all have the ability to trigger a magical chain of events that appeared outrageously improbable only moments earlier.

As one might expect, a section on Test cricket's all-time record-breakers contains a legion of the game's most revered names – Donald Bradman, Garfield Sobers, Sachin Tendulkar and Shane Warne to name but four – but there are also some more unusual, less heralded entrants. Who, for example, was the first bowler to take nine wickets in an innings, or which wicketkeeper holds the record for the highest score in Test cricket?

Melbourne, the site for the first Test match in 1877 and still selling out on the big occasion.

TEAM RECORDS

RESULTS SUMMARY

Team	Span	Mat	Won	Lost	Tied	Draw	W/L	%W	%L	%D
Australia	1877–2014	767	360	203	2	202	1.77	46.94	26.47	26.34
Bangladesh	2000–14	83	4	68	0	11	0.05	4.82	81.93	13.25
England	1877–2014	945	336	273	0	336	1.23	35.56	28.89	35.56
India	1932–2014	478	121	151	1	205	0.80	25.31	31.59	42.89
New Zealand	1930–2014	391	75	158	0	158	0.47	19.18	40.41	40.41
Pakistan	1952–2014	380	118	107	0	155	1.10	31.05	28.16	40.79
South Africa	1889–2014	384	140	129	0	115	1.08	36.46	33.59	29.95
Sri Lanka	1982–2014	227	68	81	0	78	0.83	29.96	35.68	34.36
West Indies	1928–2013	495	160	166	1	168	0.96	32.32	33.54	33.94
Zimbabwe	1992–2013	93	11	56	0	26	0.19	11.83	60.22	27.96
ICC World XI	2005	1	0	1	0	0	0.00	0.00	0.00	100.00*

* An ICC World XI played a one-off "Super" Test against Australia in 2005 – the match was given official Test status by the ICC and so appears in all Test records.

The 40-year wait

No country has been forced to endure a longer wait for a series victory than New Zealand. Between the country's first-ever Test match (against England) in 1929 and 1969, they suffered 21 series defeats (with nine drawn) before a draw in the Third Test against Pakistan in Dacca (now in Bangladesh) in November 1969 secured a 1–0 series victory to end their record-breaking sequence of 30 Test series without a victory.

England crush sorry Australia

England, inspired by 22-year-old **Len Hutton** (who made a world record 364), put on a batting masterclass for two-and-a-half days of the final Test of the 1938 Ashes series, played at The Oval. Trailing 1–0 in the series, the home side compiled a massive 903 for 7 in their first innings to leave Australia with a daunting mountain to climb. They failed miserably, falling to 201 all out in their first innings and 123 all out in their second. The margin of defeat – an innings and 579 runs – is the largest (by an innings) in Test history.

The West Indies by a whisker

When Australia's off-spinner Tim May took 5 for 9 in 6.5 overs to help dismiss the West Indies for 146 in the Fourth Test at Adelaide in January 1993, it left the home side needing a modest 186 runs for a victory that would hand them an unassailable 2–0 lead in the five-match series. Australia slipped to 144 for 9, before a rearguard action from May and Craig McDermott brought them within agonizing reach of the winning line. Then tragedy struck: a **Courtney Walsh** (right) delivery found the edge of McDermott's bat; Junior Murray claimed the catch; and the West Indies had won one of the greatest Test matches in history by a single run – the smallest margin of victory (by runs) in Test history.

England off to a flyer

A fine innings of 169 by **Patsy Hendren** helped England to a commanding first-innings score of 521 all out in the first Test of the 1928–29 Ashes series, played at Brisbane. In reply, Australia – featuring debutant Donald Bradman – limped to 122 all out – 399 runs in arrears. England, declining to enforce the follow-on, piled on the pressure, hitting 342 for 8 in their second innings to set Australia an unlikely victory target of 742. The home side wilted under the pressure, subsiding to 66 all out in 25.3 overs to lose by 675 runs – the largest losing margin (by runs) in Test history.

First whitewash

The 1920–21 Ashes series was nothing short of a nightmare for England. They were trounced by 377 runs in Sydney, by an innings and 91 runs in Melbourne, by 119 runs in Adelaide, by eight wickets back in Melbourne, and by nine wickets back in Sydney to become the first team in history to suffer a "whitewash" in a five-

The taming of the Tigers

Having attained Test status in June 2000, Bangladesh's cricketers struggled to establish themselves in the highest echelon of the game. After losing their first-ever Test match (and series) to India, the Tigers went a further 36 Tests and a record-breaking 16 series before recording their first series win. When it finally happened – following a 1–0 series victory against Zimbabwe in January 2005 – it sparked mass celebrations on the streets of cricket-mad Bangladesh.

Pick and mix for England

England simply could not find a winning formula in the 1921 home Ashes series. Defeat by ten wickets at Trent Bridge prompted six changes for the Second Test at Lord's; Australia won the match by eight wickets. Seven changes ensued for the Third Test at Headingley, as well as the appointment of **Lionel Tennyson** as captain; Australia won by 219 runs. Six changes were made at Old Trafford (match drawn) and a further two at The Oval (match drawn), and in all England used 30 different players, a record for a five-match series.

The first tied Test match

In December 1960, in the First Test against the West Indies at Brisbane, the Australians, after holding a 52-run first-innings lead, were set 233 runs to win. They slipped to 92 for 6 before a record-breaking 134-run seventh-wicket stand between Alan Davidson (who became the first player to score 100 runs and take 10 wickets in a Test match) and captain Richie Benaud brought them to within six runs of victory. Then disaster struck: Davidson was run out for 80 and Benaud (52) followed two runs later. Panic set in, and Australia lost their last two wickets – both run-outs – for only four runs. The match had ended in a tie: the first of only two instances of a tied match in Test cricket.

Longest unbeaten streak

With a battery of fast bowlers capable of intimidating any opposition line-up and an array of batting talent to rival any in the game, the West Indies side of the 1980s and early 1990s was the most formidable in modern cricket and, for a period, they were virtually unbeatable. Following their 1–0 series win over England in 1980, the Caribbean side did not lose a series over a 15-year period (in which they lost only 15 Test matches) before finally losing to Australia at home (2–1), in May 1995.

Honours even

When England ended Zimbabwe's second innings on 234 at Bulawayo in December 2006, it left them with a target of 205 runs off 37 overs to secure a 1–0 lead in the two-match series. Often up with the rate, but never comfortably ahead of it, England eventually needed three runs off the final delivery (from Heath Streak) for victory. Nick Knight only managed two and the match – with England on 204 for 6 – ended in a draw. On two occasions a Test has been tied (the side batting last having been bowled out), but this was the first Test match ever to end in a draw with the scores level; the second came between India and the West Indies at Mumbai in November 2011.

A come-from-behind victory for England

Being forced to follow on in the opening Test of the 1894–95 Ashes series, at Sydney, could have left England floundering, but instead it inspired them. Trailing by 263 runs, a fine 117 from Albert Ward was the basis of a fighting second-innings total of 437, before **Bobby Peel** took 6 for 67 to help England dismiss Australia for 166, 11 runs short of their victory target. It was the first of only three instances in Test cricket of a side coming back to win the match after being forced to follow on.

HIGH INNINGS TOTALS: TOP 10

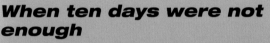

	Team	Score	Overs	RR	Inns	Opposition	Venue	Match start
1	Sri Lanka	952/6d	271.0	3.51	2	India	Colombo	2 Aug 1997
2	England	903/7d	335.2	2.69	1	Australia	The Oval	20 Aug 1938
3	England	849	258.2	3.28	1	West Indies	Kingston	3 Apr 1930
4	West Indies	790/3d	208.1	3.79	2	Pakistan	Kingston	26 Feb 1958
5	Pakistan	765/6d	248.5	3.07	2	Sri Lanka	Karachi	21 Feb 2009
6	Sri Lanka	760/7d	202.4	3.75	2	India		16 Nov 2009
7	Australia	758/8d	245.4	3.08	2	West Indies	Kingston	11 Jun 1955
8	Sri Lanka	756/5d	185.1	4.08	2	South Africa	Colombo	27 Jul 2006
9	West Indies	751/5d	202.0	3.71	1	England	St John's	10 Apr 2004
10	West Indies	749/9d	194.4	3.84	2	England	Bridgetown	26 Feb 2009

When ten days were not enough

Before the 1938–39 series, England and South Africa had agreed to make the Fifth Test, at Durban, "timeless" – played to a conclusion – if the scores going into the final match were level or if either side was one up in the series. England led 1–0. Play got under way on a bright, sunny morning on 3 March 1939. The batsmen had a field day. Ten days later, with the pitch showing few discernible signs of wear, England, chasing 696 for victory, had battled their way to 654 for 5 before play was abandoned at tea on 13 March to allow the England players time to undertake a two-day journey to Cape Town to catch the mail boat home. It remains the highest fourth-innings score in history.

India's batsmen prosper

For six Test matches, between October 1986 and February 1987, all played on Indian soil, India's batsmen were on fire, notching up an all-time record six consecutive scores of 400-plus – with a highest of 676 for 7 declared, including centuries for **Mohammad Azharuddin** (199), Sunil Gavaskar (176) and Kapil Dev (163) against Sri Lanka at Kanpur – before the run finally came to an end after they declared their second innings on 181 for 3 in the drawn Second Test against Pakistan at Kolkata in February 1987.

Digging deep

Faced with a mighty West Indies first-innings total of 575 for 9 declared in the First Test at Bridgetown, Barbados, in January 1958, Pakistan produced a woeful reply, limping to a paltry 106 all out in 42.2 overs. To their great credit, however, they dug deep in spectacular fashion second time round, thanks in no small part to **Hanif Mohammad**'s massive 337, to score 657 for 8 and hold out for a remarkable draw. The difference in runs between the two innings, 551, is the largest in history.

Indian wickets tumble

Already two matches down to England in a four-match series, India travelled to Old Trafford in July 1952 in understandably low spirits. And it showed. After England compiled a steady 347 for 9 declared over two rain-interrupted days, on the third day India slipped to 58 all out and, following on, 82 all out to lose by a mighty innings and 207 runs. They became the first of three Test teams ever to lose all 20 wickets in a single day. **Fred Trueman**, Alec Bedser and Tony Lock took nine, seven and four wickets, respectively.

BELOW: Captains **Andrew Strauss** (right) and **Chris Gayle** (left) discuss the state of play with the umpires. Moments later, the Second Test at Antigua was abandoned.

The shortest match

Much to the West Indies Cricket Board's chagrin, just ten deliveries, 1.4 overs, of the Second Test between the West Indies and England at the Sir Vivian Richards Stadium in Antigua were enough to establish that the sandy outfield was unsafe for bowlers and the match, amid much embarrassment and blame, was abandoned as a draw. The fiasco did produce one record, however: it remains the shortest completed Test match in history.

History-making run-chase

Australia may have slipped from 242 for 0 to 417 all out in their second innings in the Fourth Test against the West Indies at St John's, Antigua, in May 2003, but they would still have fancied their chances of winning the match and securing a 4–0 series victory. The West Indies batsmen had other ideas, however. Chasing 418 – the scores were level after completion of the first innings – and helped by centuries from **Ramnaresh Sarwan** (105) and Shivnarine Chanderpaul (104), the home side cantered to the target with three wickets to spare. It remains the highest successful run-chase in Test history.

Blink and you've missed it

South Africa's 1924 tour to England got off to a dreadful start at Edgbaston. After England had compiled 438 all out, South Africa subsided to a meagre 30 all out in just 12.3 overs – at 75 balls, it remains the shortest completed innings in Test history. They did better second time around (scoring 390), but England still went on to win the game by an innings and 18 runs.

LOWEST TOTALS: TOP 10

	Score	Team	Overs	RR	Inns	Opposition	Venue	Match start
1	26	New Zealand	27.0	0.96	3	England	Auckland	25 Mar 1955
2	30	South Africa	18.4*	1.91	4	England	Port Elizabeth	13 Feb 1896
=	30	South Africa	12.3	2.40	2	England	Birmingham	14 Jun 1924
4	35	South Africa	22.4*	1.84	4	England	Cape Town	1 Apr 1899
5	36	South Africa	23.2	1.54	1	Australia	Melbourne	12 Feb 1932
=	36	Australia	23.0	1.56	2	England	Birmingham	29 May 1902
7	42	New Zealand	39.0	1.07	1	Australia	Wellington	29 Mar 1946
=	42	Australia	37.3#	1.66	2	England	Sydney	10 Feb 1888
=	42	India	17.0	2.47	3	England	Lord's	20 Jun 1974
10	43	South Africa	28.2#	2.26	3	England	Cape Town	25 Mar 1889

* match played with five-ball overs; # match played with four-ball overs

The longest wait for victory

Following an eight-wicket defeat by England in their first-ever Test match, at Christchurch in January 1930, life was tough for New Zealand cricketers. For the next 26 years, over a period of 44 Test matches (a record), New Zealand failed to produce a single Test victory. The magic moment, which saw local offices close and crowds stream into Eden Park, finally arrived in Auckland on 13 March 1956, as New Zealand, already three down in the four-match series, bowled out the West Indies for 77 in the second innings to record their first-ever Test victory, by 190 runs.

Bangladesh just can't shake that losing feeling

The argument that a team can only improve by pitting themselves against the best in the business was sorely tested when Bangladesh were granted Test status in June 2000. The country may have been a mine of untapped talent, but the Tigers' initial forays into Test cricket were nothing short of disastrous. Between 15 November 2001 and 19 February 2004, Bangladesh crashed to a record 21 consecutive defeats (12 of them by an innings or more) before the run came to an end following a rain-hit draw against Zimbabwe in Bulawayo in March 2004.

Australia's record-breaking run without a draw included a 4–1 series win over England in the 2001 Ashes series. **Steve Waugh** holds the trophy after Australia's innings-and-25-run victory in the Fifth Test at The Oval.

Forcing a result

Having a rich, deep seam of talent at their disposal may have been the principal factor, but a large, and much heralded, part of Australia's success in world cricket in recent times was the positive manner in which they approached the game. Their philosophy was one based on attack: to score runs as quickly as possible to give yourself time to bowl out an opponent and force a result. As a consequence, it comes as little surprise that, between October 1999 and August 2001, Australia played out 23 Test matches (20 wins, three defeats) – an all-time record – without recording a single draw.

Most miss-able day's play

The most turgid five-and-a-half hours' play in Test cricket? Look no further than the first day's play of the first-ever Test match between Pakistan and Australia, played at Karachi between 11 and 17 October 1956. Australia won the toss, elected to bat and, mesmerized by the guile of opening bowlers **Fazal Mahmood** (who took 6 for 34 off 27 overs) and Khan Mohammad (4 for 43 off 26.1 overs), produced a 53.1-over crawl to 80 all out. By the close of play, Pakistan had reached 15 for 2 and the day had produced a meagre 95 runs.

Most consecutive draws

In recent times, pitches throughout the Caribbean have come under fire for their inability to produce a result, but this is no new phenomenon. It seems that wickets in the islands were equally lifeless back in the 1970s. Between the last three Tests of the West Indies' five-match series against India in 1970–71, a drawn five-match series against New Zealand in 1971–72, and the first two Test matches of the 1972–73 series against Australia, the West Indies played out ten consecutive draws (all of them at home). The record drawing streak finally came to an end in the Third Test against Australia at Port of Spain in March 1973, which the West Indies lost by 44 runs.

Taking the positive approach

During the 1902–03 Test series in South Africa, Australia's reply to South Africa's first-innings total of 454 in the First Test, played at the Old Wanderers ground in Johannesburg, was all-out attack. And, although they fell for 296 – to trail by 158 runs – and were forced to follow on, they had compiled their total at a record rate of 5.80 runs per over (a record that stands to this day). Australia rallied in their second innings, hitting 372 for 7 – at a more leisurely rate of 4.76 runs per over – to force a draw.

MOST RUNS IN A DAY: TOP 10

	Runs	Team	Opposition	Day	Wkts	Venue	Date
1	588	England	India	2	6	Manchester	25 Jul 1936
2	522	England	South Africa	2	2	Lord's	28 Jun 1924
3	509	Sri Lanka	Bangladesh	2	9	Colombo	21 Jul 2002
4	508	England	South Africa	3	8	The Oval	17 Aug 1935
5	496	England	Pakistan	2	4	Nottingham	1 Jul 1954
6	494	Australia	South Africa	1	6	Sydney	9 Dec 1910
7	492	England	South Africa	2	8	The Oval	17 Aug 1935
8	491	England	New Zealand	3	7	Leeds	11 Jun 1949
9	482	Australia	India	3	10	Sydney	2 Jan 2000
=	482	Australia	South Africa	1	5	Adelaide	22 Nov 2012

RIGHT: Walter Hammond scored 167 of England's 588 runs on the second day of the Second Test against India at Old Trafford in July 1936.

Hitting an all-time low

Just when New Zealand cricket fans thought things could not get much worse – their side had remained winless in 32 matches since the country's first-ever Test match, against England in 1930 – their players hit an all-time low. Facing a meagre first-innings deficit of 46 against England at Auckland in March 1955, and very much in with a chance of getting something out of the match, they capitulated to an all-time Test low score of 26 all out – compiled at an all-time low run-rate of 0.96 runs per over – to hand England victory by an innings and 20 runs.

All in a day's play

There has been no harder day to bat in Test history than on 16 July 1888, the second day of the First Test (of three) between England and Australia, at Lord's. Resuming on 18 for 3 on the second morning, after a rain-affected first day had seen Australia amass a less than confident 116 all out, England limped their way to 53 all out. Australia made 60 in their second innings to set England an achievable 124 runs for victory, but the home side did not come close, slipping to 62 all out to lose the match by 61 runs. A total of 27 wickets fell on the second day, which remains an all-time record in Test cricket.

Beat us if you can

For a period in the early 1980s, the West Indies – powered with the bat by **Viv Richards**, Gordon Greenidge, Desmond Haynes and co at their peak and with the ball by the most fearsome attack in the game's history – were literally unbeatable. From January 1982 (a drawn match against Australia at Sydney) to December 1984 (a draw against the same opposition in Melbourne), the men from the Caribbean did not lose a single one of their 27 matches. It remains the longest unbeaten streak in Test history.

Record-breakers

With a heady mix of batting talent, a world-class wicketkeeper-batsman and a bowling attack (including **Glenn McGrath** and legendary leg-spinner Shane Warne) as complete as any the game has ever seen, Australia dominated world cricket in the late 1990s and the first decade of the new millennium. Twice during that period (between October 1999 and February 2001, and again between December 2005 and January 2008) they put together a sequence of 16 consecutive victories. It is an all-time record in Test cricket.

MOST SIXES IN A MATCH: TOP 10

	6s	Team 1	Team 2	Match winner	Venue	Match start
1	27	Pakistan	India	drawn	Faisalabad	21 Jan 2006
=	27	Bangladesh	New Zealand	drawn	Chittagong	9 Oct 2013
3	23	New Zealand	England	England	Christchurch	13 Mar 2002
4	22	Pakistan	New Zealand	drawn	Karachi	30 Oct 1976
=	22	West Indies	South Africa	drawn	Basseterre	18 June 2010
6	21	Australia	England	Australia	Adelaide	5 Dec 2013
7	20	India	Sri Lanka	India	Mumbai	2 Dec 2009
=	20	Zimbabwe	New Zealand	New Zealand	Dhaka	1 Nov 2011
=	20	Bangladesh	Sri Lanka	Sri Lanka	Dhaka	27 Jan 2014

There have 19 sixes in a match on nine occasions.

LEFT: **Brad Haddin** hit five of Australia's 21 sixes in the match during the Second Test against England at Adelaide in December 2013.

Most ducks recorded in a single innings

The record for the most ducks in a single innings is six, an event that has occurred on three occasions, all of them in the subcontinent. First in December 1980, when Pakistan slipped to 128 all out against the West Indies in the First Test in Karachi; second when South Africa collapsed to 105 all out and defeat in their fourth innings against India in Ahmedabad in November 1996; and third when Bangladesh slumped to 80 all out in their second innings against the West Indies in Dacca in December 2002 to lose by a mighty innings and 310 runs.

Chipping in for the cause

Facing a first-innings deficit of 48 (which could have been far worse given that they were all out for 75 on the first day), England required a more fruitful second innings in the second Test against Australia at Melbourne in December 1894 if they wanted to maintain or extend their 1–0 series lead. Their 475 all out was significant for two reasons: it helped them seal a 2–0 Ashes series lead and was the first instance in Test history (of 12) of all 11 batsmen making double figures in a single innings.

Finding the boundary rope

High-scoring draws are not always the most palatable affairs for spectators, but the drawn Fourth Test match between Australia and India at Sydney in January 2004 was notable for more than the consistently high standard of batting on display. Of the 1,747 runs scored in the match, 952 of them came from 238 fours – the most in Test history.

Sixes galore

Aided in no small part by **Matthew Hayden**'s then world record contribution of 380, Australia's massive first-innings total of 735 for 6 declared (the 12th highest innings total of all time) against Zimbabwe at Perth in October 2003 contained a single-innings record 17 sixes – Hayden struck 11 of them, Steve Waugh and Darren Lehmann hit one each, and wicketkeeper-batsman Adam Gilchrist plundered the other four.

All 11 fail to make a mark

South Africa's sorry 75-ball capitulation to 30 all out against England in the First Test in June 1924, at Edgbaston – the shortest completed innings (by balls) in history – was significant for another reason: it remains the only instance in Test history in which all 11 batsmen failed to make a double-figure score (extras were the top scorer with 11).

Record-shattering performance

Memorable principally for being the highest innings total and containing the highest partnership in Test history (**Mahela Jayawardene**, left, and **Kumar Sangakkara**'s, facing camera, epic second-wicket stand of 624), Sri Lanka's colossal first-innings total of 952 for 6 declared in the First Test against India at Colombo in July 2006 also broke the record for the most fours scored in a single innings (109) as well as the record for the most runs scored in an innings from fours and sixes (448).

Running riot

There have been two instances in Test cricket of five batsmen scoring a century in a single innings. The first came at Kingston, Jamaica, in June 1955, when Australia's Colin McDonald (127), Neil Harvey (204), Keith Miller (109), Ron Archer (128) and Richie Benaud (121) all passed three figures against the West Indies in the Fifth Test. The second came at Multan, Pakistan, in August 2001, when the home side's Saeed Anwar (101), Taufeeq Umar (104), Inzamam-ul-Haq (105), Mohammad Yousuf (102 not out) and Abdul Razzaq (110 not out) ran riot against an inexperienced Bangladesh attack in the First Test.

Combining to great effect

Remembered as the match in which Arthur Morris (182) and Don Bradman (173) combined with devastating effect in the fourth innings to chase down a then world record victory target of 404 to secure an unassailable 3–0 lead in the 1948 Ashes series, the Third Test at Headingley – in which England, despite defeat, scored a commendable 861 runs – also saw the record for the most century partnerships in a single Test match (eight – five by England and three by Australia).

Getting off to a good start

The maxim that the foundations of a good innings are more than often based on a solid opening partnership has been around for many years, but it wasn't until August 1899 – 22 years and 63 matches after the first-ever Test match – that two openers from the same team both scored a century in the same innings in a Test match. Stanley Jackson (118) and **Tom Hayward** (137) got England off to a flying start against Australia in the Fifth Test at The Oval, posting an opening partnership of 185. England could not capitalize on the situation, however, the match ended in a draw and Australia clinched the series 1–0.

A run-fest in Antigua

Already holding an unassailable 2–0 lead in the four-Test series, South Africa would have been more than happy with their first-innings total of 588 for 6 – including centuries for A.B. de Villiers (114), Graeme Smith (126), Jacques Kallis (147) and Ashwell Prince (131) – in the Fourth Test at St John's, Antigua, in April–May 2005. But rather than capitulating, the West Indies batsmen dug deep and carved out a magnificent 747 in reply, with **Chris Gayle** (317), Ramnaresh Sarwan (127), Shivnarine Chanderpaul (127) and Dwayne Bravo (107) all passing three figures. The eight centuries scored in the match (which ended in a draw) is an all-time record.

Giving everyone a go

With the game long since destined for a draw, the Third Test (of five) between South Africa and England, at Cape Town in January 1965, produced a cricket peculiarity. During South Africa's second innings, which put the result beyond doubt, all ten England fielders had bowled. Then, with England needing an impossible 406 runs to win off eight overs, South Africa's captain **Trevor Goddard** elected to bowl the four members of his side who had not bowled in the first innings. For the only time in Test history, all 20 fielders had bowled in the match.

Unwanted record for makeshift keeper

In the final Test at The Oval in 1934, with the Ashes series locked at 1–1, England went in to bat facing a massive Bradman- and Ponsford-inspired Australian first-innings total of 701. Things really started to unravel for the home side after their wicket-keeper Les Ames was forced to retire hurt with a strained back and took no further part in the game. England fell to 321 all out. Australia, electing not to enforce the follow-on, batted again, scoring 327 – an innings that saw 47-year-old Frank Woolley take over the gloves for England (and concede a world record 37 byes) – to set England an improbable 708 runs for victory. They did not come close, capitulating to 145 all out as Australia won by 562 runs to regain the Ashes.

Combining to great effect

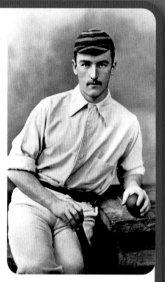

It is a captain's dream: not one but two of his bowlers firing on all cylinders to send an opponent packing. There have been 52 instances in Test cricket of two bowlers taking five wickets in the same innings, the first of which occurred in February 1887, in the 26th Test match in history, when Australia's **J.J. Ferris** (5 for 71) and Charlie Turner (5 for 41) combined to dismiss England for 151 in their first innings at Sydney. Not that the pair's effort changed the course of the match, however. England's George Lohmann took 10 wickets of his own (for 87 runs) as the visitors won the match by 71 runs to take a 2–0 series lead.

Most wides in a match

The opening second-innings stand of 223 between **Phil Jacques** (left, 108) and **Simon Katich** (right, 157), which effectively batted the West Indies out of the game, took all the plaudits as Australia won the Third and final Test match by 87 runs at Bridgetown, Barbados, in June 2008 to win the series 2–0. Newspaper reports at the time failed to point the finger of blame at the West Indies' bowling attack, but perhaps they should have done, as during the match they bowled an all-time record 34 wides.

Most players out caught

A more common phenomenon than one might think, there have been 58 instances in Test cricket – the first happening in the Second Test between Australia and England at Melbourne in January 1904 – in which all ten batsmen have been out caught in the same innings. The record for the most players caught in a match is 33, in the Fifth Test between Australia and India at Perth in February 1992.

Finding the target

It may be that batsmen's techniques have improved over the years or that modern-day cricketers simply do not bowl straight enough, but both instances in Test history of nine players being bowled out in the same innings occurred in the 19th century. First at Cape Town in March 1889, when England bowled out South Africa for 43 in their second innings; and then in August 1890, when England dismissed Australia for 102 in the second innings of the Second Test, played at The Oval.

MOST EXTRAS IN AN INNINGS: TOP 10

	Extras	(b, lb, w, nb)	Team	Opposition	Venue	Match start
1	76	(35, 26, 0, 15)	Pakistan	India	Bangalore	8 Dec 2007
2	74	(35, 12, 11, 16)	West Indies	England	Port of Spain	6 Mar 2009
3	71	(21, 8, 4, 38)	Pakistan	West Indies	Georgetown	2 Apr 1988
4	68	(29, 11, 0, 28)	Pakistan	West Indies	Bridgetown	18 Feb 1977
5	65	(10, 18, 1, 36)	Zimbabwe	Sri Lanka	Harare	11 Oct 1994
6	64	(4, 18, 6, 36)	South Africa	Pakistan	Johannesburg	19 Jan 1995
=	64	(18, 11, 1, 34)	England	West Indies	Manchester	27 Jul 1995
=	64	(12, 25, 0, 27)	India	West Indies	Kolkata	26 Dec 1987
=	64	(25, 21, 5, 13)	South Africa	England	Lord's	31 Jul 2003
10	63	(11, 34, 3, 15)	England	India	Birmingham	10 Aug 2011

An incidental record

The Third Test between England and South Africa at Edgbaston in July–August 2008 will best be remembered for the ruthless manner in which South Africa, inspired by captain Graeme Smith's unbeaten 154, chased down a victory target of 281. The five-wicket win saw South Africa take an unassailable 2–0 lead in the four-match series, prompting the tearful resignation of long-standing England captain Michael Vaughan. It is South Africa's first-innings total of 314 all out that makes the record books, however, as it contained a world record 35 leg-byes.

Most players out lbw in a single Test match

Umpires Billy Bowden and Tony Hill had never been busier than during the First Test between the West Indies and Pakistan at Guyana in May 2011. During the match, which the West Indies won by 40 runs to take a 1–0 lead in the two-match series, the pair combined to give 20 players out lbw – a record for a Test match. The record for the most batsmen out lbw in a single Test innings is seven, an event that has occurred on two occasions: Zimbabwe against England at Chester-le-Street in June 2003; and New Zealand against Australia at Christchurch in March 2005.

Overstepping the mark

The First Test of the five-match series between the West Indies and Pakistan in 1976–77 got off to an exhilarating start at the Kensington Oval, Bridgetown, Barbados. In a high-scoring match, the home side – set 306 runs for victory – clung on for a hard-fought draw. The game has forced its way into the record books for another reason, however. As bowlers strained every sinew to force a breakthrough, no-balls blighted the game, a staggering 103 of them, an all-time record. The total number of extras conceded in the match – 173 (b37, lb31, w2, nb103) – is also a record.

RIGHT: *The 35 byes conceded by wicketkeeper* **Dinesh Kartik** *was a major factor in India conceding a world-record 35 byes against Pakistan in December 2007.*

Run-out madness

The run-out is possibly the most demoralizing dismissal in cricket; a basic misjudgement that leads to the cheap loss of a wicket. Losing one player to a run-out in an innings may be bad enough, but over the years four players have been run out in a single innings on two occasions: India against Pakistan at Peshawar in February 1955; and Australia against the West Indies at Adelaide in January 1969. On both occasions the match ended in a draw.

Two-man attack

Monty Noble (left, 7 for 17 and 6 for 60) and **Hugh Trumble** (right, 3 for 38 and 4 for 49) were the scourge of England's batsmen in the Second Test at Melbourne in January 1902, combining to devastating effect as Australia won the match by 229 runs to level the Ashes series at 1–1. It was the first of six instances in Test cricket in which two bowlers have taken all 20 wickets in a match.

GROUND RECORDS

Ground	Span	Mat
Lord's, London, England	1884–2013	127
Melbourne Cricket Ground, Australia (below left)	1877–2013	106
Sydney Cricket Ground, Australia	1882–2014	102
Kennington Oval, London, England (below, right)	1880–2013	96
Old Trafford, Manchester, England	1884–2013	75
Adelaide Oval, Australia	1884–2013	72
Headingley, Leeds, England	1899–2013	72
Trent Bridge, Nottingham, England	1899–2013	59
Queen's Park Oval, Port of Spain, Trinidad, West Indies	1930–2012	58
Woolloongabba, Brisbane, Australia	1931–2013	56
Basin Reserve, Wellington, New Zealand	1930–2014	56
Newlands, Cape Town, South Africa	1889–2014	51
Kensington Oval, Bridgetown, Barbados, West Indies	1930–2013	49
Eden Park, Auckland, New Zealand	1930–2014	49
Edgbaston, Birmingham, England	1902–2012	47
Sabina Park, Kingston, Jamaica, West Indies	1930–2012	46
National Stadium, Karachi, Pakistan	1955–2009	41
W.A.C.A. Ground, Perth, Australia	1970–2013	41
AMI Stadium, Christchurch, New Zealand	1930–2006	40
Gaddafi Stadium, Lahore, Pakistan	1959–2009	40
Kingsmead, Durban, New Zealand	1923–2013	40
Eden Gardens, Kolkata, India	1934–2013	39
Sinhalese Sports Club Ground, Colombo, Sri Lanka	1984–2012	36
The Wanderers Stadium, Johannesburg, South Africa	1956–2013	35
Feroz Shah Kotla, Delhi, India	1948–2013	32
MA Chidambaram Stadium, Chepauk, Chennai, India	1934–2013	31
Harare Sports Club, Harare, Zimbabwe	1992–2013	31
Bourda, Georgetown, Guyana, West Indies	1930–2005	30
St George's Park, Port Elizabeth, South Africa	1889–2014	25
Iqbal Stadium, Faisalabad, Pakistan	1978–2006	24
Wankhede Stadium, Mumbai, India	1975–2013	24
Old Wanderers, Johannesburg, South Africa	1896–1939	22
Antigua Recreation Ground, St John's, Antigua, W.Indies	1981–2009	22
Galle International Stadium, Galle, Sri Lanka	1998–2013	22
Green Park, Kanpur, India	1952–2009	21
Asgiriya Stadium, Kandy, Sri Lanka	1983–2007	21
M.Chinnaswamy Stadium, Bangalore, India	1974–2012	20
Seddon Park, Hamilton, New Zealand	1991–2013	20
Queens Sports Club, Bulawayo, Zimbabwe	1994–2011	19
SuperSport Park, Centurion, South Africa	1995–2014	19
Brabourne Stadium, Mumbai, India	1948–2009	18
Bangabandhu National Stadium, Dhaka, Bangladesh	1955–2005	17
P Sara Oval, Colombo, Sri Lanka	1982–2012	17
Sardar Patel (Gujarat) Stadium, Ahmedabad, India	1983–2012	12
Bellerive Oval, Hobart, Australia	1989–2012	11
Punjab C.A. Stadium, Mohali, Chandigarh, India	1994–2013	11
Z.A. Chowdhury Stadium, Chittagong, Bangladesh	2006–2014	11
Shere Bangla National Stadium, Dhaka, Bangladesh	2007–2014	11
Carisbrook, Dunedin, New Zealand	1955–1997	10
McLean Park, Napier, New Zealand	1979–2012	10
Nehru Stadium, Madras, India	1956–1965	9
Vidarbha C.A. Ground, Nagpur, India	1969–2006	9
R.Premadasa Stadium, Colombo, Sri Lanka	1992–2013	8
Rawalpindi Cricket Stadium, Rawalpindi, Pakistan	1993–2004	8

Ground	Span	Mat
M.A. Aziz Stadium, Chittagong, Bangladesh	2001–2005	8
Ellis Park, Johannesburg, South Africa	1948–1954	6
Arbab Niaz Stadium, Peshawar, Pakistan	1995–2003	6
Sharjah C.A. Stadium, Sharjah, UAE	2002–2014	6
University Oval, Dunedin, New Zealand	2008–2013	6
Dubai International Cricket Stadium, Dubai, UAE	2010–2014	6
Niaz Stadium, Hyderabad, India	1973–1984	5
Multan Cricket Stadium, Multan, Pakistan	2001–2006	5
Riverside Ground, Chester-le-Street, England	2003–2013	5
Sheikh Zayed Stadium, Abu Dhabi, UAE	2010–2014	5
Lord's, Durban, South Africa	1910–1921	4
Jinnah Stadium, Sialkot, Pakistan	1985–1995	4
Tyronne Fernando Stadium, Moratuwa, Sri Lanka	1992–1993	4
Chevrolet Park, Bloemfontein, South Africa	1999–2008	4
Vidarbha Cricket Association Stadium, Nagpur, India	2008–2012	4
Bagh-e-Jinnah, Lahore, Pakistan	1955–1959	3
Lal Bahadur Shastri Stadium, Hyderabad, India	1955–1988	3
Colombo Cricket Club Ground, Colombo, Sri Lanka	1984–1987	3
Beausejour Cricket Ground, Gros Islet, St Lucia, W.Indies	2003–2006	3
Warner Park, Basseterre, St Kitts, West Indies	2006–2011	3
Sir Vivian Richards Stadium, North Sound, Antigua	2008–2012	3
Rajiv Gandhi International Stadium, Hyderabad, India	2010–2013	3
Pallekele International Cricket Stadium, Sri Lanka	2010–2012	3
Windsor Park, Roseau, Dominica, West Indies	2011–2013	3
Exhibition Ground, Brisbane, Australia	1928–1931	2
Barabati Stadium, Cuttack, India	1987–1995	2
Sheikhupura Stadium, Sheikhupura, Pakistan	1996–1997	2

Ground	Span	Mat
Arnos Vale Ground, Kingstown, St Vincent, W.Indies	1997–2009	2
National Cricket Stadium, St George's, Grenada	2002–2009	2
Marrara Cricket Ground, Darwin, Australia	2003–2004	2
Cazaly's Stadium, Cairns, Australia	2003–2004	2
Providence Stadium, Guyana, West Indies	2008–2011	2
Sophia Gardens, Cardiff, Wales	2009–2011	2
Bramall Lane, Sheffield, England	1902–1902	1
Gymkhana Ground, Mumbai, India	1933–1933	1
University Ground, Lucknow, India	1952–1952	1
Bahawal Stadium, Bahawalpur, Pakistan	1955–1955	1
Peshawar Club Ground, Peshawar, India	1955–1955	1
Pindi Club Ground, Rawalpindi, Pakistan	1965–1965	1
Ibn-e-Qasim Bagh Stadium, Multan, Pakistan	1980–1981	1
Gandhi Stadium, Jalandhar, India	1983–1983	1
Sawai Mansingh Stadium, Jaipur, India	1987–1987	1
Sector 16 Stadium, Chandigarh, India	1990–1990	1
Jinnah Stadium, Gujranwala, Pakistan	1991–1991	1
Bulawayo Athletic Club, Bulaway, Zimbabwe	1992–1992	1
Southend Club Cricket Stadium, Karachi, Pakistan	1993–1993	1
K.D.Singh 'Babu' Stadium, Lucknow, India	1994–1994	1
Buffalo Park, East London, South Africa	2002–2002	1
Senwes Park, Potchefstroom, South Africa	2002–2002	1
Shaheed Chandu Stadium, Bogra, Bangladesh	2006–2006	1
Narayanganj Osmani Stadium, Fatullah, Bangladesh	2006–2006	1
The Rose Bowl, Southampton, England	2011–2011	1
Sheikh Abu Naser Stadium, Khulna, Bangladesh	2012–2012	1

BATTING RECORDS

MOST CAREER RUNS: TOP 10

Pos	Player	Span	Mat	Inns	NO	Runs	HS	Ave	100	50	0
1	S.R. Tendulkar (Ind)	1989–2013	200	329	33	15,921	248*	53.78	51	68	14
2	R.T. Ponting (Aus)	1995–2012	168	287	29	13,378	257	51.85	41	62	17
3	J.H. Kallis (ICC/SA)	1995–2013	166	280	40	13,289	224	55.37	45	58	16
4	R. Dravid (ICC/Ind)	1996–2012	164	286	32	13,288	270	52.31	36	63	8
5	B.C. Lara (ICC/WI)	1990–2006	131	232	6	11,953	400*	52.88	34	48	17
6	D.P.M.D. Jayawardene (SL)	1997–2014	143	240	15	11,319	374	50.30	33	46	14
7	S. Chanderpaul (WI)	1994–2013	153	261	45	11,219	203*	51.93	29	62	14
8	A.R. Border (Aus)	1978–1994	156	265	44	11,174	205	50.56	27	63	11
9	K.C. Sangakkara (SL)	2000–14	122	209	17	11,151	319	58.07	35	45	9
10	S.R. Waugh (Aus)	1985–2004	168	260	46	10,927	200	51.06	32	50	22

Lindsay's heroics help South Africa sink Australia

South Africa's epic 3–1 home series victory over Australia in 1966–67 created many legends – Graeme Pollock (with 537 runs) and Trevor Goddard (with 26 wickets) for example – but the real star of the series was South Africa wicketkeeper Denis Lindsay, whose 606 runs at an average of 86.57 (with three centuries, including an innings of 182 in the First Test at Johannesburg) remains the highest series total by a wicket-keeper in Test history.

Prospering on home turf

It would be safe to assume that the Sinhalese Sports Club ground in Colombo is the former Sri Lanka captain **Mahele Jayawardene**'s favourite venue. Since playing there for the first time in 1997, the right-hander has scored ten centuries and eight 50s at the ground (with a highest score of 374 against South Africa in July 2006) and amassed 2,698 runs (at an average of 77.08). It is the highest amount of runs scored by a player at a single ground in Test history.

Gillespie shows the way

Under normal circumstances, the most one could expect from a nightwatchman would be to see out the last few overs of a day and then to add a few quick runs the following morning before leaving the serious business of batting to the batsmen. But after successfully negotiating the final 6.4 overs of the first day (5 not out overnight) of the Second Test against Bangladesh at Chittagong in April 2006, and adding a further 14 runs on a rain-affected second day, Australia's nightwatchman Jason Gillespie had other ideas. The next day, Gillespie added 83 runs to record his first Test century; on day four, incredibly, he reached 201 not out before Australia decided to declare. It is the highest-ever score by a night-watchman in Test cricket.

Gooch's Indian summer

Graham Gooch, the 11th-highest run-scorer of all time in Test cricket, reached the peak of his considerable powers in the First Test (of three) against India, at Lord's, in 1990. Leading by example, the England captain smashed 333 in the first innings and plundered a 113-ball 125 in the second as England romped to victory by 247 runs. The Essex man's 456 runs in the match is an all-time Test record.

A year to remember

In 2006, **Mohammad Yousuf** produced the best 12 months of batting form Test cricket has ever seen. He started the year with a century (173 against India in Lahore) and ended it in the same fashion (with a match-winning 124 against the West Indies in Karachi). In between times, the Pakistan right-hander registered nine centuries (a record for a calendar year), with a highest of 202 against England at Lord's, and amassed 1,788 runs – an all-time Test record for runs scored in a calendar year.

Test cricket's most productive over

While six sixes in an over have been achieved in one-day international cricket (Herschelle Gibbs), Twenty20 international cricket (Yuvraj Singh) and first-class cricket (Garfield Sobers and Ravi Shastri), to date no one has completed the feat in Test cricket. The most runs scored off an over is 28, achieved on two occasions: by Brian Lara off South Africa's slow left-armer Robin Peterson at Johannesburg in December 2003 and by Australia's George Bailey equalled Lara's feat off the bowling of England's James Anderson at Perth in the 2013–14 Ashes series.

Lone resistance

It is not often that a batsman of a team that has just lost a Test match early on the fifth day takes all the plaudits, but the whole world knew that Sri Lanka's ten-wicket victory over the West Indies in the Third Test at Colombo in November–December 2001 would have been far greater had it not been for the efforts of Brian Lara. The Trinidad left-hander hit 221 (of 390) in the first innings and 130 (of 262) in the second. His 351 runs in the match are the most in Test history by any player to end up on the losing side.

The Don plunders the England attack

That Australia recovered from losing the opening match of the 1930 series against England to regain the Ashes had much to do with the formidable talent of **Donald Bradman**. Not that the New South Wales batsman could have been blamed in any way for the 93-run defeat at Trent Bridge, scoring as he did 195 of Australia's 479 runs. His good form continued at Lord's, where his first-innings 254 did much to secure an Australian seven-wicket victory. At a drawn match at Headingley, the Don plundered a then world record score of 334 (including a record 309 runs on the first day). He failed in the rain-affected Fourth Test at Old Trafford, but resumed normal service with a sublime 232 runs in the deciding Test at The Oval; the innings was a major factor in Australia's innings-and-39-run victory. Bradman's 974 runs in the series (at an average of 139.14) is an all-time record.

Flower blooms in Nagpur

If you had to pick one innings to confirm Zimbabwe wicket-keeper-batsman Andy Flower's credentials as a Test player of the highest quality, the obvious choice would be his second-innings performance against India in the Second Test at Nagpur in November 2000. Striding to the crease with his side in dire straits at 61 for 3, still 156 runs behind after following on, Flower dug deep for over nine hours, hitting an unbeaten 232 to take his side to 503 for 6 and safety. It is the highest individual score by a wicketkeeper in Test history.

Lara's moment of magic

England's bowlers had every reason to be sick of the sight of **Brian Lara** in the 1990s and after the turn of the century. In April 1994, at St John's, Antigua, the left-hander had plundered a world record 375 off their bowlers; a decade later at the same venue – having lost his record to Australia's Matthew Hayden (380 v Zimbabwe at Perth in October 2003) – the West Indies maestro did it again, smashing England's frustrated bowlers for 43 fours and four sixes en route to a world record score of 400 not out.

HIGHEST CAREER BATTING AVERAGE: TOP 10

Pos	Ave	Player	Career span	Mat	Inns	NO	Runs	HS	100	50	0
1	99.94	D.G. Bradman (Aus)	1928–48	52	80	10	6,996	334	29	13	7
2	60.97	R.G. Pollock (SA)	1963–70	23	41	4	2,256	274	7	11	1
3	60.83	G.A. Headley (WI)	1930–54	22	40	4	2,190	270*	10	5	2
4	60.73	H. Sutcliffe (Eng)	1924–35	54	84	9	4,555	194	16	23	2
5	59.23	E. Paynter (Eng)	1931–39	20	31	5	1,540	243	4	7	3
6	58.92	C.A. Pujara (Ind)	2010–14	19	32	4	1,650	206*	6	4	0
7	58.67	K.F. Barrington (Eng)	1955–68	82	131	15	6,806	256	20	35	5
8	58.61	E.D. Weekes (WI)	1948–58	48	81	5	4,455	207	15	19	6
9	58.45	W.R. Hammond (Eng)	1927–47	85	140	16	7,249	336*	22	24	4
10	58.07	K.C. Sangakkara (SL)	2000–14	122	209	17	11,151	319	35	45	9

Foster in tip-top form

One of seven brothers to represent Worcestershire before the First World War, **Tip (Reginald Erskine) Foster** was undoubtedly the most talented of them. The highlight of his brief eight-Test career came at Sydney, in the opening Test of the 1903–04 Ashes series, when he became the first player in Test history to pass the 250-run mark, hitting 287 – a figure that would remain as Test cricket's highest individual score for the next 26 years.

Bowing out in style

Often forced to play second fiddle to opening partner Jack Hobbs during his England career, **Andy Sandham** bowed out of Test cricket (after 14 Tests over nine years) with a truly headline-grabbing performance. As England piled on a massive 849 in their first innings against the West Indies at Kingston, Jamaica, in April 1930, Sandham, in his 40th year, batted for 10 hours, faced 640 balls and hit 28 fours en route to becoming the first player in Test history to score a triple-century. His innings of 325 remained a Test best for less than three months.

Top of the class

In the history of Test cricket, two players have scored a hundred in both innings of a Test match on three separate occasions: Sunil Gavaskar (124 and 220, India against the West Indies at Port of Spain in April 1971; 111 and 137, India against Pakistan at Karachi in November 1978; 107 and 182 not out, India against the West Indies at Kolkata in December 1978); and **Ricky Ponting** (149 and 104 not out, Australia against the West Indies at Brisbane in November 2005; 120 and 143 not out, Australia against South Africa at Sydney in January 2006; 103 and 116, Australia against South Africa at Durban in March 2006).

Dramatic debuts

Five players have made a double-century in their first-ever Test match: Tip Foster (287 for England against Australia at Sydney in December 1903); Lawrence Rowe (214 for the West Indies against New Zealand at Kingston, Jamaica, in February 1972); Brendon Kuruppu (201 not out for Sri Lanka against New Zealand at Colombo in April 1987); **Mathew Sinclair** (214 for New Zealand against the West Indies at Wellington in December 1999); and Jacques Rudolph (222 not out for South Africa against Bangladesh at Chittagong in April 2003).

Off to a blistering start

Test cricket did not have to wait long to witness the first-ever century. Indeed, the man who faced the first-ever ball in Test cricket, Australia's **Charles Bannerman** (against England at Melbourne in March 1877), went on to bat for a further four-and-three-quarter hours before retiring hurt on 165 (out of an Australian total of 245 all out). Australia went on to win the low-scoring match by 45 runs.

Starting as you mean to go on

Hometown boy Lawrence Rowe made the most impressive start to an international career in Test history against New Zealand at Sabina Park, Kingston, Jamaica, in February 1972. Unleashing a barrage of trademark cuts and pulls, the elegant right-hander made 214 in the first innings of the match and an unbeaten century in the second; his 314 runs in the match are the most by any player on debut in Test history. Rowe went on to make 30 Test appearances for the West Indies over eight years.

Finishing with a flourish

Having seen his side reach an overwhelmingly dominant position in the Second Test against South Africa at Auckland in March 2004 – requiring just 54 runs for victory in their second innings – Kiwi captain **Stephen Fleming** decided to produce some fireworks. His 31 off 11 balls, which took his side past the winning line for the first time against South Africa on home soil, was hit at a rate of 281.81 runs per 100 balls – the highest strike-rate in an innings in Test history.

Two hundreds in a match

That Australia held out for a draw in serene fashion in the Fifth Test of the 1909 Ashes campaign at The Oval to complete a 2–1 series victory had much to do with the history-making performance of opener, Warren Bardsley. The New South Wales left-hander hit 136 in the first innings and 130 in the second to become the first player in Test history to score a century in both innings of a match, a feat since repeated on 71 occasions.

Leading by example

His country's finest batsman of the early 1880s and team captain, Billy Murdoch led the way as Australia put England's bowlers to the sword in the first innings of the Third Test at The Oval in August 1884. As the visitors compiled an accomplished 551 all out, Murdoch batted for 490 minutes, faced 525 balls and struck 24 fours en route to becoming the first player in Test history to score a double-century (211). England recovered well, however, to claim a draw and a 1–0 series win.

Ending a 92-year wait

In February 1969, at Sydney, Australia's Doug Walters made history. In the first innings of the Fifth Test against the West Indies he struck a majestic 242; he then crafted a patient 103 in the second innings to become, in the 646th Test match, the first player in 92 years of Test cricket to record a double-century and a century in the same match. Six players (Sunil Gavaskar, Lawrence Rowe, Greg Chappell, Graham Gooch, Brian Lara and Kumar Sangakkara) have gone on to emulate the feat.

MOST HUNDREDS IN A CAREER: TOP 10

Pos	100s	Player	Career span	Mat	Inns	NO	Runs	HS	Ave	50	0
1	51	**S.R. Tendulkar** (India)	1989–2013	200	329	33	15,921	248*	53.78	68	14
2	45	J.H. Kallis (ICC/SA)	1995–2013	166	280	40	13,289	224	55.37	58	16
3	41	R.T. Ponting (Aus)	1995–2012	168	287	29	13,378	257	51.85	62	17
4	36	R. Dravid (ICC/Ind)	1996–2012	164	286	32	13,288	270	52.31	63	8
5	35	K.C. Sangakkara (SL)	2000–14	122	209	17	11,151	319	58.07	45	9
6	34	S.M. Gavaskar (Ind)	1971–87	125	214	16	10,122	236*	51.12	45	12
=	34	B.C. Lara (ICC/WI)	1990–2006	131	232	6	11,953	400*	52.88	48	17
8	33	D.P.M.D. Jayawardene (SL)	1997–2014	143	240	15	11,319	374	50.30	46	14
9	32	S.R. Waugh (Aus)	1985–2004	168	260	46	10,927	200	51.06	50	22
10	30	M.L. Hayden (Aus)	1994–2009	103	184	14	8,625	380	50.73	29	14

MOST HUNDREDS AGAINST ONE TEAM: TOP 10

Pos	100	Player	Opponent	Mat	Inns	NO	Runs	HS	Ave
1	19	D.G. Bradman (Aus)	England (1928–48)	37	63	7	5,028	334	89.78
2	13	S.M. Gavaskar (Ind)	West Indies (1971–83)	27	48	6	2,749	236*	65.45
3	12	J.B. Hobbs (Eng)	Australia (1908–30)	41	71	4	3,636	187	54.26
4	11	S.R. Tendulkar (Ind)	Australia (1991–2012)	35	67	7	3,438	241*	57.30
5	10	G.S. Sobers (WI)	England (1954–74)	36	61	8	3,214	226	60.64
=	10	S.R. Waugh (Aus)	England (1986–2003)	46	73	18	3,200	177*	58.18
7	9	S.R. Tendulkar (Ind)	Sri Lanka (1990–2010)	25	36	3	1,995	203	60.45
=	9	R.B. Richardson (WI)	Australia (1984–95)	29	48	4	2,175	182	49.43
=	9	W.R. Hammond (Eng)	Australia (1928–47)	33	58	3	2,852	251	51.85
=	9	B.C. Lara (ICC/WI)	Australia (1992–2005)	31	58	2	2,856	277	51.00
=	9	G.S. Chappell (Aus)	England (1970–83)	35	65	8	2,619	144	45.94
=	9	D.I. Gower (Eng)	Australia (1978–91)	42	77	4	3,269	215	44.78
=	9	K.C. Sangakkara (SL)	Pakistan (2002–14)	19	37	6	2,486	230	80.19

A good morning's work

There have been four instances in history of a player scoring a century before lunch on the first day of a Test match: Victor Trumper, 103 not out for Australia against England at Lord's in 1902; Charlie Macartney, 112 not out for Australia against England at Leeds in 1926; Donald Bradman, 105 not out for Australia against England at Leeds in 1930; and Majid Khan, 108 not out for Pakistan against New Zealand at Karachi in 1976.

Six in a row

When **Donald Bradman** passed three figures (103) in Australia's first innings against England at Headingley in July 1938, he achieved something that no player before or since has equalled. Starting with the Third Test match of the 1936–37 Ashes series at Melbourne, Bradman had recorded a century in six consecutive matches. Three players (Jacques Kallis, Mohammad Yousuf and Gautham Gambhir) have scored centuries in five consecutive matches.

Test cricket's youngest-ever centurion

In general, Bangladesh's early forays in the Test arena brought them nothing but disappointment, but there were some brighter moments, notably in September 2001 in the Second Test against Sri Lanka at Colombo. The record books may show that the home side cantered to an innings-and-137-run victory, but Bangladesh's second-innings score of 328 (after a pitiful 90 all out in their first innings) provided a moment of history. Playing in his first Test match, Mohammad Ashraful crafted a 212-ball 114 to become, aged 17 years 61 days, the youngest centurion in Test history.

Bradman leads the way for Australia

If the mark of a good batsman is to push on once settled and register a big score, then there has been no finer exponent than **Donald Bradman**. The Australian maestro made an all-time record 12 double-centuries in his 20-year Test career – including a record three in a series against England in 1930 – and is one of only four batsmen in the game's history (along with Brian Lara, Virender Sehwag and Chris Gayle) to have passed 300 runs in a single innings twice in his Test career.

Brutal Richards destroys England

With England already 4–0 down in the five-match series and facing a first-innings deficit of 164, West Indies captain **Viv Richards** strode to the crease with his side on 100 for 1 in the Fifth Test at St John's, Antigua, and decided to put on a batting masterclass for the home fans. By the time he declared his side's innings on 246 for 2, Richards had plundered an unbeaten 110 off 58 balls – he reached three figures off a mere 56 balls, to record the fastest century Test cricket has ever seen.

Sobers strides into the history books

Garfield Sobers's first-innings score of 365 not out in the Third Test against Pakistan at Sabina Park, Kingston, Jamaica, in February–March 1958 was remarkable for a number of reasons. It was the highest-ever maiden century in the history of the game (in 16 previous Tests Sobers's highest score had been 80), it broke the world record for the highest individual score (Len Hutton's 364 against Australia in 1938) and meant that, at 21 years 213 days, Sobers had become the youngest player in Test history to score a triple-century.

Resilient in defeat

The West Indies may have crashed to a 3–0 loss in their home five-match series against Australia in the spring of 1955, but one of their defeated team could hold his head up high. Stylish right-hander Clive Walcott scored 698 runs in the series – including a series record five centuries in the five Tests (108 in the First, 126 and 110 in the Second and 155 and 110 in the Fifth) – at an average of 87.25.

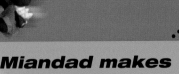

Miandad makes his mark

Javed Miandad's introduction to Test cricket was nothing short of remarkable. In his very first innings for Pakistan at the highest level of the game, he scored 163 against New Zealand at Lahore on 9–13 October 1976; three weeks later, in only his third Test – against the same opponents, in Karachi – he hit a brilliant 206 to become, aged 19 years 140 days, the youngest double-centurion in Test history.

Five in five for Weekes

A fine second-innings knock of 141 by Everton Weekes in the Fourth Test against England at Kingston, Jamaica, in March 1948 did much to guide the West Indies to a ten-wicket victory and a 2–0 series win. Eight months later, the stocky right-hander picked up in the three-match series against India where he had left off against England, rattling off scores of 128 (in the First Test), 194 (in the Second Test) and 162 and 101 (in the Third Test) to become the first, and to date only, player in Test history to score five centuries in five consecutive innings.

The oldest centurion in Test history

The 1928–29 Ashes series was an unqualified success for England, who won the first four Tests, but for **Jack Hobbs** (left) looking to bow out of his final overseas tour in style (21 years after making his Test debut), those matches had been a bitter disappointment – he had scored just 224 runs in seven innings. That all changed in Melbourne: in the first innings Hobbs hit a peerless 142 to become, aged 46 years 82 days, the oldest centurion in Test history.

Making Test cricket look easy

Mohammad Azharuddin's initial forays into Test cricket for India were the most spectacular in the game's history. Handed his debut in the Third Test against England at Kolkata in January 1985, the 21-year-old hit a sublime first-innings 110 before the match ended in a draw. Retaining his place for the Fourth Test at Chennai, he hit a second-innings 105, only to see India lose the match by nine wickets. His first-innings 122 in the drawn fifth and final Test at Kanpur meant he had become the first, and to date only, player in Test history to register three centuries in his first three matches.

The Lahore crawl

Pakistan's crawl to 407 for 9 over the first two-and-a-half days of the First Test against England at Lahore in December 1977 may have been painful to watch, but it did contain a moment of history. When opener **Mudassar Nazar** finally reached three figures – after 9 hours and 57 minutes of batting – he had recorded the slowest Test century in history.

MOST SCORES OF 50-PLUS IN A CAREER: TOP 10

Pos	50+	Player	Span	Mat	Inns	NO	Runs	HS	Ave	100	50
1	119	S.R. Tendulkar (Ind)	1989–2013	200	329	33	15,921	248*	53.78	51	68
2	103	R.T. Ponting (Aus)	1995–2012	168	287	29	13,378	257	51.85	41	62
=	103	J.H. Kallis (ICC/SA)	1995–2013	166	280	40	13,289	224	55.37	45	58
4	99	R. Dravid (ICC/Ind)	1996–2012	164	286	32	13,288	270	52.31	36	63
5	91	S. Chanderpaul (WI)	1994–2013	153	261	45	11,219	203*	51.93	29	62
6	90	A.R. Border (Aus)	1978–94	156	265	44	11,174	205	50.56	27	63
7	82	B.C. Lara (ICC/WI)	1990–2006	131	232	6	11,953	400*	52.88	34	48
=	82	S.R. Waugh (Aus)	1985–2004	168	260	46	10,927	200	51.06	32	50
9	80	K.C. Sangakkara (SL)	2000–14	122	209	17	11,151	319	58.07	35	45
10	79	S.M. Gavaskar (Ind)	1971–87	125	214	16	10,122	236*	51.12	34	45

Getting off the mark

It is ironic given he was always seen as a nervous starter, but the record for the most consecutive innings in Test cricket without a duck is 119, set by England's **David Gower** between August 1982 and December 1990.

Left stranded on 99

There are few more frustrating feelings for a batsman than being left stranded on 99 not out. The phenomenon has occurred five times in Test cricket: Geoffrey Boycott (England against Australia at Perth in December 1979); Steve Waugh (Australia against England at Perth in February 1995); Alex Tudor (England against New Zealand at Birmingham in July 1999); Shaun Pollock (South Africa against Sri Lanka at Centurion in November 2002); and Andrew Hall (South Africa against England at Headingley in August 2003). One player has been left stranded on 199 not out (Andy Flower, Zimbabwe against South Africa at Harare in September 2001), and one player on 299 not out (Donald Bradman, Australia against South Africa at Adelaide in January–February 1932).

Duck avoidance

Now one of the first names on the South Africa team-sheet, **A.B. de Villiers**'s first forays in Test cricket were smooth if not spectacular. He scored a maiden century in his fifth Test (against England at Centurion in January 2005) and endured the highs and lows every Test player suffers. Unremarkable in every way but one: between his debut in December 2004 and November 2008, he went a record 78 innings before recording his first duck (against Bangladesh at Centurion).

New heights for De Villiers

One of the sweetest timers of the ball in world cricket, A.B. de Villiers has become one of the most important members of South Africa's much-feted batting line-up. And from November 2012 to February 2014 he was in the form of his life, scoring a 50 or more in a record-breaking 12 consecutive Test matches. The run started with a majestic 169 against Australia in that November 2012 Third Test at Perth, included four centuries and ended in March 2014 when he could only manage 14 and 43 against Australia in the Third Test at Cape Town. His feat broke Viv Richards' record that had stood for 38 years.

Out in the nervous 90s

Three players hold the record for being out in the 90s the most times in a career: India's Rahul Dravid and Sachin Tendulkar and Australia's Steve Waugh have all been out in the 90s on 10 occasions.

Most times dismissed on 99 in Test cricket

Five players have been dismissed on 99 twice in their Test careers: Richie Richardson (West Indies against India at Port of Spain in April 1989; West Indies against Australia at Bridgetown in April 1991); John Wright (New Zealand against Australia at Melbourne in December 1987; New Zealand against England at Christchurch in January 1992); **Michael Atherton** (England against Australia at Lord's in June 1993; England against South Africa at Headingley in August 1994); Greg Blewett (Australia against the West Indies at Adelaide in January 1997; Australia against New Zealand at Hobart in November 1997); and Sourav Ganguly (India against Sri Lanka at Nagpur in November 1997; India against England at Trent Bridge in August 2002).

Fastest 50

A sorry mismatch between South Africa and Zimbabwe at Cape Town in March 2005, which the home side won by an innings and 21 runs inside two days, provided **Jacques Kallis** with a record-breaking opportunity. Coming to the crease with his side on a commanding 234 for 2 (already 184 ahead), Kallis reached his 50 off just 24 balls (ending on 54 not out): it is the fastest half-century (by balls faced) in Test history.

True grit

Trailing by 52 runs in the First Test of the 1958–59 Ashes series at Brisbane, England needed to dig deep in their second innings if they were going to post a remotely challenging victory target. And nobody dug deeper than Trevor Bailey (batting). The Essex all-rounder limped to 50 off a record slow (by balls faced) 350 balls before falling for a commendable 68. Sadly for England, Bailey's efforts made little difference to the outcome of the match: Australia won by eight wickets.

The first to fall short

Lower-order resistance was the key to Australia's 229-run victory over England at Melbourne in the Second Test of the 1901–02 Ashes campaign, which saw the home side level the series at 1–1. Reggie Duff's battling 104 may have grabbed the majority of the headlines, but it was Clem Hill's innings that stole a place in the record books. The left-hander was out for 99; the first of 79 instances of such a feat.

Most ducks in a series

Not only was the 1978–79 Ashes series one to forget for Australia, England having crushed them 5–1, it was also a record-breaking one for Alan Hurst. The renowned Victorian fast bowler batted 12 times during the campaign, scored a meagre 44 runs and recorded six ducks – an all-time record in a series.

MOST DUCKS IN A CAREER: TOP 10

Pos	0	Player	Span	Mat	Inns	NO	Runs	HS	Ave	100	50
1	43	C.A. Walsh (WI)	1984–2001	132	185	61	936	30*	7.54	0	0
2	36	C.S. Martin (NZ)	2000–13	71	104	52	123	12*	2.36	0	0
3	35	G.D. McGrath (Aus)	1993–2007	124	138	51	641	61	7.36	0	1
4	34	S.K. Warne (Aus)	1992–2007	145	199	17	3,154	99	17.32	0	12
5	33	M. Muralitharan (ICC/SL)	1992–2009	130	159	54	1,203	67	11.45	0	1
6	29	Zaheer Khan (Ind)	2000–14	92	127	24	1,231	75	11.95	0	3
7	26	M. Dillon (WI)	1997–2004	38	68	3	549	43	8.44	0	0
=	26	C.E.L. Ambrose (WI)	1988–2000	98	145	29	1,439	53	12.40	0	1
9	25	Danish Kaneria (Pak)	2000–10	61	84	33	360	29	7.05	0	0
10	23	D.K. Morrison (NZ)	1987–97	48	71	26	379	42	8.42	0	0

Mr Maximum

In all probability the finest wicketkeeper-batsman Test cricket has ever seen, **Adam Gilchrist** played for Australia on 96 occasions, scoring 5,570 runs (at an average of 47.60, including a highest score of 204 not out against South Africa in Johannesburg) and struck an all-time career Test record 100 sixes.

Consecutive fours

The record for the most consecutive fours is six. Three players have achieved the feat: Chris Gayle (off Matthew Hoggard, West Indies against England at The Oval in 2004); Ramnaresh Sarwan (off Munaf Patel, West Indies against India at St Kitts in 2006); and Sanath Jayasuriya (off James Anderson, Sri Lanka against England at Kandy in 2007).

Stealing the limelight

Eight players have batted on each day of a five-day match: Motganhalli Jaisimha (India against Australia at Kolkata in January 1960); Geoffrey Boycott (England against Australia at Trent Bridge in July 1977); Kim Hughes (Australia against England at Lord's in August 1980); Allan Lamb (England against the West Indies at Lord's in June 1984); Ravi Shastri (India against England at Kolkata in December 1984); Adrian Griffith (West Indies against New Zealand at Hamilton in December 1999); Andrew Flintoff (England against England at Mohali in March 2006); and Alviro Petersen (South Africa against New Zealand at Welling in March 2012).

The worst of starts

Two players share the record for being dismissed by/off the first ball of a Test match. India's Sunil Gavaskar (against England by Geoff Arnold at Birmingham in 1974, against Pakistan by Imran Khan in Jaipur in 1986–87, and against the West Indies by Malcolm Marshall in Kolkata in 1983–84) and Bangladesh's Hannan Sarkar (each time against the West Indies by Pedro Collins, at Dhaka in 2002–03, at Gros Islet in 2004 and at Kingston in 2004) have both suffered the ignominious fate on three occasions.

Waqar's unusual record

One of the game's deadliest operators with the ball, where his ability to swing the ball late and at pace created havoc among opposition batsmen, Waqar Younis claimed 373 wickets in 87 Test matches between 1989 and 2003. His batting skills also found a place in the record books: with a highest score of 45, he remains the only player in history to score 1,000 career runs in Test cricket without scoring a single half-century.

Most fours in an innings

A selector's dream – a technically gifted opening batsman who knew both his limitations and which ball to put away – **John Edrich** played 77 Test matches for England between 1963 and 1976, scoring 5,138 runs. The highlight of his career came against New Zealand at Headingley in July 1965, when he batted for eight minutes short of nine hours and faced 450 balls en route to compiling an unbeaten 310: the innings contained a world record 52 fours (and five sixes).

HIGHEST SCORES BY BATTING POSITION

Pos	Player	Runs	Mins	Balls	4s	6s	Team	Opposition	Venue	Match start
1/2	M.L. Hayden	380	622	437	38	11	Australia	Zimbabwe	Perth	9 Oct 2003
1/2	L. Hutton	364	797	847	35	0	England	Australia	The Oval	20 Aug 1938
3	B.C. Lara	400*	778	582	43	4	West Indies	England	St John's	10 Apr 2004
4	D.P.M.D. Jayawardene	374	752	572	43	1	Sri Lanka	South Africa	Colombo	27 Jul 2006
5	M.J. Clarke	329*	609	468	39	1	Australia	India	Sydney	3 Jan 2012
6	K.D. Walters	250	394	342	30	2	Australia	New Zealand	Christchurch	18 Feb 1977
7	D.G. Bradman	270	458	375	22	0	Australia	England	Melbourne	1 Jan 1937
8	Wasim Akram	257*	490	363	22	12	Pakistan	Zimbabwe	Sheikhupura	17 Oct 1996
9	I.D.S. Smith	173	237	136	23	3	New Zealand	India	Auckland	22 Feb 1990
10	W.W. Read	117	120	155	20	0	England	Australia	The Oval	11 Aug 1884
11	A.C. Agar	98	134	101	14	2	Australia	England	Nottingham	10 Jul 2013

UNUSUAL DISMISSALS

Player	Dismissal	Runs	Team	Opposition	Venue	Match start
L. Hutton	obstructing the field	27	England	South Africa	The Oval	16 Aug 1951
W.R. Endean	handled the ball	3	South Africa	England	Cape Town	1 Jan 1957
A.M.J. Hilditch	handled the ball	29	Australia	Pakistan	Perth	24 Mar 1979
Mohsin Khan	handled the ball	58	Pakistan	Australia	Karachi	22 Sep 1982
D.L. Haynes	handled the ball	55	West Indies	India	Mumbai	24 Nov 1983
G.A. Gooch	handled the ball	133	England	Australia	Manchester	3 Jun 1993
S.R. Waugh	handled the ball	47	Australia	India	Chennai	18 Mar 2001
M.S. Atapattu	retired out	201	Sri Lanka	Bangladesh	Colombo	6 Sep 2001
D.P.M.D. Jayawardene	retired out	150	Sri Lanka	Bangladesh	Colombo	6 Sep 2001
M.P. Vaughan	handled the ball	64	England	India	Bangalore	19 Dec 2001

Consecutive sixes

The record for the most consecutive sixes in Tests is four. Three players have achieved the feat: Shahid Afridi (off Harbhajan Singh, for Pakistan against India at Lahore in 2006); Kapil Dev (off Eddie Hemmings, for India against England at Lord's in 1990); and A.B. de Villiers (off Andrew McDonald, for South Africa against Australia at Cape Town in 2008–09).

Fastest to 10,000 runs

Eleven players in the history of Test cricket have achieved the heady feat of accumulating more than 10,000 runs. Three men reached the 10,000 runs mark in their 195th Test innings: Brian Lara, Sachin Tendulkar and Kumar Sangakkara, the last doing so in December 2012.

Hitting the most boundaries

No batsman in Test history has struck more fours than the sport's all-time leading run-scorer, **Sachin Tendulkar**. The Mumbai-born maestro has found the boundary on 2,058 occasions in 200 Tests between 1989 and 2013.

Des stands his ground

Desmond Haynes holds the all-time Test record for carrying his bat (batting throughout his side's innings and remaining not out) on the most occasions. The right-handed opener stood firm while all around him capitulated three times during his Test career: 88 not out of the West Indies' 211 all out against Pakistan in Karachi in November 1986; 75 not out of the West Indies' 176 all out against England at The Oval in August 1991; and 143 not out of the West Indies' 382 all out against Pakistan at Port of Spain in April 1993.

The longest individual innings in Test history

Len Hutton's legendary innings of 364 against Australia at The Oval in August 1938 was not only the highest individual score in Test history at the time (Garfield Sobers broke it in 1958 with 365 not out against Pakistan), but it was also, and remains, the longest Test innings of all time. Hutton faced 847 balls.

Most sixes in an innings

Wasim Akram showed his true credentials as a genuine all-rounder in spectacular fashion in the First Test against Zimbabwe at Sheikhupura in October 1996. The Pakistan captain smashed an imperious 257 off 363 balls (the highest innings by a No. 8 in Test history), an innings that included a world record 12 sixes.

BOWLING RECORDS

MOST WICKETS IN A CAREER: TOP 10

Pos	Wkts	Player	Span	Mat	Balls	Runs	BBI	BBM	Ave	5	10
1	800	M. Muralitharan (ICC/SL)	1992–2010	133	44,039	18,180	9/51	16/220	22.72	67	22
2	708	S.K. Warne (Aus)	1992–2007	145	40,705	17,995	8/71	12/128	25.41	37	10
3	619	A. Kumble (Ind)	1990–2008	132	40,850	18,355	10/74	14/149	29.65	35	8
4	563	G.D. McGrath (Aus)	1993–2007	124	29,248	12,186	8/24	10/27	21.64	29	3
5	519	C.A. Walsh (WI)	1984–2001	132	30,019	12,688	7/37	13/55	24.44	22	3
6	434	Kapil Dev (Ind)	1978–94	131	27,740	12,867	9/83	11/146	29.64	23	2
7	431	R.J. Hadlee (NZ)	1973–90	86	21,918	9,611	9/52	15/123	22.29	36	9
8	421	S.M. Pollock (SA)	1995–2008	108	24,353	9,733	7/87	10/147	23.11	16	1
9	414	Wasim Akram (Pak)	1985–2002	104	22,627	9,779	7/119	11/110	23.62	25	5
10	413	Harbhajan Singh (India)	1998–2013	101	28,293	13,372	8/84	15/217	32.37	25	5

Walsh flattens Kiwis

New Zealand's batsmen could find no answers to the many questions posed to them by Courtney Walsh in the Second Test at Wellington in February 1995. The West Indies captain took 7 for 37 in the first innings and 6 for 18 in the second to lead his side to a colossal innings-and-322-run victory. Walsh's 13 for 55 are the best match figures by a captain in Test history.

Laker's Test

England's innings-and-71-run victory over Australia in the Fourth Test at Old Trafford in July 1956 to retain the Ashes will always be remembered as **Jim Laker**'s Test. The Surrey off-break bowler took 9 for 37 in Australia's first innings and 10 for 53 in the second to become the first person in Test history to take ten wickets in an innings (a feat repeated only once, by Anil Kumble, who took 10 for 74 against Pakistan in 1999). Laker's match figures of 19 for 90 remain the best in Test history. It was also the first of six instances of a bowler dismissing all 11 batsmen in a match.

There's no place like home

Despite being the leading wicket-taker (with 800 wickets) and the record-holder for the most five-wicket (67) and 10-wicket hauls (22) in Test history, the argument against Muttiah Muralitharan being the greatest bowler of all time is that he has the good fortune to play the majority of his games on the helpful wickets of Sri Lanka. And how he has prospered in his homeland: his 166 wickets at Colombo's Sinhalese Sports Club Ground, his 117 Test wickets at the Asgiriya Stadium in Kandy and his 111 Test wickets at Galle's International Stadium occupy the top three places on the all-time list for the most Test wickets taken by a player at a single ground.

Lone resistance

Javagal Srinath's commendable effort of taking 5 for 46 in the first innings and 8 for 86 in the second were not enough to prevent India from slipping to a 46-run defeat in the First Test against Pakistan in Kolkata in February 1999. The paceman's 13 for 132 are the best match figures by a player who has ended up on the losing side in Test history.

First nine-wicket haul

The chief architect of England's comprehensive innings-and-197-run victory over South Africa at Johannesburg in March 1896 was George Lohmann. The Surrey man ripped the heart out of their batting line-up to take 9 for 28. It was the first instance (of 15) in Test history of a bowler taking nine wickets in an innings.

England's Briggs casts a spell on South Africa

Dismissed for 292 in their first innings against South Africa in the Second and final Test at Cape Town in March 1889, England knew that, barring an outstanding performance with the ball, they would have to bat again. Cue Johnny Briggs. The Lancashire slow left-armer bewitched the hosts, taking 7 for 17 in the first innings and 8 for 11 in the second to secure an England victory by an innings and 202 runs and to become the first player (of 12) in Test history to take 15 wickets or more in a match.

Going out on a high

The star of England's 4–0 series win over South Africa in 1913–14 was S.F. Barnes. Despite playing in only four of the five Tests, the Staffordshire-born fast bowler was unplayable, taking an all-time record 49 wickets in the series, including seven five-wicket hauls – with a best of 9 for 103 in the Second Test at Johannesburg – and three ten-wicket match hauls. It turned out to be some swansong: these were the final Test matches of Barnes's career.

All in vain

Nobody could point the finger of blame at Kapil Dev following India's 138-run defeat to the West Indies in the Third Test at Ahmedabad in November 1983. India's captain led from the front in the West Indies' second innings, taking 9 for 83: the best bowling performance in an innings by a captain and the best figures in an innings by a bowler who has ended up on the losing side in Test history.

Fiery Fred the first to 300

No one will ever know how much more **Fred Trueman** could have achieved had not an insubordinate nature and a sharp tongue stood in his way. The Yorkshireman, a bowler with genuine pace, was selected for only 67 of a possible 118 Tests throughout his career, but when he played, he prospered. In his 65th Test, against Australia at The Oval in August 1964, he dismissed Neil Hawke (above) to become the first bowler in history to take 300 Test wickets.

The world's first great leg-spinner

Clarrie Grimmett moved from New Zealand to Australia at the age of 17 to pursue a dream of playing Test cricket (New Zealand was not a Test-playing nation at the time), made his debut (against England) 16 years later, and soon set about establishing his legend as the world's first great leg-spinner. Baffling batsmen around the world, he claimed his 200th Test wicket (the first player in history to do so) in only his 36th Test, the fewest in history.

Golden year

The legendary zip of his leg-spinner's action may have diminished over the years, but, by 2005, **Shane Warne**'s experience, craft and guile were more than a match for his opponents. In the 15 Tests he played during that year, the spin wizard took 96 wickets – including a sensational 40 in a losing Ashes campaign – to set the record for the most Test wickets in a calendar year.

BEST ECONOMY RATE IN AN INNINGS: TOP 10
(minimum of 10 overs)

Pos	Econ	Player	O	M	R	W	Team	Opposition	Venue	Match start
1	0.15	R.G. Nadkarni	32.0	27	5	0	India	England	Chennai	10 Jan 1964
2	0.21	G.S. Sobers	14.0	11	3	1	West Indies	New Zealand	Wellington	3 Mar 1956
=	0.21	R.G. Nadkarni	14.0	11	3	0	India	England	Mumbai (BS)	21 Jan 1964
4	0.30	Majid Khan	10.0	8	3	0	Pakistan	West Indies	Port of Spain	1 Apr 1977
5	0.32	R.E.S. Wyatt	13.0	10	4	3	England	South Africa	Durban	21 Jan 1928
=	0.32	H. Verity	13.0	11	4	0	England	South Africa	Leeds	13 Jul 1935
7	0.37	J.C. Laker	14.1*	9	7	2	England	South Africa	Cape Town	1 Jan 1957
8	0.40	J.W. Burke	15.0*	10	8	0	Australia	South Africa	Johannesburg	7 Feb 1958
9	0.41	H. Verity	12.0	9	5	2	England	South Africa	Leeds	13 Jul 1935
=	0.41	Pervez Sajjad	12.0	8	5	4	Pakistan	New Zealand	Rawalpindi	27 Mar 1965

* The match was played using eight-ball overs.

The best bowler in history?

The first bowler to take nine wickets in a Test match innings and the fastest to the 100 Test wickets milestone (a mere 16 matches), on statistics alone **George Lohmann** has a rightful claim to being Test cricket's greatest ever bowler. In 18 Tests between 1886 and 1896, the medium-pacer took 112 wickets at 10.75 – the lowest-ever average – and his a strike-rate of a wicket every 34.1 balls is also the best in history.

The mean machine

Few players in the history of the game have frustrated batsmen as much as William Attewell, a bowler of metronomic accuracy who relied on the principle of bowling the ball at off stump and setting an off-side field. In ten Tests between 1884 and 1894, the Nottinghamshire medium-pacer bowled 2,850 balls in Test cricket (taking 28 wickets) at an economy rate of 1.31 runs per over. Of bowlers to have bowled 2,000 balls or more in Test cricket, it is the lowest economy rate in the game's history.

Lean times with the ball

Now considered one of his country's finest umpires, Asoka de Silva did not enjoy the best of careers as a player. Capped ten times for Sri Lanka between 1985 and 1991, the left-arm googly bowler set two dubious records: of bowlers to have bowled 2,000 balls or more, he has the worst career bowling average (129.00 – 8 wickets for 1,032 runs) and the worst career strike-rate (a wicket every 291.0 balls).

On a hot streak

Although Australia lost the 1888 Ashes series 2–1 to England, none of the team's detractors would have apportioned any blame to Charlie Turner. Despite the loss, the fast-medium bowler was in inspired form with the ball, taking 5 for 44, 7 for 43, 5 for 27, 5 for 36, 6 for 112 and 5 for 86 to become the only player in Test history to claim five-wicket hauls in six consecutive innings.

Taking the brunt of it

Len Hutton and the rest of his England team-mates were not the only ones to enter the record books following their historic innings-and-579-run victory over Australia at The Oval in August 1938. The main victim of England's massive first-innings 903 for 7 declared was Australia's **Chuck Fleetwood-Smith**. The left-arm chinaman bowler delivered 87.0 overs and took just one wicket; his strike-rate of 522.0 is the worst in a single innings in Test history.

Best strike-rate in an innings

It took just 19 balls in India's first innings of the First Test at Brisbane in November–December 1947 for Australia's **Ernie Toshack** to claim a place in the record books. The left-arm medium-pace bowler took five wickets for two runs in 2.3 eight-ball overs to help reduce India to 58 all out. At 3.8 balls per wicket, it is the best strike-rate in Test history of any bowler who has taken four or more wickets in an innings.

Lacking a cutting edge

Renowned more for his batting (he has scored 416 runs at an average of 32.00 in eight Tests for Bangladesh, 2008–12), Naeem Islam has bowled 95.4 overs of off-spin in Test cricket, but has taken only one wicket (New Zealand's Daniel Flynn, with his fifth ball on his debut). He thus holds the record for the worst career bowling average of any Test wicket-taker in history, 303.00.

Making an early mark

With Australia already 2–0 down in the 1894–95 Ashes series, it was time to make changes for the Third Test at Adelaide. In came Albert Trott, and the Victoria slow bowler got off to a blistering start, taking a match-winning 8 for 43 in England's second innings to lead Australia to a 382-run victory. They are the best single-innings figures by a player on debut in the game's history.

Into the lion's den

Fast-tracked into the Bangladesh Test side as an 18-year-old in 2005 after being discovered at a talent-spotting camp, fast bowler **Shahadat Hossain** found his early forays in international cricket to be a chastening experience. In all, he claimed 70 wickets in 35 matches, but, of all the bowlers to have bowled 2,000 or more balls in Test cricket, he holds the record for the worst career economy rate (4.20 runs per over) and for the worst economy rate in an innings (8.41 – against England at Lord's in May 2005, when his figures were 12-0-101-0).

Youngest and oldest

The youngest player to take five wickets in an innings is Nasim-ul-Ghani, who took 5 for 116 for Pakistan against the West Indies at Georgetown in March 1958 aged 16 years 303 days. The oldest player to achieve the feat is **Bert Ironmonger**, who took 6 for 18 for Australia against South Africa in Melbourne in February 1932 aged 49 years 311 days. The performance also saw Ironmonger become the oldest player to take ten wickets in a match.

Hirwani's heroics

Drafted into the India team for the first time for the Fourth Test against the West Indies at Chennai in January 1988, **Narendra Hirwani**'s introduction to Test cricket was the most spectacular in the game's history. The slow left-armer took 8 for 61 in the first innings and 8 for 75 in the second as India won by 255 runs to draw the series 1–1. Hirwani's match figures of 16 for 136 are a record for a Test debutant.

MOST RUNS CONCEDED IN A CAREER: TOP 10

Pos	Runs	Player	Span	Mat
1	18,355	A. Kumble (Ind)	1990–2008	132
2	18,110	**M. Muralitharan** (ICC/SL)	1992–2010	133
3	17,995	S.K. Warne (Aus)	1992–2007	145
4	13,372	Harbhajan Singh (Ind)	1998–2013	101
5	12,867	Kapil Dev (Ind)	1978–94	131
6	12,688	C.A. Walsh (WI)	1984–2001	132
7	12,392	D.L. Vettori (ICC/NZ)	1997–2012	112
8	12,186	G.D. McGrath (Aus)	1993–2007	124
9	11,242	M. Ntini (SA)	1998–2009	101
10	10,878	I.T. Botham (Eng)	1977–92	102

Hitting the right spot

Anil Kumble, India's legendary leg-spinner who, with 619 Test wickets, stands third on the all-time list of wicket-takers, may not have been the biggest turner of a cricket ball, but what he may have lacked in zip, he more than made up for with a nagging accuracy. The reward for his unremitting line-and-length policy was 156 lbw victims (25.2 per cent of his wickets) and 35 caught-and-bowled victims (5.65 per cent of his wickets). Both are an all-time Test record (the latter shared with Sri Lanka's Muttiah Muralitharan).

All-time leader

Perhaps not surprising given his status as the leading Test wicket-taker of all time, **Muttiah Muralitharan** holds the record for the most wickets taken bowled (167, 20.87 per cent of his wickets), the most wickets taken caught (435 – 54.37 per cent of his wickets) and for most wickets stumped (47, 5.87 per cent of his wickets). He also shares the record (with Anil Kumble) for the most caught-and-bowled victims (35).

Most deliveries

No bowler has bowled more deliveries in Test cricket than **Muttiah Muralitharan**. Sri Lanka's spinning legend, the all-time leading Test wicket-taker and the holder of numerous other records, has completed 44,039 deliveries in 133 Test matches between 1992 and 2010.

Spofforth's strikes leave England reeling

Australia may already have been in dreamland after reducing England to 26 for 4 on the opening morning of the only Ashes Test of the tour, played at Melbourne in January 1879, but even better things were to follow. Fast bowler **Fred Spofforth** dismissed Vernon Royle, Francis Mackinnon and Tom Emmett in successive deliveries to leave England on a desperate 26 for 7 (a position from which they never recovered; Australia won the game by ten wickets) and record the first of 39 hat-tricks in Test history.

Most wickets taken hit-wicket

Australia's best fast bowler of the 1960s, **Graham McKenzie** had a languid action and surprising pace, which brought him 246 Test wickets in a ten-year career between 1961 and 1971. Uniquely, an all-time Test record four of those scalps were out hit-wicket.

Two hat-tricks in a day

The triangular tournament between England, Australia and South Africa – held in England – in 1912 may have been an unusual occurrence in itself, but the match between Australia and South Africa at Old Trafford provided a unique moment in Test history. In South Africa's first innings, leg-break bowler Jimmy Matthews took the eighth hat-trick in Test history. Later in the day, with South Africa following on, he took another. Bizarrely they were the only wickets he took in the match, but Matthews remains the only man in history to have achieved the feat of taking two hat-tricks in a single Test match.

Earning a crust

Trailing the West Indies by a massive 288 runs after the first innings in the First Test at Edgbaston in May–June 1957, England had to dig deep. And no one dug deeper than captain Peter May (285 not out) and Colin Cowdrey (154 not out) as the home side ground out a patient 583 for 4 declared off a mighty 258 overs; Sonny Ramadhin delivered 98 of those overs (588 deliveries) – a single-innings record – to take 2 for 179. The match ended in a draw.

Four wickets in five balls

There have been three instances in Test cricket of a bowler taking four wickets in five balls: Maurice Allom, W-WWW, on debut for England against New Zealand at Christchurch in 1929–30; **Chris Old**, WW-WW, for England against Pakistan at Birmingham in 1978; and Wasim Akram, WW-WW, for Pakistan against the West Indies at Lahore in 1990–91.

Finding the corridor of uncertainty

The most successful fast bowler in the game's history and fourth on the all-time list of wicket-takers, **Glenn McGrath** used methods not based on express pace but on a metronomic ability to bowl the ball on the line of off stump or just outside. As a result, a record 152 of his 563 Test victims (26.99 per cent of his career haul) were out caught behind.

BOWLER/BATSMAN COMBINATION: TOP 10

Pos	Wkts	Bowler	Batsman	Span	Mat	Ave	Ducks
1	19	**G.D. McGrath** (Aus)	**M.A. Atherton** (Eng)	1994–2001	17	9.89	3
2	18	A.V. Bedser (Eng)	A.R. Morris (Aus)	1946–54	21	32.11	2
3	17	C.E.L. Ambrose (WI)	M.A. Atherton (Eng)	1991–2000	26	25.76	4
=	17	C.A. Walsh (WI)	M.A. Atherton (Eng)	1991–2000	27	22.64	1
5	16	M.D. Marshall (WI)	G.A. Gooch (Eng)	1980–91	21	28.50	2
6	15	H. Trumble (Aus)	T.W. Hayward (Eng)	1896–1904	22	26.26	4
=	15	C.E.L. Ambrose (WI)	M.E. Waugh (Aus)	1991–99	22	35.06	3
=	15	G.D. McGrath (Aus)	B.C. Lara (ICC/WI)	1995–2005	24	41.40	2
=	15	C.A. Walsh (WI)	I.A. Healy (Aus)	1988–99	28	12.53	5
10	14	G.F. Lawson (Aus)	D.I. Gower (Eng)	1981–89	21	40.85	0
=	14	S.K. Warne (Aus)	A.J. Stewart (Eng)	1993–2002	23	26.64	2
=	14	M.A. Noble (Aus)	A.F.A. Lilley (Eng)	1899–1909	29	14.85	2

BOWLERS NO-BALLED FOR THROWING

Bowler	Team	Opposition	Venue	Year
E. Jones	Australia	England	Melbourne	1898
G.A.R. Lock	England	West Indies	Kingston	1954
G.M. Griffin	South Africa	England	Lord's	1960
Haseeb Ahsan	Pakistan	India	Mumbai	1960
I. Meckiff	Australia	South Africa	Brisbane	1963
Abid Ali	India	New Zealand	Christchurch	1968
S.M.H. Kirmani	India	West Indies	Bridgetown	1983
D.I. Gower	England	New Zealand	Nottingham	1986
H. Olonga	Zimbabwe	Pakistan	Harare	1995
M. Muralitharan	Sri Lanka	Australia	Melbourne	1995
G.W. Flower	Zimbabwe	New Zealand	Bulawayo	2000

The most unusual hat-trick

In the Second Test of the 1988–89 series between Australia and the West Indies, at Perth, **Merv Hughes** dismissed Gus Logie with the final ball of his 36th over of the first innings, and then Patrick Patterson with the first ball of his 37th over to end the West Indies' innings. When he trapped Gordon Greenidge lbw first ball in the West Indies' second innings, he had completed Test cricket's most unusual hat-trick.

Players to take a hat-trick on Test debut

Three players in Test history have taken a hat-trick on debut: Maurice Allom, for England against New Zealand at Christchurch in 1929–30; Peter Petherick, for New Zealand against Pakistan at Lahore in 1976–77, and Damien Fleming, for Australia against Pakistan at Rawalpindi in 1994–95.

A spectacular introduction

Picture the scene. A bowler is appearing in his first Test match. The captain has just thrown him the ball; he is standing at the end of his run-up, ball in sweaty hand; the crowd is hushed, and the nerves are jangling. But the debutant gets off to the perfect start: he takes a wicket with his first-ever ball. Eighteen players in Test history have enjoyed such an experience.

Fastest to 250 and 300

After breaking on to the international scene in the early 1970s, with his fearsome pace and legendary stamina it did not take **Dennis Lillee** long to win the hearts of Australian cricket fans or to strike terror into batsmen around the world. As the fans chanted his name, Lillee responded in style: no player has taken 250 (48 matches) or 300 Test wickets (56 matches) in a shorter time.

Fastest to 50

One of the best bowlers Australia has ever produced, Charlie Turner was a skilful right-arm fast-medium bowler with an effortless action. He made a blistering start to his Test career, reaching the 50-wicket milestone in only his sixth Test match and remains the fastest to achieve the feat in Test history.

Fastest to 150

The finest bowler of the early part of the 20th century, England's **S.F. Barnes** was one of the first bowlers to make use of a new ball's seam and, as a result, terrorized batsmen throughout his 13-year, 27-Test career. He claimed his 150th scalp in only his 24th Test – it is a record that stands to this day.

ALL-TIME LEADING TEST WICKET-TAKER: PROGRESSIVE RECORD HOLDERS FROM THE START OF 20TH CENTURY

Record broken	Player	New record
1900	Johnny Briggs (England)	119
January 1904	Hugh Trumble (Australia)	141
December 1913	Sydney (S.F.) Barnes (England)	189
January 1936	Clarrie Grimmett (Australia)	216
July 1953	Alec Bedser (England)	236
January 1963	Brian Statham (England)	242
March 1963	Fred Trueman (England)	307
February 1976	Lance Gibbs (West Indies)	309
December 1981	Dennis Lillee (Australia)	355
August 1986	Ian Botham (England)	383
November 1988	**Richard Hadlee** (New Zealand)	431
January 1994	Kapil Dev (India)	434
March 2000	Courtney Walsh (West Indies)	519
May 2004	Muttiah Muralitharan (Sri Lanka)	520
July 2004	Shane Warne (Australia)	527*
August 2004	Muttiah Muralitharan (Sri Lanka)	532
October 2004	Shane Warne (Australia)	708
December 2007	Muttiah Muralitharan	800

* Warne equalled Muralitharan's total of 527 wickets, before the Sri Lankan moved ahead in the race in August 2004.

More Murali records

Among Sri Lanka spin wizard Muttiah Muralitharan's many records is the speed at which he has reached various wicket milestones. He took his 350th Test wicket in a record low 66 matches; his 400th wicket in a record 72 matches; his 450th Test wicket in a record 80 matches; his 500th Test wicket in a record 87 matches; his 600th wicket in a record 101 matches; his 700th wicket in a record 113 matches; and, of course, he is the only player in history to have reached the 800-wicket milestone (in 133 Tests).

No need for change

For two bowlers to bowl unchanged throughout an innings is a rare event in Test cricket; there have been only 24 such occurrences in the game's history (and only three since 1956). It usually occurs only when opening bowlers get into an unplayable groove and dismiss a side cheaply, but that is not always the case. In the first-ever instance of the feat, in the Second Test of the 1881–82 Ashes series, at Melbourne, Australia's Joey Palmer and Edwin Evans combined for an unchanged 115 (four-ball) overs in England's first innings.

Split Test hat-tricks

There have been three instances of a bowler taking a hat-trick split over two Test innings, strangely all involving Australia and the West Indies. It first occurred in the First Test at Brisbane, in November 1988, when Courtney Walsh had Tony Dodemaide caught behind with the last ball of Australia's first innings and Mike Veletta and Graeme Wood with his first two balls of the second. Two weeks later, Merv Hughes emulated Walsh (see opposite page). The third occasion was at Bridgetown, Barbados, in May 2003, when Jermaine Lawson bowled Brett Lee and Stuart MacGill with the last two balls of Australia's first innings and trapped Justin Langer lbw with the first ball of the second innings.

BEST FIGURES IN AN INNINGS: PROGRESSIVE RECORD

Rank	Bowling	Player	Match	Venue	Season
1	7–55	Tom Kendall (Aus)	Australia v England	Melbourne	1876–77*
2	7–44	Fred Spofforth (Aus)	England v Australia	The Oval	1882
3	7–28	Billy Bates (Eng)	Australia v England	Melbourne	1882–83
4	8–35	George Lohmann (Eng)	Australia v England	Sydney	1886–87
5	8–11	Johnny Briggs (Eng)	South Africa v England	Cape Town	1888–89
6	8–7	George Lohmann (Eng)	South Africa v England	Port Elizabeth	1895–96
7	9–28	George Lohmann (Eng)	South Africa v England	Johannesburg	1895–96
8	10–53	Jim Laker (Eng)	England v Australia	Manchester	1956

* Kendall took his 7 for 55 in the inaugural Test Match

WICKETKEEPING RECORDS

MOST DISMISSALS IN A CAREER: TOP 10

Pos	Dismissals	Player	Span	Mat	Inns	Ct	St	Dis/Inn
1	555	**M.V. Boucher** (ICC/SA)	1997–2012	147	281	532	23	1.97
2	416	A.C. Gilchrist (Aus)	1999–2008	96	191	379	37	2.178
3	395	I.A. Healy (Aus)	1988–99	119	224	366	29	1.763
4	355	R.W. Marsh (Aus)	1970–84	96	182	343	12	1.950
5	270	P.J.L. Dujon (WI)	1981–91	81	150	265	5	1.800
6	269	A.P.E. Knott (Eng)	1967–81	95	174	250	19	1.545
7	263	M.S. Dhoni (India)	2005–14	83	155	226	37	1.696
8	241	A.J. Stewart (Eng)	1990–2003	133	141	227	14	1.709
9	233	B.J. Haddin (Aus)	2008–14	57	110	228	5	2.118
10	230	M.J. Prior (Eng)	2007–13	75	138	217	13	1.666

Tragic end for Boucher

Mark Boucher's career sadly was cut short after he was struck in the eye by a bail during a warm-up match for South Africa's 2012 tour of England. The all-time leader in Test dismissals, with 555, suffered serious eye damage in the freak incident – similar to the one in 1990 which forced England wicketkeeper Paul Downton to hang up his gloves.

Bore draw brings a record

At first glance, the Second Test between the West Indies and New Zealand at St John's, Antigua, in April 1996 was an inspiring draw brought to life, only briefly, by the West Indies' mini-collapse in the second innings, only for New Zealand to run out of time in their chase for victory. However, dig deeper and you will find that the match was a record-breaking one: the 1,299 runs scored in the match did not contain a single bye; it is the highest match aggregate with no byes conceded in Test history.

Record-breaking Brad

Australia had a series to forget against England in 2013, losing 3–0 to suffer their third consecutive Ashes defeat, but no one could criticize the efforts of Brad Haddin. The New South Wales keeper bagged 29 dismissals in the series (all caught) to break Rod Marsh's 31-year record for the most dismissals by a keeper in a series.

Most dismissals in a single Test match

The Second Test between England and South Africa at Johannesburg in November–December 1995 was a memorable one for Jack Russell. The England wicketkeeper took six catches in the first innings and five in the second to set the all-time record for the most dismissals in a match (11). South Africa's A.B. de Villiers equalled Russell's record during his country's 21-run victory over Pakistan at Johannesburg in February 2013 (also with 11 catches).

Most dismissals in an innings

The record for the most dismissals in an innings by a wicketkeeper is seven, a feat that has been achieved on four occasions: Wasim Bari (7ct), Pakistan against New Zealand at Auckland in February 1979; Bob Taylor (7ct), England against India at Mumbai in February 1980; Ian Smith (7ct), New Zealand against Sri Lanka at Hamilton in February 1991; and Ridley Jacobs (7ct), West Indies against Australia at Melbourne in December 2000.

Setting a series benchmark

The West Indies may have crashed to a 2–1 home series defeat against Australia in 1960–61, but it was not for any lack of effort by Gerry Alexander. The wicketkeeper-batsman not only topped the West Indies' batting averages, with 484 runs at an average of 60.50, he also excelled behind the stumps, taking 16 catches: it was the first time of 19 instances in history that a wicketkeeper has scored 300 runs and taken 15 dismissals in a series.

Dujon's standout performances

The only wicketkeeper in Test history to score 300-plus runs and take 15-plus dismissals in a series on three occasions is **Jeff Dujon**. The West Indies keeper achieved the feat against India in 1983–84 (367 runs and 16 dismissals), against Australia in 1984–85 (341 runs and 19 dismissals) and against England in the 1988 series (305 runs and 20 dismissals).

Evans sets a career benchmark

By the time **Godfrey Evans** finished his 91-match, 13-year England career in 1959 he was considered a true technician behind the stumps and one of the greatest wicketkeepers the game has ever seen. His career haul of 219 dismissals (173ct, 46st) and 2,439 runs became a target for other keepers to aim at. In modern times, 200 dismissals and 2,000 career runs is considered a fair benchmark by which to judge a wicketkeeper. Evans was the first of 14 players in Test history to achieve the feat.

Most stumpings in a career

With his rapid reflexes and boundless enthusiasm, Australia's Bert Oldfield was the first of the game's great wicketkeepers. A master of the stumping – he is the only man to have taken four stumpings in an innings on four occasions – he made more stumpings in his 17-year, 54-Test career (1920–37) than any other wicketkeeper in history (52).

Most stumpings in a match

The main beneficiary of Narendra Hirwani's record-breaking 16-wicket haul on debut for India in the Fourth Test against the West Indies on an under-prepared, spinner-friendly surface at Chennai in January 1988 was wicketkeeper Kiran More. As the West Indies batsmen floundered against the spinning ball throughout the match, More picked up an all-time record six stumpings – one of them in the first innings and five of them coming in the second.

Scant consolation for Prasanna Jayawardene

Sri Lanka may ultimately have lost the match (by an innings and 24 runs) and with it the series (2–0) in the third Test against India at the Brabourne Stadium in Mumbai in December 2009, but for their wicketkeeper **Prasanna Jayawardene** the bitterness of defeat was offset by the fact that his performances behind the stumps earned him a place in the history books. During India's massive first-innings total of 726 for 9 declared (in which Virender Sehwag top-scored with 293), Jayawardene did not concede a single bye. It is the largest innings total in Test history in which no byes were conceded.

Most stumpings in a series

The record for the most stumpings in a series is jointly held by two players: Percy Sherwell, with nine stumpings for South Africa against Australia in the 1910–11 series in Australia; and Dick Lilley, with nine stumpings for England against Australia in the 1903–04 Ashes series.

SCORING 100 AND FIVE DISMISSALS IN AN INNINGS

Player	Bat	Field	Team	Opposition	Venue	Match start
D.T. Lindsay	182	6ct/0st	South Africa	Australia	Johannesburg	23 Dec 1966
I.D.S. Smith	113*	4ct/1st	New Zealand	England	Auckland	10 Feb 1984
S.A.R. Silva	111	5ct/0st	Sri Lanka	India	Colombo	6 Sep 1985
A.C. Gilchrist	133	4ct/1st	Australia	England	Sydney	2 Jan 2003
M.J. Prior	118	5ct/0st	England	Australia	Sydney	3 Jan 2011
A.B. de Villiers	103*	6ct/0st	South Africa	Pakistan	Johannesburg	1 Feb 2013
M.J. Prior	110*	5ct/0st	England	New Zealand	Auckland	22 Mar 2013
B.J. Watling	124	5ct/0st	New Zealand	India	Wellington	14 Feb 2014

FIELDING RECORDS

MOST CATCHES IN A CAREER: TOP 10

Pos	Catches	Player	Span	Mat	Inns	Ct/Inn
1	210	**R. Dravid** (Ind/ICC)	1996–2012	164	301	0.697
2	200	J.H. Kallis (SA/ICC)	1995–2013	166	315	0.634
3	196	R.T. Ponting (Aus)	1995–2012	168	328	0.597
4	194	D.P.M.D. Jayawardene (SL)	1997–2014	143	258	0.751
5	181	M.E. Waugh (Aus)	1991–2002	128	245	0.738
6	171	S.P. Fleming (NZ)	1994–2008	111	199	0.859
7	169	G.C. Smith (SA/ICC)	2002–14	117	225	0.751
8	164	B.C. Lara (WI/ICC)	1990–2006	131	241	0.680
9	157	M.A. Taylor (Aus)	1989–99	104	197	0.796
10	156	A.R. Border (Aus)	1978–94	156	277	0.563

Most catches in an innings by a fielder (not keeping wicket)

The record for the most catches in an innings by a fielder is five, a feat achieved seven times: Vic Richardson for Australia against South Africa at Durban in February 1936; Yajurvindra Singh for India against England at Bangalore in January 1977; Mohammad Azharuddin for India against Pakistan at Karachi in November 1989; Kris Srikkanth for India against Australia at Perth in February 1992; Stephen Fleming for New Zealand against Zimbabwe at Harare in September 1997; Graeme Smith for South Africa against Australia at Perth in November 2012; and Darren Sammy for the West Indies against India at Mumbai in November 2013.

Most catches in a match

The record for the most catches in a match is seven, a feat that has been achieved on five occasions: by Greg Chappell for Australia against England at Perth in December 1974; by Yajurvindra Singh for India against England at Bangalore in January 1977; by Hashan Tillakaratne for Sri Lanka against New Zealand at Colombo in December 1992; by Stephen Fleming for New Zealand against Zimbabwe at Harare in September 1997, and by Matthew Hayden for Australia against Sri Lanka at Galle in March 2004.

Slip-fielding all-time greats: MARK WAUGH (Australia)

An elegant and gifted strokemaker with the bat (scoring 8,029 runs at an average of 41.81 for Australia in 128 Test matches between 1991 and 2002) and a talented off-spinner (with 59 Test wickets), **Mark Waugh** was equally at home in the hotbed of the slip cordon. By the time he finished his career, the younger of the Waugh twins had taken 128 catches, a mark that stood as a world record until Rahul Dravid broke it in April 2009.

Most catches in a series

There were many heroic Australian performances during their 5–0 whitewash of England in the 1920–21 series. Warwick Armstrong's three centuries and Arthur Mailey's 36 wickets in the series won the highest acclaim, but one perhaps more obscure performance entered the record books and has stood the test of time: Jack

Fielding all-time greats: JONTY RHODES (South Africa)

A man selected as much for his prowess in the field as for his ability with the bat (particularly in the one-day game), South Africa's **Jonty Rhodes** inspired more fear in batsmen than almost any other fielder in the game's history. Razor-sharp reflexes, dives like a leaping salmon at backward point and deadly accurate throws even when off balance became the trademark of his eight-year, 52-Test career between 1992 and 2000.

Fielding all-time greats: ROGER HARPER (West Indies)

He was neither a world-beating off-spinner (25 Tests between 1983 and 1993 brought him a mere 46 wickets) nor a great batsman (he averaged 18.44 with the bat), but there have been few finer fielders in the game than Roger Harper. Just ask Graham Gooch. Batting for the MCC against the World XI at Lord's in 1987, the England opener drilled an on-drive off Harper's bowling and stepped out of his crease in anticipation, only to see Harper's telescopic arm reach down, grab the ball and throw down Gooch's stumps to run him out.

Slip-fielding all-time greats: BOBBY SIMPSON (Australia)

A first-rate opening batsman (he scored 4,869 runs at an average of 46.81 in 62 Tests for Australia between 1957 and 1978) and, with 71 Test wickets to his name, a handy leg-break bowler, Bobby Simpson also had electric reflexes – demonstrated in his youth when he used to catch flies with his bare hands to amuse his school-mates – that turned him into arguably the greatest slip fielder in the history of the game. He ended his career with 110 Test catches.

Fielding all-time greats: COLIN BLAND (South Africa)

The hours spent honing his skills by throwing at a single stump certainly paid dividends for **Colin Bland**, who was born in Zimbabwe (then Rhodesia). Although a more than capable batsman (he scored 1,669 runs at an average of 49.08 for South Africa in a 21-Test career between 1961 and 1966), it was his speed, balance and powerful arm in the field that thrilled spectators and opponents around the world in equal measure. He was the world's first truly great fielder.

Proving a point

Left out of the side and watching on from the sidelines as five of his team-mates went on to score centuries in the First Test against newcomers Bangladesh at Multan in August 2001, Pakistan's Younis Khan must have been kicking his heels. And when his chance to impress in the field finally came (on as a substitute for Inzamam-ul-Haq), he grabbed it with both hands, literally, taking an all-time record (for a substitute fielder) four catches in Bangladesh's second innings.

Most catches by a substitute in a match

The record for most catches in a match by a substitute is four, a feat that has been achieved on three occasions: by Gursharan Singh for India against the West Indies at Ahmedabad in November 1983; by Younis Khan for Pakistan against Bangladesh at Multan in August 2001; and by Virender Sehwag for India against Zimbabwe at Nagpur in February 2002.

Perfect partners

The most successful bowler-fielder combination in Test history is that of Sri Lanka's Muttiah Muralitharan and Mahela Jayawardene. The pair combined for a world-record 77 dismissals between 1997 and 2010.

ALL-ROUND RECORDS

ALL-ROUNDERS TO HAVE SCORED 3,000 RUNS AND TAKEN 200 TEST WICKETS (RANKED BY ORDER OF DEBUT)

Player	Span	Mat	Runs	HS	Ave	100	Wkts	BBI	Ave	5	Ct	St
G.S. Sobers (WI)	1954–74	93	8,032	365*	57.78	26	235	6/73	34.03	6	109	0
Imran Khan (Pak)	1971–92	88	3,807	136	37.69	6	362	8/58	22.81	23	28	0
R.J. Hadlee (NZ)	1973–90	86	3,124	151*	27.16	2	431	9/52	22.29	36	39	0
I.T. Botham (Eng)	1977–92	102	5,200	208	33.54	14	383	8/34	28.40	27	120	0
Kapil Dev (Ind)	1978–94	131	5,248	163	31.05	8	434	9/83	29.64	23	64	0
C.L. Cairns (NZ)	1989–2004	62	3,320	158	33.53	5	218	7/27	29.40	13	14	0
S.K. Warne (Aus)	1992–2007	145	3,154	99	17.32	0	708	8/71	25.41	37	125	0
W.P.U.J.C. Vaas (SL)	1994–2009	111	3,089	100*	24.32	1	355	7/71	29.58	12	31	0
S.M. Pollock (SA)	1995–2008	108	3,781	111	32.31	2	421	7/87	23.11	16	72	0
J.H. Kallis (SA/ICC)	1995–2013	166	13,289	224	55.37	45	292	6/54	32.65	5	200	0
D.L. Vettori (NZ/ICC)	1997–2012	112	4,516	140	30.10	6	360	7/87	34.42	20	58	0
A. Flintoff (Eng/ICC)	1998–2009	79	3,845	167	31.77	5	226	5/58	32.78	3	52	0

100 runs and ten wickets in a match

Only three players in Test history have achieved the feat of scoring 100 runs and taking ten wickets in a Test match: **Alan Davidson**, 124 runs and 11 wickets for Australia against the West Indies at Brisbane in December 1960; Ian Botham, 114 runs and 13 wickets for England against India at Mumbai in February 1980; and Imran Khan, 117 runs and 11 wickets for Pakistan against India at Faisalabad in January 1983.

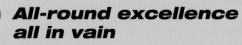

All-round excellence all in vain

Working on the basic principle of hitting the ball as hard and bowling the ball as fast as he could, Jimmy Sinclair did much to put South African cricket on the map. The peak of his 15-year, 25-match career came against England at Cape Town in April 1899 when – despite an eventual 210-run win for England – he took 6 for 26 in England's first innings and then scored 106 to become the first player ever to score 100 and take five wickets in an innings in a Test match. This feat has been repeated on 28 occasions.

A cut above the rest

The only player in history to score 100 runs and take five wickets in an innings on five occasions is Ian Botham. The legendary England all-rounder achieved the feat against New Zealand at Christchurch in February 1978 (103 and 5 for 73); against Pakistan at Lord's in June 1978 (108 and 8 for 34); against India at Mumbai in February 1980 (114 and 6 for 58/7 for 48); against Australia at Headingley in July 1981 (149 not out and 6 for 95); and against New Zealand at Wellington in January 1984 (138 and 5 for 59).

The first great all-rounder

A fine batsman in defence, an excellent driver of the ball and a right-arm medium-pace bowler who relied on spin, guile and variations in flight and pace, Australia's **George Giffen** was Test cricket's first truly great all-rounder. In 31 Tests between 1881 and 1896, he became the first of 54 players in history to score 1,000 runs (1238) and take 100 wickets (103).

Major contributions

A cornerstone of the England team for 58 Tests over 31 years from the turn of the 20th century, Wilfred Rhodes was the greatest slow left-armer of his day and a capable batsman (he once shared an opening stand of 323 with Jack Hobbs), who more than held his own in the field. He was the first of 22 players in history to score 1,000 runs (2,325), take 50 wickets (127) and snare 50 catches (60) in Test cricket.

The first of the fielding all-rounders

A superb batsman (scoring 7,249 runs for England at an average of 58.45, including 22 centuries), Walter Hammond ranks among the finest players ever to have played the game. A naturally gifted athlete, he also proved his worth in the field, taking 110 catches in his 20-year, 85-Test career to become the first of 66 players in history to score 5,000 runs and take 50 catches in Test cricket.

All-time great all-rounders: IAN BOTHAM (England)

Few players in the game's history have been able to galvanize a crowd like **Ian Botham**. A fast-medium swing bowler with an almost unique wicket-taking ability (by the time he ended his 15-year Test career in 1992 he was the world's leading wicket-taker with 383 wickets), Botham was also a hard-hitting batsman capable of turning a match on its head (few who saw it will ever forget his Ashes-turning 149 not out against Australia at Headingley in July 1981) and a world-class slip fielder, who bagged 120 catches in 102 matches.

All-time great all-rounders: KAPIL DEV (India)

Without doubt the finest fast bowler India has ever produced, **Kapil Dev** also made some hefty contributions to the Indian cause with the bat, plundering 5,238 runs – with a highest score of 163 against Sri Lanka at Kanpur in December 1986 – in a 16-year, 131-Test career between 1978 and 1994. However, it was Kapil Dev's relentless march to, and beyond, Richard Hadlee's then world record haul of 431 Test wickets that guaranteed his status among the game's all-time greats.

All-time great all-rounders: GARFIELD SOBERS (West Indies)

Garfield Sobers was the most complete cricketer in the game's history. In a 93-Test career for the West Indies spanning 20 years, he was a world-class performer with both bat (scoring 8,032 runs at an average of 57.78, including a then world record score of 365 not out against Pakistan at Kingston in February 1958), and ball (taking 235 wickets, as either a left-arm fast-medium or slow left-arm bowler), and also excelled in the field, taking 109 catches.

PARTNERSHIP RECORDS

HIGHEST PARTNERSHIPS BY WICKET: TOP 10

Wkt	Runs	Partners	Match	Venue	Match date
1st	415	N.D. McKenzie/G.C. Smith	SA v Bang	Chittagong (CDS)	29 Feb 2008
2nd	576	S.T. Jayasuriya/R.S. Mahanama	SL v Ind	Colombo (RPS)	2 Aug 1997
3rd	624	K.C. Sangakkara/D.P.M.D. Jayawardene	SL v SA	Colombo (SSC)	27 Jul 2006
4th	437	D.P.M.D. Jayawardene/T.T. Samaraweera	SL v Pak	Karachi	21 Feb 2009
5th	405	S.G. Barnes/D.G. Bradman	Aus v Eng	Sydney	13 Dec 1946
6th	352	B.B. McCullum/B.J. Watling	NZ v Ind	Wellington	14 Feb 2014
7th	347	D.S. Atkinson/C.C. Depeiaza	WI v Aus	Bridgetown	14 May 1955
8th	332	**I.J.L. Trott/S.C. Broad**	Eng v Pak	Lord's	26 Aug 2010
9th	195	M.V. Boucher/P.L. Symcox	SA v Pak	Johannesburg	14 Feb 1998
10th	163	P.J. Hughes/A.C. Agar	Aus v Eng	Nottingham	10 Jul 2013

Golden pair show Australia the way

Australia's Matthew Hayden and Ricky Ponting loved batting together in the 2005–06 season. Between 14 October 2005 and 9 April 2006 the pair batted together on 12 occasions, notching up seven century stands (the highest: 201 v South Africa in Durban) to amass 1,317 runs – a partnership record for a calendar year.

The Karachi kids

The best partnership in Test history (by average) not involving an opening pair is that of Pakistan's Javed Miandad and Shoaib Mohammad (both Karachi-born). The duo batted together 23 times between 1984 and 1993, hitting eight century and seven 50 partnerships and amassing 2,117 runs at a record average of 91.82 runs per partnership.

Mammoth effort is all in vain

A valiant 363-run partnership between Pakistan's **Mohammad Yousuf** (left, 192) and **Younis Khan** (right, 173) on days two and three of the Third Test against England at Headingley in August 2006 ultimately counted for little. The home side went on to win the match by 167 runs to take an unassailable 2–0 lead in the four-Test series, and the pair's 83.5-over effort remains the highest partnership in a losing cause in Test history.

Stuck in the middle with you

It's a fielding side's worst nightmare. Pakistan were floundering on 176 for 9 chasing Sri Lanka's first-innings 273 in the First Test at Colombo in June 2000. Then Wasim Akram (78) and Arshad Khan (9 not out off 95 balls) held on for 257 balls (42.5 overs in three hours four minutes) to add 90 runs – it is the longest tenth-wicket stand (by balls faced) in Test history.

Standing firm

The record for the most successful partnership in a series (868) is jointly held by England's great opening pair **Jack Hobbs** (left) and **Herbert Sutcliffe** (right) (against Australia in 1924–25, with four century stands) and Australia's Donald Bradman and Bill Ponsford (against England in 1934, including a then world record stand of 451 at Headingley).

Leading from the front

Between 2 October 1964 and 14 May 1965, in ten Tests against India, Pakistan and the West Indies, Australia's **Bill Lawry** (right) and **Bobby Simpson** (left) averaged 66.94 runs when they batted together (with a highest of 382 v West Indies in Barbados), to become the first opening partnership to register 1,000 runs (1,205) in a calendar season.

The best opening pair in history

By some distance, the best opening partnership in Test history (in terms of average runs scored) was that of England's Jack Hobbs and Herbert Sutcliffe. The pair batted together on 38 occasions between 1924 and 1930, recording 15 century stands (highest of 283 v Australia at Melbourne in January 1925) at an average of 87.81 runs per innings – only one other pair in Test history (West Indies' Allan Rae and Jeffrey Stollmeyer) has averaged over 70.

Solid as a rock

The legend of the great West Indies sides of the late 1970s and '80s may have been built on a battery of formidable fast bowlers, but a crucial, if unheralded, factor in the success of those teams was the firm foundation provided by a rock-solid opening partnership. Gordon Greenidge and Desmond Haynes batted together on 148 occasions over 14 years and scored 6,482 runs – the most scored by any partnership in Test history.

Perfect partners

Rahul Dravid and Sachin Tendulkar, who formed the backbone of India's batting line-up for approaching 16 years, and in Tendulkar's case considerably more, hold the all-time Test record for the most century partnerships. The pair added 100 runs or more together on 20 occasions between 1996 and 2012, with a highest effort of 249 (for the third wicket) in the Second Test against Zimbabwe at Nagpur in November 2000.

Test cricket's first century partnership

Test cricket had to wait three years and four matches before witnessing the first century partnership. On the opening morning of the 1880 Oval Test against Australia, England's W.G. Grace (152) put on 91 for the first wicket with his brother, E.M. Grace, and then added 120 runs with Bunny Lucas (55) for the second wicket to lead England to a commanding first-innings score of 420 and an eventual five-wicket victory.

Rescue act

Chasing South Africa's first-innings 169 in the First Test at Colombo on 27 July 2006, Sri Lanka had slipped to 14 for 2 when **Mahele Jayawardene** (right) joined **Kumar Sangakkara** (left) at the crease. 157 overs later, the pair – Sangakkara, 285; Jayawardene, 309 – had amassed a mighty 624-run partnership, smashing the partnership record for any wicket (576) set by compatriots Sanath Jayasuriya and Roshan Mohanama in 1997. Sri Lanka went on to win the match by an innings and 153 runs.

TEST RECORDS: BY TEAM

The spread of the game around the world was not instantaneous. Australia and England first locked horns in March 1877, but it took 123 years before we reached today's complement of ten Test-playing nations as South Africa (1889), West Indies (1928), New Zealand (1930), India (1932), Pakistan (1952), Sri Lanka (1982), Zimbabwe (1992) and Bangladesh (2000) joined the party. This section looks at the leading Test players on a country-by-country basis and tells you, among other things, who is Australia's all-time leading Test batsman and which Pakistan player has taken the most Test catches.

Australia followed up their 5–0 Ashes white-wash over England with an impressive 2–1 series win over South Africa in 2013–14.

AUSTRALIA

One of international cricket's original two participants, Australia hosted the first-ever Test match, against England at Melbourne in March 1877. England have appeared in more matches than the other Test-playing nations, but no other country in the game's history has enjoyed as many Test wins (360) or as high a winning percentage (46.93) as Australia.

RESULT SUMMARY

Opposition	Span	Mat	Won	Lost	Tied	Draw	W/L	%W	%L	%D
Bangladesh	2003–06	4	4	0	0	0	-	100.00	0.00	0.00
England	1877–2014	336	138	105	0	93	1.31	41.07	31.25	27.67
ICC World XI	2005	1	1	0	0	0	-	100.00	0.00	0.00
India	1947–2013	86	38	24	1	23	1.58	44.18	27.90	26.74
New Zealand	1946–2011	52	27	8	0	17	3.37	51.92	15.38	32.69
Pakistan	1956–2010	57	28	12	0	17	2.33	49.12	21.05	29.82
South Africa	1902–2014	91	50	21	0	20	2.38	54.94	23.07	21.97
Sri Lanka	1983–2013	26	17	1	0	8	17.00	65.38	3.84	30.76
West Indies	1930–2012	111	54	32	1	24	1.68	48.64	28.82	21.62
Zimbabwe	1999–2003	3	3	0	0	0	-	100.00	0.00	0.00

Largest victories

By an innings: by an innings and 360 runs against South Africa in Johannesburg in February 2002.

By runs: by 562 runs against England at The Oval in 1934.

By wickets: by ten wickets on 28 occasions.

Smallest victories

By runs: by three runs against England at Manchester in July 1902.

By wickets: by one wicket against the West Indies at Melbourne in December 1951.

Heaviest defeats

By an innings: by an innings and 579 runs against England at The Oval in August 1938.

By runs: by 675 runs, against England at Brisbane in November 1928.

By wickets: by ten wickets on ten occasions.

Hitting an all-time low

Australia did not get off to the most convincing of starts in their 1902 Ashes-winning series. In the First Test, at Edgbaston, after England had reached 376 in their first innings, Australia, on a wicket affected by a heavy downpour, crashed to a cataclysmic 36 all out (the lowest total in the country's history), with only Victor Trumper (18) reaching double figures. The rain came back to save Australia, however, and the three-day match ended in a draw.

Australia end Caribbean tour on an all-time high

After watching the West Indies compile 357 in their first innings of the Fifth Test at Kingston, Jamaica, in June 1955, Australia – already holding an unassailable 2–0 series lead – were determined to bow out of their first-ever tour to the Caribbean in style and put on a spectacular show. Centuries from Colin McDonald (127), **Neil Harvey** (204), Keith Miller (109), Ron Archer (128) and Richie Benaud (121) saw them reach an Australian record total of 758 for 8. They went on to win the match by an innings and 82 runs.

Hayden hits the heights

By the end of the second day of the First Test between Australia and Zimbabwe at Perth in October 2003, the fact that Australia had amassed a mighty first-innings score of 735 for 6 – the highest total on Australian soil in 126 years of Test cricket – was all but forgotten. Every one of the following day's headlines would be reserved for one man: Matthew Hayden. The Queensland left-handed opener smashed a then world record 380 (off 437 balls); it remains the highest individual score by an Australian in Test history.

BATTING – MOST RUNS: TOP 10

Pos	Runs	Player	Span	Mat	Inns	NO	HS	Ave	100	50	0
1	13,378	R.T. Ponting	1995–2012	168	287	29	257	51.85	41	62	17
2	11,174	A.R. Border	1978–94	156	265	44	205	50.56	27	63	11
3	10,927	S.R. Waugh	1985–2004	168	260	46	200	51.06	32	50	22
4	8,625	M.L. Hayden	1994–2009	103	184	14	380	50.73	30	29	14
5	8,240	M.J. Clarke	2004–14	105	180	20	329*	51.50	27	27	9
6	8,029	M.E. Waugh	1991–2002	128	209	17	153*	41.81	20	47	19
7	7,696	J.L. Langer	1993–2007	105	182	12	250	45.27	23	30	11
8	7,525	M.A. Taylor	1989–99	104	186	13	334*	43.49	19	40	5
9	7,422	D.C. Boon	1984–96	107	190	20	200	43.65	21	32	16
10	7,110	G.S. Chappell	1970–84	87	151	19	247*	53.86	24	31	12

All-time great: DONALD BRADMAN

Donald Bradman made his Test debut for Australia aged 20 against England in the 1928–29 Ashes series and registered the first of his 29 Test centuries in his second Test match. From that moment, he became the scourge of bowlers around the world. In the 1930 Ashes series, he plundered a record 974 runs (including a memorable and Test record-breaking knock of 334 at Headingley) at an average of 139.14 – it was the first of five times he would score 500-plus runs in a series. Going into his final Test, against England at The Oval in 1948, with his legend as the greatest batsman of all time confirmed, he needed a mere four runs to end with a career average of 100.00. Sensationally he was out for 0, but his career average of 99.94 still stands as the greatest of all time.

Ponting's record haul

Australia's best batsman of modern times and the heartbeat of one of his country's best-ever teams, **Ricky Ponting** had a talismanic approach to batting, in which every shot is played with a flourish of the bat, and it brought him rich rewards. In 168 Tests for his country (77 of them as captain) he plundered 13,378 runs (at an average of 51.85) with 41 centuries. Both the runs and centuries are all-time national records.

Struggling to get off the mark

The leading wicket-taker of all fast bowlers in Test history (with 563 wickets), Glenn McGrath may well have struck fear into opponents when he had the ball in his hand, but it was an altogether different story when he came out to bat. In 124 Test matches between 1993 and 2007, McGrath amassed just 671 runs (at an average of 7.36) and recorded an Australian record 35 ducks.

BOWLING – MOST WICKETS: TOP 10

Pos	Wkts	Player	Span	Mat	Balls	Runs	BBI	BBM	Ave	Econ	SR	5	10
1	708	S.K. Warne	1992–2007	145	40,705	17,995	8/71	12/128	25.41	2.65	57.4	37	10
2	563	G.D. McGrath	1993–2007	124	29,248	12,186	8/24	10/27	21.64	2.49	51.9	29	3
3	355	D.K. Lillee	1971–84	70	18,467	8,493	7/83	11/123	23.92	2.75	52.0	23	7
4	310	B. Lee	1999–2008	76	16,531	9,554	5/30	9/171	30.81	3.46	53.3	10	0
5	291	C.J. McDermott	1984–96	71	16,586	8,332	8/97	11/157	28.63	3.01	56.9	14	2
6	264	M.G. Johnson	2007–14	59	13,227	7,240	8/61	12/127	27.42	3.28	50.1	12	3
7	259	J.N. Gillespie	1996–2006	71	14,234	6,770	7/37	9/80	26.13	2.85	54.9	8	0
8	248	R. Benaud	1952–64	63	19,108	6,704	7/72	11/105	27.03	2.10	77.0	16	1
9	246	G.D. McKenzie	1961–71	60	17,681	7,328	8/71	10/91	29.78	2.48	71.8	16	3
10	228	R.R. Lindwall	1946–60	61	13,650	5,251	7/38	9/70	23.03	2.30	59.8	12	0

Magical Mailey destroys downbeat England

Already 3–0 up in the 1921 Ashes series, Australia went into the Fourth Test at Melbourne looking to ram home their advantage over England, and nobody did so more effectively than Arthur Mailey. The New South Wales leg-break bowler took 9 for 121 off 47 overs in England's second innings – the best-ever bowling figures in an innings by an Australian – as the home side went on to win the match by eight wickets to take a 4–0 series lead.

Fantastic Ferris

Of all Australian bowlers to have bowled 2,000 or more deliveries in Test cricket, nobody has a better average than J.J. Ferris. In eight matches between 1887 and 1892, the left-arm swing bowler took 61 wickets – with a best return of 7 for 37 against South Africa in Cape Town in March 1892 (in his final appearance for his country) – at an amazing average of 14.25.

Burke produces the most miserly bowling spell

As South Africa battled in vain to avoid defeat against Australia at Johannesburg in the Fourth Test in 1957–58, Australian off-break bowler Jim Burke made history. His 15 (wicketless, eight-ball) overs cost a mere ten runs – the best economy rate in an innings by an Australian bowler in history (0.40).

Bob Massie's magical debut

With the exception of India's Narendra Hirwani, no bowler has enjoyed a more spectacular start to his Test career than **Bob Massie**. Playing at Lord's in the Second Test of the 1972 Ashes series, the fast-medium swing bowler destroyed England, taking 8 for 84 in the first innings and 8 for 53 in the second to help Australia to an eight-wicket win. His match figures of 16 for 137 are the best by an Australian bowler in Test history.

All-time great: SHANE WARNE

From the moment at Old Trafford in June 1993 when Shane **Warne** ripped a massive leg-break from outside leg stump past a bemused Mike Gatting's defensive push and into off stump with his first delivery in Ashes cricket, the world knew it was witnessing a bowler with supreme ability. His major tools may have changed over the years as a result of injuries – the frequency of the big-spinning deliveries was replaced with more craft and guile – but Warne's ability to hypnotize opponents continued unabated. By the time he finished his 145-match, 15-year Test career in 2007, Warne had taken more five-wicket hauls (37), more ten-wicket hauls (10) and more wickets (708) than any other Australian bowler in history.

WICKETKEEPER – MOST DISMISSALS: TOP 5

Pos	Dis	Player	Span	Mat	Inns	Ct	St	Dis/Inn
1	416	**A.C. Gilchrist**	1999–2008	96	191	379	37	2.178
2	395	I.A. Healy	1988–99	119	224	366	29	1.763
3	355	R.W. Marsh	1970–84	96	182	343	12	1.950
4	233	B.J. Haddin	2008–14	57	110	228	5	2.118
5	187	A.T.W. Grout	1957–66	51	98	163	24	1.908

MOST DISMISSALS: INNINGS/MATCHES/SERIES

Three players (Wally Grout, Rod Marsh and Ian Healy) hold the Australian record for the most dismissals in an innings with six. **Adam Gilchrist** holds the record for the most dismissals in a match with ten (all caught), achieved against New Zealand at Hamilton in March 2000, while Brad Haddin holds the record for the most dismissals in a series, with 29 (all catches) in the 2013–14 Ashes series.

FIELDING – MOST CATCHES: TOP 5

Pos	Ct	Player	Span	Mat	Inns	Max	Ct/Inn
1	196	**R.T. Ponting**	1995–2012	165	328	3	0.597
2	181	M.E. Waugh	1991–2002	128	245	4	0.738
3	157	M.A. Taylor	1989–99	104	197	4	0.796
4	156	A.R. Border	1978–94	156	277	4	0.563
5	128	M.L. Hayden	1994–2009	103	205	4	0.624

MOST CATCHES: INNINGS/MATCHES/SERIES

Vic Richardson holds the Australian record for the most catches in an innings with five, against South Africa at Durban in February 1936. Greg Chappell (against England at Perth in December 1974) and Matthew Hayden (against Sri Lanka at Galle in March 2004) hold the record for the most catches in a match, with seven; and Jim Gregory holds the record for the most catches in a series, having taken 15 against England in 1920–21.

LONGEST-SERVING CAPTAINS: TOP 10

Pos	Mat	Player	Span	W-L-T-D	%W
1	93	**A.R. Border**	1984–94	32-22-1-38	34.40
2	77	R.T. Ponting	2004–10	48-16-0-13	62.33
3	57	S.R. Waugh	1999–2004	41-9-0-7	71.92
4	50	M.A. Taylor	1994–99	26-13-0-11	52.00
5	48	G.S. Chappell	1975–83	21-13-0-14	43.75
6	39	R.B. Simpson	1964-78	12-12-0-15	30.76
7	37	M.J. Clarke	2011–14	19-11-0-7	51.35
8	30	I.M. Chappell	1971–75	15-5-0-10	50.00
9	28	R. Benaud	1958–63	12-4-1-11	42.85
=	28	K.J. Hughes	1979–84	4-13-0-11	14.28

Most successful captain

A natural successor to Steve Waugh when he took over Australia's Test captaincy in 2004, Ricky Ponting went on to become the most successful captain in his country's history. In his 77 Tests in charge, Ponting recorded 48 wins (seven more than Waugh) with a winning percentage of 62.33.

Record partnership

Australia posted an intimidating and series-clinching first-innings total in the final 1934 Ashes Test at The Oval. Bill Ponsford (266) and Donald Bradman (244) put on 451 for the second wicket (the highest Test partnership by an Australian pair) to help their side to 701 all out and an eventual 562-run win.

ENGLAND

The home of cricket and the nation that gave the game to the world, England played in the first-ever Test match, against Australia at Melbourne in 1877, and have since gone on to play in more Test matches than any other country (945). There have been many highs and lows along the way: England's 331 victories (second only to Australia) are balanced out by a record number of defeats (273).

RESULT SUMMARY

Opposition	Span	Mat	Won	Lost	Tied	Draw	W/L	%W	%L	%D
Australia	1877–2014	336	105	138	0	93	0.76	31.25	41.07	27.67
Bangladesh	2003–10	8	8	0	0	0	-	100.00	0.00	0.00
India	1932–2012	107	40	20	0	47	2.00	37.38	18.69	43.92
New Zealand	1930–2013	99	47	8	0	44	5.87	47.47	8.08	44.44
Pakistan	1954–2012	74	22	16	0	36	1.37	29.72	21.62	48.64
South Africa	1889–2012	141	56	31	0	54	1.80	39.71	21.98	38.29
Sri Lanka	1982–2012	26	10	7	0	9	1.42	38.46	26.92	34.61
West Indies	1928–2012	148	45	53	0	49	0.84	30.40	35.81	33.78
Zimbabwe	1996–2003	6	3	0	0	3	-	50.00	0.00	50.00

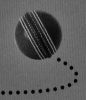

Low points

There have been a few too many calamitous days for English cricket fans over the years – 46 all out against the West Indies at Port of Spain in March 1994; 51 all out against the same opposition at Bridgetown in January 2009 – but the lowest point in their history came in the first innings of the First Test of the 1886–87 Ashes series, at Melbourne, when they crashed to a miserable 45 all out. Astonishingly, however, England rallied to win the match by 13 runs.

Largest victories

By an innings: by an innings and 579 runs against Australia at The Oval in August 1938.

By runs: by 675 runs against Australia at Brisbane in November 1928.

By wickets: by ten wickets on 20 occasions.

Smallest victories

By runs: by two runs against Australia at Edgbaston in August 2005.

By wickets: by one wicket on three occasions: against Australia at The Oval in August 1902, against Australia at Melbourne in January 1908 and against South Africa in Cape Town in January 1923.

Heaviest defeats

By an innings: by an innings and 332 runs against Australia at Brisbane in November 1946.

By runs: by 562 runs against Australia at The Oval in August 1934.

By wickets: by ten wickets on 20 occasions.

Records tumble in Ashes finale at The Oval

England's spectacular batting performance in the first innings of the Fifth Test against Australia at The Oval in August 1938, which led to them squaring the Ashes series 1–1, set several benchmarks for future generations of England cricketers to aspire to. The team total (903 for 7 declared) is the highest by an England team in history; **Len Hutton's** majestic innings of 364 has never been bettered by an Englishman; and the victory margin – by an innings and 579 runs – is the largest (by an innings) in England's history.

BATTING – MOST RUNS: TOP 10

Pos	Runs	Player	Span	Mat	Inns	NO	HS	Ave	100	50	0
1	8,900	G.A. Gooch	1975–95	118	215	6	333	42.58	20	46	13
2	8,463	A.J. Stewart	1990–2003	133	235	21	190	39.54	15	45	14
3	8,231	D.I. Gower	1978–92	117	204	18	215	44.25	18	39	7
4	8,181	K.P. Pietersen	2005–14	104	181	8	227	47.28	23	35	10
5	8,114	G. Boycott	1964–82	108	193	23	246*	47.72	22	42	10
6	8,047	A.N. Cook	2006–14	102	183	10	294	46.51	25	35	7
7	7,728	M.A. Atherton	1989–2001	115	212	7	185*	37.69	16	46	20
8	7,624	M.C. Cowdrey	1954–75	114	188	15	182	44.06	22	38	9
9	7,249	W.R. Hammond	1927–47	85	140	16	336*	58.45	22	24	4
10	7,037	A.J. Strauss	2004–12	100	178	6	177	40.91	21	27	15

Best opening partnership

Between 1924 and 1930 England were blessed with the greatest opening partnership in their history. During that seven-year span, Jack Hobbs and Herbert Sutcliffe batted together on 38 occasions and scored 3,249 runs with 15 century stands (only Gordon Greenidge and Desmond Haynes of the West Indies, with 16, have done better in Test history – taking 148 innings to achieve the feat). Hobbs and Sutcliffe's average partnership of 87.81 is the best in Test history.

All-time great: WALTER HAMMOND

Without doubt one of the finest batsmen to play the game, Walter Hammond was also one of the first players to bring a real sense of dash to Test cricket. A naturally gifted athlete, he was quick on his feet, a dashing stroke player and a sweet timer of the ball who was equally dynamic off both the front and back foot, particularly when driving the ball. In 85 Tests for England between 1927 and 1947, Hammond scored 7,249 runs at an impressive average of 58.45. He also set the national record for the most centuries (22, since passed by Alastair Cook and Kevin Pietersen) and for the most runs in a series (905 against Australia in 1928–29).

Sutcliffe: One of England's very best

Revered for his astounding powers of concentration and an exemplary technique, the outbreak of the First World War may have delayed **Herbert Sutcliffe's** entry into county cricket (he was 24 when he made his debut for Yorkshire in 1919), but the Harrogate-born batsman more than made up for lost time, breaking into the England team by 1924 and going on to form one half (alongside Jack Hobbs) of his country's most successful opening partnership of all time. His first century (of 16) came in only his second Test (122 against South Africa at Lord's in June 1924) and by the time he bowed out of international cricket 11 years later (after 54 matches) he had amassed 4,555 runs (with a highest score of 194 against Australia at Sydney in December 1932) at an average of 60.73 – the highest by any England batsman in Test history.

Captain Cook tops hundreds list

Tipped for greatness from an early age, former England U19 captain **Alastair Cook** was drafted into the senior England squad touring India in March 2006 and seemed set to fulfil the earlier prophecies by scoring 60 and an unbeaten 104 on his Test debut. The tall, stylish left-hander has not looked back since: two further centuries followed against Pakistan the next summer and by the time he had reached his 25th birthday in December 2009 he had scored more runs (3,536) and more centuries (nine) than any other England player of a comparable age. He was in irrepressible form during England's successful 2010–11 Ashes campaign, scoring 766 runs in the series and passing 5,000 Test runs (the second youngest player in Test history, after Sachin Tendulkar, to do so). Cook succeeded Andrew Strauss, who retired as England captain in August 2012, having let the team in for a short series in May 2011, and recorded his highest Test score (294 against India) later that summer. Cook notched his English record 23rd Test century during England's winter 2012 tour to India. By 2014, Cook had already notched up his 25th Test century – one would expect plenty more to follow.

BOWLING - MOST WICKETS: TOP 10

Pos	Wkts	Player	Span	Mat	Balls	Runs	BBI	BBM	Ave	Econ	SR	5	10
1	383	I.T. Botham	1977–92	102	21,815	10,878	8/34	13/106	28.40	2.99	56.9	27	4
2	343	J.M. Anderson	2003–14	92	20,350	10,522	7/43	11/71	30.67	3.10	59.3	15	2
3	325	R.G.D. Willis	1971–84	90	17,357	8,190	8/43	9/92	25.20	2.83	53.4	16	0
4	307	F.S. Trueman	1952–65	67	15,178	6,625	8/31	12/119	21.57	2.61	49.4	17	3
5	297	D.L. Underwood	1966–82	86	21,862	7,674	8/51	13/71	25.83	2.10	73.6	17	6
6	255	G.P. Swann	2008–14	60	15,349	7,642	6/65	10/132	29.96	2.98	60.1	17	3
7	252	J.B. Statham	1951–65	70	16,056	6,261	7/39	11/97	24.84	2.33	63.7	9	1
8	248	M.J. Hoggard	2000–08	67	13,909	7,564	7/61	12/205	30.50	3.26	56.0	7	1
9	238	S.C.J. Broad	2007–14	67	13,896	7,125	7/44	11/121	30.31	3.11	58.3	11	2
10	236	A.V. Bedser	1946–55	51	15,918	5,876	7/44	14/99	24.89	2.21	67.4	15	5

Most five-wicket hauls

A talismanic all-rounder with an uncanny ability to bring a crowd to its feet through his deeds with both bat and ball, Ian Botham ended his 15-year, 102-Test career in 1992 as the world's leading wicket-taker, with 383 wickets, including 27 five-wicket hauls. Both marks still stand as all-time England Test records.

Laker's record return

No player in history, let alone one from England, has been able to match **Jim Laker**'s amazing achievements with the ball during the Fourth Test against Australia at Old Trafford in July 1956. In an Ashes-retaining performance of sublime quality, the Yorkshire off-spinner took 9 for 37 in the first innings and an all-time best 10 for 53 in the second. His match figures of 19 for 90 are also an all-time record in Test cricket.

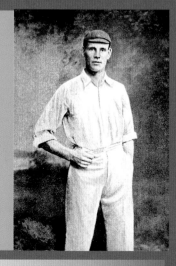

Toiling in the summer sun

Not every day for **Ian Botham** was one to remember, however. As Pakistan prospered on a batsman-friendly surface in the Fifth Test at The Oval in August 1987, England's bowlers suffered, and none more so than Botham. The Somerset all-rounder's 52 overs eventually brought him three wickets, but they also cost 217 runs – the most ever conceded in a Test innings by an England bowler.

Keeping it tight

Two players share the England record (0.30) for the most economic spell of bowling (minimum of ten overs) in Test history: Bob Wyatt, who took 3 for 4 off 13 overs against South Africa at Durban in January 1928; and Hedley Verity, who took 0 for 4 off 13 overs against South Africa at Leeds in July 1935

All-time great: S.F. BARNES

England have produced some world-class bowlers over the years – Fred Trueman and Ian Botham to name but two – but none of them has struck as much fear into the hearts of opposing batsmen as the legendary **S.F. Barnes**, the greatest fast bowler of the early part of the 20th century. One of the first bowlers to make full use of the ball's seam and capable of swinging the ball both ways, at pace, Barnes took 189 wickets for England (including a national record seven ten-wicket match hauls) in 27 Tests between 1901 and 1914. In his final Test series, against South Africa, he took a world record 49 wickets in the series, in only four Tests.

WICKETKEEPER – MOST DISMISSALS: TOP 5

Pos	Dis	Player	Span	Mat	Inns	Ct	St	Dis/Inn
1	269	**A.P.E. Knott**	1967–81	95	174	250	19	1.545
2	241	A.J. Stewart	1990–2003	133	141	227	14	1.709
3	230	M.J. Prior	2007–13	75	138	217	13	1.666
4	219	T.G. Evans	1946–59	91	175	173	46	1.251
5	174	R.W. Taylor	1971–84	57	106	167	7	1.641

MOST DISMISSALS: INNINGS/MATCHES/SERIES

The record for the most dismissals in an innings by an England wicketkeeper is seven by Bob Taylor (7ct) against India in Mumbai in February 1980. Jack Russell holds the record both for the most dismissals in a match – 11 catches in the Second Test of 1995–96 series against South Africa in Johannesburg – and for the most dismissals in a series – 27 (25ct, 2st) against South Africa in the 1995–96 series.

FIELDING - MOST CATCHES: TOP 5

Pos	Ct	Player	Span	Mat	Inns	Max	Ct/Inn
1	121	A.J. Strauss	2004–12	100	189	3	0.640
2	120	I.T. Botham	1977–92	102	179	3	0.670
=	120	M.C. Cowdrey	1954–75	114	214	3	0.560
4	110	W.R. Hammond	1927–47	85	154	3	0.714
5	105	G.P. Thorpe	1993–2005	100	179	4	0.586

MOST CATCHES: INNINGS/MATCHES/SERIES

The England record for the most catches in an innings is four, a feat achieved on 20 occasions; the record for the most catches in a match is six, a feat achieved on seven occasions; and the record for the most catches in a series is 12, a feat achieved on five occasions.

Most successful captain

His sudden resignation following a five-wicket defeat to South Africa at Edgbaston in August 2008 prevented **Michael Vaughan** from surpassing Michael Atherton as England's longest-serving captain (51 Tests to Atherton's 54), but the history books will record that Vaughan was the most successful England captain in history, recording 26 wins. The highlight of his captaincy came in 2005, when England won the Ashes for the first time in 18 years.

LONGEST-SERVING CAPTAINS: TOP 10

Pos	Mat	Player	Span	W-L-T-D	%W
1	54	M.A. Atherton	1993–2001	13-21-0-20	24.07
2	51	M.P. Vaughan	2003–08	26-11-0-14	50.98
3	50	A.J. Strauss	2006–12	24-11-0-15	48.00
4	45	N. Hussain	1999–2003	17-15-0-13	37.77
5	41	P.B.H. May	1955–61	20-10-0-11	48.78
6	34	G.A. Gooch	1988–93	10-12-0-12	29.41
7	32	D.I. Gower	1982–89	5-18-0-9	15.62
8	31	R. Illingworth	1969–73	12-5-0-14	38.70
=	31	J.M. Brearley	1977–81	18-4-0-9	58.06
10	30	E.R. Dexter	1961–64	9-7-0-14	30.00

INDIA

A Test-playing nation since 1932, India's rise towards the top of world cricket's ranks was gradual. First they became competitive at home, where overseas batsmen struggled against India's legion of spin bowlers on slow, low, turning wickets, and then, with the emergence of an array of batting talent, such as Sunil Gavaskar and Sachin Tendulkar, they started to make waves around the world.

RESULT SUMMARY

Opposition	Span	Mat	Won	Lost	Tied	Draw	W/L	%W	%L	%D
Australia	1947–2013	86	24	38	1	23	0.63	27.90	44.18	26.74
Bangladesh	2000–10	7	6	0	0	1	-	85.71	0.00	14.28
England	1932–2013	107	20	40	0	47	0.50	18.69	37.38	43.92
New Zealand	1955–2014	54	18	10	0	26	1.80	33.33	18.51	48.14
Pakistan	1952–2007	59	9	12	0	38	0.75	15.25	20.33	64.40
South Africa	1992–2013	29	7	13	0	9	0.53	24.13	44.82	31.03
Sri Lanka	1982–2010	35	14	6	0	15	2.33	40.00	17.14	42.85
West Indies	1948–2013	90	16	30	0	44	0.53	17.77	33.33	48.88
Zimbabwe	1992–2005	11	7	2	0	2	3.50	63.63	18.18	18.18

Plummeting to new depths

A trip to Lord's is considered the pinnacle of many players' careers, but that was far from being the case when India played England at the home of cricket in June 1974. Forced to follow on in their second innings, still 327 runs behind, they crashed to a disastrous 42 all out to lose by an innings and 285 runs. It remains India's lowest-ever Test total.

Stellar Sehwag steals the show

After watching South Africa compile a handsome 540 all out in their first innings of the First Test at Chennai in March 2008, India needed a confident performance with the bat if they were to stay in the game. And **Virender Sehwag** duly obliged, batting for 8 hours and 50 minutes, facing 304 balls and hitting 42 fours and five sixes en route to a score of 319. It is the 17th highest score in Test history and the highest by an Indian batsman.

Starting off in style

Sunil Gavaskar, India's first great batsman, burst on to the international scene in spectacular fashion against the West Indies, in the Caribbean, between February and April 1971. Handed his debut in the Second Test of the five-match series, the diminutive opener hit four centuries (with a highest score of 220 in the Fifth Test) and three half-centuries to help India to a sensational 1–0 series win. His haul of 774 runs in the series (at an average of 154.80) is an all-time Indian record.

Largest victories

By an innings: by an innings and 239 runs against Bangladesh in Dhaka in May 2007.

By runs: by 320 runs against Australia at Mohali in October 2008.

By wickets: by ten wickets on seven occasions.

Smallest victories

By runs: by 13 runs against Australia at Mumbai in November 2004.

By wickets: by one wicket against Australia at Mohali in October 2010.

Heaviest defeats

By an innings: by an innings and 336 runs against the West Indies at Kolkata in December 1958.

By runs: by 342 runs against Australia at Nagpur in October 2004.

By wickets: by ten wickets on 17 occasions.

BATTING – MOST RUNS: TOP 10

Pos	Runs	Player	Span	Mat	Inns	NO	HS	Ave	100	50	0
1	15,921	S.R. Tendulkar	1989–2013	200	329	33	248*	53.78	51	68	14
2	13,265	R. Dravid	1996–2012	163	284	32	270	52.63	36	63	7
3	10,122	S.M. Gavaskar	1971–87	125	214	16	236*	51.12	34	45	12
4	8,781	V.V.S. Laxman	1996–2012	134	225	34	281	45.97	17	56	14
5	8,503	V. Sehwag	2001–13	103	178	6	319	49.43	23	31	16
6	7,212	S.C. Ganguly	1996–2008	113	188	17	239	42.17	16	35	13
7	6,868	D.B. Vengsarkar	1976–92	116	185	22	166	42.13	17	35	15
8	6,215	M. Azharuddin	1984–2000	99	147	9	199	45.03	22	21	5
9	6,080	G.R. Viswanath	1969–83	91	155	10	222	41.93	14	35	10
10	5,248	Kapil Dev	1978–94	131	184	15	163	31.05	8	27	16

All-time great: SACHIN TENDULKAR

Arguably the biggest icon the game has ever seen, **Sachin Tendulkar** is the most complete batsman of his age, capable of playing every shot in the coaching manual with equal aplomb and scoring heavily in every part of the world against any type of attack. A star from the moment he made his Test debut as a 16-year-old in 1989, Tendulkar, known as the "Little Master", made the first of his all-time record 51 Test centuries aged 17, against England in 1990, and has gone on to enjoy a spectacular career, achieving almost godlike status in cricket-mad India. In 2008 he surpassed Brian Lara as Test cricket's all-time leading run-scorer, with 15,921 runs (at an average of 53.78).

Batting their way to a series win

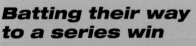

Already one-nil up in the three-match series and having seen Sri Lanka compile 393 all out in their first innings in the Third Test at Mumbai in December 2009, the equation for India was a simple one: to occupy the crease for as long as possible and bat Sri Lanka out of the game. They did so in record-breaking fashion, as a mighty innings of 293 from Virender Sehwag plus an unbeaten century from Mahendra Singh Dhoni saw them compile a massive 726 for 9 declared – the highest total in India's history – en route to an eventual innings-and-24-run victory and a 2–0 series win.

Sign of things to come

Having played first-class cricket for nine years without international recognition, many thought Shikhar Dhawan's chance of playing for India had gone. But when it finally arrived – against Australia in the Third Test at Mohali in March 2013 – he grabbed it in style. The Delhi-born opener reached his century off 85 balls (a record for a Test debutant) and went on to score 187 – the highest-ever score by an Indian on debut.

Hit and miss with the bat

He may have been a huge hit with the ball (taking an impressive 311 wickets in 92 Test matches), but Zaheer Khan has endured more fluctuating fortunes with the bat: he has struck three half-centuries (with a highest score of 75, against Bangladesh at Dhaka in December 2004), but has also failed to trouble the scorers on 29 occasions – a record number of ducks for an India batsman in Tests.

Mankad and Roy power India to series win

One–nil up in the five-match series with one Test to go, at Chennai in January 1956, India won the toss, elected to bat and would have pinned their hopes of series success on their batsmen batting New Zealand out of the game. Their openers, **Vinoo Mankad** (231) and Pankaj Roy (173), responded in spectacular fashion, putting on 413 for the opening wicket – the highest partnership in India's Test history. It provided the perfect foundation for India, who went on to win the match by an innings and 109 runs to take the series 2–0.

BOWLING – MOST WICKETS: TOP 10

Pos	Wkts	Player	Span	Mat	Balls	Runs	BBI	BBM	Ave	Econ	SR	5	10
1	619	A. Kumble	1990–2008	132	40,850	18,355	10/74	14/149	29.65	2.69	65.9	35	8
2	434	Kapil Dev	1978–94	131	27,740	12,867	9/83	11/146	29.64	2.78	63.9	23	2
3	413	Harbhajan Singh	1998–2013	101	28,293	13,372	8/84	15/217	32.37	2.83	68.5	25	5
4	311	Z. Khan	2000–14	92	18,785	10,247	7/87	10/149	32.94	3.27	60.4	11	1
5	266	B.S. Bedi	1966–79	67	21,364	7,637	7/98	10/194	28.71	2.14	80.3	14	1
6	242	B.S. Chandrasekhar	1964–79	58	15,963	7,199	8/79	12/104	29.74	2.70	65.9	16	2
7	236	J. Srinath	1991–2002	67	15,104	7,196	8/86	13/132	30.49	2.85	64.0	10	1
8	189	E.A.S. Prasanna	1962–78	49	14,353	5,742	8/76	11/140	30.38	2.40	75.9	10	2
9	164	I. Sharma	2007–14	55	11,025	6,161	6/51	10/108	37.56	3.35	67.2	5	1
10	162	M.H. Mankad	1946–59	44	14,686	5,236	8/52	13/131	32.32	2.13	90.6	8	2

Record-breaking achievements with the ball

The fourth and final day of the Second Test match between India and Pakistan at Delhi in February 1999 was a day to remember for Anil Kumble. With Pakistan set an unlikely 420 runs for victory, the leg-spinner became the first Indian, and only the second bowler in Test history, to take all ten wickets in an innings, finishing with 10 for 74 off 26.3 overs. The best match figures by an Indian bowler are 16 for 136, achieved by Narendra Hirwani against the West Indies at Chennai in January 1988.

A miser with the ball

Renowned for his tireless efforts in practice, where he would spend hours bowling at a coin placed on a good length, Bapu Nadkarni was the most miserly bowler in Test history. The left-arm spinner holds the Indian record for both the best economy rate in an innings (0.15 against England at Chennai in January 1964, when his spell of 32-27-5-0 included 22 consecutive maidens) and the best economy rate in a career (his 1,527.3 overs cost him just 1.67 runs per over).

Chandrasekhar too much for England

The star of India's 2–1 home series win over England in 1972–73 was, without doubt, Bhagwath Chandrasekhar. The leg-spinner bewitched England's batsmen throughout, taking four five-wicket hauls (with a best of 8 for 79 in the First Test at Delhi) and ended the series with 35 wickets to his name – an all-time record series haul by an Indian bowler.

All-time great: ANIL KUMBLE

A determined performer who has probably won more matches for India than other bowler in history, **Anil Kumble** owed his success more to a high action that was capable of achieving both metronomic accuracy and an awkward bounce than an inherent ability to turn the ball. After making his debut against England at Old Trafford in 1990, the leg-spinner went on to break virtually every single Indian bowling record. In a 132-Test, 18-year international career he set records for the most wickets (619), the most five-wicket hauls in an innings (35) and the most ten-wicket hauls in a match (8).

India's latest spin star

Left-arm spinner **Ravindra Jadeja** made his Test debut against England at Nagpur in December 2012, bowling 70 overs and taking three wickets. He has since emerged as an economical, wicket-taking bowler who can deliver a huge number of overs and by March 2014 had taken 36 wickets in eight Tests at an average of 26.30 – the best by an Indian bowler in Test history.

WICKETKEEPER – MOST DISMISSALS: TOP 5

Pos	Dis	Player	Span	Mat	Inns	Ct	St	Dis/Inn
1	263	**M.S. Dhoni**	2005–14	83	155	226	37	1.696
2	198	S.M.H. Kirmani	1976–86	88	151	160	38	1.311
3	130	K.S. More	1986–93	49	90	110	20	1.444
4	107	N.R. Mongia	1994–2001	44	77	99	8	1.389
5	82	F.M. Engineer	1961–75	46	83	66	16	0.987

MOST DISMISSALS: INNINGS/MATCHES

The Indian record for the most dismissals in an innings is six, a feat achieved on two occasions: by Syed Kirmani (5ct, 1st) against New Zealand at Christchurch in February 1976; and by M.S. Dhoni (6ct) against New Zealand at Wellington in April 2009. The Indian record for the most dismissals in a match is eight, a feat achieved on five occasions – twice by Nayan Mongia and three times by Dhoni.

FIELDING – MOST CATCHES: TOP 5

Pos	Ct	Player	Span	Mat	Inns	Max	Ct/Inn
1	209	**R. Dravid**	1996–2012	163	299	3	0.698
2	135	V.V.S. Laxman	1996–2012	134	248	4	0.544
3	115	S.R. Tendulkar	1989–2013	200	366	3	0.314
4	108	S.M. Gavaskar	1971–87	125	216	3	0.500
5	105	M. Azharuddin	1984–2000	99	177	5	0.593

MOST CATCHES: INNINGS/MATCHES/SERIES

The Indian record for the most catches in an innings is five, achieved on three occasions; the record for the most catches in a match is seven, by Yajurvindra Singh against England at Bangalore in January 1977; the record for the most catches in a series is 13, by **Rahul Dravid** against Australia in 2004–05.

LONGEST-SERVING CAPTAINS: TOP 10

Pos	Mat	Player	Span	W-L-T-D	%W
1	53	M.S. Dhoni	2008–14	26-14-0-13	49.05
2	49	S.C. Ganguly	2000–05	21-13-0-15	42.85
3	47	M. Azharuddin	1990–99	14-14-0-19	29.78
=	47	S.M. Gavaskar	1976–85	9-8-0-30	19.14
5	40	Nawab of Pataudi	1962–75	9-19-0-12	22.50
6	34	Kapil Dev	1983–87	4-7-1-22	11.76
7	25	R. Dravid	2003–07	8-6-0-11	32.00
=	25	S.R. Tendulkar	1996–2000	4-9-0-12	16.00
9	22	B.S. Bedi	1976–78	6-11-0-5	27.27
10	16	A.L. Wadekar	1971–74	4-4-0-8	25.00

Most dismissals in a series

The Indian record for the most dismissals by a wicketkeeper in a series is 19, held jointly by Naren Tamhane (12ct, 7st), against Pakistan in the 1954–55 series in Pakistan, and by Syed Kirmani (17ct, 2st) against Pakistan in 1979–80 in India.

India's most successful captain

Many people believe that wicket-keepers do not make good captains because their work behind the stumps every ball takes too much concentration for them to look at the bigger picture. India's M.S. Dhoni has exploded that myth in recent years. Not only are his personal figures better, but also under his captaincy, India rose to No.1 in the ICC World Test Rankings and enjoyed some spectacular success. In 2013, Dhoni became India's first captain to have a winning percentage in excess of 50 (51.06), although by 2014 that had dropped to 49.05.

NEW ZEALAND

New Zealand were granted Test status in 1929–30, but it took them 26 years and 44 Tests to record their first victory and 40 years before they could celebrate a first series win. However, the emergence of world-class all-rounder Richard Hadlee in the 1970s inspired a new generation of players to the extent that, today, New Zealand are one of the most competitive sides on the international circuit.

RESULT SUMMARY

Opposition	Span	Mat	Won	Lost	Tied	Draw	W/L	%W	%L	%D
Australia	1946–2011	52	8	27	0	17	0.29	15.38	51.92	32.69
Bangladesh	2001–13	11	8	0	0	3	-	72.72	0.00	27.27
England	1930–2013	99	8	47	0	44	0.17	8.08	47.47	44.44
India	1955–2014	54	10	18	0	26	0.55	18.51	33.33	48.14
Pakistan	1955–2011	50	7	23	0	20	0.30	14.00	46.00	40.00
South Africa	1932–2013	40	4	23	0	13	0.17	10.00	57.50	32.50
Sri Lanka	1983–2012	28	10	8	0	10	1.25	35.71	28.57	35.71
West Indies	1952–2013	42	11	12	0	19	0.91	26.19	28.57	45.23
Zimbabwe	1992–2012	15	9	0	0	6	-	60.00	0.00	40.00

BATTING – MOST RUNS: TOP 10

Pos	Runs	Player	Span	Mat	Inns	NO	HS	Ave	100	50	0
1	7,172	S.P. Fleming	1994–2008	111	189	10	274*	40.06	9	46	16
2	5,444	M.D. Crowe	1982–95	77	131	11	299	45.36	17	18	9
3	5,334	J.G. Wright	1978–93	82	148	7	185	37.82	12	23	7
4	5,219	B.B. McCullum	2004–14	84	145	8	302	38.09	9	28	11
5	4,702	N.J. Astle	1996–2006	81	137	10	222	37.02	11	24	11
6	4,508	D.L. Vettori	1997–2012	111	171	22	140	30.25	6	23	19
7	4,178	L.R.L. Taylor	2007–14	54	98	9	217*	46.94	11	21	4
8	3,448	B.E. Congdon	1965–78	61	114	7	176	32.22	7	19	9
9	3,428	J.R. Reid	1949–65	58	108	5	142	33.28	6	22	5
10	3,320	C.L. Cairns	1989–2004	62	104	5	158	33.53	5	22	7

Turner triumphs in the Caribbean

Five consecutive draws between the West Indies and New Zealand in the 1971–72 series played in the Caribbean may not have made for the most entertaining of cricket viewing, but for New Zealand's Glenn Turner the tour was a triumphant one. The right-handed opener's haul of 672 runs in the series, including a highest score of 259 in the Fourth Test at Georgetown, is a New Zealand record.

Largest victories

By an innings: by an innings and 301 runs against Zimbabwe in Napier in January 2012.

By runs: by 204 runs against the West Indies at Bridgetown in June 2002.

By wickets: by ten wickets on four occasions.

Smallest victories

By runs: by 7 runs against Australia at Hobart in December 2011.

By wickets: by one wicket against the West Indies at Dunedin in February 1980.

Heaviest defeats

By an innings: by an innings and 324 runs against Pakistan at Lahore in May 2002.

By runs: by 358 runs against South Africa in Johannesburg in November 2007.

By wickets: by ten wickets on 12 occasions.

Plumbing the depths

New Zealand, still chasing the first Test victory in their history, were still very much in the match after both sides had completed their first innings in the Second Test at Auckland in March 1955, trailing England by just 46 runs. But what followed was the most dramatic collapse in Test history. New Zealand folded to a pitiful 26 all out – the lowest total in Test history – to lose by an innings and 20 runs.

Magic McCullum

At 94 for 5 and still trailing India by 152 runs, New Zealand were in huge trouble in their second innings in the Second Test at Wellington in February 2014 and their captain **Brendon McCullum** needed to deliver. He did so in record-breaking fashion: supported by BJ Watling (124) and Jimmy Neesham (137) he scored a national record 302 to lead his side to the highest total in their history – 680 for 8 – and to safety.

All-time great: MARTIN CROWE

Born into a cricketing family (his father Dave played first-class cricket and his elder brother Jeff played 39 Tests for New Zealand), **Martin Crowe** was the most complete batsman his country has ever produced. A right-hander who possessed every shot in the book, and a seemingly limitless amount of time in which to play them, he scored 5,444 runs (at an average of 45.36) in 77 Tests for his country – including a national record 17 centuries and a highest score of 299 before injury brought a premature end to his career in 1995.

Taylor tops New Zealand averages list

Ross Taylor did not make the greatest start to his Test career in 2007, scoring just 44 runs in his first four innings (all against South Africa), but a well-crafted century in his fifth Test match innings against England at Hamilton in March 2008 marked him out as a player of huge potential. And he has gone on to deliver the goods for his country: by 2014, he had scored 4,178 runs in 54 matches (with 11 centuries and a highest score of 217 not out) at an average of 46.94 – the highest by any New Zealand player in Test history.

Most fifties

A sweet timer of the ball and equally strong through the offside or off his pads, **Stephen Fleming** will enter the history books as one of New Zealand's best-ever batsmen. His sole weakness was an inability to convert good starts into big scores. In a 111-Test career for his country between 1994 and 2008, Fleming, New Zealand's most-capped player and all-time leading run-scorer, passed 50 on 55 occasions (a national record), but only managed to convert nine of them into three-figure scores – a conversion rate of just 16.36 per cent.

A rabbit with the bat

In a 71-Test career since making his debut for New Zealand against South Africa in November 2000, **Chris Martin** has taken a commendable 233 wickets, but his hapless performances with the bat are almost as remarkable as his feats with the ball. In 104 innings for his country, Martin has scored just 123 runs (at an average of 2.36, including a national record 36 ducks.

BOWLING – MOST WICKETS: TOP 10

Pos	Wkts	Player	Span	Mat	Balls	Runs	BBI	BBM	Ave	Econ	SR	5	10
1	431	R.J. Hadlee	1973–90	86	21,918	9,611	9/52	15/123	22.29	2.63	50.8	36	9
2	359	D.L. Vettori	1997–2012	111	28,508	12,281	7/87	12/149	34.20	2.58	79.4	20	3
3	233	C.S. Martin	2000–13	71	14,026	7,878	6/26	11/180	33.81	3.37	60.1	10	1
4	218	C.L. Cairns	1989–2004	62	11,698	6,410	7/27	10/100	29.40	3.28	53.6	13	1
5	160	D.K. Morrison	1987–97	48	10,064	5,549	7/89	8/83	34.68	3.30	62.9	10	0
6	130	B.L. Cairns	1974–85	43	10,628	4,280	7/74	10/144	32.92	2.41	81.7	6	1
7	123	E.J. Chatfield	1975–89	43	10,360	3,958	6/73	10/124	32.17	2.29	84.2	3	1
8	116	R.O. Collinge	1965–78	35	7,689	3,393	6/63	9/166	29.25	2.64	66.2	3	0
9	112	T.G. Southee	2008–14	31	6,527	3,438	7/64	10/108	30.69	3.16	58.2	4	1
10	111	B.R. Taylor	1965–73	30	6,334	2,953	7/74	9/182	26.60	2.79	57.0	4	0

A taste for wickets

Among the fastest bowlers on the circuit before his retirement in 2010, **Shane Bond**'s career has been blighted by a succession of injuries since he made his debut against Australia at Hobart in November 2001. When he was able to make it on to the pitch, however, he excelled. In 18 matches for the Blackcaps, Bond took 87 wickets at an average of 22.09 with a wicket every 38.7 balls – the best strike-rate by any New Zealand bowler in history.

Best economy rate: career/innings

Although Jeremy Coney's 52 Test matches brought him only a modest 27 wickets, no bowler (to have bowled more than 2,000 balls) in New Zealand's history can match his economy rate – a mere 2.04 runs per over. The best economy rate in an innings by a New Zealand bowler was achieved by Bev Congdon, whose 18 eight-ball overs against England at Christchurch in February 1978 went for just 14 runs (0.58 runs per over).

The first great Kiwi bowler

After Hadlee, the second best fast bowler New Zealand has ever produced, Jack Cowie played in all nine of New Zealand's Test matches between 1937 and 1949 (by which time he was 37 years old) and prospered, taking 45 wickets (with best figures of 6 for 40 against Australia at Wellington in March 1946) at an average of 21.53 – the best by a New Zealand bowler in history.

Pakistan's batsmen take a liking to Boock

As Pakistan, driven on by Javed Miandad's imperious 271, piled on the runs to reach 616 for 5 in the first innings against New Zealand in the Third Test at Auckland in February 1989, the Blackcaps' slow left-armer Stephen Boock found himself in the record books. His 70 overs in the innings, which brought him one wicket, cost an all-time New Zealand record 229 runs.

All-time great: RICHARD HADLEE

Certainly the finest fast bowler his country has ever produced and one of the greatest all-rounders of all time, **Richard Hadlee** almost single-handedly changed New Zealand's cricket fortunes. In short, when Hadlee was firing on all cylinders with the ball, New Zealand had every chance of winning the game. By the time he ended his 86-match, 17-year Test career, he had taken 431 wickets (at the time an all-time record) and he still holds the New Zealand records for the best bowling in an innings (9 for 52 against Australia at Brisbane in November 1985), the best bowling in a match (15 for 123 in the same match), the most wickets in a series (33 against Australia in the 1985–86 series), the most five-wicket hauls in an innings (36) and the most ten-wicket hauls in a match (9).

WICKETKEEPER – MOST DISMISSALS: TOP 5

Pos	Dis	Player	Span	Mat	Inns	Ct	St	Dis/Inn
1	201	**A.C. Parore**	1990–2002	78	121	194	7	1.661
2	179	B.B. McCullum	2004–14	84	95	168	11	1.884
3	176	I.D.S. Smith	1980–92	63	109	168	8	1.614
4	96	K.J. Wadsworth	1969–76	33	59	92	4	1.627
5	59	W.K. Lees	1976–83	21	42	52	7	1.404

MOST DISMISSALS: INNINGS/MATCHES/SERIES

The New Zealand record for the most dismissals in an innings is seven, achieved by Ian Smith (7ct) against Sri Lanka at Hamilton in February 1991. The record for the most dismissals in a match is nine, set by Brendon McCullum (8ct, 1st) against Pakistan at Napier in December 2009 and BJ Watling (9ct) against India at Auckland in February 2014. The record for the most dismissals in a series is 23, by Artie Dick (21ct, 2st) against South Africa in South Africa in 1961–62.

FIELDING – MOST CATCHES: TOP 5

Pos	Ct	Player	Span	Mat	Inns	Max	Ct/Inn
1	171	S.P. Fleming	1994–2008	111	199	5	0.859
2	90	L.R.P.L. Taylor	2007–14	54	99	3	0.909
3	71	M.D. Crowe	1982–95	77	130	4	0.546
4	70	N.J. Astle	1996–2006	81	147	2	0.476
5	64	J.V. Coney	1974–87	52	97	3	0.659

LONGEST-SERVING CAPTAINS: TOP 10

Pos	Mat	Player	Span	W-L-T-D	%W
1	80	S.P. Fleming	1997–2006	28-27-0-25	35.00
2	34	J.R. Reid	1956–65	3-18-0-13	8.82
3	32	**D.L. Vettori**	2007–11	6-16-0-10	18.75
4	30	G.P. Howarth	1980–85	11-7-0-12	36.66
5	19	G.T. Dowling	1968–72	4-7-0-8	21.05
6	18	K.R. Rutherford	1993–95	2-11-0-5	11.11
7	17	B.E. Congdon	1972–75	1-7-0-9	5.88
8	16	M.D. Crowe	1990–93	2-7-0-7	12.50
9	15	J.V. Coney	1984–87	5-4-0-6	33.33
10	14	J.G. Wright	1988–90	3-3-0-8	21.42
=	14	B.B. McCullum	2013–14	3-4-0-7	21.42

MOST CATCHES: INNINGS/MATCHES/SERIES

The New Zealand record for the most catches in an innings is five, achieved by **Stephen Fleming** against Zimbabwe at Harare in September 1999; he went on to take seven catches in the match (also a national record). Fleming also holds the record for the most catches in a series (10), a feat he achieved twice: against Zimbabwe in 1997–98 and against England in 1999.

Most successful captain

Stephen Fleming proved an inspirational choice as New Zealand captain when, aged just 23 years 321 days, he took over from Lee Germon in 1997. He went on to captain the Blackcaps on 80 occasions and recorded 28 wins – the most, by some distance, of any New Zealand captain in history.

PAKISTAN

Granted Test status in July 1952, following a recommendation from arch-rivals India, Pakistan are one of the most unpredictable Test teams: they can be world-beaters on one day and spectacularly ordinary on another. The country has produced some of Test cricket's all-time great players, such as Javed Miandad and Hanif Mohammad with the bat and Imran Khan, Wasim Akram and Waqar Younis with the ball.

RESULT SUMMARY

Opposition	Span	Mat	Won	Lost	Tied	Draw	W/L	%W	%L	%D
Australia	1956–2010	57	12	28	0	17	0.42	21.05	49.12	29.82
Bangladesh	2001–11	8	8	0	0	0	-	100.00	0.00	0.00
England	1954–2012	74	16	22	0	36	0.72	21.62	29.72	48.64
India	1952–2007	59	12	9	0	38	1.33	20.33	15.25	64.40
New Zealand	1955–2011	50	23	7	0	20	3.28	46.00	14.00	40.00
South Africa	1995–2013	23	4	12	0	7	0.33	17.39	52.17	30.43
Sri Lanka	1982–2014	46	17	11	0	18	1.54	36.95	23.91	39.13
West Indies	1958–2011	46	16	15	0	15	1.06	34.78	32.60	32.60
Zimbabwe	1993–2013	17	10	3	0	4	3.33	58.82	17.64	23.52

Pakistan slump to record low

Having dismissed South Africa for a below-par 253 in the first innings of the first Test at Johannesburg in February 2013, Pakistan had the chance to establish a solid platform for victory in their reply; instead they fell apart. Only two of their batsmen (Azhar Ali and Misbah-ul-Haq) reached double figures as they crashed to 49 all out (the lowest score in Pakistan's history) and ultimately lost the match by 211 runs.

Making hay against the old enemy

There was little doubt as to who was the star of the show during Pakistan's triumphant and comprehensive 3–0 home series victory over arch-rivals India in 1982–83. Mudassar Nazar hit four centuries and one 50 (with a highest score of 231 in the Fourth Test at Faisalabad) to end the six-match series with an all-time Pakistan record haul of 761 runs at an impressive average of 126.83.

A record-breaking response

Any hopes of victory Sri Lanka had after compiling 644 for 7 declared in their first innings of the First Test against Pakistan at Karachi in February 2009 soon turned to frustration. The home side, led by **Younis Khan** (313) and Kamran Akmal (158 not out), responded by posting 765 for 6 declared – the highest score in their history – as the match petered out into a draw.

Largest victories

By an innings: by an innings and 324 runs against New Zealand at Lahore in May 2002.

By runs: by 341 runs against India at Karachi in January 2006.

By wickets: by ten wickets on 11 occasions.

Smallest victories

By runs: by 12 runs against India at Chennai in January 1999.

By wickets: by one wicket on two occasions: against Australia at Karachi in September 1994; and against Bangladesh at Multan in September 2003.

Heaviest defeats

By an innings: by an innings and 225 runs against England at Lord's in August 2010.

By runs: by 491 runs against Australia at Perth in December 2004.

By wickets: by ten wickets on nine occasions.

BATTING – MOST RUNS: TOP 10

Pos	Runs	Player	Span	Mat	Inns	NO	HS	Ave	100	50	0
1	8,832	Javed Miandad	1976–93	124	189	21	280*	52.57	23	43	6
2	8,829	Inzamam-ul-Haq	1992–2007	119	198	22	329	50.16	25	46	14
3	7,530	Mohammad Yousuf	1998–2010	90	156	12	223	52.29	24	33	11
4	7,399	Younis Khan	2000–14	89	158	14	313	51.38	23	28	15
5	5,768	Saleem Malik	1982–99	103	154	22	237	43.69	15	29	12
6	5,062	Zaheer Abbas	1969–85	78	124	11	274	44.79	12	20	10
7	4,114	Mudassar Nazar	1976–89	76	116	8	231	38.09	10	17	7
8	4,052	Saeed Anwar	1990–2001	55	91	2	188*	45.52	11	25	8
9	3,931	Majid Khan	1964–83	63	106	5	167	38.92	8	19	9
10	3,915	Hanif Mohammad	1952–69	55	97	8	337	43.98	12	15	5

Kaneria's unfortunate record

In his ten-year Test career Danish Kaneria has had considerable success with the ball – he has taken 261 wickets in 61 Tests for his country since making his debut in 2000 – but he has enjoyed few high points with the bat: he has been dismissed without scoring on 25 occasions, an all-time record for a Pakistan player.

All-time great: JAVED MIANDAD

Far from conventional (he was one of the first to perfect the reverse sweep) and often at the centre of controversy, **Javed Miandad**'s greatest ability with the bat was his uncanny tendency to score runs at will under any conditions. He burst on to the international scene as a fresh-faced 19-year-old against New Zealand in 1976, scoring 504 runs in three Tests (including 203 in the Third Test to become the game's youngest-ever double centurion) and became a mainstay of Pakistan's batting line-up for the next 17 years. In 124 Tests he scored a Pakistan record 8,832 runs (including 23 centuries) at an average of 52.57 (also a national record).

Yasir hits the ground running

An exquisite timer of the ball whose game is built around a solid technique, Yasir Hameed's Test career got off to a blistering start when he scored 170 in his first-ever Test innings for Pakistan against Bangladesh at Karachi in August 2003 to break Khalid Ibadulla's 39-year national record for the highest score on debut. Not that the right-hander was finished there: he went on to score 105 in the second innings to become only the second player in history (joining the West Indies' Lawrence Rowe) to score two centuries in his debut Test.

Hanif digs Pakistan out of a hole

The first real star of Pakistan cricket, and the first player in Test history to be labelled "The Little Master", Hanif Mohammad showed star quality when his side really needed it in the First Test against the West Indies at Bridgetown in January 1958. With Pakistan forced to follow on in their second innings, still 473 runs in arrears, Hanif played the longest innings in Test history, taking 970 minutes to compile 337 – still the highest individual score by a Pakistan batsman – to help his side save the game.

Inzamam's record haul

Javed Miandad may have edged him out as his country's leading all-time run-scorer, but no Pakistan batsman in history has scored more hundreds or more 50s than **Inzamam-ul-Haq**. In 119 Tests for Pakistan between 1992 and 2007 the right-hander passed the half-century mark on 71 occasions and went on to reach three figures 25 times.

BOWLING – MOST WICKETS: TOP 10

Pos	Wkts	Player	Span	Mat	Balls	Runs	BBI	BBM	Ave	Econ	SR	5	10
1	414	Wasim Akram	1985–2002	104	22,627	9,779	7/119	11/110	23.62	2.59	54.6	25	5
2	373	Waqar Younis	1989–2003	87	16,224	8,788	7/76	13/135	23.56	3.25	43.4	22	5
3	362	Imran Khan	1971–92	88	19,458	8,258	8/58	14/116	22.81	2.54	53.7	23	6
4	261	Danish Kaneria	2000–10	61	17,697	9,082	7/77	12/94	34.79	3.07	67.8	15	2
5	236	Abdul Qadir	1977–90	67	17,126	7,742	9/56	13/101	32.80	2.71	72.5	15	5
6	208	Saqlain Mushtaq	1995–2004	49	14,070	6,206	8/164	10/155	29.83	2.64	67.6	13	3
7	185	Mushtaq Ahmed	1990–2003	52	12,532	6,100	7/56	10/106	32.97	2.92	67.7	10	3
8	178	Shoaib Akhtar	1997–2007	46	8,143	4,574	6/11	11/78	25.69	3.37	45.7	12	2
9	177	Sarfraz Nawaz	1969–84	55	13,951	5,798	9/86	11/125	32.75	2.49	78.8	4	1
10	171	Iqbal Qasim	1976–88	50	13,019	4,807	7/49	11/118	28.11	2.21	76.1	8	2

The prince of Pakistan

Wasim Akram may have been a fine all-rounder, but it was his performances with the ball that will leave an indelible mark in the history books. The most effective left-arm fast bowler Test cricket has ever produced, Wasim ended his 104-Test match career in 2003 as Pakistan's all-time leading wicket-taker (with 414 wickets), including a national record 25 five-wicket hauls (with a best of 7 for 119 against New Zealand at Wellington in March 1994).

Keeping things tight

Pervez Sajjad holds the Pakistan record for the best economy rate in a career. In 19 matches for his country between 1964 and 1973, the slow left-armer took 59 wickets at an average of 23.89 and conceded just 2.04 runs per over. Majid Khan holds the record for the best economy rate in an innings. In the West Indies' second innings of the Fourth Test at Port of Spain in April 1977, the off-spinner bowled ten overs for just three runs (0.30 runs per over) with eight maidens.

The wicket machine

Waqar Younis was the finest exponent of reverse-swing bowling Test cricket has ever seen. In 87 matches for his country between 1989 and 2003, the fast bowler took 373 wickets at 23.56 with a strike-rate of a wicket every 43.4 balls – the best by a Pakistan bowler, the eighth best of all time and the second-best (behind South Africa's Dale Steyn) by any bowler to have bowled more than 10,000 deliveries in Test history.

On the wrong end of a Sobers pummelling

While the Third Test of the 1957–58 series between the West Indies and Pakistan, at Kingston, Jamaica, was one to remember for Garfield Sobers (the 21-year-old hit a then world record score of 365 not out), it was certainly one to forget for two of Pakistan's bowlers. Khan Mohammad's 54 wicketless overs went for 259 runs (an all-time national record) while his team-mate Fazal Mahmood went for 247 runs off 85.2 overs – the second highest number of runs conceded in an innings by a Pakistan bowler.

All-time great: IMRAN KHAN

With his good looks and limitless ability, **Imran Khan** did much to confirm cricket's status as the number-one sport in Pakistan from the moment he made his debut against England in 1971. He was worth a place in the Pakistan side for his ability with the bat alone (he scored 3,807 runs at an average of 37.69), but it was his bowling that made him a truly world-class performer, his bounding, athletic run, high-leaping delivery stride and a huge variety of deliveries – all produced at express pace – striking fear into the hearts of batsmen around the world. In 88 Tests for his country, 48 of them as captain, he set numerous national records: the best bowling figures in a match (14 for 116 against Sri Lanka at Lahore in March 1982), the most ten-wicket match hauls (6), the most wickets in a series (40 against India in Pakistan in 1982–83) and the best career average (22.81).

WICKETKEEPER – MOST DISMISSALS: TOP 5

Pos	Dis	Player	Span	Mat	Inns	Ct	St	Dis/Inn
1	228	**Wasim Bari**	1967–84	81	146	201	27	1.561
2	206	Kamran Akmal	2002–10	53	99	184	22	2.080
3	147	Moin Khan	1990–2004	69	118	127	20	1.245
4	130	Rashid Latif	1992–2003	37	69	119	11	1.884
5	104	Saleem Yousuf	1982–90	32	58	91	13	1.793

MOST DISMISSALS: INNINGS/MATCHES/SERIES

The Pakistan record for the most dismissals in an innings is seven, by **Wasim Bari** (7ct) against New Zealand at Auckland in February 1979. The record for the most dismissals in a match is nine, by Rashid Latif (9ct) against New Zealand at Auckland in February 1994 and by Kamran Akmal (9ct) against the West Indies at Kingston in June 2005. The record for the most dismissals in a series is 18 (17ct, 1st), by Rashid Latif against Bangladesh in 2003.

FIELDING – MOST CATCHES: TOP 5

Pos	Ct	Player	Span	Mat	Inns	Max	Ct/Inn
1	93	**Javed Miandad**	1976–93	124	218	3	0.426
2	91	Younis Khan	2000–13	82	152	3	0.598
3	81	Inzamam-ul-Haq	1992–2007	119	217	4	0.373
4	65	Majid Khan	1964–83	63	116	3	0.560
=	65	Saleem Malik	1982–99	103	184	3	0.353
=	65	Mohammad Yousuf	1998–2010	90	168	3	0.386

MOST CATCHES: INNINGS/MATCHES/SERIES

The Pakistan record for the most catches in an innings is four, a feat achieved on eight occasions. The national record for the most catches in a match is six, set by Taufeeq Umar against South Africa in Faisalabad in October 2003. Umar went on to take nine catches in the series, a record matched by Younis Khan (against South Africa in 2006–07) and Wallis Mathias (against the West Indies in 1957–58).

LONGEST-SERVING CAPTAINS: TOP 10

Pos	Mat	Player	Span	W-L-T-D	%W
1	48	**Imran Khan**	1982–92	14-8-0-26	29.16
2	34	Javed Miandad	1980–93	14-6-0-14	41.17
3	31	Inzamam-ul-Haq	2001–07	11-11-0-9	35.48
4	27	Misbah-ul-Haq	2010–14	12-7-0-8	44.44
5	25	Wasim Akram	1993–99	12-8-0-5	48.00
6	23	A.H. Kardar	1952–58	6-6-0-11	26.08
7	19	Mushtaq Mohammad	1976–79	8-4-0-7	42.10
8	17	Intikhab Alam	1969–75	1-5-0-11	5.88
=	17	Waqar Younis	1993–2003	10-7-0-0	58.82
10	14	Zaheer Abbas	1983–84	3-1-0-10	21.42

Most successful captains

Two Pakistan captains have achieved 14 career wins: **Javed Miandad** (14 wins in 34 Tests as captain with a win percentage of 41.17) and **Imran Khan** (14 wins in 48 matches with a win percentage of 29.16).

SOUTH AFRICA

A 21-year ban from Test cricket between 1970 and 1991 as a result of the South African government's oppressive apartheid policy may have stopped several potentially glittering international careers in their tracks, but since the country's return to the international fold, they have quickly resumed their position as one of the game's most competitive nations.

RESULT SUMMARY

Opposition	Span	Mat	Won	Lost	Tied	Draw	W/L	%W	%L	%D
Australia	1902–2014	91	21	50	0	20	0.42	23.07	54.94	21.97
Bangladesh	2002–08	8	8	0	0	0	-	100.00	0.00	0.00
England	1889–2012	141	31	56	0	54	0.55	21.98	39.71	38.29
India	1992–2013	29	13	7	0	9	1.85	44.82	24.13	31.03
New Zealand	1932–2013	40	23	4	0	13	5.75	57.50	10.00	32.50
Pakistan	1995–2013	23	12	4	0	7	3.00	52.17	17.39	30.43
Sri Lanka	1993–2012	20	10	5	0	5	2.00	50.00	25.00	25.00
West Indies	1992–2010	25	16	3	0	6	5.33	64.00	12.00	24.00
Zimbabwe	1995–2005	7	6	0	0	1	-	85.71	0.00	14.28

Largest victories

By an innings: by an innings and 229 runs against Sri Lanka at Cape Town in January 2001.

By runs: by 358 runs against New Zealand at Johannesburg in November 2007.

By wickets: by ten wickets on eight occasions.

Smallest victories

By runs: by five runs against Australia at Sydney in January 1994.

By wickets: by one wicket against England at Johannesburg in January 1906.

Heaviest defeats

By an innings: by an innings and 360 runs against Australia at Johannesburg in February 2002.

By runs: by 530 runs against Australia at Melbourne in February 1911.

By wickets: by ten wickets on 12 occasions.

Hitting an all-time low

South Africa have crashed to a sorry 30 all out on two occasions: in the First Test against England at Port Elizabeth in February 1896; and against the same opposition in the First Test at Birmingham in June 1924 (an innings in which extras was the highest scorer with 11).

Lording it at the home of cricket

South Africa dominated England in crushing fashion in the Second Test at Lord's in July–August 2003. After dismissing the hosts for 173 in their first innings, the Proteas, led by captain **Graeme Smith** (259) and Gary Kirsten (108), amassed a mighty 682 for 6 declared – the highest score by a South Africa side in history – en route to an innings-and-92-run victory.

BATTING – MOST RUNS: TOP 10

Pos	Runs	Player	Span	Mat	Inns	NO	HS	Ave	100	50	0
1	13,206	J.H. Kallis	1995–2013	16	278	39	224	55.25	45	58	16
2	9,253	G.C. Smith	2002–14	116	203	13	277	48.70	27	38	10
3	7,289	G. Kirsten	1993–2004	101	176	15	275	45.27	21	34	13
4	7,168	A.B. de Villiers	2004–14	92	154	16	278*	51.94	19	35	3
5	6,214	H.M. Amla	2004–14	76	132	11	311*	51.35	21	27	7
6	6,167	H.H. Gibbs	1996–2008	90	154	7	228	41.95	14	26	11
7	5,498	M.V. Boucher	1997–2012	146	204	24	125	30.54	5	35	16
8	4,554	D.J. Cullinan	1993–2001	70	115	12	275*	44.21	14	20	10
9	3,781	S.M. Pollock	1995–2008	108	156	39	111	32.31	2	16	9
10	3,714	W.J. Cronje	1992–2000	68	111	9	135	36.41	6	23	11

All-time great: JACQUES KALLIS

The history books will record that **Jacques Kallis** is one of the greatest batting all-rounders of all time. While his right-arm fast-medium bowling has brought him 292 wickets in a 165-match career, it is his performances with the bat that make him a truly outstanding performer. Not necessarily the most flamboyant of players, he shows a determined, limpet-like resolve at the batting crease that has brought him a national record 13,206 runs (only three players in history have scored more), 45 centuries and 58 half-centuries.

Pollock cut short in his prime

One of a number of exceptional players whose international career was cut short by South Africa's expulsion from international cricket, **Graeme Pollock** was, with the exception of Garfield Sobers, arguably the best left-handed batsman Test cricket has ever seen. In 23 matches for his country between 1963 and 1970, he scored 2,256 runs (with a highest score of 274 against Australia at Durban in February 1970) at an average of 60.97, the highest by any South African player in history to have completed 20 innings.

Amla masterclass puts South Africa in control

It was, without doubt, the series of the 2012 summer, with the winner becoming the no.1 ranked Test nation, and South Africa found themselves under pressure after England had posted 385 in the first innings of the First Test at The Oval – and that pressure only grew when, in reply, they slipped to 1 for 1. But then Hashim Amla took control: the classy right-hander batted for over 13 hours and faced 529 balls to score 311 not out – the highest score by a South African batsman in Test history – to guide his side to a mighty 637 for 2. His innings stopped England in their tracks: they fell to 240 all out in the second innings as South Africa won by an innings and 12 runs.

Faulkner flourishes as South Africa fold

Few players in Test cricket have emerged with as much credit following a crushing series defeat as Aubrey Faulkner. As South Africa, struggling on fast, bouncy wickets, crashed to a 4–1 series defeat against Australia in 1910–11, only Faulkner stood tall, hitting 732 runs in the five Tests (a staggering 26.3 per cent of his team's total runs), with a highest score of 204 in the Second Test at Melbourne. His series haul remains a South African record to this day.

Makhaya's misfortune with the bat

The first black African cricketer to play for South Africa when he made his Test debut against Sri Lanka at Cape Town in March 1998, Makhaya Ntini has enjoyed considerable success with the ball in his 101-match career, taking 390 wickets. His performances with the bat have been less impressive, however. His tally of 21 ducks is an all-time South African record.

BOWLING – MOST WICKETS: TOP 10

Pos	Wkts	Player	Span	Mat	Balls	Runs	BBI	BBM	Ave	Econ	SR	5	10
1	421	S.M. Pollock	1995–2008	108	24,353	9,733	7/87	10/147	23.11	2.39	57.8	16	1
2	390	M. Ntini	1998–2010	101	20,834	11,242	7/37	13/132	28.82	3.23	53.4	18	4
3	362	D.W. Steyn	2004–14	72	15,261	8,333	7/51	11/60	23.01	3.27	42.1	22	5
4	330	A.A. Donald	1992–2002	72	15,519	7,344	8/71	12/139	22.25	2.83	47.0	20	3
5	291	J.H. Kallis	1995–2013	165	20,172	9,497	6/54	9/92	32.63	2.82	69.3	5	0
6	189	M. Morkel	2006–14	56	10,968	5,855	6/23	8/196	30.97	3.20	58.0	6	0
7	170	H.J. Tayfield	1949–60	37	13,568	4,405	9/113	13/165	25.91	1.94	79.8	14	2
8	134	P.R. Adams	1995–2004	45	8,850	4,405	7/128	10/106	32.87	2.98	66.0	4	1
9	123	T.L. Goddard	1955–70	41	11,736	3,226	6/53	8/92	26.22	1.64	95.4	5	0
=	123	A. Nel	2001–08	36	7,630	3,919	6/32	10/88	31.86	3.08	62.0	3	1

Philander bursts onto Test scene

South Africa already possessed the considerable talents of Dale Steyn and Morne Morkel, but the addition of **Vernon Philander** to their attack has done much to propel the Springboks to the top of the Test rankings. Drafted into the Test squad to play against Australia in 2010–11, the left-armer grabbed his chance with both hands, producing match figures of 8 for 78 on debut. His persistent line and length has continued to worry batsmen and he raced to 50 Test wickets in only his seventh Test (only Australia's Charlie Turner, back in the 1880s, has done better). To date, Philander holds the all-time South African Test record for the best career bowling average (20.11) with a strike-rate of one wicket every 42.3 deliveries.

All-time great: SHAUN POLLOCK

Born into a South African cricketing dynasty – his father Peter and uncle Graeme both starred for the country in the 1960s – **Shaun Pollock** made his Test debut against England in 1996, went on to form an effective new-ball partnership with Allan Donald and soon established himself as an international cricketer of the highest class. His meticulous line-and-length bowling saw him become the first, and to date only, South African bowler to pass the 400-wicket milestone, and he ended his 108-Test match career (26 of them as captain) with 421 scalps to his name.

Makhaya marches into the record books

With an action based on that of Malcolm Marshall, Makhaya Ntini has enjoyed considerable success for South Africa. One of only three of his countrymen to have taken more than 300 Test scalps, the right-arm fast bowler holds the national record for the best figures in a match (13 for 132 against the West Indies at Port of Spain in April 2005) and shares the record for the most ten-wicket match hauls (four) with Dale Steyn.

Tayfield spins his way into the record books

It seems strange given that their recent success has been based on a battery of talented fast bowlers that the best single-innings Test figures recorded by a South African were delivered by an off-spinner. Hugh Tayfield, perhaps his country's best-ever spinner, was the man to achieve them, taking 9 for 113, against England in the fourth Test at Johannesburg in February 1957, to lead his side (who were already 2–0 down in the five-match series) to a morale-boosting 12-run victory.

Steyn's greed for wickets

Fast-tracked into the South African side to face England in 2004 little more than a year after making his first-class debut, Dale Steyn's inexperience was exposed, but once he found his feet, he demonstrated just how effective he could be. Genuinely fast, with aggression to match, his first 72 Test matches brought him 362 wickets with 22 five-wicket hauls and five match hauls of over ten wickets – both all-time South African records.

Goddard turns the screw

Renowned more in a 41-Test career between 1955 and 1970 as a solid left-handed opening batsman, Trevor Goddard was as miserly as he was effective with the ball. His left-arm medium pace brought him 123 wickets at an average of 26.22, with his overs costing just 1.64 runs – the best economy rate by any South African to have bowled 2,000 balls or more in Test cricket.

WICKETKEEPER – MOST DISMISSALS: TOP 5

Pos	Dis	Player	Span	Mat	Inns	Ct	St	Dis/Inn
1	553	**M.V. Boucher**	1997–2012	146	279	530	23	1.982
2	152	D.J. Richardson	1992–98	42	77	150	2	1.974
3	141	J.H.B. Waite	1951–65	50	92	124	17	1.532
4	83	AB de Villiers	2002–14	92	40	80	3	2.075
5	56	D.T. Lindsay	1963–70	19	28	54	2	2.000

MOST DISMISSALS: INNINGS/MATCHES/SERIES

The South Africa record for the most dismissals in an innings is six, a feat achieved by Denis Lindsay (6ct) against Australia at Johannesburg in December 1966, by **Mark Boucher** on four occasions and by AB de Villiers (6 ct) against Pakistan at Johannesburg in February 2013. De Villiers went to equal the world record and set a national best 11 dismissals in the match (all caught). The most dismissals in a series is 26, set by John Waite (23ct, 3st) against New Zealand in 1960–61 and by Mark Boucher (25ct, 1st) against England in 1998.

FIELDING – MOST CATCHES: TOP 5

Pos	Ct	Player	Span	Mat	Inns	Max	Ct/Inn
1	196	**J.H. Kallis**	1995–2013	165	313	4	0.626
2	166	G.C. Smith	2002–14	116	223	5	0.744
3	94	H.H. Gibbs	1996–2008	90	173	4	0.543
4	89	AB de Villiers	2004–14	92	135	3	0.659
5	83	G. Kirsten	1993–2004	101	191	4	0.434

MOST CATCHES: INNINGS/MATCHES/SERIES

The South African record for the most catches in an innings is five, set by Graeme Smith against Australia at Perth in November/December 2012. Smith went on to take six catches in the match, a record euqalled by Bert Vogler against England at Durban in January 1910, Bruce Mitchell against Australia at Melbourne in December 1931 and by Jacques Kallis against Sri Lanka at Cape Town in January 2012. Vogler and Mitchell went on to take 12 catches in the series, a national record equalled by Trevor Goddard against England in 1956–57.

LONGEST-SERVING CAPTAINS: TOP 10

Pos	Mat	Player	Span	W-L-T-D	%W
1	108	**G.C. Smith**	2003–14	53-28-0-27	49.07
2	53	W.J. Cronje	1994–2000	27-11-0-15	50.94
3	26	S.M. Pollock	2000–03	14-5-0-7	53.84
4	18	H.W. Taylor	1913–24	1-10-0-7	5.55
5	16	K.C. Wessels	1992–94	5-3-0-8	31.25
6	15	J.E. Cheetham	1952–55	7-5-0-3	46.66
=	15	A.D. Nourse	1948–51	1-9-0-5	6.66
8	14	D.J. McGlew	1955–62	4-6-0-4	28.57
9	13	T.L. Goddard	1963–65	1-2-0-10	7.69
=	13	P.W. Sherwell	1906–11	5-6-0-2	38.46

Smith silences the critics

He may have been a surprise choice as South African captain following the Proteas' dismal showing at the 2003 ICC World Cup, but **Graeme Smith**, just 23 years old at the time of his appointment, has gone on to become the most successful captain in South Africa's history, winning 53 of his 108 Tests in charge between 2003 and his retirement in 2014.

SRI LANKA

Sri Lanka were granted Test status in 1981 to become the eighth Test-playing nation and, such were the strides they made, by the mid-1990s, they were considered a major force in international cricket. Their success has been founded on the emergence of a host of world-class batsmen and, in Muttiah Muralitharan, the most prolific bowler Test cricket has ever seen.

RESULT SUMMARY

Opposition	Span	Mat	Won	Lost	Tied	Draw	W/L	%W	%L	%D
Australia	1983–2013	26	1	17	0	8	0.05	3.84	65.38	30.76
Bangladesh	2001–14	16	14	0	0	2	-	87.50	0.00	12.50
England	1982–2012	26	7	10	0	9	0.70	26.92	38.46	34.61
India	1982–2010	35	6	14	0	15	0.42	17.14	40.00	42.85
New Zealand	1983–2012	28	8	10	0	10	0.80	28.57	35.71	35.71
Pakistan	1982–2014	46	11	17	0	18	0.64	23.91	36.95	39.13
South Africa	1993–2012	20	5	10	0	5	0.50	25.00	50.00	25.00
West Indies	1993–2010	15	6	3	0	6	2.00	40.00	20.00	40.00
Zimbabwe	1994–2004	15	10	0	0	5	-	66.66	0.00	33.33

Capitulation in Kandy

Trailing 1–0 in the series going into the Third and final Test against Pakistan at Kandy in August 1994, Sri Lanka got off to the worst possible start. After losing the toss and being put in to bat, they wilted in the face of some excellent fast bowling from Wasim Akram (4 for 32) and Waqar Younis (6 for 34) and crashed to 71 all out in just 28.2 overs – the lowest total in their history. Pakistan went on to win the match by an innings and 52 runs.

Batting for fun

With India having amassed an impressive 537 for 8 declared in the first innings of the First Test in Colombo in August 1997, it was time for Sri Lanka to produce a batting masterclass of their own if they wanted to stay in the match. They did just that. Bolstered by centuries from **Sanath Jayasuriya** (340), Roshan Mahanama (225) and Aravinda de Silva (126), they reached 952 for 6 declared – the highest total in Test history.

Jayasuriya prospers against India

An explosive performer in all formats of the game, **Sanath Jayasuriya** reserved his best performances in the Test arena for the two-match series against India in August 1997. In three innings he scored 340 (at the time a new national record), 32 and 199. His series haul of 571 runs (at an unbelievable average of 190.33) is an all-time Sri Lankan record.

Murali's struggles with the bat

While Muttiah Muralitharan holds virtually every Sri Lankan bowling record in the book, his performances with the bat have been less eyebrow-raising: in 132 Tests for his country between 1992 and 2010 he has scored 1,259 runs at an average of 11.87 including a national record 32 ducks.

BATTING – MOST RUNS: TOP 10

Pos	Runs	Player	Span	Mat	Inns	NO	HS	Ave	100	50	0
1	11,319	D.P.M.D. Jayawardene	1997–2014	143	240	15	374	50.30	33	46	14
2	11,151	K.C. Sangakkara	2000–14	122	209	17	319	58.07	35	45	9
3	6,973	S.T. Jayasuriya	1991–2007	110	188	14	340	40.07	14	31	15
4	6,361	P.A. de Silva	1984–2002	93	159	11	267	42.97	20	22	7
5	5,502	M.S. Atapattu	1990–2007	90	156	15	249	39.02	16	17	22
6	5,492	TM Dilshan	1999–2013	87	145	11	193	40.98	16	23	14
9	5,462	T.T. Samaraweera	2001–13	81	132	20	231	48.76	14	30	11
8	5,105	A. Ranatunga	1982–2000	93	155	12	135*	35.69	4	38	12
9	4,545	H.P. Tillakaratne	1989–2004	83	131	25	204*	42.87	11	20	9
10	3,089	W.P.U.J.C. Vaas	1994–2009	111	162	35	100*	24.32	1	13	12

Largest victories

By an innings: by an innings and 254 runs against Zimbabwe at Bulawayo in May 2004.

By runs: by 465 runs against Bangladesh at Chittagong in January 2009.

By wickets: by ten wickets on eight occasions.

Smallest victories

By runs: by 42 runs against Pakistan at Faisalabad in September 1995.

By wickets: by one wicket against South Africa at Colombo in August 2006.

Heaviest defeats

By an innings: by an innings and 229 runs against South Africa at Cape Town in January 2001.

By runs: by 301 runs against Pakistan at Colombo in August 1994.

By wickets: by ten wickets on four occasions.

Super Sangakkara

Hauled into the Test side in 2000 at the age of 22 despite modest performances in first-class cricket, **Kumar Sangakkara** has more than repaid the faith the Sri Lankan selectors showed in him. In 122 Tests for his country, the classy left-hander has scored 11,151 runs (with a highest score of 319 against Bangladesh at Chittagong in February 2014) at an average of 58.07 – the highest by any Sri Lankan batsman in history.

All-time great: MAHELA JAYAWARDENE

From the moment **Mahela Jayawardene** stepped into the Test arena, with his side on 790 for 4 against India at Colombo in August 1997, he knew the benchmark to which he must aspire. And he has not disappointed in a 143-match career spanning 17 years. A well-organized right-hand batsman with limitless concentration and application, Jayawardene has consistently delivered the goods and holds the Sri Lankan record for the most runs scored (11,319), the highest individual score (a stunning knock of 374 against South Africa at Colombo in July 2006, as part of an all-time record partnership of 624 with Kumar Sangakkara.

BOWLING – MOST WICKETS: TOP 10

Pos	Wkts	Player	Span	Mat	Balls	Runs	BBI	BBM	Ave	Econ	SR	5	10
1	795	M. Muralitharan	1992–2010	132	43,715	18,023	9/51	16/220	22.67	2.47	54.9	67	22
2	355	W.P.U.J.C. Vaas	1994–2009	111	22,438	10,501	7/71	14/191	29.58	2.68	66.0	12	2
3	217	H.M.R.K.B. Herath	1999–2014	51	13,933	6,514	7/89	12/157	30.01	2.80	64.2	17	3
4	101	S.L. Malinga	2004–10	30	5,209	3,349	5/50	9/210	33.15	3.85	51.5	3	0
5	100	C.R.D. Fernando	2000–12	40	6,181	3,784	5/42	7/95	37.84	3.67	61.8	3	0
6	98	S.T. Jayasuriya	1991–2007	110	8,188	3,366	5/34	9/74	34.34	2.46	83.5	2	0
7	85	G.P. Wickramasinghe	1991–2001	40	7,260	3,559	6/60	6/80	41.87	2.94	85.4	3	0
8	73	R.J. Ratnayake	1983–92	23	4,961	2,563	6/66	9/125	35.10	3.09	67.9	5	0
9	70	B.A.W. Mendis	2008–14	18	4,526	2,349	6/99	10/209	33.55	3.11	64.6	4	1
10	69	H.D.P.K. Dharmasena	1993–2004	31	6,939	2,920	6/72	8/183	42.31	2.52	100.5	3	0

Mr Economy

Don Anurasiri found it difficult to cement a permanent place in the Sri Lanka side after making his Test debut at the age of 20 against Pakistan in Colombo in March 1986 (he played just 18 times for his country over a 12-year period), but when the slow left-armer did play, he was the epitome of both accuracy and economy. He holds the Sri Lanka record for both best career economy rate (2.33) and for the best economy rate in an innings – 0.60 (15-11-9-0) in the Third Test against Pakistan at Colombo in March 1986.

Part-time success

Tillakaratne Dilshan is renowned chiefly for his prowess with the bat (he has scored 4,722 runs in 79 Tests at an average of 40.01), but his part-time off-spin has earned him a place in the record books. The figures for his spell of bowling in the Second Test against Bangladesh at Chittagong in January 2009 – 4.2-1-10-4 – represent the best strike-rate by a Sri Lanka bowler in Test history (a wicket every 6.5 deliveries).

Slinga Malinga

The fastest bowler Sri Lanka has ever produced, **Lasith Malinga** was a batsman's worst nightmare. Generating genuine pace with an old or new ball, his low-slung, round-arm action made him almost impossible to pick up, and when he was fit – injuries kept him out of Test cricket between December 2007 and July 2010 before he retired from Test cricket in April 2011 – he was deadly: he took 101 wickets in 30 Tests at a strike-rate of a wicket every 51.5 deliveries, an all-time Sri Lankan record.

All-time great: MUTTIAH MURALITHARAN

Predictably enough, **Muttiah Muralitharan**, Test cricket's all-time leading wicket-taker with 800 wickets (which includes the five wickets he took for the ICC), holds virtually every single Sri Lankan bowling record. He leads the way for the best bowling figures in an innings (9 for 51 against Zimbabwe at Kandy in January 2002), the best bowling figures in a match (16 for 220 against England at The Oval in August 1998), the best average of any Sri Lanka bowler to have bowled 2,000 or more balls in Test cricket (22.67), the most five-wicket hauls in an innings (67), the most ten-wicket hauls in a match (22) and the most runs conceded in an innings (224 against Australia in Perth in December 1995).

Sri Lanka's hat-trick man

The only Sri Lanka bowler in Test history to take a hat-trick is Nuwan Zoysa. The left-arm fast-medium bowler dismissed Trevor Gripper (lbw), Murray Goodwin (caught behind) and Neil Johnson (lbw) in the first innings of the Second Test against Zimbabwe in Harare in November 1999 to create his own slice of Sri Lankan cricket history.

WICKETKEEPER – MOST DISMISSALS: TOP 5

Pos	Dis	Player	Span	Mat	Inns	Ct	St	Dis/Inn
1	151	**K.C. Sangakkara**	2000–14	122	90	131	20	1.677
2	147	H.A.P.W. Jayawardene	2000–14	55	96	115	32	1.531
3	119	R.S. Kaluwitharana	1992–2004	49	85	93	26	1.400
4	35	H.P. Tillakaratne	1989–2004	83	18	33	2	1.944
5	34	S.A.R. Silva	1983–88	9	15	33	1	2.266

MOST DISMISSALS: INNINGS/MATCHES/SERIES

The Sri Lanka record for the most dismissals in an innings is six, by Amal Silva (6ct) against India at the Sinhalese Sports Club Ground in Colombo in August 1985; he went on to achieve nine dismissals in the match and repeated the feat in the following Test (8ct, 1s) at the P. Sara Oval ground in Colombo to end the series with a record 22 dismissals to his name.

FIELDING – MOST CATCHES: TOP 5

Pos	Ct	Player	Span	Mat	Inns	Max	Ct/Inn
1	194	D.P.M.D. Jayawardene	1997–2014	143	258	4	0.751
2	89	H.P. Tillakaratne	1989–2004	83	123	4	0.723
3	78	S.T. Jayasuriya	1991–2007	110	196	3	0.397
4	77	T.M. Dilshan	1999–2013	85	149	4	0.516
5	70	M. Muralitharan	1992–2009	131	229	2	0.305

MOST CATCHES: INNINGS/MATCHES/SERIES

The Sri Lanka record for the most catches in an innings is four, a feat achieved on ten occasions. The record for the most catches in a match is seven, by Hashan Tillakaratne against New Zealand in Colombo in December 1992. Mahela Jayawardene holds the Sri Lanka record for the most catches in a series, with ten against Bangladesh in 2007.

LONGEST-SERVING CAPTAINS: TOP 10

Pos	Mat	Player	Span	W-L-T-D	%W
1	56	**A. Ranatunga**	1989–99	12-19-0-25	21.42
2	38	S.T. Jayasuriya	1999–2002	18-12-0-8	47.36
=	38	D.P.M.D. Jayawardene	2006–13	18-12-0-8	47.36
4	19	L.R.D. Mendis	1982–87	2-8-0-9	10.52
5	18	M.S. Atapattu	2002–05	8-6-0-4	44.44
6	15	K.C. Sangakkara	2009–11	5-3-0-7	33.33
7	11	H.P. Tillakaratne	1999–2004	1-4-0-6	9.09
=	11	T.M. Dilshan	2011–12	1-5-0-5	9.09
9	7	A.D. Mathews	2013–14	3-1-0-3	42.85
10	6	P.A. de Silva	1991–99	0-4-0-2	0.00

Most successful captains

Sanath Jayasuriya and Mahela Jayawardene share an identical record as Sri Lanka captain. The both captained their country in 38 Tests and led the side to 18 wins, with 12 draws and 12 defeats.

WEST INDIES

Granted Test status in 1928 to become the fourth Test-playing nation, the West Indies enjoyed only sporadic success until the late 1970s and early '80s, when a mix of dashing stroke players and fearsome fast bowlers took them to the top of the world game. In recent years, however, the men from the Caribbean have struggled to recapture the glorious successes of those golden years.

RESULT SUMMARY

Opposition	Span	Mat	Won	Lost	Tied	Draw	W/L	%W	%L	%D
Australia	1930–2012	111	32	54	1	24	0.59	28.82	48.64	21.62
Bangladesh	2002–12	10	6	2	0	2	3.00	60.00	20.00	20.00
England	1928–2012	148	53	45	0	50	1.17	35.81	30.40	33.78
India	1948–2013	90	30	16	0	44	1.87	33.33	17.77	48.88
New Zealand	1952–2013	42	12	11	0	19	1.09	28.57	26.19	45.23
Pakistan	1958–2011	46	15	16	0	15	0.93	32.60	34.78	32.60
South Africa	1992–2010	25	3	16	0	6	0.18	12.00	64.00	24.00
Sri Lanka	1993–2010	15	3	6	0	6	0.50	20.00	40.00	40.00
Zimbabwe	2000–03	8	6	0	0	2	-	75.00	0.00	25.00

Harmison blows the Windies away

It was a collapse of spectacular proportions. Trailing England by just 28 runs after the first innings in the First Test at Kingston, Jamaica, in March 2004, the West Indies capitulated to 47 all out in 25.3 overs, with Steve Harmison doing most of the damage for England, taking 7 for 12. It remains the lowest total in the islanders' history.

Sobers and Hunte lead the way at Kingston

Garfield Sobers's then world record score of 365 not out in the Third Test against Pakistan at Kingston, Jamaica, in February–March 1958, coupled with Conrad Hunte's innings of 260 (the pair added 446 for the second wicket), provided the platform for the West Indies' highest-ever total – 790 for 3 declared. It is one of four 700-plus scores by the islanders.

Largest victories

By an innings: by an innings and 336 runs against India at Kolkata in December 1958.

By runs: by 425 runs against England at Manchester in July 1976.

By wickets: by ten wickets on 23 occasions.

Smallest victories

By runs: by one run against Australia at Adelaide in January 1993.

By wickets: by one wicket on two occasions – against Australia at Bridgetown in March 1999 and against Pakistan at St John's in May 2000.

Heaviest defeats

By an innings: by an innings and 283 runs against England at Leeds in May 2007.

By runs: by 382 runs against Australia at Sydney in February 1969.

By wickets: by ten wickets on 15 occasions.

Walsh's woes with the bat

You never knew quite what to expect when Courtney Walsh marched to the wicket with a bat in his hands, but the odds were that it would be as brief as it would be entertaining. In 132 Test matches between 1984 and 2001, Test cricket's one-time leading wicket-taker racked up an all-time record 43 ducks.

BATTING – MOST RUNS: TOP 10

Pos	Runs	Player	Span	Mat	Inns	NO	HS	Ave	100	50	0
1	11,912	B.C. Lara	1990–2006	130	230	6	400*	53.17	34	48	17
2	11,219	S. Chanderpaul	1994–2013	153	261	45	203*	51.93	29	62	14
3	8,540	I.V.A. Richards	1974–91	121	182	12	291	50.23	24	45	10
4	8,032	G.S. Sobers	1954–74	93	160	21	365*	57.78	26	30	12
5	7,558	C.G. Greenidge	1974–91	108	185	16	226	44.72	19	34	11
6	7,515	C.H. Lloyd	1966–85	110	175	14	242*	46.67	19	39	4
7	7,487	D.L. Haynes	1978–94	116	202	25	184	42.29	18	39	10
8	6,933	C.H. Gayle	2000–13	99	174	9	333	42.01	15	34	15
9	6,227	R.B. Kanhai	1957–74	79	137	6	256	47.53	15	28	7
10	5,949	R.B. Richardson	1983–95	86	146	12	194	44.39	16	27	8

All-time great: BRIAN LARA

No player since Don Bradman has had such an appetite for building big scores and few players have broken as many records during their career as **Brian Lara**. Twice the left-hander broke the record for the all-time highest score in Test cricket, first with a brilliant knock of 375 against England at St John's, Antigua, in April 1994 and then with a blistering 400 not out against the same opponents at the same venue almost exactly a decade later. He finished his 131-Test, 16-year career in 2006 as the leading run-scorer of all time (his tally of 11,912 runs has since been broken by Sachin Tendulkar) and as the holder of several West Indian records: the most hundreds (34) and the most scores of 50 plus (82).

The "Black Bradman"

The first of the great black batsmen to emerge from the islands at a time when the West Indies team comprised mostly white players, **George Headley** performed such feats with the bat that he was dubbed the "Black Bradman". In 22 Tests for the islanders between 1930 and 1954 he scored 2,190 runs, including 10 centuries (with a highest score of 270 not out against England at Kingston, Jamaica, in March 1935), at an average of 60.83 – the highest by any West Indian batsman in history.

The master blaster runs riot

Viv Richards was at his swaggering best during the West Indies' 3–0 series win over England in 1976. In seven innings during the five-match series – he missed the Second Test at Lord's through injury – the master blaster smashed three centuries and two half-centuries (with a highest score of 291 at The Oval in the Fifth Test) en route to amassing 829 runs at an average of 118.42. It remains the highest series haul by any West Indian batsman.

BOWLING – MOST WICKETS: TOP 10

Pos	Wkts	Player	Span	Mat	Balls	Runs	BBI	BBM	Ave	Econ	SR	5	10
1	519	C.A. Walsh	1984–2001	132	30,019	12,688	7/37	13/55	24.44	2.53	57.8	22	3
2	405	C.E.L. Ambrose	1988–2000	98	22,103	8,501	8/45	11/84	20.99	2.30	54.5	22	3
3	376	M.D. Marshall	1978–91	81	17,584	7,876	7/22	11/89	20.94	2.68	46.7	22	4
4	309	L.R. Gibbs	1958–76	79	27,115	8,989	8/38	11/157	29.09	1.98	87.7	18	2
5	259	J. Garner	1977–87	58	13,169	5,433	6/56	9/108	20.97	2.47	50.8	7	0
6	249	M.A. Holding	1975–87	60	12,680	5,898	8/92	14/149	23.68	2.79	50.9	13	2
7	235	G.S. Sobers	1954–74	93	21,599	7,999	6/73	8/80	34.03	2.22	91.9	6	0
8	202	A.M.E. Roberts	1974–83	47	11,135	5,174	7/54	12/121	25.61	2.78	55.1	11	2
9	192	W.W. Hall	1958–69	48	10,421	5,066	7/69	11/126	26.38	2.91	54.2	9	1
10	165	F.H. Edwards	2003–12	55	9,602	6,249	7/87	8/132	37.87	3.9	68.1	12	0

Whispering Death destroys England

Nicknamed "Whispering Death" for his graceful, stealth-like approach to the bowling crease and an effortless action that produced deliveries at a blistering pace, **Michael Holding** was one of the most feared bowlers of his day. In 60 Tests for the West Indies between 1975 and 1987 he took 249 wickets, with his best performance coming against England at The Oval in August 1976. He took 8 for 92 in the first innings and 6 for 57 in the second: his match haul of 14 for 149 is an all-time West Indies record.

Brief but mightily effective for Lawson

After bursting on to the international scene in December 2002, with 6 for 3 in only his third Test match, against Bangladesh at Chittagong, followed by a career-best 7 for 78 against the all-conquering Australians the following May, Jermaine Lawson's career started to unravel. As the ICC started to question the legitimacy of his action, he struggled to hold a place in the West Indies line-up and by 2005 his international career was over. However, his 51 wickets in 13 Tests came at a strike-rate of a wicket every 46.3 deliveries – an all-time record for a West Indies bowler.

Keeping it tight

Gerry Gomez was the most economical bowler in West Indies cricket history. In 29 Tests for the islanders between 1939 and 1954, his 5,236 deliveries of medium-pace bowling went for just 1.82 runs per over. Garfield Sobers holds the national record for the best economy rate in an innings: he produced a spell of 14-11-3-1 against New Zealand at Wellington in March 1956 – an economy rate of just 0.21 runs per over.

All-time great: MALCOLM MARSHALL

Of the battery of world-class fast bowlers to have emerged from the Caribbean islands over the years, **Malcolm Marshall** was the best of them. Relatively short for a fast bowler, standing at just 5ft 9in, he made up for any lack of height with express pace and an ability to swing the ball both ways. In 81 Tests for the West Indies between 1978 and 1991 he took 376 wickets and set national records for: the best average (20.94), the best strike-rate in an innings (6.5 – against Pakistan at Faisalabad in November 1990, where his figures were 4.2-0-24-4), the most five-wicket hauls (22, shared with Curtly Ambrose and Courtney Walsh), the most ten-wicket match hauls (4) and the most wickets in a series (35, against England in 1988).

Bucking the trend

Given that the golden years of cricket in the Caribbean were based on a fearsome, four-pronged pace attack, it may seem strange that the best bowling figures ever recorded by a West Indian bowler were produced by an off-spinner. In only his second Test match, against India at Port of Spain, Trinidad, in March 1971, 35-year-old Jack Noreiga took 9 for 95. It remains the only nine-wicket innings haul in West Indies cricket history.

WICKETKEEPER – MOST DISMISSALS: TOP 5

Pos	Dis	Player	Span	Mat	Inns	Ct	St	Dis/Inn
1	270	**P.J.L. Dujon**	1981–91	81	150	265	5	1.800
2	219	R.D. Jacobs	1998–2004	65	122	207	12	1.795
3	189	D.L. Murray	1963–80	62	119	181	8	1.588
4	161	D. Ramdin	2005–13	56	100	156	5	1.610
5	101	J.R. Murray	1993–2002	33	57	98	3	1.771

MOST DISMISSALS: INNINGS/MATCHES/SERIES

The West Indies record for the most dismissals in an innings is seven, achieved by Ridley Jacobs (7ct) against Australia at Melbourne in December 2000. Jacobs went on to take a national record nine dismissals in the match (8ct, 1st), equalling previous performances by David Murray (9ct) against Australia at Melbourne in December 1981 and by Courtney Browne against England at Nottingham in August 1995. Murray also holds the record for the most dismissals in a series, 24 (22ct, 2st) against England in 1963.

FIELDING – MOST CATCHES: TOP 5

Pos	Ct	Player	Span	Mat	Inns	Max	Ct/Inn
1	164	**B.C. Lara**	1990–2006	130	239	4	0.686
2	122	I.V.A. Richards	1974–91	121	232	4	0.525
3	115	C.L. Hooper	1987–2002	102	189	4	0.608
4	109	G.S. Sobers	1954–74	93	172	4	0.633
5	96	C.G. Greenidge	1974–91	108	208	3	0.461

MOST CATCHES: INNINGS/MATCHES/SERIES

The West Indies record for the most catches in an innings is four, a feat achieved on 12 occasions. The record for most catches in a match is six, by Garfield Sobers against England at Lord's in August 1973 and by Jimmy Adams against England at Kingston in February 1994. **Brian Lara** holds the national record for the most catches in a series with 13, a feat he achieved on two occasions (against England in 1997–98 and against India in 2006).

LONGEST-SERVING CAPTAINS: TOP 10

Pos	Mat	Player	Span	W-L-T-D	%W
1	74	C.H. Lloyd	1974–85	36-12-0-26	48.64
2	50	I.V.A. Richards	1980–91	27-8-0-15	54.00
3	47	B.C. Lara	1997–2006	10-26-0-11	21.27
4	39	G.S. Sobers	1965–72	9-10-0-20	23.07
5	30	D.J.G. Sammy	2010–13	8-12-0-10	26.66
6	24	R.B. Richardson	1992–95	11-6-0-7	45.83
7	22	J.D.C. Goddard	1948–57	8-7-0-7	36.36
=	22	C.L. Hooper	2001–02	4-11-0-7	18.18
=	22	C.A. Walsh	1994–97	6-7-0-9	27.27
10	20	C.H. Gayle	2007–10	3-9-0-8	15.00

Golden times under Lloyd

Blessed no doubt by having a myriad of world-class talent at his disposal, **Clive Lloyd** is the most successful captain in the West Indies' long cricket history. Between 1974 and 1985 he captained the islanders on 74 occasions, notching up 36 wins with a winning percentage of 48.64.

BANGLADESH

Test cricket's newest incumbents – they were granted Test status in 2000, to become the game's tenth Test-playing nation – Bangladesh have struggled to find their feet in the hotbed of the Test arena. In 77 matches to date, the Tigers have won just four times: twice against struggling Zimbabwe and twice against a severely weakened West Indies outfit.

RESULT SUMMARY

Opposition	Span	Mat	Won	Lost	Tied	Draw	W/L	%W	%L	%D
Australia	2003–06	4	0	4	0	0	0.00	0.00	100.00	0.00
England	2003–10	8	0	8	0	0	0.00	0.00	100.00	0.00
India	2000–10	7	0	6	0	1	0.00	0.00	85.71	14.28
New Zealand	2001–13	11	0	8	0	3	0.00	0.00	72.72	27.27
Pakistan	2001–03	8	0	8	0	0	0.00	0.00	100.00	0.00
South Africa	2002–08	8	0	8	0	0	0.00	0.00	100.00	0.00
Sri Lanka	2001–14	16	0	14	0	2	0.00	0.00	87.50	12.50
West Indies	2002–12	10	2	6	0	2	0.33	20.00	60.00	20.00
Zimbabwe	2001–13	11	2	6	0	3	0.33	18.18	54.54	27.27

Mushfiqur breaks new ground for the Tigers

By the time Bangladesh faced Sri Lanka in the First Test in Galle in March 2013, they had lost all 13 previous meetings between the two countries. And so when Sri Lanka posted an imposing 570 for 4 declared in their first innings, one might have forgiven the Bangladesh players for fearing the worst. Instead they responded in style, posting 638 all out (their highest total in Tests). Captain Mushfiqur Rahim led the way with a 321-ball 200 – the first-ever double hundred by a Bangladesh player in Tests – as the match ended in a draw.

Bangladeshi bowling bests

Shakib Al Hasan showed his true all-round potential when he took 7 for 36 against New Zealand at Chittagong in December 2008 with his slow left-arm spin bowling. They are the best figures in an innings ever recorded by a Bangladesh bowler. Another slow left-arm bowler, Enamul Haque Jr, holds the record for the best figures in a match: his 12 for 200 against Zimbabwe at Dhaka in January 2005 did much to ensure his country's first-ever series win.

All-time great: HABIBUL BASHAR

One of the few Bangladesh players of genuine Test quality, **Habibul Bashar** carried his side's batting in their early days as a Test-playing nation. The Tigers' longest-serving captain (he led them on 18 occasions between 2004 and 2007) and one of only two Bangladesh players to have played in 50 Tests (Mohammad Ashraful is the other), the right-hander (and former captain) holds the national record for the most runs (3,026) and the most scores of 50 or over (27).

Leading gloveman

A regular behind the stumps for Bangladesh between 2000 and 2007, Khaled Mashud holds the national record for the most dismissals with 87 (78ct, 9st) in 44 Tests.

Shakib lifts the gloom

His team-mates may have been floundering around him, but Shakib Al Hasan has been a leading light for Bangladesh in recent times with both bat and ball. Arguably the finest all-round cricketer his country has ever produced – in March 2013 he was ranked the best all-rounder in one-day international cricket and was second only to South Africa's Jacques Kallis in Test cricket – since making his debut in 2007 he has scored 2,278 runs in 34 Tests for Bangladesh (only three of his fellow countrymen have ever scored more) and has taken a national record 122 wickets with his slow left-arm orthodox bowling.

ZIMBABWE

Zimbabwe became the ninth Test-playing nation in 1992 and were perennial strugglers in the longest format of the game until the turn of the century when, although never strong, they were at least competitive. Zimbabwe's political problems, however, led to their expulsion from the Test arena in January 2006, and they have played only nine Test matches since then (three in 2011, one in 2012 and six in 2013).

RESULT SUMMARY

Opposition	Span	Mat	Won	Lost	Tied	Draw	W/L	%W	%L	%D
Australia	1999–2003	3	0	3	0	0	0.00	0.00	100.00	0.00
Bangladesh	2001–13	11	6	2	0	3	3.00	54.54	18.18	27.27
England	1996–2003	6	0	3	0	3	0.00	0.00	50.00	50.00
India	1992–2005	11	2	7	0	2	0.28	18.18	63.63	18.18
New Zealand	1992–2012	13	0	9	0	6	0.00	0.00	60.00	40.00
Pakistan	1993–2013	17	3	10	0	4	0.30	17.64	58.82	23.52
South Africa	1995–2005	7	0	6	0	1	0.00	0.00	85.71	14.28
Sri Lanka	1994–2004	15	0	10	0	5	0.00	0.00	66.66	33.33
West Indies	2000–13	8	0	6	0	2	0.00	0.00	75.00	25.00

Leading from the front

Dave Houghton, Zimbabwe's first Test captain, led by example in the Second Test against Sri Lanka at Bulawayo in October 1994. Coming to the crease with his side precariously placed on 5 for 2, the right-hander batted for over 11 hours and faced 541 balls en route to amassing 266 runs – the highest score ever made by a Zimbabwe batsman.

A cut above the rest

The second most capped player in Zimbabwe's history (behind Grant Flower) with 65 appearances for his country between 1993 and 2005 (21 of them as captain), Heath Streak was a fast-medium bowler of genuine quality with a heart and stamina to match. The only Zimbabwe bowler in history to reach the 100-wicket milestone, he ended his career with 216 Test scalps to his name. He is also his country's longest-serving captain, leading his side on 21 occasions (a record shared with Alistair Campbell), and its most successful one, recording four victories with a winning percentage of 19.04 per cent.

All-time great: ANDY FLOWER

The finest batsman Zimbabwe has produced and ranked for a short time in 2000 as the number-one batsman in the world, **Andy Flower** set numerous national records in a 63-Test career spanning a decade between 1992 and 2002. Of all Zimbabwe batsmen he has scored the most runs (4,794), has the highest average (an exceptional 51.54), has scored the most hundreds (12), has the most scores of 50 plus (39) and also holds the national record for the most runs in a series (540 in the two-match series against India in 2000–01). He is also the leading wicketkeeper in Zimbabwe's history with 151 (142ct, 9st) Test victims.

Best bowling in an innings/match

A leg-spinner with the full repertoire, Paul Strang is Zimbabwe's second most prolific wicket-taker of all time with 70 Test wickets to his name in 24 Tests between 1994 and 2001. He holds the record for the best bowling figures in an innings: 8 for 109 against New Zealand at Bulawayo in September 2000. Adam Huckle holds the record for the best match figures: the leg-spinner took 11 for 255 against New Zealand at Bulawayo in September 1997.

AUSTRALIA v ENGLAND

It is the oldest and the most eagerly anticipated rivalry in world cricket. England and Australia have been locking horns on a cricket pitch since 1877, and matches between the two countries have become the stuff of legend. Australia lead the way with 138 wins, to England's 105 (with 93 draws), and matches between the game's oldest rivals remain the highlight of the cricket calendar.

Proving their point

In 1938, with any hopes of regaining the Ashes already dashed, England went into the final Test at The Oval 1–0 down in the series and determined to prove a point. They had a plan: to bat the Australians into submission. England won the toss, batted and, over the next two-and-a-half days, ground out a mammoth 903 for 7, a then world record score and still the highest team total in Ashes history. England went on to win the match by an innings and 579 runs (the largest victory margin in Ashes history).

OVERALL SERIES RECORDS

(336 Tests between 1877 and 2014)

	W	L	T	D	W/L	%W	%L	%D
Australia	136	105	0	93	1.31	41.07	31.25	27.68
England	105	136	0	93	0.76	31.25	41.07	27.68

First match: 15–19 March 1877, Melbourne Cricket Ground

Marsh tops dismissals list

An ever-present behind the stumps for Australia for over a decade, Rod Marsh is the most successful wicketkeeper in Ashes history. The combative Western Australian took 141 catches – c. Marsh b. Lillee became a part of cricket folklore Down Under – and seven stumpings in 42 Ashes Tests between 1970 and 1983.

A Herculean effort from 22-year-old Hutton

The main architect of England's Ashes record 903 for 7 and subsequent innings-and-579-run victory over Australia at The Oval in 1938 was **Len Hutton**. The Yorkshire opener faced 847 balls and batted for 13 hours and 17 minutes to compile an innings of 364 – breaking Walter Hammond's world record score of 336 not out (broken by Garfield Sobers in 1958) and setting an all-time Ashes record.

Captain fantastic

The most successful captain in Ashes history? **Allan Border**. The Queensland batsman reluctantly took over the Australian captaincy in 1984–85, but led the side with great distinction to the top of the world game. He captained Australia in 29 Tests against England over five series between 1985 and 1993, winning three of them and an Ashes record 13 matches.

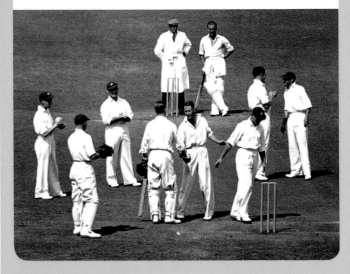

*ABOVE: **Len Hutton** receives the congratulations of the Australia players after breaking Walter Hammond's world-record score of 336 at The Oval in 1938.*

Best in the business

In 37 Tests between 1928 and 1948, **Donald Bradman** terrorized English bowling attacks and set numerous Ashes records along the way. No other batsman in history has scored more runs in Ashes encounters (5,028), no batsman has recorded a higher career average (89.78) and no one has scored more Ashes centuries (19) – his nearest rival on the all-time Ashes centuries list is Steve Waugh, with ten.

Making hay at the top of the order

The most productive partnership in all Tests between Australia and England is that of England's Jack Hobbs and Herbert Sutcliffe. The legendary opening pair combined to score 2,452 runs in 30 innings between 1924 and 1930 at an average of 84.55, with 11 century partnerships and nine half-century partnerships.

Australia get off to the worst of starts

It was the first match of five in the 1902 Ashes series, at Edgbaston, and a chance for England to avenge the crushing 4–1 series defeat they had suffered in Australia just two months earlier. England batted first and scored 376. Australia, embarrassingly, subsided to a sorry 36 all out – the lowest score in Ashes history. Amazingly, however, because it was only a three-day game, they managed to hold out for the draw, and went on to win the series 2–1.

Ponsford and Bradman dash England's hopes

The outcome of the 1934 Ashes series was still hanging in the balance when the two teams arrived for the Fifth and final Test at The Oval locked at 1–1, but by the end of the first day's play, thanks to stunning performances from Bill Ponsford (266) and Donald Bradman (244), there was only going to be one winner. The pair combined to add an Ashes record 451 runs for the second wicket to propel Australia to a mighty first-innings total of 701 all out and an eventual series-clinching 562-run victory.

MOST RUNS: TOP 10

Pos	Player	Runs
1	D.G. Bradman (Australia, 1928–48)	5,028
2	J.B. Hobbs (England, 1908–30)	3,636
3	A.R. Border (Australia, 1978–93)	3,548
4	D.I. Gower (England, 1978–91)	3,269
5	S.R. Waugh (Australia, 1986–2003)	3,200
6	G. Boycott (England, 1964–81)	2,945
7	W.R. Hammond (England, 1928–47)	2,852
8	H. Sutcliffe (England, 1924–34)	2,741
9	C. Hill (Australia, 1896–1912)	2,660
10	J.H. Edrich (England, 1964–75)	2,644

MOST WICKETS: TOP 10

Pos	Player	Wickets
1	**S.K. Warne** (Australia, 1993–2007)	195
2	D.K. Lillee (Australia, 1971–82)	167
3	G.D. McGrath (Australia, 1994–2007)	157
4	I.T. Botham (England, 1977–89)	148
5	H. Trumble (Australia, 1890–1904)	141
6	R.G.D. Willis (England, 1971–83)	128
7	M.A. Noble (Australia, 1898–1909)	115
8	R.R. Lindwall (Australia, 1946–59)	114
9	W. Rhodes (England, 1899–1926)	109
10	S.F. Barnes (England, 1901–12)	106
=	C.V. Grimmett (Australia, 1925–34)	106

Chappell claims the most catches

The outstanding Australian batsman of his generation and a fine captain (he led his country to Ashes success in 1982–83), Greg Chappell is also the most successful fielder in all matches between England and Australia, taking 61 catches in 35 Ashes Tests between 1970 and 1983.

Laker puts Australia in a spin

It was the finest performance by a bowler in Test history. With the 1956 Ashes series locked at 1–1 going into the Fourth Test, off-spinner Jim Laker took 9 for 37 in the first innings and 10 for 53 in the second (the best single-innings haul in Test history) as England romped to victory by an innings and 170 runs. Laker's match haul of 19 for 90 is the best in Test history and his series haul of 49 wickets remains an all-time Ashes record.

S. AFRICA v ENGLAND

The first fixture between the two sides took place in March 1889, making this the second-oldest fixture in Test cricket. England enjoyed an early supremacy over South Africa, but matches in recent times, particularly since the Proteas' readmission to international cricket in 1992, have been much closer affairs with South Africa claiming 13 wins to England's ten.

Best partnership

Jacques Kallis joined Hashim Amla at the crease during the first Test against England at The Oval in July 2012 with South Africa already on a comfortable 260 for 2, having dismissed England for 385. They put on 377 runs, a record partnership in matches between the countries, with Amla amassing the highest Test score ever by a South African, 311 not out. Kallis was unbeaten on 182 not out as South Africa declared on 637 for 2. It was too much for England as they were bowled out for 240 to go 1–0 down in the three-match series.

OVERALL SERIES RECORDS

(141 Tests between 1889 and 2012)

	W	L	T	D	W/L	%W	%L	%D
South Africa	31	56	0	54	0.55	21.99	39.72	38.30
England	56	31	0	54	1.80	39.72	21.99	38.30

First match: 12–13 March 1889, Port Elizabeth

Brilliant Barnes too good for South Africa

If statistics alone can be proof of greatness, then S.F. Barnes was the best fast bowler England has ever produced and he was at his electrifying best against South Africa during England's 1913–14 tour when, playing on matting wickets, he was virtually unplayable. In the Second Test at Johannesburg, which England won by an innings and 12 runs, he produced match figures of 17 for 159 (a record in Tests between the two countries) and ended the series (despite missing the fifth and final Test match) with 49 wickets to his name (an all-time Test record for a five-match series).

Smith is most successful captain

Graeme Smith has come a long way since he first assumed the South African captaincy in the wake of his country's disastrous showing at the 2003 ICC World Cup and has led his country with distinction to this day. He is the most successful captain in South Africa-England Tests, leading his side to eight wins in 21 matches between 2003 and 2010.

Compton's magical series

Denis Compton's battling 163 in the second innings of the First Test against South Africa at Trent Bridge in 1947 not only helped England save the match (the home side had been forced to follow on still 325 runs in arrears), but also changed the course of the series. England went on to win the five-match series 3–0 with Compton's fine form continuing: he hit 208 at Lord's in the Second Test, 115 at Old Trafford in the Third Test and 113 in the Fifth and final Test at The Oval. The Middlesex star's series haul of 753 runs (at an average of 94.12) is an all-time record in matches between the two countries.

Lohmann rips through South Africa

The South African batsmen had no answer to George Lohmann on the matting wicket at the Old Wanderers ground in Johannesburg in March 1896. The right-arm fast-medium bowler, who was renowned for his accuracy, took 9 for 28 in South Africa's first innings as England went on to win the match by an innings and 197 runs. Lohmann's effort remains the best bowling performance in an innings in matches between the two sides.

Kicking England when they were down

Following the sudden resignation of Nasser Hussain as England captain after a drawn First Test at Edgbaston in 2003, South Africa piled more misery on to England when the two sides reconvened at Lord's for the Second Test. First they skittled the home side for 173, then, led by captain **Graeme Smith** (259) and Gary Kirsten (108), they compiled 682 for 6 declared – the highest total in all matches between the two sides – en route to completing a convincing innings-and-92-run victory.

Most catches

A stalwart of the South Africa side who appeared in 42 consecutive Tests for his country between 1929 and 1949, **Bruce Mitchell** was a fine batsman (scoring 1,380 Test runs at an average of 51.11) and an excellent fielder. He holds the record for the most catches by a player in Tests between England and South Africa, with 43 in 30 Tests between 1929 and 1949.

South African lows

South Africa may hold the upper hand in Tests against England in recent times, winning five and losing only two of the last ten matches played, but that has not always been the case. In fact, in the early years, they won only eight and lost 24 of the 39 Tests played between 1889 and 1924 and suffered some horror shows along the way. Twice they were dismissed for a paltry 30 – at Port Elizabeth in February 1896 and at Edgbaston in June 1924: they are the lowest totals ever recorded in Test matches between the two countries.

Edrich finally masters the South Africans

Having scored a meagre 21 runs in his first five innings against South Africa on the 1938–39 tour, it could be argued that a battling 219 in the Fifth "timeless" Test at Durban saved Bill Edrich's career. He was full of confidence when South Africa toured England in 1947, hitting two half-centuries in the First Test, 189 in the Second Test at Lord's and a brilliant 191 in the Third Test at Old Trafford. In 12 innings against South Africa, Edrich scored 792 runs at an average of 72.00, the highest average of any player to have batted ten times or more in Tests between the two countries.

Most dismissals

A standout performer for South Africa for over a decade, and one of the finest wicketkeeper-batsmen in history, Mark Boucher holds the all-time record for the most dismissals in Test matches between England and South Africa. The East London-born keeper has claimed 105 dismissals (103 catches and two stumpings) in 25 Tests against England between 1998 and 2010.

Most productive partnership

The most productive partnership in all Tests between England and South Africa is that between Len Hutton and Cyril Washbrook. In 19 innings between 1947 and 1949, the pair combined to score 1,371 runs at an average of 80.64.

MOST WICKETS: TOP 10

Pos	Player	Wickets
1	**S.M. Pollock** (South Africa, 1995–2005)	91
2	A.A. Donald (South Africa, 1994–2000)	86
3	S.F. Barnes (England, 1912–14)	83
4	H.J. Tayfield (South Africa, 1955–60)	75
5	C.L. Vincent (South Africa, 1927–35)	72
6	M. Ntini (South Africa, 1998–2009)	70
7	J.B. Statham (England, 1951–65)	69
8	G.A. Faulkner (South Africa, 1906–24)	68
9	T.L. Goddard (South Africa, 1955–65)	63
10	A.E.E. Vogler (South Africa, 1906–10)	60

MOST RUNS: TOP 10

Pos	Player	Runs
1	B. Mitchell (South Africa, 1929–49)	2,732
2	H.W. Taylor (South Africa, 1912–31)	2,287
3	D.C.S. Compton (England, 1947–57)	2,205
4	W.R. Hammond (England, 1927–39)	2,188
5	J.H. Kallis (South Africa, 1995–2012)	2,141
6	G.C. Smith (South Africa, 2003–12)	2,051
7	A.D. Nourse (South Africa, 1935–51)	2,037
8	G. Kirsten (South Africa, 1994–2003)	1,608
9	L. Hutton (England, 1938–51)	1,564
10	J.B. Hobbs (England, 1910–29)	1,562

S. AFRICA v AUSTRALIA

Australia hold a dominating lead in all Tests between the two countries, with 50 wins to South Africa's 21, but in recent times clashes between the two sides have been close affairs, with the series-winning side often considered the best team on the planet.

Classy Grimmett leaves South Africa in a spin

South Africa's batsmen continually failed to come to terms with Clarrie Grimmett's mastery of leg-spin bowling. In ten Tests against the South Africans, the spin wizard claimed 77 scalps (35.65 per cent of his Test victims), including 14 for 199 in the Fourth Test at Adelaide in January–February 1932 (a record match haul in Tests between the two countries) and a series record 44 wickets in the home series in 1935–36.

OVERALL SERIES RECORDS

(91 Tests between 1902 and 2014)

	W	L	T	D	W/L	%W	%L	%D
South Africa	21	50	0	20	0.42	23.08	54.95	21.98
Australia	50	21	0	20	2.38	54.95	23.08	21.98

First match: 11–14 October 1902, Johannesburg

Prolific Ponting an all-round record-breaker

Ricky Ponting has enjoyed some great moments against South Africa. He is the leading run-scorer in all Tests between the two countries (2,132 runs), the most successful captain (eight wins) and a member (along with Matthew Hayden) of the most productive partnership. He also holds the record for the most catches, with 35 in 26 Tests between 1997 and 2012.

Australian batsmen find their form

The Australians made a huge statement of intent in the opening Test of their 2001–02 tour to South Africa at Johannesburg. Having won the toss and elected to bat they put South Africa's bowlers to the sword, with Adam Gilchrist (204), Damien Martyn (133) and Matthew Hayden (122) all making hefty contributions as Australia amassed the highest-ever total in all Tests between the two countries – 652 for 7 declared. Australia went on to win the match by an innings and 360 runs.

Brilliant Boucher leads the way

The most prolific wicketkeeper in history, **Mark Boucher** leads the dismissals list in Tests between Australia and South Africa. In 20 Tests against the Aussies between 2001 and 2011, the South Africa gloveman claimed 66 dismissals, with 64 catches and two stumpings.

South Africa down and out

Already 4–0 down in the series, the South African tourists had any urge to continue the fight knocked out of them as they returned to Melbourne for the Fifth and final Test against Australia in February 1932. And how it showed. After winning the toss and choosing to bat, they collapsed to a miserable 36 all out in a little under 90 minutes – the lowest-ever total in matches between the two sides. Australia went on to win the Test by an innings and 72 runs to complete a series whitewash.

Best partnership

When **Greg Blewett** (left) joined **Steve Waugh** (right) with Australia on 174 for 4, still 128 runs behind South Africa in the First Test at Johannesburg in February–March 1997, the home side would have felt very much as though they were still in the game. Not for long, however. Over the next day and a half the pair – Waugh (160), Blewett (214) – combined to add an Australia-South Africa Test-best partnership of 385 runs to help Australia to 628 for 8 declared and an eventual innings-and-196-run victory.

Most productive partnership

The most productive partnership in all Tests between South Africa and Australia is that of Matthew Hayden and Ricky Ponting. The pair combined to score 1,136 runs in 14 innings between 2001 and 2009 at an average of 87.38.

Most successful captain

The second most successful Test captain of all time (with 48 wins), Ricky Ponting enjoyed considerable success as Australia's skipper against South Africa. In 12 Tests as captain between 2005 and 2009, the Tasmanian led his side to a record eight wins.

The Don's batting masterclass

Having already posted scores of 226 and 112 in his first two Tests against South Africa, Donald Bradman reserved his best performance of the 1931–32 series for the Fourth Test at Adelaide, hitting a magnificent unbeaten 299 – the highest individual score in all matches between the two countries. Ironically, he was left stranded after running out No. 11 Pud Thurlow in a scrambled, and ultimately misguided, attempt to reach 300.

Harvey's heroics in vain in drawn series

An electrifying batsman who thrilled crowds with his stunning strokeplay and frustrated opponents with his seemingly limitless powers of concentration, Neil Harvey was at his best during the scintillating 2–2 series draw against South Africa in 1952–53. The left-hander hit four centuries and three half-centuries (with a highest score of 205 in the Fifth Test at Melbourne) to end the series with 834 runs at an average of 92.66. His tally remains the highest series haul by any batsman in all Tests between the two countries. He also holds the record for the highest batting average of all batsmen to have batted in at least ten innings in matches between Australia and South Africa, scoring 1,625 runs at an average of 81.25 in 23 innings against South Africa between 1949 and 1958.

MOST RUNS: TOP 10

Pos	Player	Runs
1	**R.T. Ponting** (Australia, 1997–2011)	2,132
2	J.H. Kallis (South Africa, 1997–2011)	1,978
3	AB de Villiers (South Africa, 2005–14)	1,641
4	R.N. Harvey (Australia, 1949–58)	1,625
5	M.J. Clarke (Australia, 2008–14)	1,487
6	M.L. Hayden (Australia, 1994–2009)	1,486
7	R.G. Pollock (South Africa, 1963–70)	1,453
8	H.M. Amla (South Africa, 2008–14)	1,280
9	G.C. Smith (South Africa, 2002–14)	1,226
10	E.J. Barlow (South Africa, 1963–70)	1,149

MOST WICKETS: TOP 10

Pos	Player	Wickets
1	S.K. Warne (Australia, 1993–2006)	130
2	C.V. Grimmett (Australia, 1931–36)	77
3	D.W. Steyn (South Africa, 2008–14)	69
4	H.J. Tayfield (South Africa, 1949–58)	64
=	M.G. Johnson (Australia, 2008–14)	64
6	M. Ntini (South Africa, 2001–09)	58
7	G.D. McGrath (Australia, 1994–2006)	57
8	T.L. Goddard (South Africa, 1957–70)	53
=	A.A. Donald (South Africa, 1993–2002)	53
10	R. Benaud (Australia, 1952–64)	52
=	P.M. Pollock (South Africa, 1963–70)	52

Johnson's record-breaking performance

Mitchell Johnson produced one of the most devastating spells of fast bowling in recent times in the First Test against South Africa at Perth in December 2008, taking five wickets for two runs in 21 balls to end with figures of 8 for 61 – the best in all matches between the two countries. His record-breaking efforts were all in vain, however, as the Proteas rallied to win the match by six wickets.

ENGLAND v W. INDIES

Behind the Ashes this is the second most contested fixture in international cricket. Fortunes have wavered for both England and the West Indies since the two countries played a Test match for the first time in 1928, with both sides enjoying periods of dominance, none more extreme than when the West Indies went unbeaten in 29 straight Tests against England between June 1976 and February 1990.

OVERALL SERIES RECORDS

(148 Tests between 1928 and 2012)

	W	L	T	D	W/L	%W	%L	%D
England	45	53	0	59	0.84	30.41	35.81	33.78
West Indies	53	45	0	50	1.17	35.81	30.41	33.78

First match: 23–6 June 1928, Lord's

Most catches

Brian Lara not only terrorized England with the bat between 1994 and 2004, he also caused havoc in the field. In 30 Tests against the English, the Trinidad star snared 45 catches, an all-time record for any player in Tests between the two countries.

Most productive partnership

The most productive partnership in all Tests between England and the West Indies is that between Gordon Greenidge and Desmond Haynes, who combined to score 1,862 runs in 37 innings at an average of 51.72.

The master blaster's golden summer

Viv Richards established himself as a player of true international class during the West Indies' 1976 tour to England. He hit 232 in the First Test at Trent Bridge, 135 in the Third Test at Old Trafford (after missing the Second Test through injury) and a magnificent 291 in the Fifth and final Test at The Oval. His series haul of 829 runs (at an average of 118.42) remains an all-time high in all matches between the two countries.

Lara's love-in at Antigua

Brian Lara seemed to reserve his greatest performances for matches against England at St John's, Antigua. In April 1994 he plundered the England attack for a then world record 375. A decade later he was at it again, this time amassing a new all-time Test record score of 400 not out (off 582 balls) with 43 fours and four sixes.

Murray the master behind the stumps

A regular behind the stumps for the West Indies for 17 years between 1963 and 1980, Deryck Murray holds the record for the most dismissals in Tests between England and the West Indies. In 28 matches against England, the Trinidad keeper claimed 94 scalps (90 catches and four stumpings).

Most successful captain

Viv Richards had the good fortune to captain the West Indies during the islanders' golden era, and remains the most successful captain in Test matches between the two countries, leading his side to 13 wins in 19 Tests between 1980 and 1991.

MOST RUNS: TOP 10

Pos	Player	Runs
1	G.S. Sobers (West Indies, 1954–74)	3,214
2	B.C. Lara (West Indies, 1994–2004)	2,983
3	I.V.A. Richards (West Indies, 1976–91)	2,869
4	D.L. Haynes (West Indies, 1980–94)	2,392
5	S. Chanderpaul (W. Indies, 1994–2012)	2,359
6	C.G. Greenidge (West Indies, 1976–90)	2,318
7	R.B. Kanhai (West Indies, 1957–74)	2,267
8	G. Boycott (England, 1966–81)	2,205
9	G.A. Gooch (England, 1980–91)	2,197
10	C.H. Lloyd (West Indies, 1968–84)	2,120

MOST WICKETS: TOP 10

Pos	Player	Wickets
1	C.E.L. Ambrose (W. Indies, 1988–2000)	164
2	C.A. Walsh (West Indies, 1986–2000)	145
3	M.D. Marshall (West Indies, 1980–91)	127
4	G.S. Sobers (West Indies, 1954–74)	102
5	L.R. Gibbs (West Indies, 1963–74)	100
6	M.A. Holding (West Indies, 1976–86)	96
7	J. Garner (West Indies, 1980–86)	92
8	F.S. Trueman (England, 1954–63)	86
9	S. Ramadhin (W. Indies, 1950–60)	80
10	J.A. Snow (England, 1966–76)	72

England prosper in Kingston

With the 1929–30 series locked at 1–1, it was decided that the Fourth and final Test match, at Kingston, Jamaica, should be a timeless one. England won the toss, elected to bat and, led by Andy Sandham's 325, batted themselves into an impregnable position, amassing 849 all out. The score remains the highest total in all matches between the two countries, but it wasn't enough to win the match. After rain on days eight and nine prevented any further play, the two teams agreed on a draw.

Marshall produces his menacing best

The sheer pace and consistent excellence that became the trademark of **Malcolm Marshall**'s career proved too much for England's batsmen during the West Indies' comprehensive 4–0 series win in 1988. Using his unorthodox, open-chested action to swing the ball both ways at frightening pace, Marshall took 35 wickets in the series (an all-time record in Tests between the two countries) with a best of 7 for 22 in the Third Test at Old Trafford.

Cowdrey and May rescue England with record-breaking partnership

With England trailing the West Indies by a mighty 288 runs after the completion of the first innings of the First Test at Edgbaston in May–June 1957, Colin Cowdrey and Peter May came to the rescue when their country truly needed them. The pair added a record 411 runs for the fourth wicket to lead England to 583 for 4 declared and the eventual safety of a draw.

Hutton tops the averages

One of the finest batsmen Test cricket has produced, Len Hutton enjoyed some particularly good times against the West Indies. In 13 matches against the islanders he hit five centuries – with a highest score of 202 not out at The Oval in August 1950 – and amassed 1,661 runs at an average of 79.09 – the highest of any player to have batted in ten innings in matches between England and the West Indies.

Whispering Death makes his deadly mark

Nicknamed "Whispering Death" because of his stealth-like approach to the bowling crease, Michael Holding truly found his stride in the Fifth Test against England at The Oval in August 1976. The Jamaican paceman took 8 for 92 in the first innings and 6 for 57 in the second to end up with match figures of 14 for 149: an all-time West Indian record and a record in all Tests between England and the West Indies.

Sorry England capitulate in Trinidad

Set just 194 runs to win the Third Test of the 1993–94 series at Port of Spain, Trinidad, England collapsed in spectacular and record-breaking style. The tone was set when they lost captain Michael Atherton to the first ball of the innings. Just 19.1 overs later, they had been dismissed for a paltry 46 all out – the lowest score in England–West Indies matches – with Curtly Ambrose (6 for 24) the chief destroyer.

Ambrose the destroyer

English batsmen could find few answers to the hostile pace and bounce of **Curtly Ambrose** over a 12-year period between 1988 and 2000. In 34 Tests against England, the 6ft 7in Antiguan took 164 wickets (40.49 per cent of his career Test wicket haul) with a best of 8 for 45 (at Bridgetown, Barbados, in April 1990). Both are all-time records in Test matches between the two countries.

NZ v ENGLAND

It took New Zealand 47 Test matches over 48 years before they finally managed to record their first-ever victory over England – at Wellington in February 1978 – but, helped by the emergence of several players of true international class, matches between the two countries have been more closely fought encounters in recent years.

OVERALL SERIES RECORDS

(99 Tests between 1930 and 2013)

	W	L	T	D	W/L	%W	%L	%D
New Zealand	8	47	0	44	0.17	8.08	47.47	44.44
England	47	8	0	44	5.87	47.47	8.08	44.44

First match: 10–13 January 1930, Christchurch

Lock's spell in the limelight

An aggressive left-arm spinner who for the most part had to play second fiddle to Jim Laker throughout his 49-Test match career, Tony Lock enjoyed a spell in the limelight against New Zealand in 1958. The Surrey left-arm spinner took 34 wickets in the series (with three five-wicket hauls and a best return of 7 for 35 in the Fourth Test at Old Trafford). No bowler has taken more wickets in an England-New Zealand series.

Most catches

One of the most prolific slip catchers Test cricket has ever seen, **Stephen Fleming** has bagged more catches in England–New Zealand Test matches than any other player. The former Kiwi captain took 33 catches in 19 Tests against England between 1994 and 2008.

The Edrich and Barrington show

Already 2–0 up in the 1965 series going into the Third Test at Headingley in July 1965, England were able to build on their advantage over New Zealand thanks to the batting of John Edrich (310 not out) and Ken Barrington (163). Coming together in the first innings with the score on 13 for 1, the pair added 369 for the second wicket – an all-time record partnership in matches between the two countries – to propel England to a first-innings total of 546 for 4 declared and an eventual innings-and-187-run victory.

Happy days for Vaughan

Michael Vaughan is the most successful captain in the history of Test cricket between England and New Zealand. The Yorkshire star led England to six wins over the Kiwis in eight Tests between 2004 and 2008.

Most productive partnership

The most productive partnership in all Tests between England and New Zealand is that between Michael Atherton and Alec Stewart. The England opening pair combined to score 809 runs in 14 innings at an average of 57.78 (with a highest partnership of 182 runs in the First Test at Auckland in January 1997).

Starting as you mean to go on

There is no better time to make a statement of intent than in the first innings of the opening Test of a series and, in February 1975 at Auckland, England, recently arrived in New Zealand licking their wounds following a 4–1 thumping in the Ashes series, did just that. Helped by superb innings from Keith Fletcher (216) and captain Mike Denness (181), they compiled 593 for 6 declared – the highest innings total in all matches between the two countries – en route to winning the match by an innings and 83 runs.

MOST RUNS: TOP 10

Pos	Player	Runs
1	**J.G. Wright** (New Zealand, 1978–92)	1,518
2	M.D. Crowe (New Zealand, 1983–94)	1,421
3	S.P. Fleming (New Zealand, 1994–2008)	1,229
4	G.A. Gooch (England, 1978–94)	1,148
5	A.J. Stewart (England, 1990–99)	1,145
6	B.E. Congdon (New Zealand, 1965–78)	1,143
7	M.C. Cowdrey (England, 1955–71)	1,133
8	M.A. Atherton (England, 1990–99)	1,088
9	D.I. Gower (England, 1978–86)	1,051
10	B. Sutcliffe (New Zealand, 1947–65)	1,049

MOST WICKETS: TOP 10

Pos	Player	Wickets
1	R.J. Hadlee (New Zealand, 1973–90)	97
2	I.T. Botham (England, 1978–92)	64
3	R.G.D. Willis (England, 1971–84)	60
4	R.O. Collinge (New Zealand, 1965–78)	48
=	**D.L. Underwood** (England, 1969–75)	48
6	G.A.R. Lock (England, 1958–59)	47
=	C.L. Cairns (New Zealand, 1992–2004)	47
=	A.R. Caddick (England, 1997–2002)	47
9	J.M. Anderson (England, 2008–13)	46
10	D.L. Vettori (New Zealand, 1997–2008)	45

Underwood spins England to a comprehensive victory

England's most successful spin bowler of all time, **Derek Underwood** produced a match-winning performance of star quality in the First Test against New Zealand at Lord's in July 1969. With New Zealand set an improbable 362 runs to win, the Kent left-arm spinner took 7 for 32 off 31 overs to propel England to a 230-run victory. They are the best single-innings figures in England–New Zealand Tests.

Kiwis out of their depth

Early matches between England and New Zealand were a sorry mismatch and the Kiwis hit an all-time low in the Second Test of the 1954–55 series at Auckland. Trailing England by 46 runs after the completion of the first innings, they crashed to the lowest score in Test history: a miserable 26 all out in 27 overs.

Classy Hammond the pick of the crop

One of Test cricket's all-time great batsmen, **Walter Hammond** flourished against all opponents in the Test arena, but particularly against New Zealand. In the Second Test against the Kiwis in Auckland in March–April 1933, he struck a then world record score of 336 not out (still the highest individual score in all matches between the two countries), an innings that included ten sixes (a world record that stood for 63 years). He ended the series with 563 runs (another all-time high in England-New Zealand Tests) and finished his Test career averaging 112.77 against New Zealand (the highest average of any player to have completed ten or more innings in matches between the two countries).

Deadly Derek strikes again

Nicknamed "Deadly" by his team-mates because of his effectiveness on rain-affected pitches, **Derek Underwood** lived up to his reputation in the First Test match against New Zealand at Christchurch in February 1971. On a damp wicket, he took 6 for 12 in the first innings and 6 for 85 in the second to lead England to an eight-wicket victory. His match haul of 12 for 97 is an all-time record in matches between the two countries.

The most successful keeper? That's Parore

An able performer with the bat and, arguably, the most consistent wicketkeeper in world cricket in the 1990s, Adam Parore claimed more dismissals in England-New Zealand Test matches than any other keeper in history. In 15 matches against England between 1990 and 2002, the Auckland gloveman bagged 46 scalps (45 catches and one stumping).

AUSTRALIA v W. INDIES

This is the sixth-oldest fixture in international cricket and, over the years, one of the most closely contested. Australia lead the way with 54 wins to the West Indies' 32 and in recent times have enjoyed a period of dominance over the islanders, but that has not always been the case.

Walters's West Indian love affair

Renowned as much for his off-the-field antics as for his skills on a cricket pitch, Doug Walters liked nothing more than a battle and reserved some of his best performances for matches against the West Indies fast bowlers. In nine matches against the islanders between 1968 and 1973, the New South Wales stroke player hit six centuries (with a highest score of 242 in the Fifth Test at Sydney in February 1969) and scored 1,196 runs at an average of 92.00 – the highest of any player to have completed ten innings or more in matches between the two countries.

OVERALL SERIES RECORDS

(111 Tests between 1930 and 2012)

	W	L	T	D	W/L	%W	%L	%D
Australia	54	32	1	24	1.68	48.64	28.82	22.52*
West Indies	32	54	1	24	0.59	28.82	48.64	22.52*

First match: 12–16 December 1930, Adelaide
* One match tied

West Indies crash to a record-breaking low in crushing defeat

The golden years of West Indian dominance seemed like a distant memory in the First Test of the 1999 series against Australia at Port of Spain, Trinidad. Set 364 runs to win the opening rubber, the West Indies crashed in spectacular style to 51 all out in a paltry 19.1 overs and a crushing 312-run defeat. It is the lowest team total in all Tests between the two countries.

Most productive partnership

The most productive partnership in all Tests between Australia and the West Indies is that of Gordon Greenidge and Desmond Haynes. The legendary opening batsmen combined to score 2,252 runs in 48 innings between 1978 and 1991 at an average of 53.61.

Captain Lloyd leads the way

Clive Lloyd is the most successful of all captains in the history of Test matches between Australia and the West Indies. In 22 Tests against Australia between 1975 and 1985, Lloyd led the islanders to 12 victories.

Lawry and Simpson dig deep

Having lost two of the first three matches of the 1964–65 series against the West Indies, Australia needed to show considerably more fight when the two teams arrived at Bridgetown, Barbados, for the Fourth Test in May 1965. And Bill Lawry (210) and captain Bobby Simpson (201) did just that, putting on 382 runs for the opening wicket – the best partnership in the history of Australia–West Indies Tests. Unfortunately for the tourists, the West Indies held out for a draw to secure a series victory.

Lone defiance from Walcott

Rarely has a player prospered so much in a losing cause. Australia may have eased to a 3–0 victory over the West Indies in the 1954–55 series in the Caribbean, but they did so despite the best efforts of **Clyde Walcott**. The Bajan right-hander hit five centuries and two half-centuries (with a highest score of 155 in the Fifth Test at Kingston, Jamaica) to end the series with 827 runs at an average of 82.70. It remains the highest series run haul by any batsman in the history of Australia-West Indies matches.

Australia bow out of tour in record-breaking style

In June 1955 Australia held an unassailable 2–0 lead going into the Fifth and final Test at Kingston, Jamaica, and with the series already in the bag, and the pressure off, the tourists put on a show. After watching the home side compile a steady 357 all out, five Australian batsmen passed three figures as they amassed a mighty 758 for 8 declared (the highest total in all Tests between the two sides) on the way to an innings-and-82-run victory.

McKenzie makes the most of helpful conditions

Garth McKenzie took full advantage of both the bitterly cold Boxing Day conditions and the green tinge of the Melbourne wicket in the Second Test against the West Indies in December 1968. The Western Australian fast bowler took 8 for 71 – the best single-innings figures by any bowler in Australia–West Indies Tests – to help his side to an innings-and-30-run victory.

Trio share record for most wickets in a series

Three bowlers hold the record for the most wickets in a series between Australia and the West Indies with 33: Clarrie Grimmett in Australia's 4–1 series victory in the Caribbean in 1930–31; Alan Davidson, in Australia's 2–1 home series win in 1960–61; and Curtly Ambrose, in the West Indies 2–1 series win in Australia in 1992–93.

Most catches

The possessor of one of the safest pairs of hands in Test history, Mark Waugh holds the record for the most catches in Test matches between Australia and the West Indies: the younger of the Waugh twins took 45 catches in 28 Test matches against the islanders between 1991 and 2001.

Most dismissals

Jeff Dujon heads the list of most successful wicketkeepers in matches between Australia and the West Indies. The Jamaican keeper claimed 86 scalps (85 catches and one stumping) in 23 matches against Australia between 1981 and 1991.

Lara makes a name for himself

It was in the Third Test at Sydney, in January 1993, that **Brian Lara** announced himself to the world as a player of exceptional talent. With the West Indies under intense pressure following Australia's first-innings total of 503 for 9 declared, the Trinidad star produced a batting display of breathtaking quality, facing 372 balls and hitting 38 fours en route to compiling a magnificent 277 – the highest individual score in all matches between the two countries.

MOST RUNS: TOP 10

Pos	Player	Runs
1	**B.C. Lara** (West Indies, 1992–2005)	2,815
2	I.V.A. Richards (West Indies, 1975–91)	2,266
3	D.L. Haynes (West Indies, 1978–93)	2,233
4	C.H. Lloyd (West Indies, 1968–85)	2,211
5	S.R. Waugh (Australia, 1988–2003)	2,192
6	R.B. Richardson (West Indies, 1984–95)	2,175
7	A.R. Border (Australia, 1979–93)	2,052
8	R.T. Ponting (Australia, 1996–2012)	1,977
9	M.E. Waugh (Australia, 1991–2001)	1,858
10	C.G. Greenidge (West Indies, 1975–91)	1,819

Big Merv batters the Windies at Perth

A lion-hearted fast bowler who played a major role in helping Australia to climb to the top of world cricket, **Merv Hughes** was at his menacing best in the Second Test against the West Indies at Perth in December 1988. He took 5 for 130 in the first innings and a magnificent 8 for 87 in the second to propel his side to a 169-run victory. His match figures of 13 for 217 are the best by any bowler in all Test matches between the two countries.

MOST WICKETS: TOP 10

Pos	Player	Wickets
1	**C.A. Walsh** (West Indies, 1984–2001)	135
2	C.E.L. Ambrose (West Indies, 1988–99)	128
3	G.D. McGrath (Australia, 1995–2005)	110
4	L.R. Gibbs (West Indies, 1961–76)	103
5	J. Garner (West Indies, 1978–85)	89
6	M.D. Marshall (West Indies, 1984–91)	87
7	M.A. Holding (West Indies, 1975–85)	76
8	S.K. Warne (Australia, 1992–2005)	65
9	B. Lee (Australia, 2000–08)	64
10	J.R. Thomson (Australia, 1975–82)	62

NZ v S. AFRICA

A combination of New Zealand's geographical isolation and South Africa's ostracism from world cricket meant that Test matches between the two countries were few and far between for decades following the sides' first meeting in 1932. In recent times, however, they have met on a more regular basis and South Africa have dominated the encounters, winning 14 out of 23 Tests since 1995.

OVERALL SERIES RECORDS

(40 Tests between 1932 and 2013)

	W	L	T	D	W/L	%W	%L	%D
New Zealand	4	23	0	13	0.17	10.00	57.50	32.50
South Africa	23	4	0	13	5.75	57.50	10.00	32.50

First match: 27 February–1 March 1932, Christchurch, New Zealand

Amla and Kallis conquer batting demons in Johannesburg

After 22 wickets had fallen over the first day-and-a-half of the First Test between South Africa and New Zealand at Johannesburg in November 2007, Hashim Amla (176 not out) and Jacques Kallis (186) finally made batting look easy. The pair added 330 for the third wicket – an all-time high in Tests between the two countries – to help South Africa to a second-innings total of 422 for 3 declared and an eventual 358-run victory. Amla and Kallis have also enjoyed the most productive partnership in South Africa-New Zealand Tests, combining to score 756 runs in six innings at an average of 126.00.

Goofy by name but not by nature

A 6ft 5in fast bowler who relied more on hard work than on natural ability, Godfrey "Goofy" Lawrence appeared in only five Test matches for South Africa, but he more than made his mark in the second innings of the Second Test against New Zealand at Johannesburg in December 1961, taking 8 for 53 – the best single-innings figures in all Tests between South Africa and New Zealand. Unfortunately for Lawrence and South Africa, his performance did not turn out to be a match-winning one: the game petered out into a bore draw. Lawrence ended the series with 28 wickets to his name – another record in Tests between the two countries – but, owing to South Africa's limited Test schedule, never played for his country again.

Wicketkeeper Waite leads the way

The best wicketkeeper in South Africa's history until the arrival of Mark Boucher in the 1990s, and the first South African player to win 50 caps, Johnny Waite is the most successful keeper in the history of Test matches between South Africa and New Zealand. In 15 Tests against the Kiwis between 1953 and 1964, he claimed 57 dismissals, with 47 catches and ten stumpings.

Martin leads Kiwis to memorable victory

Chris Martin was a key figure for his country as New Zealand secured only their fourth-ever victory over South Africa, in the Second Test at Auckland in March 2004. The Kiwi paceman took 6 for 76 in the first innings and 5 for 104 in the second to help his side to a nine-wicket victory. His match haul of 11 for 180 is the best in all Tests between the two sides.

Most successful captain

Graeme Smith is the most successful captain in South Africa-New Zealand Tests. He has led South Africa to eight victories in 13 Tests – a winning percentage of 61.54. Jack Cheetham won five in seven for the Springboks 1953–54.

Reid leads by example

John Reid was the star of the show as New Zealand fought back to claim a 2–2 draw in the five-match series in South Africa in 1961–62. The New Zealand captain led from the front, hitting four half-centuries and a century (142 in the Fourth Test at Johannesburg) to end the series with 546 runs – an all-time high in series between the two countries – at an average of 60.66.

Most catches

Not only is Graeme Smith the most successful captain in the history of Test matches between South Africa and New Zealand, he is also the most successful fielder. He has snared a record 18 catches in 13 matches against the Blackcaps between 2004 and 2013.

MOST RUNS: TOP 10

	Player	Runs
1	J.H. Kallis (South Africa, 1999–2013)	1,543
2	D.J. McGlew (South Africa, 1953–62)	1,100
3	S.P. Fleming (New Zealand, 1994–2007)	1,072
4	G. Kirsten (South Africa, 1994–2004)	951
5	J.R. Reid (New Zealand, 1953–64)	914
6	H.M. Amla (South Africa, 2006–13)	889
7	G.C. Smith (South Africa, 2004–13)	847
8	D.J. Cullinan (South Africa, 1994–2000)	823
9	H.H. Gibbs (South Africa, 1999–2007)	790
10	E.J. Barlow (South Africa, 1961–64)	625

MOST WICKETS: TOP 10

	Player	Wickets
1	D.W. Steyn (South Africa, 2006–13)	58
2	C.S. Martin (New Zealand, 2000–13)	55
3	M. Ntini (South Africa, 2000–07)	46
4	S.M. Pollock (South Africa, 1999–2006)	43
5	J.R. Reid (New Zealand, 1953–64)	37
6	N.A.T. Adcock (South Africa, 1953–62)	33
7	P.M. Pollock (South Africa, 1961–64)	32
8	H.J. Tayfield (South Africa, 1953–54)	31
9	F.J. Cameron (New Zealand, 1961–64)	29
10	G.B. Lawrence (South Africa, 1961–62)	28
=	V.D. Philander (South Africa, 2012–13)	28

South Africa benefit from poor captain's choice

South Africa's batsmen made New Zealand captain Dion Nash's decision to bowl first in the First Test at Auckland in February–March 1999 look like one of Test cricket's more regrettable choices when they put on 621 for 5 over the first two-and-a-half days – the highest score in all Tests between the two countries. Fortunately for Nash, South Africa's bowlers also struggled on the lifeless pitch and the match ended in a draw.

The worst of starts

It is very important to get off to a solid start on the first morning of the first Test of a series, but New Zealand had a nightmare against South Africa at Cape Town, in January 2013. After winning the toss and electing to bat, the Black Caps slumped to a miserable 45 all out in just 19.2 overs – the lowest total in all Tests between the two countries. Only one batsmen (Kane Williamson) reached double figures. Predictably New Zealand failed to recover from such a devastating start and went on to lose the match by an innings and 27 runs.

Cullinan prospers against New Zealand

Daryll Cullinan was the main beneficiary of Dion Nash's dubious decision to put South Africa in to bat in the First Test at Auckland in February–March 1999. The elegant No. 4 batsman put New Zealand's bowlers to the sword, hitting an unbeaten 275 (off 490 balls with 27 fours and two sixes), which is not only the highest individual score in matches between the two countries but also the third highest score by a South African in Test cricket. Cullinan also holds the record for the highest average by any batsman to have completed ten or more innings in New Zealand-South Africa Tests: he scored 823 runs in 16 innings against New Zealand between 1994 and 2000 at an average of 68.58.

ENGLAND v INDIA

Since the fixture was first contested in 1932, England have enjoyed the upper hand against India in home Test matches (winning 27 of the 52 matches played and losing just five), but contests on the slow, low, spin-friendly surfaces of the subcontinent have proved to be altogether closer affairs, with India leading the way with 15 wins to England's 13.

OVERALL SERIES RECORDS

(107 Tests between 1932 and 2012)

	W	L	T	D	W/L	%W	%L	%D
England	40	20	0	47	2.00	37.38	18.69	43.43
India	20	40	0	47	0.50	18.69	37.38	43.43

First match: 25–28 June 1932, Lord's

The leading wicketkeeper

Arguably the most complete wicketkeeper England has ever produced and without doubt the best when standing up to spin bowlers (his partnership with Derek Underwood for both Kent and England is legendary), Alan Knott is the most successful wicketkeeper in the history of England-India Test matches. In 16 Tests against India between 1971 and 1977 he claimed 54 dismissals, with 49 catches and five stumpings.

Most productive partnership

The most productive partnership in all Tests between England and India is that between **Rahul Dravid** and Sachin Tendulkar, who combined to score 1,001 runs in 23 innings between 1996 and 2011 at an average of 43.52.

England post record total in massive win

Having dismissed India for a below-par 224 in their first innings in the third Test at Edgbaston in August 2011, England were keen to maintain their advantage over the visitors ... and how they did so. Led by Alastair Cook (294 – the second highest individual score in matches between the two sides) and Eoin Morgan (104), the home side posted 710 for 7 – the highest total in England–India Tests – and went on to win the match by an innings and 242 runs to take an unassailable 3–0 lead in the four-match series.

Beefy Botham on fire in Mumbai

The Golden Jubilee Test, played at Mumbai in February 1980, was the Test match which showed the world that, in Ian Botham, England possessed an all-rounder of the highest quality. The Somerset man took 6 for 58 in India's first innings, helped himself to 114 runs when England batted, and then took 7 for 48 in India's second to become only the second player in history (Australia's Alan Davidson being the other) to score a century and take 10 wickets in a Test match. Botham's match haul of 13 for 106 remains an all-time record in England–India Tests.

Bell and Pietersen confirm England dominance

England held an unassailable 3–0 lead over India going into the fourth and final Test at The Oval in August 2011, but there was still plenty for both sides to play for: an England victory would see them overtake India as the no.1 ranked side in Test cricket. England batted after winning the toss, but slipped to 97 for 2. Then **Ian Bell** (left, 235) and **Kevin Pietersen** (175) added an all-time series record 350 runs for the third wicket. After posting 591 for 6 declared, England won the match by an innings and 8 runs to complete a 4–0 series whitewash and claim the no.1 ranking.

Gavaskar proves his worth in the field

Not only is Sunil Gavaskar the leading run-scorer in Test matches between England and India (with 2,483 runs), he is also the most successful fielder. In 38 Tests against England between 1971 and 1986, the diminutive opening batsman took a record 35 catches.

MOST RUNS: TOP 10

Pos	Player	Runs
1	S.R. Tendulkar (India, 1990–2012)	2.535
2	S.M. Gavaskar (India, 1971–86)	2,483
3	R. Dravid (India, 1996–2011)	1,950
4	G.R. Viswanath (India, 1971–82)	1,880
5	G.A. Gooch (England, 1979–93)	1,725
6	D.B. Vengsarkar (India, 1977–90)	1,589
7	K.P. Pietersen (England, 2006–12)	1,581
8	A.N. Cook (England, 2006–12)	1,437
9	D.I. Gower (England, 1979–90)	1,391
10	K.F. Barrington (England, 1959–67)	1,355
=	Kapil Dev (India, 1979–93)	1,355

MOST WICKETS: TOP 10

Pos	Player	Wickets
1	B.S. Chandrasekhar (India, 1964–79)	95
2	A. Kumble (India, 1990–2007)	92
3	B.S. Bedi (India, 1967–79)	85
=	Kapil Dev (India, 1979–93)	85
5	D.L. Underwood (England, 1971–82)	62
=	R.G.D. Willis (England, 1974–82)	62
7	I.T. Botham (England, 1979–82)	59
8	J.M. Anderson (England, 2006–11)	57
9	M.H. Mankad (India, 1946–52)	54
10	F.S. Trueman (England, 1952–59)	53

Most successful captain

One of the quirks of England's destruction of India in the much-hyped but ultimately anti-climatic 2011 series was that Andrew Strauss became the most successful captain in England–India Test matches, having recorded four wins at the helm.

Fiery Fred routs India

Batting on an already green wicket that had been further softened by rain, India's batsmen could find no answer to the pace and hostility of **Fred Trueman** in the Third Test of the 1952 series at Old Trafford. In 8.4 electrifying overs, the legendary Yorkshire fast bowler took 8 for 31 – the best single-innings figures in all Tests between England and India – to propel England to an eventual innings-and-207-run victory.

Gooch's Indian summer

Graham Gooch, England's all-time leading run-scorer, was in the form of his life in the 1990 series against India. In the First Test at Lord's he hit 333 in the first innings (the highest individual score in all Tests between the two countries) and 123 in the second – his match aggregate of 456 runs is the highest in Test history. The Essex man's rich vein of form continued in the Second Test at Old Trafford, where he made 116 and 7, and knocks of 85 and 88 in the third and final Test at The Oval meant that he finished the three-match series with an England-India series record 752 runs to his name at the impressive average of 125.33.

India fold at the home of cricket

Trailing England by 327 runs after the completion of the first innings in the Second Test at Lord's in June 1974, India were asked to follow on and then gave up the fight in sorry fashion, subsiding to an embarrassing 42 all out in just 17 overs – the lowest total in all Test matches between England and India – and losing the match by the massive margin of an innings and 285 runs.

Barrington reserves his best for India

A player who learnt to curb his natural attacking instincts to become one of the most obdurate batsmen England has ever produced, Ken Barrington enjoyed some particularly good times against India. In 14 matches against them between 1959 and 1967 he scored 1,355 runs (with three centuries and a highest score of 172 at Kanpur in December 1961) at an average of 75.27 – the highest of any batsman to have completed ten or more innings in Test matches between the two countries.

Chandra's box of tricks confounds England

One of the major factors behind India's 2–1 series victory over England in 1972–73 was the England batsmen's continued inability to unravel the secrets of leg-spinner Bhagwath Chandrasekhar's box of tricks. The Karnataka spin wizard used his dazzling array of leg-spinners, top-spinners, googlies and sliders to great effect, taking four five-wicket hauls in five Tests (with a best of 8 for 79 in the First Test at Delhi), and ended the series with 35 wickets to his name – a record for an England-India series.

NZ v AUSTRALIA

Given that New Zealand have been playing Test cricket since 1930, it seems strange that they had to wait 16 years before playing near-neighbours Australia for the first time – at Wellington, a match they ended up losing by an innings and 103 runs. And Australia have generally dominated the Kiwis from that moment on, winning 27 of the 52 Test matches played and losing only eight.

Most productive partnership

The most productive partnership in all Tests between New Zealand and Australia is that between Matthew Hayden and Justin Langer. The Aussie pair combined to score 961 runs in 13 innings between 2000 and 2005 at an average of 73.92.

Most catches

The seventh most prolific fielder in Test history (with 156 catches), Allan Border leads the fielding list in Australia-New Zealand clashes. The former Australian captain bagged 31 catches in 23 Tests against New Zealand between 1980 and 1993.

OVERALL SERIES RECORDS

(52 Tests between 1946 and 2011)

	W	L	T	D	W/L	%W	%L	%D
New Zealand	8	27	0	17	0.29	15.36	51.42	32.69
Australia	27	8	0	17	3.37	51.42	15.36	32.69

First match: 29–30 March 1946, Wellington, New Zealand

Australia secure series win in style

Holding a 1–0 lead in the 1993–94 series going into the Third and final Test at Brisbane, Australia soon extinguished any hopes New Zealand might have had of squaring the series. First they dismissed New Zealand for 233; then, with Steve Waugh (147 not out) and Allan Border (105) starring, they batted their opponents out of the game, compiling a massive 607 for 6 declared – the highest team total in all matches between the two countries – en route to completing an innings-and-96-run victory.

Most dismissals

Rod Marsh heads the wicketkeeping list in all Tests between Australia and New Zealand. The Western Australian gloveman claimed 58 scalps in 14 Tests against New Zealand between 1973 and 1982 with 57 catches and one stumping.

Brothers in arms

Coming to the wicket with Australia in trouble at 55 for 2 in the First Test against New Zealand at Wellington in March 1974, brothers **Ian** (right, 145) and **Greg Chappell** (left, 247 not out) combined to record-breaking effect, putting on 264 runs for the third wicket (an all-time record in Australia-New Zealand Tests) to help their side to 511 for 6 declared. The match eventually fizzled out into a draw.

Ponting prospers against New Zealand

Ricky Ponting is the most successful captain in the history of Tests between Australia and New Zealand. The Australian captain, the most successful skipper in Test history, led his side to eight wins over New Zealand in nine Tests between 2004 and 2010.

Katich prospers against Black Caps

An obdurate middle-order batsman in the early part of his career who became an effective opener for Australia, Simon Katich enjoyed many highlights in matches against New Zealand. In seven Tests against the Black Caps between 2005 and 2010, the Western Australian plundered 643 runs (with three centuries and a highest score of 131 not out in the first Test at Brisbane in November 2008) at an average of 80.37 – the highest of any batsman to have completed ten or more innings in Australia-New Zealand Tests.

MOST RUNS: TOP 10

Pos	Player	Runs
1	**A.R. Border** (Australia, 1980–93)	1,500
2	J.G. Wright (New Zealand, 1980–93)	1,277
3	M.D. Crowe (New Zealand, 1982–93)	1,255
4	J.L. Langer (Australia, 1993–2005)	1,196
5	D.C. Boon (Australia, 1985–93)	1,187
6	S.R. Waugh (Australia, 1986–2001)	1,117
7	G.S. Chappell (Australia, 1973–82)	1,076
=	R.T. Ponting (Australia, 1997–2011)	1,076
9	N.J. Astle (New Zealand, 1997–2005)	930
10	A.C. Gilchrist (Australia, 2000–05)	923

MOST WICKETS: TOP 10

Pos	Player	Wickets
1	R.J. Hadlee (New Zealand, 1973–90)	130
2	S.K. Warne (Australia, 1993–2005)	103
3	D.L. Vettori (New Zealand, 1997–2011)	65
4	G.D. McGrath (Australia, 1993–2005)	57
5	C.J. McDermott (Australia, 1985–93)	48
6	B. Lee (Australia, 2000–08)	44
7	C.L. Cairns (New Zealand, 1989–2001)	39
8	D.K. Lillee (Australia, 1977–82)	38
=	J.G. Bracewell (New Zealand, 1980–90)	38
10	D.K. Morrison (New Zealand, 1987–93)	37

Inauspicious beginnings

New Zealand got off to the worst possible start in their first-ever Test match against Australia at Wellington in March 1946. Having won the toss and elected to bat, they capitulated to a sorry 42 all out in 39 overs – the lowest total in Australia-New Zealand Test matches. The Kiwis fared little better in the second innings, limping to 54 all out – the second-lowest total in the series – to lose the match by an innings and 103 runs.

Walters digs Australia out of a considerable hole

With Australia struggling on 112 for 4 in the First Test against New Zealand at Christchurch in February 1977, they were in desperate need of a rescue act from one of their batsmen. And Doug Walters came to the party in style, hitting a magnificent 342-ball 250, the highest individual score in all Australia-New Zealand Tests, to help his side to 552 all out. It wasn't enough to win the match, however, as New Zealand eventually held on to force a draw.

Chappell cashes in against the Kiwis

Greg Chappell was the star of the show as Australia came back from 1–0 down to square the series against New Zealand in 1973–74. The middle-order batsman hit two centuries in three Tests, with a highest score of 247 not out in the First Test at Wellington, and ended the series with 449 runs – a record for Test matches between the two countries – at an average of 89.80.

Sir Richard stuns Australia

One of the outstanding bowlers in Test cricket's long history, **Richard Hadlee** finished his Test career in 1990 with 431 wickets, and between 1988 and 1994 he was the game's all-time leading wicket-taker in Tests. Hadlee, perhaps more than any other bowler for any country, often carried New Zealand's fortunes on a cricket pitch and the fast bowler was often at his brilliant best against Australia. In November 1985 at Brisbane, he decimated Australia with 9 for 52 in the first innings (the best single-innings figures in all Tests between the two countries) and ended with match figures of 15 for 123 (another record). He completed the three-match series – which New Zealand won 2–1 (their only series win on Australian soil) – with 33 wickets (another record in Australia-New Zealand clashes).

AUSTRALIA v INDIA

Although Australia enjoyed a sustained period of dominance over India – they won six and drew one of the first seven series – since 1979 series wins on the subcontinent have almost proved as elusive as the Holy Grail for the men from Down Under. They have recorded only two victories (as opposed to India's nine) in 14 Tests on Indian soil since October 2004 and lost seven out of the eight series they have played.

Most dismissals

Adam Gilchrist was a hard-hitting batsman who had the ability to take a match away from the opposition in one innings, but he was also a more than capable wicketkeeper who enjoyed considerable success against India. In 18 Tests against them between 1999 and 2008 he claimed 75 scalps, with 73 catches and two stumpings – an all-time record in Tests between the two countries.

Aussies whitewashed

India not only avenged their 4–0 series defeat in Australia in 2011–12, they also completed their first-ever 4–0 whitewash of the Aussies at home in 2013.

India challenge Australia's dominance

It was decisive proof of just how much India's fortunes had improved on Australian soil. With the series tied at 1–1 going into the Fourth and final Test at Sydney in January 2004, India won the toss, elected to bat, and batted Australia out of the game. Stunning batting from **Sachin Tendulkar** (241 not out) and V.V.S. Laxman (178), helped them to compile a massive 705 for 7 over seven sessions of the match – the highest total in all Tests between the two countries. The match ended in a draw, ensuring that India retained the Border-Gavaskar trophy.

OVERALL SERIES RECORDS

(86 Tests between 1947 and 2013)

	W	L	T	D	W/L	%W	%L	%D
Australia	38	24	1	23	1.58	44.18	27.90	26.74
India	24	38	1	23	0.63	27.90	44.18	26.74

First match: 28 November–4 December 1947, Brisbane, Australia

Brilliant Bradman puts India to the sword

Just as England, South Africa and the West Indies had discovered before them, India found out how good a player **Donald Bradman** was when Test cricket's greatest-ever batsman played his one and only series against them in 1947–48. Bradman struck four centuries in six innings, with a highest score of 201 in the Fourth Test at Adelaide, and ended the series with a haul of 715 runs (a record for an Australia-India series) at the astonishing average of 178.75.

Patel powers India to historic victory

Jasubhai Patel's sensational bowling performance in the Second Test at Kanpur in December 1959 was a major factor in India's first-ever Test victory over Australia. The off-spinner took 9 for 69, the best single-innings figures in Australia-India Test matches, in the first innings and 5 for 55 in the second as India won the match by 119 runs.

Shastri shines against Australia

An obdurate batsman who enjoyed considerable success both as an opener and in the middle order, and a player of huge importance to India for over a decade, Ravi Shastri enjoyed particular success against Australia. In nine Tests against them between 1985 and 1992 he scored 622 runs, including two centuries (with a highest score of 206 at Sydney in January 1992) at an average of 77.75 – the highest of any player in history to have completed ten or more innings in all Tests between the two countries.

Most successful captain

Bobby Simpson of Australia is the most successful captain in all Australia–India Tests. In ten Tests against the Indians between 1964 and 1978 (when he emerged from retirement, aged 41, to lead a side decimated by the departure of several players to World Series cricket), he led Australia to six wins.

Clarke leads from the front

With Australia holding a 1–0 series lead after a 122-run victory in the first Test and dismissing India for a sub-standard 191 in the first innings of the second Test at Sydney in January 2012, the Aussies were ready to put the visitors to the sword. Instead, they slipped to 37 for 3. Then Michael Clarke, the Australian captain, produced an innings of the highest quality: batting for 609 minutes, he faced 468 balls and struck 329 not out – the highest innings in Australia-India Tests. Australia declared on 659 for 4 and won by an innings and 68 runs.

Most catches

The safest pair of hands in Test history – with 210 catches he has taken more catches than any other player – Rahul Dravid also heads the Australia-India fielding list, taking 46 catches in 32 Tests against Australia between 1996 and 2012.

India bewildered in Brisbane

Unfortunate in many ways to be caught on a treacherous pitch in their first-ever Test match against Australia at Brisbane in November–December 1947, India's batsmen were horribly out of their depth. Having seen Australia compile 382 for 8 declared in the first innings, India collapsed to 58 all out in 21.3 (eight-ball) overs – the lowest-ever total in Australia-India Tests. Following on, they fared little better in the second innings, dismissed for 98 to lose the match by an innings and 226 runs.

The Turbanator torments Australia

In March 2001, having sneaked a sensational come-from-behind victory to level the series in the Second Test at Kolkata, India carried their momentum into the Third and final Test of the series at Chennai, largely thanks to **Harbhajan Singh**. "The Turbanator" took 7 for 133 in Australia's first innings and 8 for 84 in the second – his match figures of 15 for 217 are the best in all matches between the two countries – to help India to a two-wicket win and a memorable series victory. Harbhajan's 32 wickets in the series is also a record in Australia-India Tests.

MOST WICKETS: TOP 10

Pos	Player	Wickets
1	**A. Kumble** (India, 1996–2008)	111
2	Harbhajan Singh (India, 1998–2013)	95
3	Kapil Dev (India, 1979–92)	79
4	Z. Khan (India, 2001–12)	61
5	E.A.S. Prasanna (India, 1967–78)	57
6	B.S. Bedi (India, 1968–78)	56
7	N.S. Yadav (India, 1979–86)	55
8	B. Lee (Australia, 1999–2008)	53
9	R. Benaud (Australia, 1956–60)	52
10	G.D. McGrath (Australia, 1996–2004)	51

MOST RUNS: TOP 10

Pos	Player	Runs
1	S.R. Tendulkar (India, 1991–2013)	3,630
2	R.T. Ponting (Australia, 1996–2012)	2,555
3	V.V.S. Laxman (India, 1998–2012)	2,434
4	R. Dravid (India, 1996–2012)	2,143
5	M.J. Clarke (Australia, 2004–13)	1,914
6	M.L. Hayden (Australia, 2001–08)	1,888
7	V. Sehwag (India, 2003–13)	1,738
8	A.R. Border (Australia, 1979–92)	1,567
9	S.M. Gavaskar (India, 1977–86)	1,550
10	G.R. Viswanath (India, 1969–81)	1,538

Partners in crime

The most productive partnership in all Tests between Australia and India has been that of Sachin Tendulkar and Rahul Dravid, The pair has batted together on 28 occasions and have produced 1,564 runs (with an average partnership of 60.15 runs and a highest of 169, in the third Test at Chennai in March 2001). The highest partnership in Tests between the two countries is 386, between Michael Clarke (210) and Ricky Ponting (221) in the fourth Test at Adelaide in January 2012; a match Australia went on to win by 298 runs.

INDIA v WEST INDIES

In the early days of this fixture, India's misfortunes were blamed on a lack of experience of playing on hard, bouncy surfaces against a battery of fast bowlers, but in recent times the balance of power has started to shift in India's favour. Of their total of 16 victories against the islanders (in contrast the West Indies have won 30 times), 11 of those have come in the 20 Tests played since 2002.

Most catches

No player in the history of India-West Indies Test matches has taken more catches than Viv Richards. The legendary Antiguan claimed 39 victims in 28 Tests against India between 1974 and 1989.

OVERALL SERIES RECORDS

(90 Tests between 1948 and 2014)

	W	L	T	D	W/L	%W	%L	%D
India	16	30	0	44	0.53	17.78	33.33	48.89
West Indies	30	16	0	44	1.87	33.33	17.78	48.89

First match: 10–14 November 1948, Delhi, India

Most productive partnership

The most productive partnership in all Tests between India and the West Indies is that of Gordon Greenidge and Desmond Haynes. The formidable opening pair combined to score 1,325 runs in 30 innings between 1983 and 1989 at an average of 45.68.

Magical debut for Hirwani

It was the most remarkable bowling performance by a debutant in Test history. In the Fourth Test against the West Indies at Chennai in January 1988, India's leg-spinner Narendra Hirwani took 8 for 61 in the first innings and 8 for 75 in the second to bowl his side to a 255-run victory. His match figures of 16 for 136 – the best by a Test debutant in history – are the best in all matches between the two countries.

Dujon heads the dismissals list

The most successful West Indian wicketkeeper in Test history (with 270 dismissals to his name), Jeff Dujon also heads the list in matches between the West Indies and India. In 19 Tests against the Indians between 1983 and 1989, he claimed 60 scalps (with 58 catches and two stumpings).

Magnificent Marshall leads the way

Malcolm Marshall played a significant role in the West Indies' 3–0 series victory in India in 1983–84. The Barbados paceman took two five-wicket hauls, the best being 6 for 37 in the Fifth Test at Kolkata, to end the series with 33 wickets – an all-time series record between the two countries.

India lose the initiative in record-breaking style

India made the worst possible start to the 1987–88 home series against the West Indies in November 1987. Having won the toss and elected to bat, they would have been planning to compile a first-innings total in the region of 400 and put the islanders under pressure; instead they folded to 75 all out – the lowest total in all matches between the two sides – and went on to lose the match by five wickets.

A maiden century to remember

A regular in a strong West Indies batting line-up for 16 years, Rohan Kanhai had to wait until his 13th Test, 19 months after making his debut, to record his first three-figure score in international cricket, but rarely has a wait been so worthwhile. In the Third Test of the 1958–59 series at Kolkata, the diminutive right-hander plundered a magnificent 256 – the highest individual score in all matches between the two countries – and the West Indies went on to win the match by an innings and 336 runs.

644 is the limit

Both sides have recorded totals of 644 in Tests between the two countries: India achieved the total (for the loss of seven wickets) in the Sixth and final Test of the 1978–79 series at Kanpur – a match which they drew to secure a 1–0 series victory; the West Indies achieved the same total (for the loss of eight wickets) in the Fifth and final Test of the 1958–59 series in Delhi – that match also ended in a draw, which was enough to see the islanders claim the series 3–0.

A record-breaker in a losing cause

The West Indies eventually emerged victorious in the Third Test against India at Ahmedabad in November 1983 (winning the match by 138 runs), but only after being on the receiving end of a record-breaking effort by Kapil Dev. The greatest fast bowler India has ever produced took 9 for 83 in the West Indies' second innings – the best single-innings figures in all Tests between the two countries – to haul his side back into the match, only to see India's batsmen (chasing 242 for victory) slip to a sorry 103 all out in 47.1 overs.

Most successful captain

Clive Lloyd is the most successful captain in the history of Test matches between India and the West Indies. The legendary leader recorded ten wins in 20 Tests against India between 1974 and 1983.

Gavaskar and Vengsarkar make hay in the Kolkata sun

Taking advantage of a lifeless pitch, **Sunil Gavaskar** (with his 182 not out, following on from 107 in the first innings, he became the first batsman in history to score two hundreds in a Test on three occasions) and Dilip Vengsarkar (157 not out) prospered in record-breaking style in the second innings of the Third Test against the West Indies at Kolkata in 1978–79. The pair added 344 for the second wicket – an all-time record in matches between the two countries – to set the West Indies 335 runs for victory. The men from the Caribbean hung on in nervous style, however, finishing on 197 for 9 to secure a draw.

Wonderful Weekes prospers against India

Rarely has a batsman enjoyed such a continued streak of fine form in Test cricket's long history. In the West Indies' 1–0 series win in India, in 1948–49, **Everton Weekes** produced successive scores of 152, 194, 162, 101, 90, 56 and 48 to end the series with 779 runs to his name – an all-time record for a series between India and the West Indies – at an average of 111.28. Weekes's career average against the Indians (106.78 in ten Tests between 1948 and 1953) is also a record.

MOST RUNS: TOP 10

Pos	Player	Runs
1	**S.M. Gavaskar** (India, 1971–83)	2,749
2	C.H. Lloyd (West Indies, 1966–83)	2,344
3	S. Chanderpaul (W. Indies, 1994–2013)	2,171
4	R. Dravid (India, 1997–2011)	1,978
5	I.V.A. Richards (West Indies, 1974–89)	1,927
6	G.S. Sobers (West Indies, 1958–71)	1,920
7	V.V.S. Laxman (India, 1997–2011)	1,715
8	R.B. Kanhai (West Indies, 1958–71)	1,693
9	C.G. Greenidge (West Indies, 1974–89)	1,678
10	S.R. Tendulkar (India, 1994–2013)	1,630

MOST WICKETS: TOP 10

Pos	Player	Wickets
1	Kapil Dev (India, 1978–89)	89
2	M.D. Marshall (West Indies, 1978–89)	76
3	A. Kumble (India, 1994–2006)	74
4	S. Venkataraghavan (India, 1966–83)	68
5	A.M.E. Roberts (West Indies, 1974–83)	67
6	W.W. Hall (West Indies, 1958–67)	65
=	B.S. Chandrasekhar (India, 1966–79)	65
=	C.A. Walsh (West Indies, 1987–97)	65
9	L.R. Gibbs (West Indies, 1958–75)	63
10	B.S. Bedi (India, 1966–79)	62

NZ v WEST INDIES

Few contests in Test cricket demonstrate more clearly how much fortunes can change than those between New Zealand and the West Indies. Having previously won just two of 23 Tests against the islanders over a period of 35 years, New Zealand have now won seven of the 11 Test matches they have played against the West Indies since April 1996.

OVERALL SERIES RECORDS

(42 Tests between 1952 and 2013)

	W	L	T	D	W/L	%W	%L	%D
New Zealand	11	12	0	19	0.91	26.19	28.57	45.24
West Indies	12	11	0	19	1.09	28.57	26.19	45.24

First match: 8–12 February 1952, Christchurch, New Zealand

Down and out in Dunedin

New Zealand's early struggles against the West Indies were epitomized in the First Test at Dunedin in February 1956. Having won the toss and elected to bat, the home side's batsmen could find no answer to the spin bowling of Sonny Ramadhin (who took 6 for 23) and were dismissed for a paltry 74 all out – the lowest total in all Test matches between the two countries.

The Turner and Jarvis Show

Having seen the West Indies reach 365 for 7 declared in their first innings in the Fourth Test against New Zealand at Georgetown, Guyana, in April 1972, Glenn Turner (259) and Terry Jarvis (182) ensured New Zealand's reply got off to the perfect start. The opening pair added 387 runs for the first wicket – an all-time record in New Zealand-West Indies matches – to help their side to 543 for 3 declared. The game, however, petered out into a bore draw.

Most successful captain

The most successful captain in the history of Test matches between New Zealand and the West Indies is **Stephen Fleming**. The former New Zealand captain led his side to five wins in seven Tests between 1999 and 2006.

West Indies batsmen find their form when it matters

There is no better way of putting an opponent under pressure than compiling a huge first-innings total, and certainly no better time to do so than in a series-deciding Test match. That is exactly what the West Indies did in the Second Test against New Zealand at Wellington in February 1995, as centuries from Jimmy Adams (151), Brian Lara (147) and Junior Murray (101 not out) propelled them to 660 for 5 declared – the highest score in all Tests between the two countries – en route to an innings-and-322-run victory and a 1–0 series success.

Cairns turns match on its head

With the West Indies cruising on 276 for 0 towards the end of the first day's play in the First Test against New Zealand at Hamilton in December 1999, the chances of a home victory seemed remote. However, they ended up winning the match by nine wickets, and it had much to do with the second-innings bowling display of **Chris Cairns**. The all-rounder bagged 7 for 27 off 22.5 overs – the best figures in New Zealand-West Indies Tests and the best figures by any New Zealand bowler other than Richard Hadlee in history – to help dismiss the West Indies for 97 and pave the way for an unlikely victory.

Turner's Caribbean triumph

Glenn Turner was outstanding for New Zealand in the country's first-ever tour to the Caribbean in 1971–72. In a drawn five-match series – a result considered a huge triumph for New Zealand at the time – the straight-batted, dogged opener hit two memorable double-centuries, with a best of 259 in the Fourth Test at Georgetown, Guyana (the highest individual score in all matches between the two countries), and ended the series with 672 runs (at an average of 96.00). It is the highest series haul in the history of New Zealand-West Indies Test matches.

Courtney ensures New Zealand crumble

With his batsmen having put his side in a commanding position in the Second Test against New Zealand at Wellington in February 1995, amassing a mighty first-innings total of 660 for 5 declared, it was time for West Indies captain Courtney Walsh to turn the screw. He took 7 for 37 in New Zealand's first innings and 6 for 18 in their second to lead his side to a series-clinching innings-and-332-run victory. His match figures of 13 for 55 are the best in all Tests between the two countries.

A record shared

The record for the most wickets in a series between the two countries is 27, a feat achieved by two bowlers: New Zealand's Bruce Taylor in the 1971–72 series in the Caribbean; and Malcolm Marshall of the West Indies in the 1984–85 series in New Zealand.

Most dismissals

West Indies wicketkeeper Danesh Ramdin leads the dismissals list in all Tests between the two countries. The Trinidad gloveman has claimed 29 scalps (all catches) in ten Tests against New Zealand between 2006 and 2013.

MOST RUNS: TOP 10

Pos	Player	Runs
1	C.H. Gayle (West Indies, 2002–12)	1,050
2	S. Chanderpaul (W. Indies, 1995–2013)	1,037
3	C.G. Greenidge (West Indies, 1980–87)	882
4	G.M. Turner (New Zealand, 1969–72)	855
5	D.L. Haynes (West Indies, 1980–87)	843
6	B.E. Congdon (New Zealand, 1969–72)	764
7	N.J. Astle (New Zealand, 1996–2006)	715
8	B.C. Lara (West Indies, 1995–2006)	704
9	**S.P. Fleming** (New Zealand, 1995–2006)	703
10	L.P.R.L. Taylor (New Zealand, 2008–13)	686

MOST WICKETS: TOP 10

Pos	Player	Wickets
1	R.J. Hadlee (New Zealand, 1980–87)	51
2	C.A. Walsh (West Indies, 1985–99)	43
3	J. Garner (West Indies, 1980–87)	36
=	M.D. Marshall (West Indies, 1985–87)	36
5	D.L. Vettori (New Zealand, 1999–2012)	34
6	B.R. Taylor (New Zealand, 1969–72)	32
=	S. Ramadhin (West Indies, 1952–56)	32
8	T.A. Boult (New Zealand, 2012–13)	24
9	A.L. Valentine (West Indies, 1952–56)	23
=	E.J. Chatfield (New Zealand, 1985–87)	23

Gayle saves his best for New Zealand

A hard-hitting left-hand opening batsman with a reputation for treating all types of bowling with contempt, **Chris Gayle** has, unlike the rest of his teammates in recent times, prospered against New Zealand. In nine Tests against the Kiwis he has hit 1,050 runs, including ttgree centuries (with a highest score of 204 at St George's, Grenada, in June 2002) at an average of 75.00 – the highest of any batsman to have completed at least ten innings in all matches between the two teams.

INDIA v PAKISTAN

Given the historic and uneasy relationship between the two countries – they were born out of the bitterness of India's partition in 1947 – this is the most tension-fuelled and politically driven fixture in international cricket. Since the contest was first played back in 1952, Pakistan lead the way with 12 wins to India's nine, although the two sides have not met since 2007.

Wasim Bari heads the keepers list

A veteran of 81 Test matches for Pakistan, Wasim Bari has claimed more dismissals than any other wicketkeeper in Tests between India and Pakistan. In 18 matches against India between 1978 and 1983, the greatest keeper his country has ever produced bagged 55 victims (with 50 catches and five stumpings).

OVERALL SERIES RECORDS

(59 Tests between 1952 and 2007)

	W	L	T	D	W/L	%W	%L	%D
India	9	12	0	38	0.75	15.25	20.34	64.41
Pakistan	12	9	0	38	1.33	20.34	15.25	64.41

First match: 16–18 October 1952, Delhi, India

Priority lies in building a big score

The fear of defeat lies at the very heart of this fixture: as a result, 38 of the 59 Tests contested between the two countries have been drawn, and the overriding mentality appears to be to bat yourself into a position of absolute safety before even thinking about trying to win the game. As a result, there have been nine scores of 600 plus in matches between the two countries, the highest of which was 699 for 5 declared, achieved by Pakistan in the Third Test at Lahore in December 1989 – a match that, not surprisingly, ended in a draw.

India all at sea as they take their bow in Pakistan

India's batsmen played like fish out of water on the jute-matting pitch used for the first-ever Test match between the two countries to be played in Pakistan. Having won the toss and elected to bat, India slipped to 106 all out in 55.1 overs in three hours 20 minutes – still the lowest-ever team total in matches between India and Pakistan – and went on to lose by an innings and 43 runs.

Kumble puts Pakistan in a spin

It will go down in history as one of the best single-innings bowling performances in Test history, bettered, indeed, only by Jim Laker's remarkable effort against Australia at Old Trafford in 1956. Having taken 4 for 75 in Pakistan's first innings in the Second Test at Delhi in February 1999, **Anil Kumble** became only the second bowler in Test history to take ten wickets in an innings (10 for 74) to bowl India to a 212-run victory. Kumble's match figures of 14 for 149 are the best in all Tests between the two countries.

Super Sehwag at his brilliant best

A stunning innings by **Virender Sehwag** was at the heart of India's innings-and-52-run victory over Pakistan in the First Test at Multan in March–April 2004. The free-scoring opener smashed a sensational 309 runs off 375 balls (with 39 fours and six sixes) – the highest individual score in all matches between the two countries – to help his side to a mighty first-innings total of 675 for 5 declared. And this was far from an isolated case of success against Pakistan: Sehwag's career average against them of 91.14 – in nine Tests between 2004 and 2006 (which includes three double-centuries) – is the highest of any player to have completed ten or more innings in India-Pakistan matches.

MOST RUNS: TOP 10

Pos	Player	Runs
1	Javed Miandad (Pakistan, 1978–89)	2,228
2	S.M. Gavaskar (India, 1978–87)	2,089
3	Zaheer Abbas (Pakistan, 1978–84)	1,740
4	**Mudassar Nazar** (Pakistan, 1978–84)	1,431
5	Younis Khan (Pakistan, 2005–07)	1,321
6	D.B. Vengsarkar (India, 1978–87)	1,284
7	V. Sehwag (India, 2004–06)	1,276
8	Mohammad Yousuf (Pakistan, 1999–2007)	1,247
9	R. Dravid (India, 1999–2007)	1,236
10	**Imran Khan** (Pakistan, 1978–89)	1,091

MOST WICKETS: TOP 10

Pos	Player	Wickets
1	Kapil Dev (India, 1978–89)	99
2	Imran Khan (Pakistan, 1978–89)	94
3	A Kumble (India, 1999–2007)	81
4	Wasim Akram (Pakistan, 1987–99)	45
5	Fazal Mahmood (Pakistan, 1952–61)	44
6	Danish Kaneria (Pakistan, 2004–07)	43
7	Mahmood Hussain (Pakistan, 1952–61)	39
8	M.H. Mankad (India, 1952–55)	37
9	Sarfraz Nawaz (Pakistan, 1978–83)	36
10	S.P. Gupte (India, 1952–61)	34
=	Iqbal Qasim (Pakistan, 1978–87)	34

Magical Mudassar piles on the runs

Mudassar Nazar laid the foundations for Pakistan's 3–0 series victory over India in 1982–83. The opener was in sensational form with the bat, hitting four centuries – with a highest score of 231 in the Fourth Test at Hyderabad – and ending the series with 761 runs to his name (at an average of 126.83), an all-time record haul in Test matches between the two countries.

Imran's record-breaking haul sparks Pakistan

Where Mudassar Nazar excelled with the bat in Pakistan's stunning 3–0 series victory over arch-rivals India in 1982–83, Imran Khan was the star of the show with the ball. The Pakistan captain took four five-wicket hauls (with a best of 8 for 60 in the Second Test at Karachi) and two ten-wicket match hauls to end the victorious series with 40 wickets – an all-time record series haul in all matches between India and Pakistan.

Imran is the most successful leader

In a fixture not renowned for producing a result – only 35.59 per cent of matches between India and Pakistan have produced a victory for either side – Pakistan's **Imran Khan** is the most successful captain in contests between the two countries, recording four wins in 15 Tests between 1982 and 1989.

Most productive partnership

The most productive partnership in all Tests between India and Pakistan is that of Younis Khan and Mohammad Yousuf. The pair have combined to score 1,372 runs in nine innings between 2005 and 2007 at an average of 171.50.

Leading Pakistan to safety in record-breaking style

With Pakistan losing two wickets in successive deliveries to fall to 60 for 2 and into potential danger against India in the Fourth Test at Hyderabad in January 1983, Mudassar Nazar (231, and in the form of his life) and Javed Miandad (280 not out) steadied the ship in spectacular style. The pair added 451 for the third wicket – the highest partnership in all matches between the two countries – paving the way to Pakistan's 581 for 3 declared and an eventual innings-and-119-run victory.

A safe pair of hands

The record for the most catches in matches between India and Pakistan is 19, a feat achieved by two players: Sunil Gavaskar (India) in 24 Tests between 1978 and 1987; and Rahul Dravid (India) in 15 Tests between 1999 and 2007.

ENGLAND v PAKISTAN

Test matches between England and Pakistan have never been short of drama – who could forget Mike Gatting's finger-pointing rant at umpire Shakoor Rana at Faisalabad in December 1987 or Pakistan's refusal to play after the tea interval following ball-tampering allegations at The Oval in August 2006? But they are also closely contested affairs, with England recording 22 wins to Pakistan's 16.

Strauss is most successful captain

England's Andrew Strauss is the most successful captain in the history of matches between England and Pakistan. He has recorded six wins in eight Tests against Pakistan between 2006 and 2010.

OVERALL SERIES RECORDS

(74 Tests between 1954 and 2012)

	W	L	T	D	W/L	%W	%L	%D
England	22	16	0	36	1.37	29.72	21.62	48.64
Pakistan	16	22	0	36	0.72	21.62	29.72	48.64

First match: 10–15 June 1954, Lord's

Most dismissals

Wasim Bari, Pakistan's most successful wicket-keeper of all time, is the most prolific keeper in all Tests between England and Pakistan. In 24 matches against England between 1967 and 1982 he claimed 54 dismissals, with 50 catches and four stumpings.

Record-breaking effort in a losing cause for Pakistan

For the time being, at least, it was a partnership that kept Pakistan in the Second Test at Headingley in August 2006. Pakistan were trailing 1–0 in the series, and having seen England compile a healthy first-innings total of 515 all out, and then both openers fall in quick succession, the visitors needed senior players Mohammad Yousuf and Younis Khan to stand up and deliver. They did so in magnificent style, putting on 363 for the third wicket (Yousuf with 192 and Khan with 173) – the highest partnership in all matches between the two countries – to help Pakistan to 538 all out. But their effort was all in vain: Pakistan's second-innings collapse (155 all out) saw England win the game by 167 runs.

Most productive partnership

The most productive partnership in all Tests between England and Pakistan is that of Mohammad Yousuf and Inzamam-ul-Haq. The pair combined to score 901 runs in nine innings between 2000 and 2006 at an impressive average of 112.62.

Compton cashes in against uncertain Pakistan

Denis Compton made the most of Pakistan's problems in adjusting to both the cold weather and a damp wicket in the Second Test at Trent Bridge in July 1954. The Middlesex star crashed his highest Test score of 278 (with 34 fours and one six) – also the highest score in matches between the two countries – to help England to a massive first-innings total of 558 for 6 declared and an eventual innings-and-129-run victory.

Dexter saves his best for Pakistan

Ted Dexter enjoyed plenty of good times with the bat against Pakistan. In ten innings he recorded his highest Test score, 205 in the Third Test at Faisalabad in February 1962, and compiled 749 runs at an average of 93.62 – the highest of any batsman to have completed ten or more innings in Tests between the two countries.

Pakistan flattened at Edgbaston

One-nil down in the four-match series going into the Second Test against England at Edgbaston in August 2010, Pakistan won the toss, elected to bat and, in the face of fine seam bowling from James Anderson (4 for 20) and Stuart Broad (4 for 38), collapsed in spectacular fashion to 72 all out – the lowest score in all Tests between the two countries. But England, set only 145 in the second innings to win the second Test of a three-match series in the UAE, equalled Pakistan's sorry feat, and lost by 72 runs.

Batsmen power Pakistan to historic series win

It was some way to secure a first-ever series victory on English soil. Holding a 1–0 lead going into the fifth and final Test at The Oval in August 1987, Pakistan won a crucial toss, elected to bat, and soon extinguished any hopes England might have had of winning the match when they compiled a massive 708 all out, with centuries from Javed Miandad (260), Saleem Malik (102) and Imran Khan (118 not out). It is the highest total in all matches between the two countries.

Underwood thrives at a rain-sodden Lord's

There has been no more destructive bowler on a rain-affected wicket in Test history than "Deadly" Derek Underwood, and the Kent left-arm spinner took full advantage of the damp conditions in the Second Test against Pakistan at Lord's in August 1974. He took 5 for 20 in the first innings and 8 for 51 in the second to end with match figures of 13 for 71 – the best in all Tests between England and Pakistan. The weather had the final say in the match, however, and it ended in a draw.

Qadir's box of tricks too much for England

England's 1987 tour to Pakistan is best remembered, sadly, for the on-the-field tensions and arguments between the English players and the match officials – all of which completely overshadowed **Abdul Qadir**'s stunning performances with the ball throughout the series. In the First Test at Lahore, the leg-spinner got Pakistan off to the perfect start, taking 9 for 56 to help dismiss England for 175 – the best single-innings figures in all matches between the two countries and a vital factor in Pakistan's eventual innings-and-87-run victory. Two further five-wicket hauls followed and Qadir ended the three-match series, which Pakistan won 1–0, with 30 wickets to his name – an all-time record in England-Pakistan matches.

Yousuf's lone resistance

Although England, the hosts, won the four-match series 3–0, many of the headlines during the 2006 series against Pakistan were reserved for the sensational batting performances of Mohammad Yousuf. The Pakistan middle-order batsman hit three centuries, with a highest score of 202 in the First Test at Lord's, and ended the series with 631 runs at an average of 90.14 – no batsman in the history of England-Pakistan Tests has scored more runs in a series.

Most catches

Javed Miandad holds the record for the most catches taken by a fielder in England-Pakistan Tests. The former Pakistan captain took 20 catches in 22 Tests against England between 1977 and 1992.

MOST RUNS: TOP 10

Pos	Player	Runs
1	Inzamam-ul-Haq (Pakistan, 1992–2006)	1,584
2	Mushtaq Mohammad (Pakistan, 1961–74)	1,554
3	Mohammad Yousuf (Pakistan, 2000–10)	1,499
4	Saleem Malik (Pakistan, 1984–96)	1,396
5	Javed Miandad (Pakistan, 1977–92)	1,329
6	D.I. Gower (England, 1978–92)	1,185
7	Zaheer Abbas (Pakistan, 1971–84)	1,086
8	Hanif Mohammad (Pakistan, 1954–69)	1,039
9	A.J. Stewart (England, 1992–2001)	994
10	T.W. Graveney (England, 1954–69)	943

MOST WICKETS: TOP 10

Pos	Player	Wickets
1	Abdul Qadir (Pakistan, 1977–87)	82
2	Wasim Akram (Pakistan, 1987–2001)	57
3	Waqar Younis (Pakistan, 1992–2001)	50
4	Intikhab Alam (Pakistan, 1961–74)	49
5	Imran Khan (Pakistan, 1971–87)	47
6	I.T. Botham (England, 1978–92)	40
7	Sarfraz Nawaz (Pakistan, 1969–84)	37
8	D.L. Underwood (England, 1967–74)	36
=	Saeed Ajmal (Pakistan, 2010–12)	36
10	G.P. Swann (England, 2010–12)	35

INDIA v NEW ZEALAND

New Zealand did not get off to the best of starts in Tests against India – it took them ten Test matches to record their first-ever victory (at Christchurch in February 1968). Overall, India have 18 Tests to New Zealand's ten, though almost half of the 54 matches between them have ended in draws.

Dravid finds the Kiwis to his liking

No player has scored more runs in India-New Zealand Test matches than Rahul Dravid. The Indian legend, who stands fourth on Test cricket's all-time run-scoring list (with 13,288 runs), scored 1,659 runs in 15 matches against the Kiwis, with six centuries and a highest score of 222 at Ahmedabad in October 2003. He also posted two centuries in a single match against New Zealand (190 and 103 not out at Hamilton in January 1999).

OVERALL SERIES RECORDS

(54 Tests between 1955 and 2014)

	W	L	T	D	W/L	%W	%L	%D
India	18	10	0	26	1.80	33.33	18.52	45.15
New Zealand	10	18	0	26	0.55	18.52	33.33	45.15

First match: 19–24 November 1955, Hyderabad, India

Most successful captain

The prime beneficiary of India's early dominance over New Zealand, the Nawab of Pataudi (India) is the most successful captain in all Tests between India and New Zealand. He led his side to five victories in 11 Tests against the Kiwis between 1965 and 1969.

Dhoni the leading gloveman

Mahendra Singh Dhoni has had plenty to smile about in Tests against New Zealand over the years. The India captain has led his side to four victories in nine Tests against the Kiwis and also holds the record for the most dismissals in Tests between the two countries: 33 (28 catches and five stumpings) in nine matches between 2009 and 2014.

Mankad and Roy lead India to comprehensive victory

India's Vinoo Mankad (231) and Pankaj Roy (173) dashed any hopes New Zealand might have had of squaring the 1955–56 series (India held a 1–0 lead) in the Fourth and final Test at Chennai. After India had won the toss and elected to bat, the pair put on an opening stand of 413 to help their side to a daunting first-innings total of 537 for 3 declared and an eventual innings-and-109-run victory. It remains the highest partnership in all Tests between the two countries.

Venkat spins India to series success

It took a record-breaking performance from **Srinivas Venkataraghavan** for India to edge to a seven-wicket victory in the Fourth and final Test against New Zealand in 1964–65 at Delhi. The off-spinner took 8 for 72 in the first innings (the best single-innings figures in all Tests between the two countries). The record for the best figures in a match belong to Ravichandran Ashwin – 12 for 85 – when India beat New Zealand by an innings and 115 runs at Hyderabad in August 20012.

Most productive partnership

The most productive partnership in all India-New Zealand Tests is that of India's **Sachin Tendulkar** (right) and **Rahul Dravid** (left). The pair have combined to score 860 runs in 16 innings against New Zealand between 1999 and 2010 at an average of 53.75.

MOST RUNS: TOP 10

Pos	Player	Runs
1	R. Dravid (India, 1998–2010)	1,659
2	S.R. Tendulkar (India, 1990–2012)	1,595
3	B.B. McCullum (New Zealand, 2009–14)	1,224
4	G.T. Dowling (New Zealand, 1965–69)	964
5	B. Sutcliffe (New Zealand, 1955–65)	885
6	V. Sehwag (India, 2002–12)	883
7	V.V.S. Laxman (India, 2002–10)	818
8	J.G. Wright (New Zealand, 1981–90)	804
9	M. Azharuddin (India, 1988–99)	796
10	M.G. Burgess (New Zealand, 1968–76)	725

MOST WICKETS: TOP 10

Pos	Player	Wickets
1	R.J. Hadlee (New Zealand, 1976–90)	65
2	B.S. Bedi (India, 1968–76)	57
3	E.A.S. Prasanna (India, 1968–76)	55
4	A. Kumble (India, 1994–2003)	50
5	Z. Khan (India, 2002–14)	47
6	S. Venkataraghavan (India, 1965–76)	44
7	Harbhajan Singh (India, 1998–2010)	43
8	D.L. Vettori (New Zealand, 1998–2010)	40
9	B.S. Chandrasekhar (India, 1965–76)	36
10	S.P. Gupte (India, 1955–56)	34

McCullum inspires record-breaking fightback

It may not have seemed possible in the early stages of the match, but New Zealand's stunning counter-attack against India in the Second Test at Wellington, earned the Kiwis a place in the record books. After capitulating to 192 all out in their first innings, seeing India post 438 all out and slipping to 94 for 5 in their second innings, New Zealand were in deep trouble. But a magnificent 302 from Brendon McCullum (the first triple-century by a New Zealand player in Tests) plus hundreds from BJ Watling (124) and Jimmy Neesham (137) led the Kiwis to a mighty 680 for 8 (the highest-ever team total in India-New Zealand Tests) and, eventually, to safety.

Fleming is the catching king

Stephen Fleming, by some distance, is the most prolific fielder in New Zealand's history – he claimed 171 catches in 111 Tests; in second place on the all-time list is Martin Crowe with 71. Fleming also holds the record for the most catches in India-New Zealand Tests: he bagged 20 catches in 13 matches against India between 1994 and 2003.

Hadlee reduces India to all-time low

Richard Hadlee had performed poorly in the Second Test against India at Christchurch in 1975–76, and with New Zealand 1–0 down in the three-match series, many considered the young paceman lucky to be in the side for the Third Test at Wellington. Hadlee's performance in the second innings, however, in only his ninth Test, proved far too much for India and gave notice of the talent that would see him become one of the game's all-time greats. He took 7 for 23 in 8.3 menacing overs as India slipped to 81 all out – the lowest team total in all Tests between the two countries – and New Zealand went on to win the game by an innings and 33 runs to square the series.

Sutcliffe shines

The outstanding New Zealand batsman of the post-war period, **Bert Sutcliffe** stood tall while others around him wilted during the 1955–56 series in India. Although the Kiwis lost the series 2–0, the opener scored two centuries, with a highest score of 203 in the Third Test at Delhi, to end the series with 611 runs – a record in any India-New Zealand series. He seemed to prosper against the Indians: in 16 innings against them, he scored 885 runs at an average of 68.07 – the highest by any batsman to have completed ten innings or more in all Tests between the two countries.

PAKISTAN v AUSTRALIA

Australia got off to a bad start against Pakistan, losing the first-ever match played between the two countries by nine wickets at Karachi in October 1956, but their overall record against them in subsequent years has been impressive: of the 57 Test matches played, Australia have recorded 28 wins to Pakistan's 12.

Most catches

Mark Waugh is the most successful fielder in all Tests between Australia and Pakistan: he took 23 catches in 15 matches against Pakistan between 1994 and 2002.

OVERALL SERIES RECORDS

(57 Tests between 1956 and 2010)

	W	L	T	D	W/L	%W	%L	%D
Pakistan	12	28	0	17	0.42	21.05	49.12	29.83
Australia	28	12	0	17	2.45	49.12	21.05	29.83

First match: 11–17 October 1956, Karachi, Pakistan

Pakistan's batsmen fulfil their side of the bargain

Trailing 1–0 in the five-match series, and having seen Australia compile a competitive first-innings score of 465 all out at Adelaide in December 1983, Pakistan knew their only hope of winning the game was to compile a monumental first-innings score and then to bowl out Australia cheaply in their second innings. They fulfilled the first requirement, as centuries from Mohsin Khan (149), Qasim Umar (113) and Javed Miandad (131) propelled them to a mighty 624 all out (the highest team total in all matches between the two countries) and a lead of 159. Their bowlers failed to deliver, however, and the match ended in a draw.

Unplayable Mahmood prospers in Karachi as Australia crumble

Australia could find no answer to the medium-pace bowling of Fazal Mahmood in the first-ever Test match between the two countries, played on a matting wicket at Karachi in October 1956. Pakistan's first great bowler took 6 for 34 in the first innings and 7 for 80 in the second to propel his side to a memorable nine-wicket victory. His match figures of 13 for 114 remain an all-time record in Tests between the two countries.

Pakistan's shocker in Sharjah

Forced to play their three-match series against Australia in October 2002 at neutral venues as a result of safety concerns in their home country, Pakistan played like fish out of water in the Second Test at Sharjah. After winning the toss and electing to bat, they crashed to a dismal 59 all out in their first innings (in 31.5 overs), the lowest score ever made in matches between the two countries. The record did not last for long, however: in the second innings Pakistan fared even worse, subsiding to a sorry 53 all out (in a mere 24.5 overs) to lose the match by an innings and 198 runs.

Super Shane's magic too much for Pakistan

Shane Warne was Pakistan's chief destroyer as Australia romped to a 3–0 series victory in 2002–03. With all the Tests played at neutral venues for safety reasons, the legendary leg-spinner took two five-wicket hauls in three Tests – with a best return of 7 for 94 in the First Test at Colombo, Sri Lanka – to end the series with 27 wickets, an all-time record in Australia-Pakistan matches.

Sensational Sarfraz stuns Australia

With Australia, seven wickets in hand, needing only 77 runs for victory on the fifth day of the First Test at Melbourne in March 1979, Sarfraz Nawaz produced one of the greatest bowling performances in Test history. The experienced fast bowler took seven wickets for one run in 33 deliveries to help Pakistan to a stunning 71-run victory and ended with figures of 9 for 86 – the best by any bowler in Australia-Pakistan Test matches.

Taylor leads the way

Mark Taylor holds the highest average of all batsmen to have completed ten or more innings in Pakistan-Australia Test matches. The former captain averaged 79.23 (with 1,347 runs) against Pakistan in 20 innings between 1990 and 1998.

Most dismissals

Rod Marsh leads the all-time dismissals list in Australia-Pakistan Test matches. The legendary gloveman pouched 68 victims (66 catches and two stumpings) in 20 Tests against Pakistan between 1972 and 1984.

Captain Taylor hits an all-time high in Peshawar

With Australia 1–0 up in the three-match series going into the Second Test at Peshawar in October 1998, Australian captain **Mark Taylor** led from the front in record-breaking style. By the end of the second day, after occupying the crease for 12 hours and facing 564 balls, Taylor stood unbeaten on 334 not out – to equal Donald Bradman's all-time highest Test score for an Australian batsman and to leave himself within sight of Brian Lara's world record 375. To the surprise of everyone, however, he made one of Test cricket's most magnanimous gestures: placing his team's need to win the game above any personal glory, he declared. The match ended in a draw, but Taylor's effort is still the highest score by any batsman in Tests between the two countries.

Magical Malik steers Pakistan to victory

Captain Saleem Malik was the star performer as Pakistan edged to a 1–0 home series victory over Australia in 1994–95. Following a modest performance in the victorious First Test at Lahore (he scored 26 and 43 in the course of Pakistan's one-wicket victory), he proceeded to prosper, saving Pakistan in both the drawn Second Test at Rawalpindi (hitting 237 in the second innings as his side was forced to follow on 261 runs in arrears) and again in the Third and final Test at Karachi (where knocks of 75 and 143 did much to secure a draw and, with it, a series victory). His series haul of 557 runs (at the impressive average of 92.83) is an all-time record in Tests between the two countries.

Perfect partners

With Australia already holding an unassailable 2–0 lead in the three-match series going into the Third and final Test against Pakistan at Hobart in January 2010, Michael Clarke joined Ricky Ponting at the crease with their side placed on a precarious 71 for 3 and proceeded to put Pakistan's bowlers to the sword. By the time Clarke (166) departed 102.4 overs later, the pair had added 352 runs for the fourth wicket – an all-time record partnership in Australia-Pakistan Test matches. Australia ended up on 519 for 8 (with Ponting reaching 209) and went on to win the match by 231 runs to secure a 3–0 series whitewash.

On-song Ponting

Ricky Ponting is the most successful captain in the history of Test matches between Australia and Pakistan, leading his side to seven victories in eight Tests against them.

MOST RUNS: TOP 10

Pos	Player	Runs
1	Javed Miandad (Pakistan, 1976–90)	1,797
2	A.R. Border (Australia, 1979–90)	1,666
3	G.S. Chappell (Australia, 1972–84)	1,581
4	R.T. Ponting (Australia, 1998–2010)	1,537
5	Zaheer Abbas (Pakistan, 1972–84)	1,411
6	M.A. Taylor (Australia, 1990–98)	1,347
7	J.L. Langer (Australia, 1994–2005)	1,139
8	Saleem Malik (Pakistan, 1983–98)	1,106
9	Ijaz Ahmed (Pakistan, 1988–99)	1,085
10	K.J. Hughes (Australia, 1979–84)	1,016

MOST WICKETS: TOP 10

Pos	Player	Wickets
1	S.K. Warne (Australia, 1994–2005)	90
2	G.D. McGrath (Australia, 1994–2005)	80
3	D.K. Lillee (Australia, 1972–84)	71
4	Imran Khan (Pakistan, 1976–90)	64
5	Iqbal Qasim (Pakistan, 1976–88)	57
6	Sarfraz Nawaz (Pakistan, 1972–84)	52
7	Wasim Akram (Pakistan, 1990–99)	50
8	Abdul Qadir (Pakistan, 1982–88)	45
9	Mushtaq Ahmed (Pakistan, 1990–99)	35
10	Danish Kaneria (Pakistan, 2002–10)	34

WEST INDIES v PAKISTAN

Having won eight of the last 13 matches played between the two countries, one could easily assume that Pakistan have enjoyed an unrelenting supremacy over the West Indies, but this is only a recent phenomenon: despite the historic ebb and flow of a team's fortunes, matches between Pakistan and the West Indies have, for the most part, been closely fought affairs.

Most dismissals

A solid if not spectacular performer behind the stumps for the West Indies in a 25-Test career, Gerry Alexander holds the record for the most dismissals in Pakistan-West Indies Test matches. In eight games against Pakistan between 1958 and 1959, the former West Indies captain captured 29 victims, with 25 catches and four stumpings.

OVERALL SERIES RECORDS

(44 Tests between 1958 and 2006)

	W	L	T	D	W/L	%W	%L	%D
West Indies	15	16	0	15	0.93	32.60	34.78	32.60
Pakistan	16	15	0	15	10.6	34.78	32.60	32.60

First match: 17–23 January 1958, Bridgetown, Barbados

Windies put on batting masterclass under the Jamaican sun

There were four main factors in the West Indies' crushing victory over Pakistan at Kingston, Jamaica, in February–March 1958: Pakistan's depleted and toothless bowling attack; Garfield Sobers's monumental innings of 365 not out (a new world record); the support Sobers received from Conrad Hunte, who scored 260 (the pair's partnership of 446 for the second wicket is an all-time record in matches between the two countries); and the home side's colossal first-innings total of 790 for 3 declared (the highest team total in Tests between the two countries). Trailing by 462 runs on first innings, Pakistan wilted to 288 all out.

Most catches

Viv Richards holds the record for the most catches in Test matches between Pakistan and the West Indies. The "Master Blaster" from Antigua bagged 23 catches in 16 Tests against Pakistan between 1975 and 1988.

Sobers achieves superstar status

The outstanding performance of a 21-year-old left-handed batsman overshadowed all other events in the Third Test between the West Indies and Pakistan at Kingston, Jamaica, in February–March 1958. **Garfield Sobers** (still waiting to score his first century and playing in his 17th Test match) compiled a peerless innings of 365 not out to break Len Hutton's world record score of 364 against Australia at The Oval in 1938 to prompt 20,000 ecstatic supporters to invade the pitch in wild celebration. He wasn't finished there: in the Fourth Test at Georgetown, Guyana, he scored 125 and 109 not out and ended the series with 824 runs to his name at an imposing average of 137.33 – the highest in any series between Pakistan and the West Indies in history.

Rich pickings against the West Indies

Mohammad Yousuf has enjoyed some good times against the West Indies. In eight Tests against the islanders since 2000 he has scored 1,214 runs, with seven centuries (a highest of 192 in the First Test of the 2006–07 series at Lahore) at an average of 101.16 – the highest of any batsman to complete ten or more innings in matches between the two sides.

West Indies felled to record low in Faisalabad

The West Indies may not have enjoyed the best of times on Pakistani soil – winning only four times in 21 attempts – but they slipped to a record-breaking low in the First Test of the 1986–87 series between the two countries at Faisalabad. Set an achievable 240 for victory, they capitulated in the face of fine bowling from Imran Khan (4 for 30) and Abdul Qadir (6 for 16), subsiding to a miserable 53 all out and a 186-run defeat. It is the lowest team total in all matches between the two countries.

Mahmood's 12-for leads Pakistan to success

Fazal Mahmood was the chief architect of Pakistan's 41-run win in the low-scoring Second Test of the 1958–59 series at Dhaka. He took 6 for 34 in the first innings and 6 for 66 in the second to end with match figures of 12 for 100, the best in all Test matches between Pakistan and the West Indies.

Croft crushes Pakistan

Perhaps the most feared of all the legendary West Indian fast bowlers over the years, owing to his penchant for, and skill at, unleashing a barrage of high-speed, short-pitched deliveries, Colin Croft flattened Pakistan's batsmen into submission in the 1976–77 series in the Caribbean. In the Second Test at Port of Spain, Trinidad, the paceman took 8 for 29 in the second innings (still the best bowling figures by a West Indian in matches between the countries) to lead his side to a six-wicket victory. He ended the series, which the West Indies won 2–1, with 33 wickets to his name, another record in Tests between the two sides.

Most productive partnership

The most productive partnership in all Tests between the West Indies and Pakistan is that between Conrad Hunte and Garfield Sobers. The pair combined to score 723 runs in five innings in the 1957–58 series (with a highest of 446 at Kingston, Jamaica) at an average of 144.60.

Most successful captain

His appointment as captain for the 1957 tour of England was not widely celebrated in the Caribbean, but white, Cambridge-educated, Barbados-born Gerry Alexander proved a popular captain for the West Indies and also a successful one: he led the islanders to four wins over Pakistan in eight Tests between 1958 and 1959 – a record in Pakistan-West Indies Tests.

MOST RUNS: TOP 10

Pos	Player	Runs
1	**Mohammad Yousuf** (Pakistan, 2000–06)	1,214
2	B.C. Lara (West Indies, 1990–2006)	1,173
3	Inzamam-ul-Haq (Pakistan, 1993–2006)	1,124
4	I.V.A. Richards (West Indies, 1975–88)	1,091
5	C.L. Hooper (West Indies, 1988–2002)	998
6	S. Chanderpaul (West Indies, 1997–2011)	986
7	G.S. Sobers (West Indies, 1958–59)	984
8	D.L. Haynes (West Indies, 1980–93)	928
9	Wasim Raja (Pakistan, 1975–81)	919
10	C.G. Greenidge (West Indies, 1977–90)	861

MOST WICKETS: TOP 10

Pos	Player	Wickets
1	**Imran Khan** (Pakistan, 1977–90)	80
2	Wasim Akram (Pakistan, 1986–2000)	79
3	C.A. Walsh (West Indies, 1986–2000)	63
4	Waqar Younis (Pakistan, 1990–2002)	55
5	C.E.H. Croft (West Indies, 1977–81)	50
=	M.D. Marshall (West Indies, 1980–90)	50
7	Abdul Qadir (Pakistan, 1980–90)	42
=	C.E.L. Ambrose (W. Indies, 1988–2000)	42
9	Fazal Mahmood (Pakistan, 1958–59)	41
10	J. Garner (West Indies, 1977–81)	35

PAKISTAN v SRI LANKA

Sri Lanka have played Pakistan on more occasions than they have played against any other Test nation and, despite losing five of their first seven Tests against them, have enjoyed considerable success against their subcontinental near-neighbours. Pakistan still lead the overall series (with 17 wins to Sri Lanka's 11) but, in recent times, series between the two are regularly competitive.

Most catches

Mahela Jayawardene holds the record for the most catches by a fielder in matches between Pakistan and Sri Lanka: the Sri Lankan has bagged 32 catches in 27 Tests against Pakistan between 1999 and 2014.

OVERALL SERIES RECORDS

(46 Tests between 1982 and 2014)

	W	L	T	D	W/L	%W	%L	%D
Pakistan	17	11	0	18	1.54	36.96	23.91	39.13
Sri Lanka	11	17	0	18	0.64	23.91	36.96	39.13

First match: 5–10 March 1982, Karachi, Pakistan

All-round excellence

Wasim Akram made an impact with both bat and ball for Pakistan in Tests against Sri Lanka. He took 63 wickets in 19 Tests against them (including three five-wicket hauls and a best of 5 for 43 in the first Test at Colombo in August 1994) and also plundered 545 runs at an average of 28.68 (with a highest score of 100 in the first Test at Galle in June 2000). He is the only player in history to have scored more than 500 runs and taken 50-plus wickets in Pakistan-Sri Lanka Tests.

Silky Sangakkara heads averages list

A talented left-handed batsman, Kumar Sangakkara has been an integral member of Sri Lanka's batting for more than a decade. He has enjoyed considerable success against Pakistan over the years, hitting nine of his 35 Test centuries in 19 matches against them – with a highest score of 230 at Lahore in March 2002 – and scoring 2,320 runs at an average of 80.19, the most runs and the highest average of any player to have completed ten or more innings in Pakistan-Sri Lanka Tests. He also holds the record for the most runs in a Test series between the countries (516 in 2010–11)

Muralitharan is the star of the show

Not for the first time in his record-breaking career, **Muttiah Muralitharan** was at the heart of Sri Lanka's 2–1 away series victory over Pakistan in 1999–2000. The wily off-spinner took a series record 26 wickets in the three Tests, with a best of 6 for 71 during Sri Lanka's 57-run, series-clinching victory in the Second Test at Peshawar.

Most dismissals

A veteran of 69 Test matches, Moin Khan is the leading wicket-keeper in Pakistan-Sri Lanka Tests. The former Pakistan captain claimed 40 victims (35 caught and five stumped) in 16 matches against Sri Lanka between 1991 and 2004.

MOST RUNS: TOP 10

Pos	Player	Runs
1	**K.C. Sangakkara** (Sri Lanka, 2002–14)	2,486
2	Younis Khan (Pakistan, 2000–14)	1,808
3	Inzamam-ul-Haq (Pakistan, 1994–2006)	1,559
4	D.P.M.D. Jayawardene (S. Lanka, 1999–2014)	1,544
5	S.T. Jayasuriya (Sri Lanka, 1991–2006)	1,490
6	P.A. de Silva (Sri Lanka, 1985–2000)	1,475
7	A. Ranatunga (Sri Lanka, 1982–2000)	1,210
8	T.T. Samaraweera (Sri Lanka, 2002–12)	1,045
9	Saeed Anwar (Pakistan, 1994–2000)	919
10	T.M. Dilshan (Sri Lanka, 2000–12)	873

MOST WICKETS: TOP 10

Pos	Player	Wickets
1	M. Muralitharan (Sri Lanka, 1994–2009)	80
2	H.M.R.K.B. Herath (Sri Lanka, 2000–14)	65
3	Wasim Akram (Pakistan, 1985–2000)	63
4	Saeed Ajmal (Pakistan, 2009–14)	57
5	Waqar Younis (Pakistan, 1991–2002)	56
6	W.P.U.J.C. Vaas (Sri Lanka, 1994–2009)	47
7	**Imran Khan** (Pakistan, 1982–92)	46
8	Junaid Khan (Pakistan, 2011–14)	40
9	Danish Kaneria (Pakistan, 2004–09)	35
10	Saqlain Mushtaq (Pakistan, 1995–2000)	34

Pakistan grind out the runs in Karachi

There have been few more turgid stalemates in Test history. On a desperately flat track – the scourge of the modern game – at Karachi in the First Test of the 2008–09 series, Sri Lanka won the toss, elected to bat, and cruised to 644 for 7 declared. Confident Sri Lanka may have been – defeat was now out of the equation – but the Pakistan batsmen, also thriving on the lifeless surface, responded in style. Aided by a magnificent 313 from captain Younis Khan (the highest individual score in Pakistan-Sri Lanka matches) and an unbeaten 158 from Kamran Akmal, Pakistan powered to 765 for 6 declared – the highest total in all matches between the two countries. To the surprise of no one, the match ended in a draw.

Perfect partners

Mahela Jayawardene (240) and Thilan Samaraweera (231) were Sri Lanka's driving force in the First Test against Pakistan at Karachi in February 2009. The pair added 437 runs for the fourth wicket to power Sri Lanka to 644 for 7 declared in their first innings and a position of impregnability. It is the highest partnership in all Tests between the two countries. The most productive partnership in Pakistan-Sri Lanka Tests is that between Mahela Jayawardena and Kumar Sangakkara. The pair have have combined to score 1,225 runs in 26 innings against Pakistan between 2002 and 2014.

Wasim and Waqar's devastating Kandy blitz

As they had done on many occasions, Pakistan's Wasim Akram and Waqar Younis combined to devastating effect in the Third Test against Sri Lanka at Kandy in August 1994. Wasim took 4 for 32 and Waqar 6 for 34 in 28.2 overs to dismiss Sri Lanka for 71 – the lowest team total in Pakistan-Sri Lanka Tests. Pakistan went on to win the match by an innings and 52 runs to take the series 2–0.

Imran magic inspires Pakistan to crushing victory

Trailing 1–0 in their first-ever series against Pakistan going into the Third and final Test at Lahore in March 1982, but buoyed by a spirited performance in the previous drawn Test at Faisalabad, Sri Lanka then had the misfortune of running into **Imran Khan** at his sublime, but devastating, best. The Pakistan paceman took 8 for 58 in the first innings – the best single-innings figures in all matches between the two countries – and 6 for 58 in the second to lead his side to an innings-and-102-run victory. His match haul of 14 for 116 is another Pakistan-Sri Lanka record.

INDIA v SRI LANKA

While India have enjoyed a prolonged period of success in Test matches against Sri Lanka on home soil – winning ten of 17 Tests and not registering a single defeat – matches in Sri Lanka have always been closer affairs, with India recording only four victories to Sri Lanka's six.

New kid on the block

Ajantha Mendis burst on to the Test cricket scene in spectacular style against India in 2008. Bowling a mixture of leg-spinners, googlies, top-spinners, flippers and speciality "caroms" (released from an unusual snap of the fingers), the Sri Lankan sensation bamboozled India's batsmen. In the First Test at Colombo he became the first Sri Lankan in history to take eight wickets on debut, and he ended the series with 26 wickets – a series record in matches between India and Sri Lanka (and also the best return for a bowler in a three-match debut series, beating Alec Bedser's record haul against India in 1946 by two).

Sehwag sparkles against Sri Lanka

A scintillating opening batsman for India with a penchant for compiling huge scores, **Virender Sehwag** has often been in prime form against Sri Lanka: in 18 innings against them he has scored 1,239 runs – including two double-centuries (201 not out at Galle in July 2008, and 293 at Mumbai in December 2009) – at an average of 72.88. It is the highest by any player to have completed ten or more innings in India-Sri Lanka Test matches.

OVERALL SERIES RECORDS

(35 Tests between 1982 and 2010)

	W	L	T	D	W/L	%W	%L	%D
India	14	6	0	15	2.33	40.00	17.14	52.86
Sri Lanka	6	14	0	15	0.42	17.14	40.00	52.86

First match: 17–22 September 1982, Chennai, India

Sri Lanka's batting fun in the Colombo sun

The First Test between Sri Lanka and India at Colombo in August 1997 turned into yet another Test match in the subcontinent in which the bat completely dominated, but at least it was a record-breaking one. Having seen India compile 537 for 8 in their first innings, Sri Lanka, helped by sublime innings from both Sanath Jayasuriya (340) and Roshan Mahanama (225), produced a mammoth response, compiling a mighty 952 for 6 declared – the highest team total in Test history – as the match petered out into an inevitable draw.

MOST RUNS: TOP 5

Pos	Player	Runs
1	S.R. Tendulkar (India, 1990–2010)	1,995
2	D.P.M.D. Jayawardene (Sri Lanka, 1997–2010)	1,822
3	R. Dravid (India, 1997–2010)	1,508
4	K.C. Sangakkara (Sri Lanka, 2001–10)	1,257
5	P.A. de Silva (Sri Lanka, 1985–99)	1,252

MOST WICKETS: TOP 5

Pos	Player	Wickets
1	M. Muralitharan (Sri Lanka, 1993–2010)	105
2	A. Kumble (India, 1993–2008)	74
3	Harbhajan Singh (India, 1999–2010)	52
4	Kapil Dev (India, 1982–94)	45
5	**B.A.W. Mendis** (Sri Lanka, 2008–10)	34

SRI LANKA v ENGLAND

Even from the first Test matches between the two countries, England have failed to dominate Sri Lanka – perhaps it was this that prompted a seeming reluctance from the ECB to schedule fixtures against the islanders (the two countries played just five Tests between 1982 and 1993) – and in the 24 Tests played have won only nine to Sri Lanka's six.

OVERALL SERIES RECORDS

(26 Tests between 1982 and 2012)

	W	L	T	D	W/L	%W	%L	%D
Sri Lanka	7	10	0	9	0.70	26.92	38.46	34.61
England	10	7	0	9	1.42	38.46	26.92	34.61

First match: 17–21 February 1982, Colombo, Sri Lanka

Sri Lanka show England how it's done in Colombo

Having seen England compile an under-par first-innings 265 all out in the decisive Third and final Test at Colombo in December 2003 (the series was locked at 0–0 as it reached its finale), Sri Lanka's batsmen put a toothless England attack to the sword, compiling a massive 628 for 8 declared – the highest team total in all matches between the two countries – en route to a comprehensive and series-clinching innings-and-215-run victory.

Lowest score

The lowest team score in the history of England-Sri Lanka matches is 81 all out, a fate that has been suffered on two occasions: by Sri Lanka at Colombo in March 2001; and by England at Galle in December 2007.

Highest individual score

The record for the highest individual score in England-Sri Lanka Test matches is 213, a feat achieved by two Sri Lankan batsmen: **Sanath Jayasuriya** (213 at The Oval in August 1998) and Mahela Jayawardene (213 not out at Galle in December 2007). Jayawardene has prospered against England: in 33 innings against them between 1998 and 2011 he has scored 1,684 runs at an average of 56.13. the record for the highest average of any batsman to have completed ten or more innings in England-Sri Lanka Test matches is held by England's Ian Bell (592 runs at an average 84.57).

MOST RUNS: TOP 5

Pos	Player	Runs
1	D.P.M.D. Jayawardene (Sri Lanka, 1998–2012)	2,038
2	K.C. Sangakkara (Sri Lanka, 2001–12)	1,226
3	A.N. Cook (England, 2006–12)	1,000
4	M.E. Trescothick (England, 2001–06)	957
5	T.M. Dilshan (Sir Lanka, 2001–12)	889

MOST WICKETS: TOP 5

Pos	Player	Wickets
1	M. Muralitharan (Sri Lanka, 1993–2007)	112
2	W.P.U.J.C. Vaas (Sri Lanka, 2001–07)	49
3	M.J. Hoggard (England, 2002–07)	37
4	A.F. Giles (England, 2001–03)	31
5	G.P. Swann (England (2011–12)	28

Best bowling in an innings/ match/series

The magical **Muttiah Muralitharan**, Test cricket's all-time leading wicket-taker, holds every major bowling record in the book in England-Sri Lanka matches: he is the only bowler to take more than 100 wickets (112); he recorded the best single-innings bowling figures (9 for 65 at The Oval in August 1998); the best match figures (16 for 220, in the same Test at The Oval); and the most wickets in a series (26 in Sri Lanka's victorious 2003–04 series against England).

NZ v SRI LANKA

That it took nine years and 11 Tests for Sri Lanka to record their first win in matches between the two countries suggests that New Zealand have a firm hold over the Sri Lankans, but while that may have been the case in early clashes, the pendulum has certainly swung back in recent times. Sri Lanka have won six of their last 12 Test matches against New Zealand (losing three times) since July 1998.

Vettori's record-breaking efforts all in vain

If only New Zealand's batsmen could have displayed with the bat the skill levels **Daniel Vettori** showed with the ball, the outcome might well have been different. With New Zealand already in trouble in the Second Test against Sri Lanka at Wellington in December 2006 (they were 138 runs behind as Sri Lanka started their second innings), the Kiwi slow left-armer did all he could to bring his side back into the match, taking 7 for 130 – the best single-innings bowling figures in New Zealand-Sri Lanka Tests – to help dismiss the visitors for 365. Set an improbable 504 runs for victory, however, New Zealand slipped to 286 all out and a heavy 217-run defeat.

OVERALL SERIES RECORDS

(28 Tests between 1983 and 2012)

	W	L	T	D	W/L	%W	%L	%D
New Zealand	10	8	0	10	1.20	35.71	28.57	35.71
Sri Lanka	8	10	0	10	0.80	28.57	35.71	35.71

First match: 4–6 March 1983, Christchurch, New Zealand

Sri Lanka stifled in alien conditions

Sri Lanka's batsmen struggled to come to terms with a rain-affected wicket in their second-ever Test against New Zealand, at Wellington in March 1983. Leading by 39 runs after the completion of the first innings, they crashed to 93 all out – the lowest-ever team total in matches between the two countries – and an eventual six-wicket defeat.

Herath's heroics halt New Zealand

New Zealand could find no answer to the guile of Rangana Herath during the first Test of the two-match series against Sri Lanka at Galle in November 2012. The veteran slow left-arm bowler was the difference between the two sides taking 5 for 65 in New Zealand's first innings and 6 for 43 in their second to help his side towards a comfortable ten-wicket victory. Herath's match haul of 11 for 108 is the best in all Tests between the two countries.

Nobody can keep up with Jones

One of the pillars upon which New Zealand built their record-breaking recovery against Sri Lanka at Wellington in January–February 1991, hitting 186 (his highest Test score), **Andrew Jones** continued to enjoy good times against Sri Lanka: in six Tests against them he scored 625 runs (with two further centuries) at an average of 62.50 – the highest by any batsman to complete ten or more innings in New Zealand-Sri Lanka Test matches.

MOST RUNS: TOP 5

Pos	Player	Runs
1	S.P. Fleming (New Zealand, 1995–2006)	1,166
2	D.P.M.D. Jayawardene (Sri Lanka, 1998–2012)	1,028
3	A. Ranatunga (Sri Lanka, 1984–98)	824
4	H.P. Tillakaratne (Sri Lanka, 1991–2003)	819
5	P.A. de Silva (Sri Lanka, 1991–98)	785

MOST WICKETS: TOP 5

Pos	Player	Wickets
1	M. Muralitharan (Sri Lanka, 1992–2009)	82
2	D.L. Vettori (New Zealand, 1997–2009)	51
3	W.P.U.J.C. Vaas (Sri Lanka, 1995–2006)	42
4	R.J. Hadlee (New Zealand, 1983–87)	37
5	H.M.R.K.B. Herath (Sri Lanka, 2005–12)	31

SRI LANKA v AUSTRALIA

Sri Lanka have not enjoyed the best of times in Tests against Australia since the two sides met for the first time in Kandy in 1983. They have won only once in 26 attempts and, sensationally at Melbourne in 1995, saw their leading bowler, Muttiah Muralitharan, become one of only 11 players in Test history (and the only Sri Lankan) to be no-balled for throwing.

OVERALL SERIES RECORDS

(26 Tests between 1983 and 2013)

	W	L	T	D	W/L	%W	%L	%D
Sri Lanka	1	17	0	8	0.05	3.85	65.38	30.77
Australia	17	1	0	8	17.00	65.38	3.85	30.77

First match: 22–26 April 1983, Kandy, Sri Lanka

MOST RUNS: TOP 5

Pos	Player	Runs
1	M.E.K. Hussey (Australia, 2007–12)	994
2	R.T. Ponting (Australia, 1995–2011)	975
3	D.P.M.D. Jayawardene (Sri Lanka, 1999–2012)	969
4	K.C. Sangakkara (Sri Lanka, 2004–12)	878
5	P.A. de Silva (Sri Lanka, 1988–99)	803

MOST WICKETS: TOP 5

Pos	Player	Wickets
1	S.K. Warne (Australia, 1992–2004)	59
2	M. Muralitharan (Sri Lanka, 1992–2007)	54
3	W.P.U.J.C. Vaas (Sri Lanka, 1995–2007)	38
4	H.M.R.K.B. Herath (Sri Lanka, 1999–2013)	38
5	G.D. McGrath (Australia, 1995–2004)	37

Sri Lanka down and out in Darwin

Before the Test it was thought that the soft, seaming wicket prepared at Darwin for the First Test of the two-match 2004 series in Australia was unlikely to bring the best out of the Sri Lankan batsmen, and so it proved. Having dismissed Australia comparatively cheaply for 207 in the first innings, Sri Lanka wilted on the unfamiliar surface to 97 all out – the lowest team total in Australia-Sri Lanka Tests. The tourists fared little better second time round: set 312 for victory, they limped to 162 all out – with Michael Kasprowicz taking 7 for 39 (the best single-innings figures in all Tests between the two countries) – and a 149-run defeat.

Australia prosper against faltering Sri Lanka

Australia's batsmen took full advantage of an under-performing Sri Lankan bowling attack dogged by accusations of ball-tampering (Sri Lanka became the first team in Test history to be charged with the offence, although the ICC reversed the decision two weeks later) in the First Test of the 1995–96 series at Perth. Led by centuries from Michael Slater, whose 219 is the highest individual score in Australia-Sri Lanka Tests, and Mark Waugh (111), they amassed a colossal 617 for 5 declared – the highest team total in all matches between the two countries – en route to an innings-and-36-run victory.

Mr Cricket shines against Sri Lanka

It was appropriate that **Mike Hussey** chose to end his 75-Test career for Australia against Sri Lanka after the final Test at Sydney in January 2013. The man dubbed "Mr Cricket" enjoyed great success against Sri Lanka, scoring 994 runs in eight Tests against them between 2007 and 2013 at a heady average of 110.44. Both the average and runs scored are records in Tests between the two countries.

W. INDIES v S. AFRICA

As the two countries first met only in 1992, by which time the shameful policy of apartheid had started to unravel, South Africa, for the most part, have played only against a troubled West Indian side whose glory days seemed far behind them. As a result, South Africa have dominated proceedings, winning 16 of the 25 Tests played to the West Indies' three.

Deadly de Villiers finds his form

A.B. de Villiers has enjoyed some of the finest moments of his already impressive Test career against the West Indies. The right-handed middle-order batsman has hit four of his ten Test centuries against the men from the Caribbean (with a best of 178 at Bridgetown, Barbados, in April 2005) and has hit 1,037 runs in 18 innings at an average of 79.76 – the highest by any batsman to have completed ten innings or more in matches between the two countries.

A run-fest in Antigua

The Antigua Recreation Ground confirmed its reputation as possessing the most benign strip in world cricket when the West Indies met South Africa in the Fourth and final Test of the 2004–05 series. South Africa, holding an impregnable 2–0 series lead, won the toss and batted the West Indies out of the game with 588 for 6 declared. But the West Indies, playing for nothing more than pride, responded bravely. Led by an imperious 317 from Chris Gayle (the highest individual score in all matches between the two countries) and centuries from Ramnaresh Sarwan (127), Shivnarine Chanderpaul (127) and Dwayne Bravo (107), they amassed a colossal 747 all out – the 11th highest team total in Test history and the highest in West Indies-South Africa clashes – as the match meandered towards an inevitable draw.

OVERALL SERIES RECORDS

(25 Tests between 1992 and 2010)

	W	L	T	D	W/L	%W	%L	%D
West Indies	3	16	0	6	0.18	12.00	64.00	24.00
South Africa	16	3	0	6	5.33	64.00	12.00	24.00

First match: 18–23 April 1992, Bridgetown, Barbados

Getting off to the worst of starts

The West Indies have endured a miserable sequence of results against South Africa in recent times (losing 5–0 in 1998–99, 2–1 in 2001 and winning only one of 11 Tests against them between 2003 and 2008), so a good start was essential for both their confidence and morale when the two sides met for the First Test (of three) at Port of Spain in June 2010. South Africa won the toss, elected to bat and reached 352 all out. In reply, the West Indies slumped to 102 all out – the lowest total in all Tests between the two countries – and went on to lose the match by 163 runs.

Most wickets in a series

The record for the most wickets in a West Indies-South Africa series is 29, a feat achieved by two South African players: Shaun Pollock, in South Africa in 1998–99; and Makhaya Ntini, in South Africa in 2003–04.

MOST RUNS: TOP 5

Pos	Player	Runs
1	J.H. Kallis (South Africa, 1998–2010)	2,356
2	B.C. Lara (West Indies, 1992–2005)	1,715
3	S. Chanderpaul (West Indies, 1998–2010)	1,619
4	G.C. Smith (South Africa, 2003–10)	1,593
5	H.H. Gibbs (South Africa, 1998–2008)	1,403

MOST WICKETS: TOP 5

Pos	Player	Wickets
1	**S.M. Pollock** (South Africa, 1998–2008)	70
2	M. Ntini (South Africa, 2001–08)	63
3	A. Nel (South Africa, 2003–08)	52
=	J.H. Kallis (South Africa, 1998–2010)	52
4	C.A. Walsh (West Indies, 1992–2001)	51

ZIMBABWE v INDIA

Apart from a pair of unexpected defeats in Harare (in October 1998 and June 2001, when Zimbabwe cricket was at its strongest), India dominated the few Tests they played against Zimbabwe between 1992 and 2005, winning seven out of 11 and drawing two.

OVERALL SERIES RECORDS

(11 Tests between 1992 and 2005)

	W	L	T	D	W/L	%W	%L	%D
Zimbabwe	2	7	0	2	0.28	18.18	63.64	18.18
India	7	2	0	2	3.50	63.64	18.18	18.18

First match: 18–22 October 1992, Harare, Zimbabwe

MOST RUNS: TOP 5

Pos	Player	Runs
1	A. Flower (Zimbabwe, 1992–2002)	1,138
2	R. Dravid (India, 1998–2005)	979
3	S.R. Tendulkar (India, 1992–2002)	918
4	G.W. Flower (Zimbabwe, 1992–2002)	565
5	S.S. Das (India, 2000–02)	560

MOST WICKETS: TOP 5

Pos	Player	Wickets
1	A. Kumble (India, 1992–2005)	38
2	Harbhajan Singh (India, 1998–2005)	31
3	J. Srinath (India, 1992–2002)	30
=	H.H. Streak (Zimbabwe, 1998–2005)	30
5	Z. Khan (India, 2000–05)	21
=	I.K. Pathan (India, 2005)	21

Records tumble in Nagpur

One-nil up in the series going into the Second and final Test at Nagpur in November 2000, India won the toss and batted Zimbabwe out of the game as centuries from Shiv Sunder Das (110), Rahul Dravid (162) and Sachin Tendulkar (201) propelled them to a mighty 609 for 6 declared – the highest team score in matches between the two sides. When, having dismissed Zimbabwe for 382, they enforced the follow-on, an Indian victory seemed the most probable outcome. In stepped **Andy Flower**, however, hitting an unbeaten 232 – the highest individual score in Zimbabwe-India Tests – to rescue the draw.

Dravid, a.k.a. "The Wall", stands firm

Although Andy Flower may have outgunned him as the all-time leading run-scorer in Zimbabwe-India Tests, no batsman played with more consistency than Rahul Dravid. In 13 innings against Zimbabwe between 1998 and 2005, the man nicknamed "The Wall" hit 979 runs, including five half-centuries and three centuries (with a highest score of 200 not out at Delhi in November 2000), at an average of 97.90 – the highest by any batsman to complete ten or more innings in matches between the two countries.

Disappointment in Delhi for Zim

Trailing India by a mere 25 runs after the completion of the first innings in the Second Test of the two-match 2001–02 series at Delhi, and still very much in the game, Zimbabwe failed to cope with the dual spin threat of Harbhajan Singh and **Anil Kumble**. The former took 6 for 62 and the latter 4 for 58 as Zimbabwe slipped to 146 all out – the lowest team total in Tests between the two countries – and an eventual four-wicket defeat.

Pathan prospers under the African sun

India's comprehensive 2–0 series win over a weak Zimbabwe side in 2005–06 was a personal triumph for Irfan Pathan. Swinging the ball prodigiously, the medium-fast bowler took 5 for 58 and 4 for 53 in India's innings-and-90-run victory in the First Test at Bulawayo, and 7 for 59 (the best single-innings bowling figures in Zimbabwe-India Tests) and 5 for 67 in India's ten-wicket win in the Second Test at Harare. His match figures of 12 for 156 at Harare and his series haul of 21 wickets are both records in matches between the two countries.

ZIMBABWE v NZ

Matches between Zimbabwe and New Zealand have been one-way affairs ever since the two sides met for the first time in Bulawayo in 1992, with New Zealand winning seven of the 13 Test matches played and Zimbabwe failing to record a single victory.

Astle tops the batting charts

A free-scoring middle-order batsman and a veteran of 81 Test matches for his country, **Nathan Astle** has been the outstanding batsman in matches betwee Zimbabwe and New Zealand. The Canterbury star is the leading run-scorer – with 813 runs in 11 Tests between 1996 and 2003 (including three centuries and a highest score of 141 at Wellington in December 2000) – and has the highest average of any batsman to have completed ten or more innings in matches between the two countries (50.81).

Huckle's spell in the limelight

The brightest moments in Adam Huckle's brief eight-Test career came in the drawn two-match series against New Zealand in 1997–98. In the Second Test at Bulawayo, the leg-spinner took 6 for 109 in the first innings and 5 for 146 in the second as New Zealand, chasing 286 for victory, hung on at 275 for 8 to force a hard-fought, if nervous, draw. Huckle's match haul of 11 for 255 is the best in Zimbabwe-New Zealand Tests, and his series haul of 16 wickets is another record in matches between the two countries.

OVERALL SERIES RECORDS

(15 Tests between 1992 and 2005)

	W	L	T	D	W/L	%W	%L	%D
Zimbabwe	0	9	0	6	0.0 0	0.0 0	60.00	40.00
New Zealand	9	0	0	6	-	60.00	0.00	40.00

First match: 1–5 November 1992, Bulawayo, Zimbabwe

Zimbabwe back with record defeat

Zimbabwe's one-off Test match against New Zealand at Napier in January 2012 was the first overseas Test they had played in since visiting South Africa in March 2005. Although it was a welcome return to the international fold, it quickly developed into a forgettable match. Having elected to field, Zimbabwe watched Ross Taylor (122) and Bradley-John Watling (102 not out) put their bowlers to the sword, posting 495 for 7 declared (the highest total in all New Zealand-Zimbabwe Tests). the Black Caps then dismissed the visitors for 51 in the first innings and 143 in the second to win by an innings and 301 runs – the largest winning margin in all Tests between the countries.

Strang shines as Zimbabwe stumble

Although Zimbabwe lost the first Test against New Zealand in Bulawayo in September 2000 by seven wickets (despite taking a 12-run first innings lead), no blame for the defeat could be apportioned to Paul Strang. The leg-spinner took 8 for 109 in New Zealand's first innings – the best single-innings figures ever recorded in Test matches between the two countries.

MOST RUNS: TOP 5

Pos	Player	Runs
1	N.J. Astle (New Zealand, 1996–2005)	813
2	G.W. Flower (Zimbabwe, 1992–2000)	780
3	A. Flower (Zimbabwe, 1992–2000)	721
4	G.J. Whittall (Zimbabwe, 1996–2000)	647
5	S.P. Fleming (New Zealand, 1996–2005)	640

MOST WICKETS: TOP 5

Pos	Player	Wickets
1	**C.L. Cairns** (New Zealand, 1996–2000)	39
2	H.H. Streak (Zimbabwe, 1996–2005)	32
=	D.L. Vettori (New Zealand, 1997–2012)	32
4	P.A. Strang (Zimbabwe, 1996–2000)	29
5	D.N. Patel (New Zealand, 1992–96)	23

S. AFRICA v INDIA

Ever since South Africa edged the historic 1992 home series against India (the first team they played against in the post-apartheid era), they have enjoyed a measure of supremacy over them, both at home and away, recording 13 victories in the 29 Tests played to India's seven.

India seize their chance

Having lost the First Test of the two-match series against South Africa in February 2010 (by an innings and 6 runs in Nagpur), it was win or bust for the home side when the two teams faced off in Kolkata a week later. And when South Africa slipped to an under-par 296 all out in their first innings, India were handed their chance. They grabbed it with both hands as centuries from **Virender Sehwag** (165), Sachin Tendulkar (106), V.V.S. Laxman (143 not out) and captain Mahendra Singh Dhoni (132 not out) propelled them to a mighty 643 for 6 declared – the highest total in all Tests between the two countries – and an eventual innings-and-57-run victory.

OVERALL SERIES RECORDS

(29 Tests between 1992 and 2013)

	W	L	T	D	W/L	%W	%L	%D
South Africa	13	7	0	9	1.85	44.83	24.14	31.03
India	7	13	0	9	0.53	24.14	44.83	31.03

First match: 13–17 November 1992, Durban, South Africa

Down and out in Durban

India's batsmen failed to cope either with an electric performance from South Africa fast bowler Allan Donald (who took 9 for 54 in the match) or with a lively Durban wicket in the First Test of the 1996–97 series. Set an unlikely 395 runs to win the low-scoring match, they crashed to 66 all out – the lowest team total in Tests between the countries – and a 328-run defeat.

Klusener's cracking debut

Lance Klusener produced one of the most scintillating debut performances in Test history to lead South Africa to a comprehensive victory over India in the Second Test of the 1996–97 series at Kolkata. With the home side set an unlikely 467 runs to win both the match and the series, the all-rounder took 8 for 64. They are the best figures by a debutant in South Africa's history and the best single-innings figures in the history of Tests between South Africa and India. Remarkably, this remained the only five-wicket haul of Klusener's 49-Test career.

Kallis is Mr Consistency

India's batting legend Sachin Tendulkar has scored the most runs (1,741), but no batsman has performed with more consistency in South Africa-India Tests than **Jacques Kallis**. South Africa's legendary all-rounder has scored 1,734 runs in 18 Tests against India since 2000 – with a highest score of 201 not out at Pretoria in December 2010 – at an average of 69.36, the highest by any batsman to complete ten or more innings in matches between the two countries.

MOST RUNS: TOP 5

Pos	Player	Runs
1	S.R. Tendulkar (India, 1992–2011)	1,741
2	J.H. Kallis (South Africa, 2000–13)	1,734
3	V. Sehwag (India, 2001–11)	1,306
4	R. Dravid (India, 1996–2011)	1,252
5	H.M. Amla (South Africa, 2004–13)	1,207

MOST WICKETS: TOP 5

Pos	Player	Wickets
1	A. Kumble (India, 1992–2008)	84
2	J. Srinath (India, 1992–2001)	64
3	D.W. Steyn (South Africa, 2006–13)	63
4	Harbhajan Singh (India, 2001–11)	60
5	A.A. Donald (South Africa, 1992–2000)	57

SRI LANKA v S. AFRICA

The difficulties faced by both sides to adapt to alien conditions have had a major bearing on matches between South Africa and Sri Lanka: South Africa, with a tendency to struggle on spin-friendly, slow, low surfaces, have won only twice in ten attempts in Sri Lanka; the islanders, exposed to fast bowling on livelier South African wickets, have won one, drawn one and lost eight of the ten Test matches.

Standout performer

Quite apart from his headline-grabbing innings of 374 in Colombo in 2006, **Mahela Jayawardene** has excelled against South Africa. In 15 Tests against them since 2000 he has scored 1,604 runs (the most by any batsman in Tests between the two countries), with five centuries (all of them in home matches), at an average of 59.40 – the highest by any batsman to have played in ten or more Test matches in the Sri Lanka-South Africa series.

OVERALL SERIES RECORDS

(20 Tests between 1993 and 2011)

	W	L	T	D	W/L	%W	%L	%D
Sri Lanka	5	10	0	5	0.50	25.00	50.00	25.00
South Africa	10	5	0	5	2.00	50.00	25.00	25.00

First match: 25–30 August 1993, Moratuwa, Sri Lanka

Sri Lanka cruise to record-breaking total in Colombo

Sri Lanka crushed South Africa in comprehensive and record-breaking style in the First Test of the 2006 series in Colombo. In the first innings, having dismissed South Africa for an under-par 169 and then slipped to a worrying 14 for 2 in reply, Sri Lanka needed something magical – and their two most gifted batsmen duly obliged. Mahela Jayawardene (374 – the fourth highest score in Test history, and the highest in Sri Lanka-South Africa Tests) and Kumar Sangakkara (287) added 624 runs for the third wicket (the highest partnership for any wicket in Test history) to propel Sri Lanka to a mighty 756 for 5 declared – the highest team total in all matches between the two countries – and an eventual innings-and-153-run victory.

Murali puts South Africa in a spin

A legion of South African batsmen have failed to fathom the wristy guile of **Muttiah Muralitharan** over the years: of his world record 792 Test wickets, 104 have come against South Africa (only against England has he taken more, 112). And Murali was at his spellbinding best in the First Test of the 2000 series against South Africa at Galle, taking 7 for 84 in the second innings to end the match with 13 for 171 (the latter is a record in Sri Lanka-South Africa Tests) as Sri Lanka won the match by an innings and 15 runs. He ended the series with 26 wickets, another record in a series between Sri Lanka and South Africa.

MOST RUNS: TOP 5

Pos	Player	Runs
1	D.P.M.D. Jayawardene (Sri Lanka, 2000–11)	1,604
2	K.C. Sangakkara (Sri Lanka, 2000–11)	1,362
3	D.J. Cullinan (South Africa, 1993–2001)	917
4	J.H. Kallis (South Africa, 1998–11)	894
5	S.T. Jayasuriya (Sri Lanka, 1993–2006)	857

MOST WICKETS: TOP 5

Pos	Player	Wickets
1	M. Muralitharan (Sri Lanka, 1993–2006)	104
2	S.M. Pollock (South Africa, 1998–2006)	48
3	M. Ntini (South Africa, 1998–2006)	35
4	N. Boje (South Africa, 2000–06)	34
5	A.A. Donald (South Africa, 1993–2001)	29

SRI LANKA v W. INDIES

Aided by a near-impeccable home record against the West Indies (that has seen them win five and draw one of the six Tests played), Sri Lanka have been the dominant force in matches played between the two countries since they met for the first time in 1993, registering six wins to the West Indies' three.

OVERALL SERIES RECORDS

(15 Tests between 1993 and 2010)

	W	L	T	D	W/L	%W	%L	%D
Sri Lanka	6	3	0	6	2.00	40.00	20.00	40.00
West Indies	3	6	0	6	0.50	20.00	40.00	20.00

First match: 8–13 December 1993, Moratuwa, Sri Lanka

Best career average

Of all the batsmen to complete ten or more innings in matches between Sri Lanka and the West Indies, Hashan Tillakaratne has the best average – 89.20 in ten innings between 1993 and 2003, including a career-best 204 not out at Colombo in November-December 2001.

MOST RUNS: TOP 5

Pos	Player	Runs
1	**B.C. Lara** (West Indies, 1993–2003)	1,125
2	K.C. Sangakkara (Sri Lanka, 2001–10)	918
2	R.R. Sarwan (West Indies, 2001–08)	749
4	D.P.M.D. Jayawardene (Sri Lanka, 2001–10)	748
5	T.T. Samaraweera (Sri Lanka, 2001–10)	644

MOST WICKETS: TOP 5

Pos	Player	Wickets
1	M. Muralitharan (Sri Lanka, 1993–2008)	82
2	W.P.U.J.C. Vaas (Sri Lanka, 2001–08)	55
3	C.E.L. Ambrose (West Indies, 1993–97)	14
=	C.D. Collymore (West Indies, 2003)	14
5	D.B.L. Powell (West Indies, 2005–08)	13
=	J.E. Taylor (West Indies, 2003–08)	13

The Colombo run-fest

Already holding an unassailable 2–0 lead in the three-match 2001–02 series going into the final Test at Colombo, Sri Lanka responded in style to the West Indies' first-innings score of 390 (of which **Brian Lara** contributed 221 – the highest individual score in all Tests between the two countries). Led by an unbeaten 204 from Hashan Tillakaratne, they compiled 627 for 9 declared – the highest team total in Sri Lanka-West Indies clashes – en route to a ten-wicket win and a 3–0 series whitewash.

Murali dashes West Indian hopes

Given that Sri Lanka had amassed 375 in their second innings, it was not inconceivable that the West Indies could chase down a victory target of 378 to win the Second Test at Kandy in July 2005 and square the series. But Muttiah Muralitharan had other ideas, hitting top form to take 8 for 46 – the best single-innings figures in Sri Lanka–West Indies Tests – to help dismiss the West Indies for 137 and lead his side to a 240-run win and a 2–0 series victory.

West Indies crawl to record-breaking low

Holding a 58-run first-innings lead and very much in the driving seat in the First Test of the 2005 series at Colombo, the West Indies then capitulated to Sri Lanka in disappointing style. Unable to withstand fine bowling from **Chaminda Vaas** (4 for 15) and Muttiah Muralitharan (6 for 36) they limped to 113 all out in 60 overs – the lowest team total in matches between the two countries – and an eventual six-wicket defeat.

ZIMBABWE v SRI LANKA

Sri Lanka may have been forced to work harder to achieve a victory on Zimbabwean soil – they won three of the eight Tests played there and drew five – but at home against the southern Africans they were invincible, recording seven wins out of seven, and most of them in dominant style.

Sri Lanka cash in against weak Zimbabwe

By 2004, what was effectively the reserve Zimbabwe team had been exposed as being completely out of its depth in international cricket, and when Sri Lanka played against them at Bulawayo in May 2004 they took full advantage. Having seen Zimbabwe struggle to 228 all out, they made the most of the batting-friendly surface. Bolstered by centuries from captain Marvan Atapattu (249), **Kumar Sangakkara** (270 – the highest individual score in Zimbabwe-Sri Lanka Tests) and Mahela Jayawardene (100 not out), they reached 713 for 3 declared (the highest team total in all Tests between the two countries) before bowling out Zimbabwe for 231 second time round to win the match by an innings and 254 runs.

Marvellous Marvan heads averages list

A veteran of 90 Test matches for Sri Lanka over a period of 17 years, **Marvan Atapattu** was a useful opening batsman who seemed to reserve his best performances for matches against Zimbabwe. In ten Test matches against them between 1998 and 2004, he scored 1,145 runs, with five centuries, at an average of 95.41 – the highest by any batsman to complete ten or more innings in matches between the two countries.

Zimbabwe gunned out at Galle

In truth, few thought Zimbabwe capable of chasing down a target of 395 runs from 125 overs to win the Third and final Test of the 2001–02 series – in which Sri Lanka already held a 2–0 lead – but their spectacular collapse still came as a surprise. Failing to come to terms with the dual spin threat of Sanath Jayasuriya (4 for 31) and Muttiah Muralitharan (4 for 24), they folded to 79 all out – the lowest team total in Tests between the countries – and defeat by 315 runs.

OVERALL SERIES RECORDS

(15 Tests between 1994 and 2004)

	W	L	T	D	W/L	%W	%L	%D
Zimbabwe	0	10	0	5	0.00	0.00	66.67	33.33
Sri Lanka	10	0	0	5	0.50	66.67	0.00	33.33

First match: 11–16 October 1994, Harare, Zimbabwe

MOST RUNS: TOP 5

Pos	Player	Runs
1	M.S. Atapattu (Sri Lanka, 1998–2004)	1,145
2	A. Flower (Zimbabwe, 1994–2002)	778
3	S.T. Jayasuriya (Sri Lanka, 1994–2004)	730
4	K.C. Sangakkara (Sri Lanka, 2001–04)	536
5	G.W. Flower (Zimbabwe, 1994–2002)	527

MOST WICKETS: TOP 5

Pos	Player	Wickets
1	M. Muralitharan (Sri Lanka, 1994–2004)	87
2	W.P.U.J.C. Vaas (Sri Lanka, 1994–2004)	48
3	H.H. Streak (Zimbabwe, 1994–2002)	33
4	S.T. Jayasuriya (Sri Lanka, 1994–2004)	20
=	K.R. Pushpakumara (Sri Lanka, 1994–99)	20

S. AFRICA v PAKISTAN

South Africa have played only 23 Test matches against Pakistan since the two sides met for the first time in 1995, but they have already gained a degree of mastery over the men from the subcontinent, recording 12 wins to Pakistan's four, with seven of the Tests drawn.

South Africa on cruise control in Cape Town

One–nil up in the two-match series against Pakistan, South Africa got off to a flying start in the Second Test at Cape Town in January 2003. Graeme Smith (151) and **Herschelle Gibbs** (228 – the highest individual score in South Africa-Pakistan clashes) put on 368 runs for the first wicket to propel the home side to 620 for 7 declared (the highest team total in matches between the two countries). Pakistan wilted under the pressure and lost the match by an innings and 142 runs.

Steyn on fire

Pakistan could find no answers to the home side's much-feted pace attack during their 3–0 series defeat to South Africa in 2012–13, and in particular to the spearhead of that attack, Dale Steyn. The Phalaborwa-born paceman took 11 for 60 in the First Test, 4 for 93 in the second and 5 for 105 in the third to end the series with 20 wickets, a record in South Africa-Pakistan Tests.

Pakistan in freefall in Johannesburg

Pakistan were delighted to dismiss South Africa for 253 in the first innings of the First Test at Johannesburg in February 2013, and thought a solid reply would give them a great chance to edge ahead in the three-match series. Instead they capitulated dramatically, slipping to a sorry 49 all out (with Dale Steyn taking 6 for 8). It was the lowest team total in Tests between the two countries, and Pakistan went on to lose the match by 211 runs.

De Villiers finds his feet

A.B. de Villiers may not have enjoyed the best of starts in matches against Pakistan, scoring just 184 runs against them in his first 11 innings, but when he finally found his feet against them, the runs just kept on coming. The turning point came when he scored 278 not out (his highest Test score) against them in Abu Dhabi in November 2010. Since then he has added three further centuries and two half-centuries in nine innings. By 2014, he had played 12 Tests against Pakistan and scored 1,112 runs against them at an average of 65.41 – the latter is a record in Tests between the two countries.

OVERALL SERIES RECORDS

(23 Tests between 1995 and 2013)

	W	L	T	D	W/L	%W	%L	%D
South Africa	12	4	0	7	3.00	52.17	17.39	30.43
Pakistan	4	12	0	7	0.33	17.39	52.17	30.43

First match: 19–23 January 1995, Johannesburg, South Africa

MOST RUNS: TOP 5

Pos	Player	Runs
1	J.H. Kallis (South Africa, 1997–2013)	1,564
2	G.C. Smith (South Africa, 2002–13)	1,259
3	AB de Villiers (South Africa, 2007–13)	1,112
4	Younis Khan (Pakistan, 2002–13)	990
5	H.M. Amla (South Africa, 2007–13)	937

MOST WICKETS: TOP 5

Pos	Player	Wickets
1	**D.W. Steyn** (South Africa, 2007–13)	47
2	S.M. Pollock (South Africa, 1997–2007)	45
3	M. Ntini (South Africa, 2002–07)	41
4	Danish Kaneria (Pakistan, 2003–07)	36
5	Mushtaq Ahmed (Pakistan, 1997–2003)	29

PAKISTAN v ZIMBABWE

It may not have been an iron grip, but Pakistan certainly held the upper hand in the 17 Test matches they played against Zimbabwe between 1993 and 2013, winning ten, drawing four and losing only three of them.

Spin-friendly surface suits Saqlain

Saqlain Mushtaq took full advantage of a wicket that offered spin from the first afternoon of the Second Test at Bulawayo in November 2002 to lay the foundations for Pakistan's ten-wicket victory over Zimbabwe to claim a 2–0 series win. The off-spinner took 7 for 66 in the first innings (the best single-innings figures in matches between the two countries) to help dismiss Zimbabwe for 178, a position from which the home side failed to recover.

Wasim's record-breaking rescue act at Sheikhupura

For a short while, with Pakistan struggling on 237 for 7, still 138 runs behind their first-innings score in the First Test of the 1996–97 series at Sheikhupura, Zimbabwe must have felt they stood a reasonable chance of winning the game. But a sensational batting performance from **Wasim Akram**, who hit an unbeaten 257 (the highest score by a No. 8 in Test history and the highest in Pakistan-Zimbabwe clashes), propelled the home side to 553 all out – still the highest team total in all matches between the two countries. Wasim's efforts were not enough to win the match, however, which ended in a draw.

Waqar extinguishes Zimbabwe challenge

Zimbabwe were unfortunate to run into **Waqar Younis** bowling at the peak of his prodigious powers when they faced Pakistan for the first time in a three-match series in 1993–94. The paceman took 7 for 91 and 6 for 44 in the First Test at Karachi (his match haul of 13 for 135 is an all-time Pakistan-Zimbabwe record), 5 for 88 and 4 for 50 in the Second Test at Rawalpindi, and 5 for 100 in the fog- and bad light-affected Third Test at Lahore. Waqar ended the series, which Pakistan won 2–0, with 27 wickets – another all-time record in matches between the two countries.

OVERALL SERIES RECORDS

(17 Tests between 1993 and 2013)

	W	L	T	D	W/L	%W	%L	%D
Pakistan	10	3	0	4	3.33	58.82	17.65	23.53
Zimbabwe	3	10	0	4	0.30	17.65	58.82	23.53

First match: 1–6 December 1993, Karachi, Pakistan

MOST RUNS: TOP 5

Pos	Player	Runs
1	G.W. Flower (Zimbabwe, 1993–2002)	961
2	A. Flower (Zimbabwe, 1993–2002)	931
3	Inzamam-ul-Haq (Pakistan, 1993–2002)	772
4	Mohammad Yousuf (Pakistan, 1998–2002)	616
5	A.D.R. Campbell (Zimbabwe, 1993–2002)	612

MOST WICKETS: TOP 5

Pos	Player	Wickets
1	Waqar Younis (Pakistan, 1993–2002)	62
2	Wasim Akram (Pakistan, 1993–98)	47
3	H.H. Streak (Zimbabwe, 1993–98)	44
4	Saqlain Mushtaq (Pakistan, 1996–2002)	28
5	G.J. Whittall (Zimbabwe, 1993–2002)	23

S. AFRICA v ZIMBABWE

Given their geographical situation as southern African neighbours, it seems strange that South Africa and Zimbabwe contested only seven Test matches in ten years between 1995 and 2005. What is less strange, however, is that South Africa dominated the matches that were played: winning all but one of the matches played and drawing the other.

Happy times in Harare

South Africa's batsmen prospered on a friendly, even surface against a weak Zimbabwe attack in the First Test of the two-match 2001–02 series at Harare. After winning the toss and electing to bat, South Africa's top three batsmen all passed three figures – Herschelle Gibbs (147), Gary Kirsten (220, the highest individual score in South Africa-Zimbabwe Tests) and **Jacques Kallis** (157 not out) – to propel their side to a substantial 600 for 3 declared (the highest team total in all Tests between the two countries) and an eventual nine-wicket win.

Flower blossoms against South Africa

A truly outstanding performer for his country in a 63-Test, decade-long international career, Andy Flower seemed, at times, to provide the sole resistance for Zimbabwe in matches against South Africa. In five Tests against them between 1995 and 2001 he scored 566 runs (with two centuries, two half-centuries and a highest score of 199 not out, at Harare in September 2001) at an average of 70.75 – the highest by any batsman to complete ten or more innings in matches between the two countries.

OVERALL SERIES RECORDS

(7 Tests between 1995 and 2005)

	W	L	T	D	W/L	%W	%L	%D
South Africa	6	0	0	1	-	85.71	0.00	14.29
Zimbabwe	0	6	0	1	0.00	0.00	85.71	14.29

First match: 13–16 October 1995, Harare, Zimbabwe

MOST RUNS: TOP 5

Pos	Player	Runs
1	J.H. Kallis (South Africa, 1999–2005)	679
2	A. Flower (Zimbabwe, 1995–2001)	566
3	G. Kirsten (South Africa, 1995–2001)	330
4	H. Masakadza (Zimbabwe, 2001–05)	278
5	H.H. Gibbs (South Africa, 2001–05)	276

MOST WICKETS: TOP 5

Pos	Player	Wickets
1	S.M. Pollock (South Africa, 1999–2005)	23
2	J.H. Kallis (South Africa, 1999–2005)	21
3	A.A. Donald (South Africa, 1995–99)	14
4	C.W. Henderson (South Africa, 2001)	11
5	B.C. Strang (Zimbabwe, 1995–99)	9
=	A. Nel (South Africa, 2001–05)	9
=	M. Zondeki (South Africa, 2005)	9

Donald at his destructive best

A blistering performance from **Allan Donald** with the ball in Zimbabwe's second innings paved the way for South Africa's victory in October 1995 at Harare. The legendary fast bowler took 8 for 71 (the best single-innings figures in South Africa-Zimbabwe Tests) to skittle Zimbabwe for 283 and leave South Africa requiring a mere 108 runs for victory; a target they achieved for the loss of three wickets. Donald's match haul (11 for 113) is also a record in South Africa-Zimbabwe matches.

ZIMBABWE v ENGLAND

A record of three victories by an innings and no defeats in the six Test matches they played against Zimbabwe between 1996 and 2000 suggests a complete English dominance over Zimbabwe, but, on occasion, particularly in home Tests, the southern Africans more than held their own.

Johnson's headline-grabbing debut

Richard Johnson made a sensational debut for England against Zimbabwe in the first-ever Test match played at Chester-le-Street in June 2003: he took two wickets in his first over and ended up with figures of 6 for 33 – the best single-innings figures in all England-Zimbabwe matches – as the home side went on to win the match by a innings and 69 runs.

Goodwin shows Zimbabwe the way

Following a comprehensive defeat at Lord's in the first match of the 2000 series, Zimbabwe showed considerable fight in the rain-affected and drawn Second Test at Trent Bridge, and no one more so than Murray Goodwin. The middle-order batsman hit 148 not out in Zimbabwe's first innings, the highest individual score in all Tests between the two countries.

England cash in at Lord's

An undisciplined performance in the field by Zimbabwe allowed England to lay the foundations for an impressive victory inside three days in the First Test of the 2003 series at Lord's. Aided by Mark Butcher's 256-ball 137, and some unforgivably loose bowling from the visitors, the home side reached 472 all out – the highest team total in all matches between the two countries. They then bowled out Zimbabwe twice (for 147 and 233) to win the match by an innings and 92 runs.

All at sea at the home of cricket

Lord's has been a far from happy hunting ground for Zimbabwe – they have played there twice over the years and lost both matches by an innings – but their first visit to the home of cricket, in May 2000, will revive particularly painful memories for the southern Africans. After losing the toss and being put in to bat, they collapsed to 83 all out in 30.3 overs (the lowest-ever total in Zimbabwe-England matches).

OVERALL SERIES RECORDS

(6 Tests between 1996 and 2003)

	W	L	T	D	W/L	%W	%L	%D
Zimbabwe	0	3	0	3	0.00	0.00	50.00	50.00
England	3	0	0	3	-	50.00	0.00	50.00

First match: 18–22 December 1996, Bulawayo, Zimbabwe

MOST RUNS: TOP 5

Pos	Player	Runs
1	**A.J. Stewart** (England, 1996–2003)	483
2	M.A. Atherton (England, 1996–2000)	259
3	N.V. Knight (England, 1996–2000)	248
4	A. Flower (Zimbabwe, 1996–2000)	200
5	N. Hussain (England, 1996–2003)	198

MOST WICKETS: TOP 5

Pos	Player	Wickets
1	**H.H. Streak** (Zimbabwe, 1996–2003)	24
2	D. Gough (England, 1996–2000)	16
3	G.J. Whittall (Zimbabwe, 1996–2000)	13
4	J.M. Anderson (England, 2003)	11
5	P.A. Strang (Zimbabwe, 1996)	10

ZIMBABWE v AUSTRALIA

Australia simply proved too strong for Zimbabwe: the two countries contested only three Test matches between 1999 and 2003 and the Australians won them all, producing some record-breaking performances along the way.

Hayden heroics light up Perth

Matthew Hayden grabbed the headlines in the First Test against Zimbabwe at Perth in October 2003. The Queensland opener, who was nursing a sore back, occupied the crease for ten hours and 22 minutes, faced 437 balls and celebrated wildly as he hit 380 runs to break Brian Lara's record for the highest score in Test cricket (a record Lara would regain seven months later). Hayden's dismissal prompted an Australian declaration: on 735 for 6 – the second-highest team total in Australia's history and the highest in all Australia-Zimbabwe matches.

Part-time bowler Katich steals the show

He went on to become an established presence at the top of the Australian order, but early in his Test career Simon Katich hit the headlines for his part-time left-arm leg-break bowling. In the Second Test against Zimbabwe at Sydney in October 2003, he took 6 for 65 in the second innings (the best bowling figures in Tests between the two countries) to help set up a nine-wicket victory for Australia. Katich also holds the record for the best match figures (6 for 90) – shared with Glenn McGrath, who achieved the feat at Harare in October 1999.

OVERALL SERIES RECORDS

(3 Tests between 1999 and 2003)

	W	L	T	D	W/L	%W	%L	%D
Zimbabwe	0	3	0	0	0.00	0.00	100.00	0.00
Australia	3	0	0	0	-	100.00	0.00	0.00

First match: 14–17 October 1999, Harare, Zimbabwe

MOST RUNS: TOP 5

Pos	Player	Runs
1	M.L. Hayden (Australia, 2003)	501
2	R.T. Ponting (Australia, 1999–2003)	290
=	S.R. Waugh (Australia, 1999–2003)	290
4	T.R. Gripper (Zimbabwe, 1999–2003)	179
5	M.A. Vermeulen (Zimbabwe, 2003)	166

Zimbabwe's highs and lows

The root of Zimbabwe's problems in Test matches against Australia has been their batsmen's inability to amass a total of any real significance: their highest total (321) came after Australia had smashed 735 runs of their own at Perth in October 2003; their lowest effort (194) came in the first-ever match between the two sides at Harare in October 1999.

MOST WICKETS: TOP 5

Pos	Player	Wickets
1	**A.J. Bichel** (Australia, 2003)	10
2	H.H. Streak (Zimbabwe, 1999–2003)	7
3	G.D. McGrath (Australia, 1999)	6
=	S.K. Warne (Australia, 1999)	6
=	S.M. Katich (Australia, 2003)	6
=	B. Lee (Australia, 2003)	6
=	R.W. Price (Zimbabwe, 2003)	6

W. INDIES V ZIMBABWE

Despite their ever-increasing woes against the strongest cricketing nations since the turn of the new millennium, the West Indies enjoyed playing against Zimbabwe. In the eight matches between the two countries since they met for the first time in 2000, the men from the Caribbean proved too strong for the southern Africans, winning six of them and drawing the other two.

Batting masterclass from Lara

An imperious innings by Brian Lara ultimately proved the difference between the two sides in the Second Test between Zimbabwe and the West Indies at Bulawayo in November 2003. The masterful left-hander crafted a brilliant 191 off 203 balls – the highest individual score in West Indies-Zimbabwe Tests – in a match the West Indies went on to win by 128 runs.

OVERALL SERIES RECORDS

(8 Tests between 1996 and 2013)

	W	L	T	D	W/L	%W	%L	%D
West Indies	6	0	0	2	-	75.00	0.00	25.00
Zimbabwe	0	6	0	2	0.00	0.00	75.00	25.00

First match: 16–20 March 2000, Port of Spain, Trinidad

MOST RUNS: TOP 5

Pos	Player	Runs
1	C.H. Gayle (WI, 2000–13)	498
2	S. Chanderpaul (WI, 2000–13)	393
3	C.B. Wishart (Zimbabwe, 2001–03)	331
4	R.R. Sarwan (West Indies, 2001–03)	297
5	H.H. Streak (Zimbabwe, 2000–03)	288

MOST WICKETS: TOP 5

Pos	Player	Wickets
1	R.W. Price (Zim, 2001–13)	24
2	H.H. Streak (Zim, 2000–03)	21
3	S. Shillingford (WI, 2013)	19
4	R.D. King (WI, 2000–01)	16
5	N.C. McGarrell (WI, 2001)	12
=	C.E.L. Stuart (WI, 2001)	12

Record-breaking rescue act

Trailing by 216 runs at the start of their second innings, Zimbabwe needed to produce an innings of huge proportions to avoid crashing to a second successive heavy defeat in the two-Test 2001 series at Harare. And they did: led by Hamilton Masakadza's 316-ball 119, and bolstered by late-order contributions from Heath Streak (83 not out) and Andy Blignaut (92), Zimbabwe battled to 563 for 9. The highest team total in all matches between the two countries enabled Zimbabwe to evade defeat for the first time against the West Indies.

Price is spot on

An impressive left-arm spinner who played 22 Tests for Zimbabwe between 1999 and 2013, **Ray Price** was at his best in the two-match series against the West Indies in November 2003. He took 6 for 73 (the best single-innings figures in West Indies-Zimbabwe matches) and 4 for 88 in the drawn First Test at Harare (his match figures of 10 for 161 are also a record in Tests between the two countries) and 5 for 199 and 4 for 36 in a losing cause in the Second Test at Bulawayo. His series haul of 24 wickets is another West Indies-Zimbabwe record.

The worst of starts

Zimbabwe crashed to a morale-crushing defeat in their first-ever Test match against the West Indies, at Port of Spain, Trinidad, in March 2000. Chasing a mere 99 runs for victory, they slumped to 63 all out – the lowest-ever total in West Indies-Zimbabwe Tests.

BANGLADESH v INDIA

India, Bangladesh's first-ever opponents in Test cricket, have dominated the few Test matches played against their subcontinental neighbours, winning six of the seven Tests played (all of them in Bangladesh) and drawing just once.

OVERALL SERIES RECORDS

(7 Tests between 2000 and 2010)

	W	L	T	D	W/L	%W	%L	%D
Bangladesh	0	6	0	1	0.00	0.00	85.71	14.29
India	6	0	0	1	-	85.71	0.00	14.29

First match: 10–13 November 2000, Dhaka, Bangladesh

MOST RUNS: TOP 5

Pos	Player	Runs
1	S.R. Tendulkar (India, 2000–10)	820
2	R. Dravid (India, 2000–10)	560
3	Mohammad Ashraful (Bangladesh, 2004–10)	386
4	G. Gambhir (India, 2004–10)	381
5	S.C. Ganguly (India, 2000–07)	371

MOST WICKETS: TOP 5

Pos	Player	Wickets
1	**Z. Khan** (India, 2000–10)	31
2	I.K. Pathan (India, 2004)	18
3	Mohammad Rafique (Bangladesh, 2000–07)	15
=	A. Kumble (India, 2004–07)	15
5	Shahadat Hossain (Bangladesh, 2007–10)	12

Pathan plagues Bangladesh

Despite Sachin Tendulkar's star turn with the bat in the First Test against Bangladesh at Dhaka in December 2004, India would not have achieved their massive innings-and-140-run victory without Irfan Pathan's considerable efforts with the ball. The young pace bowler, considered by many to have the potential to become the best Indian fast bowler since Kapil Dev, took 5 for 45 in the first innings and 6 for 51 in the second to end the match with 11 for 96 – the best match figures in all Tests between the two countries. Seven wickets in the Second Test at Chittagong saw Pathan end the series with 18 wickets – another all-time Bangladesh-India record.

India prosper in Dhaka

Having suffered the ignominy of drawing the first of the two Tests in Bangladesh in May 2007, India bounced back in style in the Second Test at Dhaka. Bolstered by centuries from each of their top four batsmen – Dinesh Karthik (129), Wasim Jaffer (138), Rahul Dravid (129) and Sachin Tendulkar (122 not out) – they reached 610 for 3 declared (the highest team total in Bangladesh-India Tests) and went on to win by an innings and 239 runs – their largest-ever Test victory.

Bangladesh let it slip

A sorry second-innings batting display by Bangladesh saw them crash to a six-wicket defeat in the first-ever Test against India at Dhaka in December 2004. The home side crashed to 91 all out – the lowest-ever total in Bangladesh-India clashes.

Tendulkar top of the bill in Dhaka

It may have come against the weakest opponents he has encountered in his illustrious Test career, but **Sachin Tendulkar** cashed in with style in the First Test against Bangladesh at Dhaka in December 2004 to record the highest score of his career (and the best individual score in Bangladesh-India matches). The Little Master faced 379 balls (hitting 35 fours) to compile an unbeaten 248 in a match that India went on to win by an innings and 140 runs.

PAKISTAN v BANGLADESH

Bangladesh's early encounters with Pakistan were humbling – they lost their first three matches against them by an innings – but, although they have lost all eight of the Test matches played, recent encounters have been more competitive as Bangladesh slowly find their feet in the Test arena.

Yousuf shows how it's done

Mohammad Yousuf was in prime batting form for Pakistan in the Second Test of the 2001–02 series against Bangladesh at Chittagong, producing a masterful innings of 204 not out – the highest individual total in matches between the two countries – as Pakistan cruised to 465 for 9. In contrast, Bangladesh's batsmen were woeful, slipping to 148 all out in both innings to lose the match by an innings and 169 runs.

OVERALL SERIES RECORDS

(8 Tests between 2001 and 2011)

	W	L	T	D	W/L	%W	%L	%D
Pakistan	8	0	0	0	-	100.00	0.00	0.00
Bangladesh	0	8	0	0	0.00	0.00	100.00	0.00

First match: 29–31 August 2001, Multan, Pakistan

MOST RUNS: TOP 5

Pos	Player	Runs
1	Taufeeq Umar (Pakistan, 2001–11)	558
2	**Habibul Bashar** (Bangladesh, 2001–03)	554
3	Mohammad Yousuf (Pakistan, 2001–03)	503
4	Mohammad Hafeez (Pakistan, 2003–11)	418
=	Younis Khan (Pakistan, 2002–11)	418

MOST WICKETS: TOP 5

Pos	Player	Wickets
1	**Danish Kaneria** (Pakistan, 2001–03)	34
2	Waqar Younis (Pakistan, 2001–02)	18
3	Umar Gul (Pakistan, 2003–11)	22
4	Shabbir Ahmed (Pakistan, 2003)	17
=	Shoaib Akhtar (Pakistan, 2002–03)	17
=	Mohammad Rafique (Bangladesh, 2003)	17

Most wickets in a series

The record for the most wickets in a Pakistan-Bangladesh series is 17, a feat achieved by two bowlers: Shabbir Ahmed (Pakistan) and Mohammad Rafique (Bangladesh), both in the 2003 series in Pakistan.

Bangladesh lose their nerve

Leading Pakistan by 66 runs after the first innings of the Second Test at Peshawar in August 2003, Bangladesh were in a strong position to win the match. But instead of pushing on to gain a first-ever victory over their subcontinental cousins, Bangladesh's batmen lost their nerve and crashed to 96 all out – the lowest total in all matches between the two sides – and a Test match they should have won was eventually lost by nine wickets.

Kaneria cashes in

One of only four Pakistan bowlers in history to take more than 250 Test wickets (254), **Danish Kaneria** has enjoyed some fine moments against Bangladesh. In the first-ever Test between the two countries at Multan in August 2001 he took 6 for 42 in the first innings and 6 for 52 in the second – his match haul of 12 for 94 is the best in all matches between the two countries – as Pakistan cruised to an innings-and-264-run victory; five months later, in Dhaka, he took 7 for 77 – the best single-innings figures in Pakistan-Bangladesh Tests.

NZ v BANGLADESH

New Zealand have dominated Bangladesh in comprehensive fashion since the two countries met for the first time at Hamilton in December 2001, winning eight of the 11 matches played – five of them by an innings – with three of the matches ending a draw.

Shakib puts New Zealand in a spin

That New Zealand won the First Test of the 2008–09 series at Chittagong by just three wickets shows both how much Bangladesh have improved in Test cricket and how much pressure New Zealand were under following a fine spell of bowling from Shakib Al Hasan. The Bangladesh left-arm spinner took 7 for 36 in New Zealand's first innings – the best single-innings figures in all Tests between the two countries – to guide his side to a 74-run first-innings lead, a position which, ultimately, they ended up squandering.

OVERALL SERIES RECORDS

(11 Tests between 2001 and 2013)

	W	L	T	D	W/L	%W	%L	%D
New Zealand	8	0	0	3	-	72.73	0.00	27.27
Bangladesh	0	8	0	3	0.00	0.00	72.73	27.27

First match: 18–22 December 2001, Hamilton, New Zealand

MOST RUNS: TOP 5

Pos	Player	Runs
1	**B.B. McCullum** (New Zealand, 2004–13)	558
2	Tamim Iqbal (Bangladesh, 2008–13)	536
3	Shakib Al Hasan (Bangladesh, 2008–13)	479
4	S.P. Fleming (New Zealand, 2001–08)	397
5	Mominul Haque (Bangladesh, 2013)	376

MOST WICKETS: TOP 5

Pos	Player	Wickets
1	**D.L. Vettori** (New Zealand, 2001–10)	51
2	Shakib Al Hasan (Bangladesh, 2008–13)	20
3	C.S. Martin (New Zealand, 2001–10)	19
4	I.E. O'Brien (New Zealand, 2008)	15
5	Mashrafe Mortaza (Bangladesh, 2001–08)	14

Fleming leads from the front

Having seen his side brush aside Bangladesh in the First Test of the 2004–05 series (New Zealand won the match at Dhaka by an innings and 90 runs), Stephen Fleming ensured his side carried the momentum into the Second Test at Chittagong. Leading from the front in imperious fashion, the Kiwi captain smashed 202 off 318 balls (the highest individual score in New Zealand-Bangladesh Tests) to help his side reach 545 for 6 declared (the highest team total in matches between the two countries) en route to a comprehensive innings-and-101-run victory.

The worst of starts

Bangladesh's batsmen were all at sea on a bowler-friendly surface at Hamilton against New Zealand in December 2001 – the first-ever Test between the two countries. Having seen the home side scramble to 365 for 9 declared in just 77.1 overs in an attempt to force a result, Bangladesh fell for 205 in the first innings and, following on, 108 in the second (the lowest total in New Zealand-Bangladesh matches) to lose by an innings and 52 runs.

Bangladesh bow to Vettori

Where Stephen Fleming, with his 202, was the star with the bat in the Second Test at Chittagong in October 2004, Daniel Vettori was New Zealand's hero with the ball. The slow left-armer took 6 for 70 in Bangladesh's first innings and 6 for 100 in their second to help bowl his side to an innings-and-101-run victory. His match figures of 12 for 170 are a record in New Zealand-Bangladesh Tests.

SRI LANKA v BANGLADESH

Those who argue that Bangladesh's elevation to Test status was premature could point to their performances against Sri Lanka. They have played 16 Tests against the Sri Lankans (more than against any other country) and have lost 14 of them – eight of them by an innings and one by 465 runs.

Super Sangakkara cashes in

Sri Lanka's almost-complete dominance in matches against Bangladesh – they have won 14 of the 16 matches played between the two countries (drawing the other two) – has often given their batsmen both the time and a free rein to post big innings. And no player has taken advantage of that set of circumstances more than **Kumar Sangakkara**. The silky left-hander has scored 1,816 runs in 15 matches against Bangladesh between 2001 and 2014 at an average of 95.57 and with a highest score of 319 (at Chittagong in February 2014). All are records in Tests between the two countries.

OVERALL SERIES RECORDS

(16 Tests between 2001 and 2014)

	W	L	T	D	W/L	%W	%L	%D
Sri Lanka	14	0	0	2	–	87.50	0.00	12.50
Bangladesh	0	14	0	2	0.00	0.00	87.50	12.50

First match: 6–8 September 2001, Colombo, Sri Lanka

MOST RUNS: TOP 5

Pos	Player	Runs
1	**K.C. Sangakkara** (SL, 2001–14)	1,816
2	D.P.M.D. Jayawardene (SL, 2001–14)	1,146
3	Mohammad Ashraful (Ban, 2001–13)	1,090
4	T.M. Dilshan (SL, 2005–13)	1,008
5	T.T. Samaraweera (SL, 2001–09)	600

MOST WICKETS: TOP 5

Pos	Player	Wickets
1	**M. Muralitharan** (Sri Lanka, 2001–09)	89
2	C.R.D. Fernando (Sri Lanka, 2002–09)	28
3	S.L. Malinga (Sri Lanka, 2005–07)	27
4	H.M.R.K.B. Herath (SL, 2005–14)	25
5	Shahadat Hossain (Ban, 2005–13)	24

Bangladesh spellbound by Murali magic

One of the arguments against **Muttiah Muralitharan** being the greatest spin bowler ever to play the game – despite his standing as Test cricket's all-time leading wicket-taker (with 792) – will be that he played the majority of his matches in favourable conditions and, in the case of Bangladesh, against favourable opposition. Murali has simply been too good for the Bangladesh batsmen – in 11 Tests he has claimed 89 wickets – and holds all manner of bowling records in matches between the two countries, including: the best bowling in a match (12 for 82 at Kandy in July 2007); the most wickets in a series (26 in 2007); and the best strike-rate (a wicket every 30.4 deliveries)

Sri Lanka cruise in Dhaka

The best way to lay down a marker in any series is to score big the first time you bat. Sri Lanka did just that in the First Test (of three) against Bangladesh at Dhaka in January 2014. Having dismissed the home side for 232, Sri Lanka duly piled on the runs. There was a double-century for Mahela Jayawardene (203) and centuries for Kuashal Silva (139) and Kithuruwan Vithanaga (103 not out) as Sri Lanka compiled a mammoth 730 for 6 declared (the highest total in all Tests between the two countries. A decisive blow delivered, Sri Lanka went on to win the match by an innings and 248 runs.

Colombo capitulation

Bangladesh's lowest point against Sri Lanka came in the First Test of the three-match 2007 series at Colombo: they fell to 62 all out in the first innings – the lowest total in all matches between the two countries.

S. AFRICA v BANGLADESH

Bangladesh have enjoyed no success in matches against South Africa: in eight matches played between the two countries since they met for the first time at East London in October 2002 they have lost every time – and on seven of those occasions they have lost by an innings.

OVERALL SERIES RECORDS

(8 Tests between 2002 and 2008)

	W	L	T	D	W/L	%W	%L	%D
South Africa	8	0	0	0	-	100.00	0.00	0.00
Bangladesh	0	8	0	0	0.00	0.00	100.00	0.00

First match: 18–21 October 2002, East London, South Africa

MOST RUNS: TOP 5

Pos	Player	Runs
1	**G.C. Smith** (South Africa, 2002–08)	743
2	J.H. Kallis (South Africa, 2002–08)	317
3	G. Kirsten (South Africa, 2002)	310
4	N.D. McKenzie (South Africa, 2003–08)	306
5	Habibul Bashar (Bangladesh, 2002–08)	301

MOST WICKETS: TOP 5

Pos	Player	Wickets
1	**M. Ntini** (South Africa, 2002–08)	35
2	D.W. Steyn (South Africa, 2008)	22
3	J.H. Kallis (South Africa, 2002–08)	17
4	Shahadat Hossain (Bangladesh, 2008)	15
5	M. Morkel (South Africa, 2008)	14

Hossein gives Bangladesh cause for hope

Although South Africa ultimately won the First Test of the 2007–08 series by five wickets, they did so only after Shahadat Hossain caused them to post their lowest-ever total against Bangladesh. The promising young fast bowler took 6 for 27 in the first innings – the best single-innings figures in matches between the two countries – to help dismiss the visitors for 170.

South Africa crush Bangladesh at Chittagong

Having won the First Test of the 2007–08 series against Bangladesh only by five wickets (thus losing their record of having won every match against them by an innings), South Africa would have been keen to reassert their total supremacy over Test cricket's newest nation in the Second Test at Chittagong. And so they did: **Graeme Smith** hit 232 (the highest individual score in South Africa–Bangladesh Tests) and Neil McKenzie 226 (the pair put on 415 runs for the opening wicket) to send South Africa on their way to a total of 583 for 7 declared (the highest in all matches between the two countries). South Africa went on to win the match by an innings and 205 runs.

Dreams dashed in Dhaka

After restricting South Africa to 330 all out in the Second Test of the 2003 series at Dhaka, Bangladesh were very much in the game, but any aspirations they may have had to win the match were soon dashed. In reply, they slipped to 102 all out – the lowest total in South Africa-Bangladesh Tests – and went on to lose by an innings and 18 runs.

Adams spins South Africa to victory

Paul Adams was South Africa's star with the ball as they crushed Bangladesh by an innings and 60 runs in the First Test at Chittagong in April 2003. The unconventional leg-spinner took 5 for 37 in the first innings and 5 for 59 in the second to record match figures of 10 for 106 – a record in South Africa-Bangladesh Test matches.

BANGLADESH v WEST INDIES

Bangladesh have enjoyed more success against the West Indies than against any other nation since their elevation to Test status in 2001, winning two of the ten Test matches played – both times, admittedly, against a much-weakened West Indies outfit.

OVERALL SERIES RECORDS

(10 Tests between 2002 and 2012)

	W	L	T	D	W/L	%W	%L	%D
Bangladesh	2	6	0	2	0.33	20.00	60.00	20.00
West Indies	6	2	0	2	3.00	60.00	20.00	20.00

First match: 8–10 December 2002, Dhaka, Bangladesh

Sarwan spearheads West Indies victory

The West Indies crushed Bangladesh in the first-ever Test between the two countries at Kingston, Jamaica, in June 2004. A brilliant unbeaten 261 from Ramnaresh Sarwan (the highest individual score in Bangladesh-West Indies Tests) led his side to 559 for 9 declared (another Bangladesh-West Indies record) and an eventual innings-and-99-run victory.

MOST RUNS: TOP 5

Pos	Player	Runs
1	S. Chanderpaul (West Indies, 2002–12)	627
2	Shakib Al Hasan (Bangladesh, 2009–12)	532
3	Tamim Iqbal (Bangladesh, 2009–12)	520
4	M.N. Samuels (West Indies, 2002–12)	486
5	R.R. Sarwan (West Indies, 2002–04)	450
=	D.M. Bravo (West Indies, 2011–12)	450

MOST WICKETS: TOP 5

Pos	Player	Wickets
1	P.T. Collins (West Indies, 2002–04)	26
2	Shakib Al Hasan (Bangladesh, 2009–11)	23
3	D.J.G. Sammy (West Indies, 2009–11)	16
4	K.A.J. Roach (West Indies, 2009–11)	14
5	J.J.C. Lawson (West Indies, 2002–04)	13

AUSTRALIA v BANGLADESH

In Test matches played between the two countries, both at home and away, Bangladesh have proved no match for Australia, losing four Tests out of four, three of them by an innings.

OVERALL SERIES RECORDS

(4 Tests between 2003 and 2006)

	W	L	T	D	W/L	%W	%L	%D
Australia	4	0	0	0	-	100.00	0.00	0.00
Bangladesh	0	4	0	0	0.00	0.00	100.00	0.00

First match: 18–20 July 2003, Darwin, Australia

Gillespie's golden innings

It was the most unexpected performance in Test cricket in recent memory. Coming in as a nightwatchman, Jason Gillespie ended the first day of the Second Test against Bangladesh at Chittagong in April 2006 on 5 not out. Three days later, remarkably, he was still batting, reaching 201 not out (the highest score by a nightwatchman in Test history and the highest individual score in Bangladesh-Australia clashes) before Australia declared on 581 for 4. Gillespie's performance was a match-winning one: the visitors went on to win the match by an innings and 80 runs.

MOST RUNS: TOP 5

Pos	Player	Runs
1	D.S. Lehmann (Australia, 2003)	287
2	Habibul Bashar (Bangladesh, 2003–06)	282
3	R.T. Ponting (Australia, 2003–06)	260
4	S.R. Waugh (Australia, 2003)	256
5	Shahriar Nafees (Bangladesh, 2006)	250

MOST WICKETS: TOP 5

Pos	Player	Wickets
1	S.C.G. MacGill (Australia, 2003–06)	33
2	J.N. Gillespie (Australia, 2003–06)	19
3	S.K. Warne (Australia, 2006)	11
=	Mohammad Rafique (Bangladesh, 2006)	11
5	B. Lee (Australia, 2003–06)	8

BANGLADESH v ENGLAND

Such has been England's dominance over Bangladesh – they have won all six of the Test matches played with ease – that they now see matches against Test cricket's new boys as an opportunity to rest some of their star players in what has become an increasingly congested international schedule.

HIGHS AND LOWS

Highest score (team): 599 for 6 dec – England v Bangladesh at Chittagong in March 2010

Lowest score (team): 104 all out – Bangladesh v England at Chester-le-Street in June 2005

OVERALL SERIES RECORDS

(8 Tests between 2003 and 2010)

	W	L	T	D	W/L	%W	%L	%D
Bangladesh	0	8	0	0	0.00	0.00	100.00	0.00
England	8	0	0	0	-	100.00	0.00	0.00

First match: 21–25 October 2003, Dhaka, Bangladesh

MOST RUNS: TOP 5

Pos	Player	Runs
1	I.R. Bell (England, 2005–10)	633
2	M.E. Trescothick (England, 2003–05)	551
3	Tamim Iqbal (Bangladesh, 2010)	505
4	A.N. Cook (England, 2010)	401
=	I.J.L. Trott (England, 2010)	401

MOST WICKETS: TOP 5

Pos	Player	Wickets
1	M.J. Hoggard (England, 2003–05)	23
2	G.P. Swann (England, 2010)	22
3	S.J. Harmison (England, 2003–05)	19
=	S.T. Finn (England, 2010)	19
5	Shakib Al Hasan (Bangladesh, 2010)	17

Trott tears into Bangladesh

Jonathan Trott produced the standout performance in a commanding display by England against Bangladesh in the First Test of the 2010 series at Lord's. Coming to the crease with England, batting first after being put into bat, the Warwickshire no.3 batted beautifully, hitting 226 – the highest individual score in Bangladesh-England clashes – to lead his side to an imposing 505 all out. England went on to win the match by eight wickets to take a 1–0 series lead.

BOWLING BESTS

Innings: 5 for 35 – S.J. Harmison (England), England v Bangladesh at Dhaka in October 2003

Match: 10 for 217 – G.P. Swann (England), England v Bangladesh at Chittagong in March 2010

Series: 16 – G.P. Swann (England), England in Bangladesh in 2009–10

PART II: ONE-DAY INTERNATIONAL CRICKET

It was thought merely to have been a one-off arrangement, a means of appeasing a cricket-hungry public following a Boxing Day Test washout, but when Australia played England in a 40-over match at Melbourne on 5 January 1971, one-day international cricket was born, and how the public loved it; 46,000 paying spectators turned up to watch this new phenomenon, and, over the years, the limited-overs game has gone on to form an increasing part of a cricket fan's diet ever since. It is also the format used to decide the game's World Cup, the first of which was contested in 1975 (and which was won by the West Indies).

Detractors would suggest a cricket fan is force-fed limited-overs cricket: in the first five years of the 1980s, 402 one-day internationals were played, as opposed to 1,382 between 2000 and 2004 – more than three times as many. But one-day international cricket, particularly in the subcontinent, has become an essential asset for the game's finances – its continued popularity has made it international cricket's cash cow. How long that situation lasts, with the meteoric rise of the Twenty20 game, remains to be seen. The game's detractors will also point out that the abbreviated form of the game brings out the worst in players; that the need for quick runs leads to the breakdown of technique. Its enduring popularity, however, suggests the one-day international game is a platform upon which the best players can dazzle and the enormous success of the 2011 ICC World Cup suggests that the 50-over format of the game will be around for a long time to come.

India celebrate their triumph over England in the final of the ICC Champions Trophy held in June 2013.

ICC WORLD CUP

The fourth most watched sporting event on the planet, the ICC World Cup is international cricket's premier 50-over tournament. It has grown in stature over the years: the first edition, held in England in 1975, featured eight pre-invited teams; the 2011 edition, staged on the Subcontinent, featured 14 nations, including four teams that had come through a qualifying tournament.

Largest victories

By runs: by 257 runs – India v Bermuda at Port of Spain, Trinidad, on 19 March 2007 (India 413 for 5 off 50 overs; Bermuda 156 all out in 43.1 overs).

By wickets: by ten wickets on 11 occasions.

Smallest victories

By runs: by one run on two occasions – Australia v India at Chennai, India, on 9 October 1987; and Australia v India at Brisbane on 1 March 1992.

By wickets: by one wicket on four occasions – West Indies v Pakistan at Birmingham on 11 June 1975; Pakistan v West Indies at Lahore on 16 October 1987; South Africa v Sri Lanka at Providence, Guyana, on 28 March 2007; and England v West Indies at Bridgetown, Barbados, on 21 April 2007.

India too hot to handle for Bermuda

One of the consequences of the ICC's commendable drive to expand the World Cup and hand cricket's lesser nations a chance to compete on the international stage has been a growing number of mismatches. When India met Bermuda at Port of Spain, Trinidad, in the 2007 tournament, they eased to 413 for 5 off their 50 overs (with **Virender Sehwag** top scoring with 114) – the highest total in World Cup history – en route to a colossal 257-run victory.

Most matches lost

No side has lost more World Cup matches than Zimbabwe. In 51 matches between 1983 and 2011, the southern Africans have lost 37 matches and won just 10 of them (with one tie and three no-results).

That winning feeling

Three-time winners Australia are the most successful side in World Cup history: in 76 matches between 1975 and 2011, the men from Down Under have won a record 55 matches – 15 more than second-placed New Zealand (with 40).

ICC WORLD CUP WINNERS

Season	Winner	Host
1975	West Indies	(England)
1979	West Indies	(England)
1983	India	(England)
1987	Australia	(India/Pakistan)
1992	Pakistan	(Australia/New Zealand)
1996	Sri Lanka	(India/Pakistan/Sri Lanka)
1999	Australia	(England/Ireland/Netherlands/Scotland)
2003	Australia	(Kenya/South Africa/Zimbabwe)
2007	Australia	(West Indies)
2011	India	(Bangladesh/India/Sri Lanka)

Honours even

There have been four tied matches in World Cup history: Australia v South Africa at Edgbaston on 17 June 1999; South Africa v Sri Lanka at Durban in March 2003; Ireland v Zimbabwe at Kingston, Jamaica, on 15 March 2007; and **India v England** at Bangalore on 27 February 2011.

Runs galore in Bangalore

India were sitting pretty at the halfway mark, as Sachin Tendulkar's 98th international century (120) hoisted them to a healthy total of 338 all out against England in Bangalore at the 2011 World Cup. But comfort soon turned to growing unease as Andrew Strauss (158) led England's noble reply. A late collapse saw the match end in a tie (the fourth in the tournament's history), but it was also a record-breaking encounter: the 676 runs scored is an all-time ICC World Cup high.

Ireland fightback stuns England

When Ireland slumped to 111 for 5 in the 25th over in reply to England's 327 for 8 in the two sides' 2011 World Cup encounter at Bangalore, the match, it seemed, was running to a predictable script. England would gain momentum in the tournament with a comfortable win. Enter **Kevin O'Brien**. The Ireland No.6 bludgeoned a 63-ball 113 – he reached his century off 50 balls (the fastest in ODI history) – to propel Ireland to an unforgettable three-wicket win. England's total (327) is the highest by a team that has gone on to lose the match in the tournament's history.

Canada collapse at Paarl

Canada, making their first World Cup appearance since 1979, proved no match for Sri Lanka when the two sides met at Paarl, South Africa, in February 2003. After losing the toss and being put into bat, they crashed to a dismal 36 all out in 18.4 overs – the lowest total in World Cup history – with **Prabath Nissanka** taking 4 for 12. Sri Lanka eased over the winning line in 4.4 overs for the loss of just one wicket.

Coming back from the dead

When Zimbabwe crashed to 134 all out in 46.1 overs in their group match against England at Albury in 1992, only the most optimistic of their players would have harboured any hopes that they could end their 18-match losing streak in the World Cup stretching back to 1983. But, aided by a bowler-friendly surface, the southern Africans struck back in headline-grabbing fashion, bowling England out for 125 to win the match by nine runs. Their total is the lowest winning total by any side batting first in World Cup history.

ICC WORLD CUP LEAGUE TABLE (RANKED BY WIN-LOSS RATIO)

Pos	Team	W/L	Mat	Won	Lost	Tied	NR
1	**Australia** (1975–2011)	2.89	76	55	19	1	1
2	South Africa (1992–2011)	2.00	47	30	15	2	0
3	England (1975–2011)	1.56	66	39	25	1	1
4	West Indies (1975–2011)	1.52	64	38	25	0	1
5	India (1975–2011)	1.50	67	39	26	1	1
6	Pakistan (1975–2011)	1.38	64	36	26	0	2
7	New Zealand (1975–2011)	1.37	70	40	29	0	1
8	Sri Lanka (1975–2011)	0.96	66	31	32	1	2
9	Bangladesh (1999–2011)	0.47	26	8	17	0	1
10	Ireland (2007–11)	0.40	15	4	10	1	0
11	Kenya (1996–2011)	0.27	29	6	22	0	1
=	Zimbabwe (1983–2011)	0.27	51	10	37	1	3
13	United Arab Emirates (1996)	0.25	5	1	4	0	0
14	Canada (1979–2011)	0.12	18	2	16	0	0
15	Netherlands (1996–2011)	0.11	20	2	18	0	0
16	Bermuda (2007)	0.00	3	0	3	0	0
=	East Africa (1975)	0.00	3	0	3	0	0
=	Namibia (2003)	0.00	6	0	6	0	0
=	Scotland (1999–2007)	0.00	8	0	8	0	0

BATTING RECORDS

MOST RUNS: TOP 10

Pos	Runs	Player	Mat	Inns	NO	HS	Ave	100	50	0
1	2,278	**S.R. Tendulkar** (Ind, 1992–2011)	45	44	4	152	56.96	6	15	2
2	1,743	R.T. Ponting (Aus, 1996–2011)	46	42	4	140*	45.86	5	6	1
3	1,225	B.C. Lara (WI, 1992–2007)	34	33	4	116	42.24	2	7	1
4	1,165	S.T. Jayasuriya (SL, 1992–2007)	38	37	3	120	34.26	3	6	0
5	1,148	J.H. Kallis (SA, 1996–2011)	36	32	7	128*	45.92	1	9	2
6	1,085	A.C. Gilchrist (Aus, 1999–2007)	31	31	1	149	36.16	1	8	1
7	1,083	Javed Miandad (Pak, 1975–96)	33	30	5	103	43.32	1	8	2
8	1,075	S.P. Fleming (NZ, 1996–2007)	33	33	3	134*	35.83	2	5	2
9	1,067	H.H. Gibbs (SA, 1999–2007)	25	23	4	143	56.15	2	8	1
10	1,064	P.A. de Silva (SL, 1987–2003)	35	32	3	145	36.68	2	6	2

King of the big hitters

Renowned for the artful manner in which he constructs an innings and guaranteed to go down in history as one of the greatest batsmen cricket has seen, Ricky Ponting could also mix it with the game's biggest hitters in one-day cricket. In 46 World Cup matches for Australia between 1996 and 2011, the Tasmanian star has struck a tournament record 31 sixes, including a record eight against India in the 2003 World Cup final at Johannesburg.

Klusener crashes his way into the record books

In his early forays in first-class cricket, **Lance Klusener** was considered nothing more than a fast bowler who would bat at No. 11. However, he developed into an all-rounder of true international class and he was at his best in one-day cricket, where his clean ball-striking often gave his side late-order impetus. In 11 World Cup innings for South Africa between 1999 and 2003, Klusener scored 372 runs at an average of 124.00 with a strike-rate of 121.17 runs per 100 balls. Both are World Cup records.

Most World Cup career ducks

The record for the most World Cup ducks is five, held by two players: Nathan Astle (in 22 matches for New Zealand between 1996 and 2003); and Ijaz Ahmed (in 29 matches for Pakistan between 1987 and 1999).

World Cup final heroics

Six players have scored a century in an ICC World Cup final: Clive Lloyd, 102 for West Indies against Australia at Lord's in 1975); Viv Richards (138 not out for West Indies against England at Lord's in 1979); Aravinda da Silva (107 not out for Sri Lanka against Australia at Lahore in 1996); Ricky Ponting (140 not out for Australia against India at Johannesburg in 2003); Adam Gilchrist (149 for Australia against Sri Lanka at Bridgetown in 2007); and Mahela Jayawardene (103 not out for Sri Lanka against India at Mumbai in 2011). The first five instances saw the star performer end up on the winning side, but there was no such luck for Jayawardene. Despite his heroics, Sri Lanka crashed to a six-wicket defeat.

Six sixes in an over

The 29th over of South Africa's 2007 World Cup Group A encounter against Netherlands at St Kitts provided a moment of cricket history. **Heschelle Gibbs** became only the fourth man in the history of the game – and the first in either a World Cup match or a one-day international – to hit six sixes in an over. The unfortunate bowler was Daan van Bunge.

Most sixes in an innings

The most sixes hit in a single innings by a player is eight, a feat achieved by three players: **Ricky Ponting** (Australia) against India at Johannesburg on 23 March 2003; Imran Nazir (Pakistan) against Zimbabwe at Kingston, Jamaica, on 21 March 2007; and by Adam Gilchrist (Australia) against Sri Lanka at Bridgetown, Barbados, on 28 April 2007.

Kirsten cashes in

Gary Kirsten made a mockery of pre-match predictions that the wicket at Rawalpindi for South Africa's 1997 Group B match against United Arab Emirates, having remained under covers for four days because of rain, would be a bowler-friendly surface. The left-handed opener smashed an unbeaten 188 off 159 balls – the highest individual score in World Cup history – as South Africa romped to a 169-run victory.

Gibbs glorious in defeat

It was one of the most scintillating batting performances of the 2003 World Cup. **Herschelle Gibbs** thrilled the partisan Johannesburg crowd with a scintillating innings of 143 to help South Africa to an imposing 306 for 6 in their Pool B encounter with New Zealand. But then the rain came and, with its arrival, South Africa's fortunes changed. New Zealand, chasing a revised target of 226 from 39 overs, and propelled by an unbeaten 134 from captain Stephen Fleming – an innings that contained the most fours in World Cup history (21) – eased to victory with 13 balls to spare. Gibbs's effort is the highest score in a losing cause in World Cup history.

The record breaker

One of the greatest batsmen ever to play the game, India's Sachin Tendulkar has shone in World Cup matches. Having played 45 matches in the tournament between 1992 and 2011, he holds the record for the most runs (2,278), the most balls faced (2,560), the most centuries (6), the most half-centuries (15), and the most runs scored in a single tournament (673 at the 2003 World Cup). The Little Master finally got his hands on a winner's medal in 2011.

Fastest World Cup 50

Although Lou Vincent, with his 101, made the headlines after New Zealand's comfortable 114-run victory over Canada in the two sides' Group C encounter at St Lucia in the 2007 World Cup, it was **Brendon McCullum**, with his late display of power hitting towards the end of New Zealand's innings of 363 for 5, who found a way into the record books. The Kiwi keeper smashed a 20-ball half-century to close out his side's innings – it was the fastest 50 in World Cup history.

BOWLING RECORDS

MOST WICKETS

Pos	Wkts	Player	Mat	O	M	R	BB	Ave	Econ	SR	4w	5w
1	71	G.D. McGrath (Aus, 1996–2007)	39	325.5	42	1292	7/15	18.19	3.96	27.5	0	2
2	68	M. Muralitharan (SL, 1996–2011)	40	343.3	15	335	4/19	19.63	3.88	30.3	4	0
3	55	Wasim Akram (Pak, 1987–2003)	38	324.3	17	1311	5/28	23.83	4.04	35.4	2	1
4	49	W.P.U.J.C. Vaas (SL, 1996–2007)	31	261.4	39	1040	6/25	21.22	3.97	32.0	1	1
5	44	J. Srinath (India, 1992–2003)	34	283.2	21	1224	4/30	27.81	4.32	38.6	2	0
=	44	Z. Khan (India, 2003–11)	23	198.5	12	890	4/42	20.22	4.47	27.1	1	0
7	38	A.A. Donald (SA, 1992–2003)	25	218.5	14	913	4/17	24.02	4.17	34.5	2	0
8	36	J.P.D. Oram (NZ, 2003–11)	23	182.2	21	768	4/39	21.33	4.21	30.3	2	0
9	35	B. Lee (Aus, 2003–11)	17	137.3	15	629	5/42	17.97	4.57	23.5	2	1
10	34	G.B. Hogg (Aus, 2003–07)	21	158.3	10	654	4/27	19.23	4.12	27.9	2	0

Snedden feels the heat

New Zealand's Martin Snedden felt the full force of a blistering England batting display during the two countries' Group A encounter at The Oval in the 1983 World Cup. The medium-pace bowler took two wickets but went for 105 runs off his 12 overs – the most runs conceded in an innings in World Cup history – as England compiled 322 for 6 (off 60 overs) en route to a comprehensive 106-run victory.

Bond's heroics all in vain

At the halfway stage of New Zealand's Super Six match-up against Australia at Port Elizabeth on 11 March 2003, the Kiwis were firmly in the driving seat after **Shane Bond**'s magnificent 6 for 23 – the best one-day international return for New Zealand – had reduced Australia to 208 for 9. But where Bond had prospered with the ball, his team-mates floundered with the bat, crashing to 112 all out in 30.1 overs – the Kiwis' lowest-ever World Cup total – to lose the match by 96 runs. Bond's return is the best spell by any bowler in World Cup history to end up on the losing side.

Super Glenn McGrath

Three-time tournament winner **Glenn McGrath** is the most successful bowler in World Cup history, with 71 wickets. The Australian paceman holds the record for the best figures in an innings (7 for 15 v Namibia at Potchefstroom on 27 February 2003), the best average (18.19), the most wickets in a single tournament (26 in the 2003 World Cup in South Africa) and for the most maidens bowled in a World Cup career (42).

Most five-wicket hauls

The record for the most five-wicket hauls in World Cup history is two, a feat achieved by five players: **Gary Gilmour** (Australia) in two matches in the 1975 World Cup; Vasbert Drakes (West Indies) in six matches in the 2003 World Cup; Ashantha de Mel (Sri Lanka) in nine matches in the 1983 and 1987 World Cups; Glenn McGrath (Australia) in 39 matches between 1996 and 2007; and Shahid Afridi (Pakistan) in 20 matches between 1999 and 2011.

Most four-wicket hauls

The greatest leg-spinner of all time, **Shane Warne** appeared in only two World Cups (he was sensationally dumped from Australia's squad for the 2003 tournament, and subsequently banned from all cricket for a year, after failing a drug test), but when he did play, he more than made his mark: in 17 World Cup matches between 1996 and 1999 he took a record four four-wicket hauls. Muttiah Muralitharan and Shahid Afridi equalled Warne's feat at the 2011 World Cup.

A giant for India

Zaheer Khan's first taste of the World Cup left a sour taste in his mouth: his first over in the 2003 final, the first of the match against Australia, went for 15, the tone was set and Australia romped to an imposing 359 for 2 – en route to a comfortable 125-run victory – with Zaheer conceding 67 off seven (a humiliating 9.57 runs per over). It was an experience that could have knocked lesser men out of their stride, but Zaheer took it in his stride, learned from it and has evolved into one of the deadliest fast bowlers on the ODI circuit; he was a cornerstone of India's bowling attack during the victorious 2011 campaign. In 23 matches in the tournament to date, the left-arm paceman has taken 44 wickets at a strike-rate of one wicket every 27.1 deliveries – the best by any bowler to have bowled 1,000 balls or more in World Cup history.

Lethal weapon

Poker-faced he may have been, but Andy Roberts was arguably the meanest and most deadly of all the great West Indian fast bowlers of the late 1970s and early '80s and played an integral role in his team's World Cup successes in 1975 and 1979. In a World Cup career spanning 16 matches between 1975 and 1983, the Antiguan paceman conceded 552 runs off 170.1 overs (taking 26 wickets) – his economy rate of 3.24 is the best by any bowler in the tournament's history.

Best economy rate in an innings by a bowler

It was the crowning performance of a commanding bowling display by England before rain robbed them of certain victory against Pakistan in the two sides' group match at Adelaide in the 1992 World Cup. As Pakistan floundered to 74 all out, England all-rounder Dermot Reeve bowled five overs for a mere two runs: his economy rate of 0.40 is the best in a single innings by any bowler to bowl five overs or more in World Cup history.

WORLD CUP HAT-TRICKS

Player	For	Against	Venue	Date
Chetan Sharma	India	New Zealand	Nagpur	31 October 1987
Saqlain Mushtaq	Pakistan	Zimbabwe	The Oval	11 June 1999
Chaminda Vaas	Sri Lanka	Bangladesh	Pietermaritzburg	14 February 2003*
Brett Lee	Australia	Kenya	Durban	15 March 2003
Lasith Malinga	Sri Lanka	South Africa	Georgetown	28 March 2007
Kemar Roach	West Indies	Netherlands	New Delhi	28 February 2011
Lasith Malinga	Sri Lanka	Kenya	Colombo	1 March 2011

* Remarkably, Vaas's hat-trick came in the first three deliveries of the match.

OTHER RECORDS

HIGHEST PARTNERSHIP BY WICKET

Wkt	Runs	Partners	Team	Opposition	Venue	Date
1st	282	W.U. Tharanga/T.M. Dilshan	Sri Lanka	Zimbabwe	Pallekele	10 Mar 2011
2nd	318	S.C. Ganguly/R. Dravid	India	Sri Lanka	Taunton	26 May 1999
3rd	237*	R. Dravid/S.R. Tendulkar	India	Kenya	Bristol	23 May 1999
4th	204	M.J. Clarke/B.J. Hodge	Australia	Netherlands	Basseterre	18 March 2007
5th	148	R.G. Twose/C.L. Cairns	New Zealand	Australia	Cardiff	20 May 1999
6th	162	K.J. O'Brien/A.R. Cusack	Ireland	England	Bangalore	2 Mar 2011
7th	98	R.R. Sarwan/R.D. Jacobs	West Indies	New Zealand	Port Elizabeth	13 February 2003
8th	117	D.L. Houghton/I.P. Butchart	Zimbabwe	New Zealand	Hyderabad	10 October 1987
9th	126*	Kapil Dev/S.M.H. Kirmani	India	Zimbabwe	Tunbridge Wells	18 June 1983
10th	71	A.M.E. Roberts/J. Garner	West Indies	India	Manchester	9 June 1983

Most catches in an innings

The record for the most catches in an innings is four, by Mohammad Kaif in India's Super Six match against Sri Lanka at Johannesburg on 10 March 2003. The feat helped India to victory by 183 runs.

Most World Cup catches

No fielder has taken more World Cup catches than Australia's Ricky Ponting. In 46 matches between 1996 and 2011 the Tasmanian has pouched 28 victims. He also holds the record for the most catches in a single tournament (11 at the 2003 World Cup in South Africa).

Most dismissals by a wicketkeeper

Adam Gilchrist was an outstanding performer with the bat for Australia during their period of World Cup dominance between 1999 and 2007 (they claimed three successive tournament wins), and his destructive hitting at the top of the order often propelled his side into an unassailable position. Gilchrist was also a mightily effective, and often underrated, performer behind the stumps. He holds the World Cup record for the most dismissals (52), the most dismissals in an innings (six v Namibia at Potchefstroom on 27 February 2003) and for the most dismissals in a single tournament (21 in the 2003 World Cup in South Africa).

Dravid and Ganguly show eases India to victory

Taking advantage of some undisciplined bowling, a batsman-friendly surface and some favourably short boundaries, **Rahul Dravid** and **Sourav Ganguly** were in record-breaking form in India's Group A encounter with Sri Lanka at Taunton in the 1999 World Cup. The pair added 318 runs in 45 overs for the second wicket – an all-time record for any wicket in one-day international cricket – to help their side to a comfortable 157-run win.

Best attended World Cup

The best attended World Cup in history was the **2003 tournament** held in Kenya, Zimbabwe and South Africa. A total of 626,845 spectators flocked through the turnstiles during the 52 matches played.

First World Cup match played under lights

The first day-night match to be played in World Cup history was the pool match between England and India at Perth during the 1992 World Cup. For the record, England won the closely fought match by nine runs.

Day-night cricket just arrived at the World Cup in 1992.

Most extras conceded in an innings

As expected, Scotland were comfortably outclassed by Pakistan in the two sides' Group A encounter at Chester-le-Street in the 1999 World Cup, losing the match by 94 runs, but indiscipline with the ball did little to help their cause. During Pakistan's innings, the Scots conceded a World Cup record 59 extras – five byes, six leg-byes, 33 wides and 15 no-balls.

Ponting sets a host of appearance records

Australia's Ricky Ponting holds the distinction of having played in more World Cup matches than any other player. The three-time tournament winner has played 46 games in the competition – 29 of them as captain (another all-time tournament record) – between 1996 and 2011.

Most matches as an umpire

Much-loved English umpire **David Shepherd**, whose death in October 2009 saddened the entire cricket world, holds the record for the most World Cup appearances as an umpire. The former Gloucestershire batsman officiated in 46 matches in the tournament, including the 1996, 1999 and 2003 World Cup finals.

Most World Cup matches staged

Headingley, in Leeds, England, has hosted more World Cup matches than any other ground in history. The home of Yorkshire CCC has staged 12 matches in the tournament between 1975 and 1999.

Most hundreds in a tournament

Big scores were the order of the day at the 2003 World Cup in Kenya, South Africa and Zimbabwe. The tournament saw a tournament record 21 centuries in the 52 matches played – the highest score was Craig Wishart's unbeaten 172 for Zimbabwe against Namibia at Harare on 10 February 2003.

MOST WINS AS CAPTAIN: TOP 5

Pos	Wins	Player
1	26	**R.T. Ponting** (Australia, 2003–11)
2	16	S.P. Fleming (New Zealand, 1999–2007)
3	15	C.H. Lloyd (West Indies, 1975–83)
4	14	Imran Khan (Pakistan, 1983–92)
5	11	A.R. Border (Australia, 1987–92)
=	11	W.J. Cronje (South Africa, 1996–99)
=	11	Kapil Dev (India, 1983–87)
=	11	G.C. Smith (South Africa, 2007–11)

ICC CHAMPIONS TROPHY

Played on a bi-annual basis and considered the second most important one-day competition in world cricket, the ICC Champions Trophy was first contested in Bangladesh in 1998 and has been held on six occasions. Australia (2006 and 2009) and India (2002 and 2013) are the tournament's only two-time winners.

ICC CHAMPIONS TROPHY WINNERS

Year	Winner	Host
1998	South Africa	(Bangladesh)
2000	New Zealand	(Kenya)
2002	India/Sri Lanka*	(Sri Lanka)
2004	West Indies	(England)
2006	Australia	(India)
2009	Australia	(South Africa)
2013	India	(England)

* The trophy was shared after the final was washed out by rain.

Maharoof mesmerizes West Indians

Bowling full and straight on a low, slow wicket at the Brabourne Stadium in Mumbai, Sri Lanka's Farveez Maharoof proved too much for the West Indies' batsmen in the two sides' qualifying group encounter at the 2002 ICC Champions Trophy. The paceman took 6 for 14 off nine overs – the best bowling figures in the tournament's history – as the West Indies slipped to 80 all out. Sri Lanka eased to victory in 13.2 overs with nine wickets in hand.

Highest individual scores

Two players hold the record for the highest individual score in ICC Champions Trophy history: New Zealand's **Nathan Astle**, 145 not out v USA at The Oval on 10 September 2004; and Zimbabwe's Andy Flower, 145 v India at Colombo on 14 September 2002.

New Zealand take advantage of Uncle Sam

New Zealand cruelly exposed a lack of depth in the USA's bowling attack in the Americans' first-ever match in the ICC Champions Trophy at The Oval on 10 September 2004. Batting first, the Kiwis – propelled by big innings from Nathan Astle (145 not out), Scott Styris (75) and Craig McMillan (64 not out) – amassed a mighty 347 for 4 off their 50 overs (the highest total in the tournament's history) en route to a crushing 210-run win – the largest in ICC Champions Trophy history.

Watson and Ponting crush humbled England

Propelled to a commendable 257 all out (after being on 101 for 6) by a battling 76-ball 80 from Tim Bresnan, England would have had high hopes of containing Australia in the two sides' ICC Champions Trophy tie at Centurion on 2 October 2009. But those hopes were soon dashed: Shane Watson (136 not out) and Ricky Ponting (111 not out) put on 252 runs for the second wicket – the highest partnership in the tournament's history – to ease Australia past the winning post with 8.1 overs to spare.

Most catches

Sri Lanka's Mahela Jayawardene is the leading fielder in all ICC Champions Trophy matches. He has bagged 15 catches in 22 matches between 2000 and 2013.

Most dismissals by a wicketkeeper

Kumar Sangakkara holds the ICC Champions Trophy record for the most dismissals by a wicketkeeper. The Sri Lankan gloveman has pouched 33 victims (28 caught and five stumped) in 18 matches in the tournament between 2000 and 2013.

Largest victories

By runs: by 210 runs – New Zealand v USA at The Oval on 10 September 2004.

By wickets: by ten wickets – West Indies v Bangladesh at Jaipur on 11 October 2006.

MOST RUNS: TOP 5

Pos	Runs	Player	M	I	NO	HS	Ave	BF	SR	100	50	0	4s	6s
1	791	C.H. Gayle (WI, 2002–13)	17	17	2	133*	52.73	891	88.77	3	1	1	101	15
2	742	D.P.M.D. Jayawardene (SL, 2000–13)	22	21	3	84*	41.22	875	84.80	0	5	0	79	6
3	683	K.C. Sangakkara (SL, 2000–13)	22	21	3	134*	37.94	957	71.36	1	4	2	68	0
4	665	S.C. Ganguly (Ind, 1998–2004)	13	11	2	141*	73.88	800	83.12	3	3	1	66	17
5	653	J.H. Kallis (SA, 1998–2009)	17	17	3	113*	46.64	843	77.46	1	3	0	63	9

MOST WICKETS: TOP 5

Pos	Wkts	Player	Mat	Overs	Mdns	Runs	BBI	Ave	Econ	SR	4	5
1	28	K.D. Mills (NZ, 2002–13)	15	112.3	7	483	4/30	17.25	4.29	24.1	2	0
2	24	M. Muralitharan (SL, 1998–2009)	17	134.1	11	484	4/15	20.16	3.60	33.5	2	0
3	22	S.L. Malinga (SL, 2006–13)	13	114.1	7	587	4/34	26.68	5.14	31.1	2	0
=	22	B. Lee (Aus, 2000–09)	16	123.1	6	591	3/38	26.86	4.79	33.5	0	0
4	21	G.D. McGrath (Aus, 2000–06)	12	102.0	13	412	5/37	19.61	4.03	29.1	0	1
5	21	J.M. Anderson (Eng, 2006–13)	12	101.2	6	457	3/20	21.76	4.50	28.9	0	0

Sorry USA collapse against Australia

On paper, the match between the USA and Australia at Southampton in the 2004 ICC Champions Trophy was always going to be a mismatch, and so it proved. Put in to bat, the USA were skittled for a paltry 65 all out in 24 overs – the lowest total in the tournament's history. Australia eased to the victory target with nine wickets and a colossal 42.1 overs to spare.

Most extras in an innings

India had an easy win over Kenya at Southampton in the 2004 ICC Champions Trophy, by 98 runs, but many questions would have been posed after their somewhat indifferent performance with the ball. During the course of the Kenyan innings, the Indians conceded a tournament record 42 extras – ten byes, nine leg-byes, a mammoth 19 wides and four no-balls.

Smallest victories

By runs: by five runs – India v England at Birmingham on 23 June 2013.

By wickets: by one wicket on three occasions – New Zealand v Sri Lanka at Cardiff on 9 June 2013.

Most successful captain

The only captain in the tournament's history to lift the cup on two occasions, Australia's **Ricky Ponting** is the most successful captain in ICC Champions Trophy history. The Australian skipper has led his side to 12 wins in 16 matches between 2002 and 2009.

ICC CHAMPIONS TROPHY LEAGUE TABLE

Pos	Team (Span)	Mat	Won	Lost	Tied	NR	%
1	India (1998–2013)	23	15	6	0	3	71.42
2	Australia (1998–2013)	21	12	7	0	2	63.15
3	New Zealand (1998–2013)	21	12	8	0	1	60.00
4	Sri Lanka (1998–2013)	24	13	9	0	2	59.09
5	West Indies (1998–2013)	24	13	10	1	0	56.25
6	South Africa (1998–2013)	21	11	9	1	0	54.76
7	England (1998–2013)	21	11	10	0	0	52.38
8	Pakistan (1998–2013)	18	7	11	0	0	38.88
9	Bangladesh (2000–06)	8	1	7	0	0	12.50
10	Kenya (2000–04)	5	0	5	0	0	0.00
=	Netherlands (2002)	2	0	2	0	0	0.00
=	USA (2004)	2	0	2	0	0	0.00
=	Zimbabwe (1998–2006)	9	0	9	0	0	0.00

ODI CRICKET

The first one-day international, a hastily arranged affair after rain washed out the Fifth Test of the 1970–71 Ashes series, was played between Australia and England at Melbourne on 5 January 1971. One-day internationals may not be universally popular, but since then they have become a mainstay of modern cricket: in 2009 alone there were 150 one-day internationals compared to 41 Test matches.

TEAM RECORDS: ONE-DAY INTERNATIONAL RESULT SUMMARY (BY COUNTRY)

Team	Mat	Won	Lost	Tied	NR	%
Afghanistan (2009–14)	31	17	14	0	0	54.83
Africa XI (2005–07)	6	1	4	0	1	20.00
Asia XI (2005–07)	7	4	2	0	1	66.66
Australia (1971–2014)	830	209	282	9	30	64.18
Bangladesh (1986–2014)	283	80	200	0	3	28.57
Bermuda (2006–09)	35	7	28	0	0	20.00
Canada (1979–2014)	77	17	58	0	2	22.66
East Africa (1975)	3	0	3	0	0	0.00
England (1971–2014)	616	299	289	7	21	50.84
Hong Kong (2004–08)	4	0	4	0	0	0.00
ICC World XI (2005)	4	1	3	0	0	25.00
India (1974–2014)	853	425	384	7	37	52.51
Ireland (2006–14)	82	37	38	3	4	49.35
Kenya (1996–2014)	154	42	107	0	5	28.18
Namibia (2003)	6	0	6	0	0	0.00
Netherlands (1996–2014)	76	28	44	1	3	39.04
New Zealand (1973–2014)	656	282	333	6	35	45.89
Pakistan (1973–2014)	817	437	355	8	17	55.12
Scotland (1999–2014)	66	24	39	0	3	38.09
South Africa (1991–2013)	504	310	174	6	14	63.87
Sri Lanka (1975–2014)	714	338	341	4	31	49.78
United Arab Emirates (1994–2014)	12	1	11	0	0	8.33
USA (2004)	2	0	2	0	0	0.00
West Indies (1973–2014)	713	365	316	8	24	53.55
Zimbabwe (1983–2013)	421	110	297	5	9	27.30

Largest victories

By runs: by 290 runs – New Zealand v Ireland at Aberdeen on 1 July 2008.

By wickets: by ten wickets on 45 occasions.

By balls remaining: 277 – England v Canada at Old Trafford on 13 June 1979.

Narrowest victories

By runs: by one run on 28 occasions.

By wickets: by one wicket on 55 occasions.

By balls remaining: off the last ball of the match on 35 occasions.

Namibia slump to record defeat

It was the biggest mismatch of the 2003 ICC World Cup. Batting first, defending champions Australia cruised to 301 for 6 off the 50-over allocation; in reply, Namibia, in the face of some fine bowling from **Glenn McGrath** (7 for 15), wilted to 45 all out in 14 overs – their innings, which lasted a mere 84 balls, is the shortest completed innings (by balls received) in one-day international cricket history.

HIGHEST TEAM TOTAL: TOP 5

Pos	Score	Team	Inns	Opposition	Venue	Date
1	443–9	Sri Lanka	1	Netherlands	Amstelveen	4 Jul 2006
2	438–9	South Africa	2	Australia	Johannesburg	12 Mar 2006
3	434–4	Australia	1	South Africa	Johannesburg	12 Mar 2006
4	418–5	South Africa	1	Zimbabwe	Potchefstroom	20 Sep 2006
=	418–5	India	1	West Indies	Indore	8 Dec 2011

LOWEST TEAM TOTAL: TOP 5

Pos	Score	Team	Overs	Inns	Opposition	Venue	Date
1	35	Zimbabwe	18.0	1	Sri Lanka	Harare	25 Apr 2004
2	36	Canada	18.4	1	Sri Lanka	Paarl	19 Feb 2003
3	38	Zimbabwe	15.4	1	Sri Lanka	Colombo	8 Dec 2001
4	43	Pakistan	19.5	1	West Indies	Cape Town	25 Feb 1993
=	43	Sri Lanka	20.1	2	South Africa	Paarl	11 Jan 2012

Tied matches

There have been 32 tied matches in one-day international cricket, most famously when **Australia tied with South Africa** in the 1999 World Cup semi-final to progress to the final.

Australia's record-breaking streak

Australia hold the all-time record for the most consecutive one-day international victories. Between 11 January 2003 (a seven-run victory over England at Hobart) and 24 May 2003 (a 67-run win against the West Indies at Port of Spain, Trinidad) they racked up 21 successive victories – a run that included success at the 2003 ICC World Cup. The record-breaking streak came to an end when they slipped to a 39-run defeat by the West Indies at Port of Spain on 25 May 2003.

Runs galore at Johannesburg

With the five-match series evenly poised at 2–2, South Africa and Australia put on a dynamic show of batting brilliance in the fifth and final one-day international at Johannesburg on 12 March 2006. Batting first, Australia romped to a mighty, and apparently match-winning, 434 for 4 off their 50 overs, helped by an innings of 164 from captain Ricky Ponting. Undaunted by the colossal total, however, South Africa, inspired by a sublime, stroke-filled, 111-ball 175 from **Herschelle Gibbs**, sensationally reached the victory target with one ball to spare. The total of 872 runs scored in the match is an all-time record in one-day international cricket.

Most consecutive defeats

Bangladesh's early struggles in the Test arena – they had to wait 35 Tests and four years three months before notching up their first victory – were replicated in one-day internationals. Between 8 October 1999 (a 73-run loss to the West Indies at Dhaka) and 9 October 2002 (a seven-wicket defeat by South Africa at Kimberley), they crashed to a record 23 consecutive defeats. Rain, rather than good play, finally brought the run to an end: their match against the West Indies at Chittagong on 29 November 2002 ended up as a no-result.

Most sixes in an innings

After rain had delayed the start of the third ODI between New Zealand and the West Indies in Queenstown on 1 January 2014, the match was reduced to a 21-over bash. The Kiwis smashed their way to 283 for 4 – an innings that included an astonishing, and record-breaking, 22 sixes (**Corey Anderson** hitting 14 of them during a 47-ball unbeaten 131. New Zealand won the match by 159 runs.

Chappell and Cosier's efforts all in vain

Greg Chappell (5 for 20) and Gary Cosier (5 for 18) created history against England at Edgbaston on 4 June 1977 – it is the only occasion in which two bowlers have taken five wickets in the same innings – but their efforts weren't enough to win Australia the match. England's bowlers rallied in spectacular style to dismiss Australia for 70 and secure a 101-run victory.

Crashing timbers

Having set New Zealand 260 to win the third one-day international at Albion, Guyana, on 14 April 1985, the West Indies' bowlers used the maxim "If you miss, I'll hit" to supreme effect: a record eight Kiwi batsmen were out bowled as the visitors slipped to 129 all out and a 130-run defeat.

Most ducks in a match

The headlines following the West Indies' 92-run victory over England in the **1979 ICC World Cup final** at Lord's were reserved for Viv Richards's stunning innings of 138 not out, but the match was also remarkable because eight batsmen in the match failed to score – an all-time record in one-day international cricket.

Most fours in an innings

Irritated at being asked by the ICC to contest two one-day internationals against the Netherlands hot on the heels of a tough tour of England, Sri Lanka unleashed their frustration in record-breaking fashion in the first of the two matches, played at Amstelveen on 4 July 2006. They smashed a one-day international record 443 for 9 off their 50 overs, an innings that included a remarkable 56 fours (50.56 per cent of their total runs) – another one-day record. Sanath Jayasuriya hit 24 of them in an innings of 157.

Most runs from fours and sixes in an innings

The record for the most runs from boundaries in a one-day international is 256, a feat achieved by two teams: Sri Lanka (43 fours and 14 sixes) v Kenya at Kandy on 6 March 1996; and Australia (43 fours and 14 sixes) v South Africa at Johannesburg on 12 March 2006. **Ricky Ponting** was South Africa's chief destroyer, hitting a majestic 164 with 13 four and nine sixes.

Runs galore in Nagpur and Lahore

Not too many centuries are scored in one-day cricket so when four are scored in a match it is a rare occurrence. It has happened only twice in ODI cricket. When Australia (Adam Gilchrist, 103, and Ricky Ponting, 124 not out) beat Pakistan (Ijaz Ahmed, 111, and Yousuf Youhana, 100) at Lahore on 10 November 1998; and when India (Shikhar Dhawan, 100, and Virat Kohli, 115 not out) beat Australia (Shane Watson, 102, and George Bailey, 156) at Nagpur on 30 October 2013.

History-making moment in Multan

Mohsin Khan (117 not out) and Zaheer Abbas (118) created a slice of history during Pakistan's 37-run victory over India in the second one-day international at Multan on 17 December 1982: it was the first time in one-day international history that two players from the same side had passed 100 in the same innings. The feat has since been repeated on 111 occasions.

ASSORTED BATTING RECORDS

Most batsmen reaching double figures: 10 – on four occasions
All 11 batsmen failing to reach double figures: two occasions
Most batsmen caught in an innings: 10 – on 15 occasions
Most batsmen lbw in an innings: 6 – on two occasions
Most batsmen run out in an innings: 5 – on ten occasions
Most batsmen stumped in an innings: 3 – on 15 occasions

Openers efforts not enough for Australia

Geoff Marsh (104) and David Boon (111) created history against India at Jaipur on 7 September 1986 – it was the first time in one-day international cricket history that both openers had scored a century in an innings (there have been 26 subsequent instances) – but it wasn't enough to win Australia the match. Chasing 251 for victory, India, thanks in no small part to Kris Srikkanth's 102, won by seven wickets with six overs to spare.

Assorted bowling records

Most bowlers used: 9 – on 13 occasions
Most bowlers taking wickets in a match: 12 – on four occasions
Most ducks in an innings: 6 – on five occasions

Most wides in an innings

The West Indies bowlers' radars were clearly malfunctioning in their Benson and Hedges World Series match against Pakistan at Brisbane on 7 January 1989: during the course of Pakistan's 258 for 7, they delivered a one-day international record 37 wides. Kenya's bowlers equalled the unfortunate feat in their match against Pakistan at Hambantota at the 2011 World Cup.

Most no-balls in an innings

A record number of no-balls (20) ultimately cost Pakistan victory against arch-rivals India in the first one-day international (of seven) at Karachi on 13 March 2004. Chasing 350 for victory, they ultimately fell six runs short.

BATTING RECORDS

MOST CAREER RUNS: TOP 10

Pos	Runs	Player	Mat	Inns	NO	HS	Ave	100	50	0
1	18,426	S.R. Tendulkar (Ind, 1989–2012)	463	452	41	200*	44.83	49	96	20
2	13,704	R.T. Ponting (Aus/ICC, 1995–2012)	375	365	39	164	42.03	30	82	20
3	13,430	S.T. Jayasuriya (Asia/SL, 1989–2011)	445	433	18	189	32.36	28	68	34
4	12,500	K.C. Sangakkara (Asia/ICC/SL, 2000–14)	369	346	37	169	40.45	18	85	14
5	11,739	Inzamam-ul-Haq (Asia/Pak, 1991–2007)	378	350	53	137*	39.52	10	83	20
6	11,574	J.H. Kallis (Afr/ICC/SA, 1996–2013)	325	311	53	139	44.86	17	86	16
7	11,512	D.P.M.D. Jayawardene (Asia/SL, 1998–2014)	412	385	38	144	33.17	16	71	27
8	11,363	S.C. Ganguly (Asia/Ind, 1992–2007)	311	300	23	183	41.02	22	72	16
9	10,889	R. Dravid (Asia/ICC/India, 1996–2011)	344	318	40	153	39.16	12	83	13
10	10,405	B.C. Lara (ICC/WI, 1990–2007)	299	289	32	169	40.48	19	63	16

The one-day international batting king

Sachin Tendulkar, known as the "Little Master", has truly lived up to his reputation in one-day cricket. A veteran of 463 matches (no player in one-day international history has played more), he has scored the most runs (18,426), has recorded the most centuries (49), the most scores of 50-plus (145), the most 90s (18), has been dismissed on 99 more times than any other batsman (3), and holds the record for the most runs in a calendar year (1,894) and the record for the most centuries in a calendar year (9).

Dhoni puts on batting master-class

It was an innings that confirmed India's **Mahendra Singh Dhoni** as a batsman of the highest class. With his side chasing an imposing 299 for victory against Sri Lanka in the third one-day international at Jaipur on 31 October 2005, Dhoni, batting at No. 3, struck an imperious, chanceless 183 not out in 145 balls to ease his side to a six-wicket victory with 23 balls to spare. It is the highest score by a wicketkeeper in one-day international history.

Misbah's steady hand crucial for Pakistan

Misbah-ul-Haq has been a calming influence on his occasionally volatile team; a player who provides consistency to what is a notoriously inconsistent team. And his middle-order runs have proved vital to Pakistan's. However, his dogged approach has seen him set a curious ODI record. Of all the players never to score an ODI century, he has scored the most runs: 4,527 in 146 matches between 2002 and 2014).

HIGHEST CAREER BATTING AVERAGE (MINIMUM OF 20 INNINGS): TOP 5

Pos	Ave	Player	M	I	NO	Runs	HS	100	50	0
1	67.00	R.N. ten Doeschate (Neth, 2006–11)	33	32	9	1,541	119	5	9	1
2	53.58	M.G. Bevan (Aus, 1994–2004)	232	196	67	6,912	108*	6	46	5
3	53.34	H.M. Amla (SA, 2008–13)	85	82	6	4,054	150	12	23	2
4	53.28	M.S. Dhoni (Ind, 2004–14)	243	214	63	8,046	183*	9	54	7
5	53.12	G.J. Bailey (Aus, 2012–14)	39	37	6	1,647	156	2	12	1

There's no place like home for Jayasuriya

After Sachin Tendulkar the most experienced one-day international cricketer of all time (444 matches) and the second-leading all-time run-scorer in the 50-over format of the game (with 13,428 runs), Sri Lanka's Sanath Jayasuriya has enjoyed considerable success at the R. Premadasa Stadium in Colombo. In 70 innings there between 1992 and 2009, the left-hander has scored 2,514 runs (with four centuries and a highest score of 130) – the most scored by a player at a single ground in ODI history.

Boom Boom Afridi

A compulsive shot-maker and clean striker of a cricket ball, Pakistan's **Shahid Afridi** is tailor-made for the shorter formats of the game. In 378 ODIs for Pakistan, ICC World XI and Asia XI between 1996 and 2014 he has scored 7,619 runs (at an average of 23.44 with six centuries) off 6,590 balls – the highest career strike-rate of any player to complete 50 innings in ODI history (115.61).

Hottest batting streaks

The record for the most centuries posted in consecutive innings is three, a feat achieved by five players: Zaheer Abbas (Pakistan) v India between 17 December 1982 and 21 January 1983; Saeed Anwar (Pakistan) v Sri Lanka, West Indies, Sri Lanka between 30 October and 2 November 1993; Herschelle Gibbs (South Africa) v Kenya, India, Bangladesh between 20 September and 3 October 2002; A.B. de Villiers (South Africa) v India (twice) and the West Indies between 24 February 2010 and 22 May 2010; and Quinton de Kok v India between 5 and 11 December 2013.

Hitting new heights

By 2012, **Sachin Tendulkar** held almost every cricket batting record in the book: he had scored the most runs in Test matches (15,470), the most runs in ODIs (18,426) and had hit more centuries in both forms of the game (100 – 51 in Tests and 49 in ODIs) than any other batsman in history. The Little Master set another record on 24 February 2010, when India played South Africa in the second one-day international at Gwalior. Opening the batting, Tendulkar smashed an unbeaten 200 off 147 balls (with 25 fours and three sixes) to become the first batsman to score 200 runs a in one-day international innings. Compatriot Virender Sehwag surpassed his total on 8 December 2011 when he scored 219 against the West Indies at Indore.

SCORING 100 ON DEBUT

Player	Runs	Balls	4s	6s	SR	Team	Opposition	Venue	Date
D.L. Amiss	103	134	9	0	76.86	England	Australia	Manchester	24 Aug 1972
D.L. Haynes	148	136	16	2	108.82	West Indies	Australia	St John's	22 Feb 1978
A. Flower	115*	152	8	1	75.65	Zimbabwe	Sri Lanka	New Plymouth	23 Feb 1992
Saleem Elahi	102*	133	7	1	76.69	Pakistan	Sri Lanka	Gujranwala	29 Sep 1995
M.J. Guptill	122*	135	8	2	90.37	New Zealand	West Indies	Auckland	10 Jan 2009
C.A. Ingram	124	126	8	2	98.41	South Africa	Zimbabwe	Bloemfontein	15 Oct 2010
R.J. Nicol	108*	131	11	0	82.44	New Zealand	Zimbabwe	Harare	20 Oct 2011
P.J. Hughes	112	129	14	0	86.82	Australia	Sri Lanka	Melbourne	11 Jan 2013
M.J. Lumb	106	117	7	2	90.59	England	West Indies	North Sound	28 Feb 2014

HIGHEST SCORE: PROGRESSIVE RECORD HOLDERS

Player	Runs	Balls	4s	6s	Team	Opposition	Venue	Date
J.H. Edrich	82	119	4	0	England	Australia	Melbourne	5 Jan 1971
D.L. Amiss	103	134	9	0	England	Australia	Manchester	24 Aug 1972
R.C. Fredericks	105	122	10	1	West Indies	England	The Oval	7 Sep 1973
D. Lloyd	116*	159	8	1	England	Pakistan	Nottingham	31 Aug 1974
G.M. Turner	171*	201	16	2	New Zealand	East Africa	Birmingham	7 Jun 1975
Kapil Dev	175*	138	16	6	India	Zimbabwe	Tunbridge Wells	18 Jun 1983
I.V.A. Richards	189*	170	21	5	West Indies	England	Manchester	31 May 1984
Saeed Anwar	194	146	22	5	Pakistan	India	Chennai	21 May 1997
C.K. Coventry	194*	156	16	7	Zimbabwe	Bangladesh	Bulawayo	16 Aug 2009
S.R. Tendulkar	200*	147	25	3	India	South Africa	Gwalior	24 Feb 2010
V. Sehwag	219	149	25	7	India	West Indies	Indore	8 Dec 2011

Afridi's spectacular entrance on to world stage

Pakistan's Shahid Afridi took the cricket world by storm. Playing in only his second one-day international, but batting for the first time (against Sri Lanka at Nairobi, Kenya, on 4 October 1996) in his fledgling career, the young star (aged just 16 years 217 days at the time) struck 102 off a mere 37 deliveries to record the fastest one-day international century of all time and become the youngest player in history to hit a century in the game's 50-over format.

Richards single-handedly flattens England

Viv Richards (right) produced a virtuoso innings to haul the West Indies into a commanding position in their one-day international against England at Old Trafford on 31 May 1984. While all around him wilted, the master blaster smashed a then one-day international record 189 not out off 170 balls to help his team to 272 for 9. His score remains the highest percentage of a team's total (69.48) in one-day history. And it was enough to secure victory: the West Indies went on to win the match by 104 runs.

Age no deterrent for Jayasuriya

Sri Lanka's **Sanath Jayasuriya**, the second-most capped one-day international cricketer of all time, proved age was no barrier when, on 28 January 2009, aged 39 years 212 days, he struck 107 against India at Dambulla to become the oldest centurion in one-day international cricket history. Sadly for the veteran, it did not turn out to be a match-winning contribution, as India cantered to victory with six wickets and 11 balls to spare.

Troubling the scorers

Kumar Dharmasena became an integral part of Sri Lanka's one-day set-up through his unorthodox, but highly effective, off-spin bowling (playing in 141 one-day internationals between 1994 and 2004), but it was his exploits with the bat that forced him into the record books: the right-hander went 72 innings before recording his first duck – an all-time record in one-day international cricket.

CARRYING BAT THROUGH A COMPLETED INNINGS

Player	Runs	Total	Inns	Team	Opposition	Venue	Date
G.W. Flower	84	205	1	Zimbabwe	England	Sydney	15 Dec 1994
Saeed Anwar	103	219	2	Pakistan	Zimbabwe	Harare	22 Feb 1995
N.V. Knight	125	246	1	England	Pakistan	Nottingham	1 Sep 1996
R.D. Jacobs	49	110	1	West Indies	Australia	Manchester	30 May 1999
D.R. Martyn	116	191	1	Australia	New Zealand	Auckland	3 Mar 2000
H.H. Gibbs	59	101†	2	South Africa	Pakistan	Sharjah	28 Mar 2000
A.J. Stewart	100	192	2	England	West Indies	Nottingham	20 Jul 2000
Javed Omar	33	103	2	Bangladesh	Zimbabwe	Harare	8 Apr 2001
Azhar Ali	81*	199	2	Pakistan	Sri Lanka	Colombo	16 June 2012

† not all ten wickets fell in the innings

Turner's one-day marathon

It was as much of a marathon innings as you could ever wish to see in a one-day international. Opening the batting for New Zealand against East Africa in the two countries' Group A encounter at Edgbaston in the 1975 World Cup, **Glenn Turner** batted through the entire 60-over innings to reach 171 not out – the 201 balls he faced is a record in one-day international cricket.

Boycott suffers unfortunate landmark

It may not have been the fastest of innings by today's standards (he faced 159 balls), but it was a record-breaking and match-winning one. Playing against Australia at The Oval on 20 August 1980, England opener Geoffrey Boycott became the first player (of 25) in one-day international history to be dismissed (caught Hughes, bowled Lillee) for 99. Buoyed by Boycott's performance, England went on to win the match by 23 runs.

FASTEST TO...

Runs	Player	Innings
1,000	I.V.A. Richards (WI);	21
	K.P. Pietersen (Eng/ICC)	
	I.J.L. Trott (Eng)	
2,000	H.M. Amla (SA)	40
3,000	H.M. Amla (SA)	57
4,000	H.M. Amla (SA)	81
5,000	I.V.A. Richards (WI)	114
	V. Kohli (India)	
6,000	I.V.A. Richards (WI)	141
7,000	S.C. Ganguly (India)	174
8,000	S.C. Ganguly (India)	200
9,000	S.C. Ganguly (India)	228
10,000	S.R. Tendulkar (India)	259
11,000	S.R. Tendulkar (India)	276
12,000	S.R. Tendulkar (India)	300
13,000	S.R. Tendulkar (India)	321
14,000	S.R. Tendulkar (India)	350
15,000	S.R. Tendulkar (India)	377
16,000	S.R. Tendulkar (India)	399
17,000	S.R. Tendulkar (India)	424
18,000	S.R. Tendulkar (India)	440

Sharma tears into Australia to set record

Rohit Sharma fell ten runs short in his pursuit of Virender Sehwag's all-time one-day international best score of 219 when he scored a magnificent, match-winning 209 (the second highest score in ODI history) against Australia at Bangalore on 2 November 2013. But the hugely impressive Indian opener's performance did outstrip that of his compatriot in one regard: Sharma's sensational 158-ball knock included 16 sixes – a record in ODI cricket, beating Shane Watson's previous record of 15 scored against Bangladesh at Dhaka on 11 April 2011.

BOWLING RECORDS

MOST WICKETS: TOP 10

Pos	Wkts	Player	M	B	R	BB	Ave	Econ	SR	4w	5w
1	534	M. Muralitharan (Asia/ICC/SL, 1993–2011)	350	18,881	12,326	7/30	23.08	3.93	35.2	15	10
2	502	Wasim Akram (Pak, 1984–2003)	356	18,186	11,812	5/15	23.52	3.89	36.2	17	6
3	416	Waqar Younis (Pak, 1989–2003)	262	12,698	9,919	7/36	23.84	4.68	30.5	14	13
4	400	W.P.U.J.C. Vaas (Asia/SL, 1994–2008)	322	15,775	11,014	8/19	27.53	4.18	39.4	9	4
5	393	S.M. Pollock (Afr/ICC/SA, 1996–2008)	303	15,712	9,631	6/35	24.50	3.67	39.9	12	5
6	381	G.D. McGrath (Aus/ICC, 1993–2007)	250	12,970	8,391	7/15	22.02	3.88	34.0	9	7
7	380	B. Lee (Aus, 2000–12)	221	11,185	8,877	5/22	23.36	4.76	29.4	14	9
8	378	Shahid Afridi (Asia/ICC/Pak, 1996–2014)	378	16,610	12,813	7/12	33.89	4.62	43.9	4	9
9	337	A. Kumble (Asia/Ind, 1990–2007)	271	14,496	10,412	6/12	30.89	4.30	43.0	8	2
10	322	S.T. Jayasuriya (Asia/SL, 1989–2009)	444	14,838	11,825	6/29	36.72	4.78	46.0	8	4

Imran stands tall as Pakistan falter

A magnificent spell of bowling from Pakistan's Imran Khan (he took 6 for 14 off his ten-over allocation) saw India crash to 125 all out in the opening match of the Four Nations Cup at Sharjah on 22 May 1985. But his magical performance was not enough to win his side the game: in reply, Pakistan slipped to 87 all out to lose the match by 38 runs. Imran's figures are the best by any bowler to end up on the losing side in one-day international cricket history.

Latecomer Harris makes his mark

He may have been a latecomer to the international fold (he was 29 when he finally made his debut for Australia), but, when fit (and numerous injuries have checked his progress), **Ryan Harris** has been the impressive spearhead of Australia's attack in all forms of the game – particularly in one-day international cricket. In 21 matches between 2009 and 2012, the Queensland tearaway fast bowler has taken 44 wickets at an average of 18.90 (with a best bowling performance of 5 for 19 against Pakistan at Perth on 26 January 2010), with a strike-rate of one wicket every 23.4 deliveries – the best by any bowler in one-day international cricket history.

Big Bird puts the breaks on opposition batsmen

There has perhaps been no more fearful sight for batsmen in cricket history: the 6ft 8in **Joel Garner** tearing into the bowling crease ready to unleash an array of searing, fast-paced deliveries from out of the clouds. And the man they called "Big Bird" was at his most potent in one-day cricket: in 98 matches for the West Indies between 1977 and 1987 he took 146 wickets for 2,752 runs at an economy rate of 3.09 runs per over – the best rate by any bowler to have bowled 1,000 deliveries or more in one-day international cricket history.

At the peak of his powers

Pakistan's most effective spin bowler of recent times, Saqlain Mushtaq enjoyed considerable success in the one-day arena. He reached the 100-, 150-, 200- and 250-wicket landmarks faster than any other bowler in history and enjoyed magical years in both 1996 (in which he took 65 one-day international wickets) and 1997 (in which he took 69 wickets – an all-time record number of wickets in a calendar year in one-day international cricket).

Record-breaking success at Sharjah

No fast bowler in history has taken more wickets in one-day international cricket than **Wasim Akram** (502 wickets in 356 matches), and the Pakistan paceman was supremely effective in his country's matches at Sharjah: in 77 matches in the emirate between 1985 and 2002 he took 122 wickets – the most wickets by any bowler at a single ground in ODI history.

A day to forget for Malinga

When he gets it right, Lasith Malinga is one of cricket's most potent bowlers; genuinely quick and with an almost unplayable in-swinging yorker, the Sri Lankan fast bowler has taken 185 wickets in 115 one-day international matches between 2004 and 2012. But even the best in the world can have a day to forget, and Malinga's nadir came against India at Hobart on 28 February 2012: his 7.4 overs went for 96 runs (12.52 runs per over) – the worst-ever economy rate in a one-day international innings.

New boy Edwards hits the headlines

Surprisingly trailing 2–1 in a five-match one-day international series against Zimbabwe in November 2003 the West Indies, desperate to change their fortunes in a match they had to win, handed young paceman Fidel Edwards his debut. It was a masterstroke: the Bajan took 6 for 22 not only to lead his side to a comfortable 72-run victory but also to record the best figures by a debutant in one-day international history.

Lacking the killer punch

A bowler who lacked the pace to make his mark in international cricket, Zimbabwe's Pommie Mbangwa holds the dubious record of having the worst career strike-rate of any bowler to have bowled 1,000 balls or more in one-day international cricket history. The medium-pace swing bowler took 11 wickets for his country in 29 matches between 1996 and 2002 at a strike-rate of a wicket every 124.4 deliveries

Magical McGrath propels Australia to victory

Glenn McGrath was in blistering form with the ball during Australia's successful campaign in the 1998–99 Carlton and United triangular series (which also involved England and Sri Lanka). The fast bowler took 27 wickets in 11 matches – the best by any bowler in history in a one-day tournament – at an average of 15.62 runs per wicket, with a best haul of 5 for 40 against Sri Lanka at Adelaide on 24 January 1999.

Miserly Simmons eases West Indies to victory

Phil Simmons's medium-pace swing bowling proved too much for Pakistan at Sydney on 17 December 1992: the West Indies all-rounder took 4 for 3 off his ten overs – the most economical figures ever recorded in a full spell of bowling in one-day international cricket – in a match the West Indies went on to win by 133 runs.

Vaas rips through Zimbabwe

Sri Lanka's **Chaminda Vaas** was inspirational against Zimbabwe at Colombo on 8 December 2001. The left-arm paceman took a wicket with the first delivery of the match and continued in a similar vein to help rout the visitors for the third lowest score in 50-over cricket (38 all out) and become the first, and to date only, bowler in one-day international cricket history to take eight wickets in an innings. He finished with the astonishing figures of 8 for 19 off eight overs.

BEST CAREER BOWLING AVERAGE: TOP 5 (QUALIFICATION: 50 WICKETS)

Pos	Ave	Player	Mat	Balls	Runs	Wkts	BBI	Econ	SR	4w	5w
1	18.84	J. Garner (WI, 1977–87)	98	5,330	2,752	146	5/31	3.09	36.5	2	3
2	20.11	L.S. Pascoe (Aus, 1977–82)	29	1,568	1,066	53	5/30	4.07	29.5	4	1
3	20.35	A.M.E. Roberts (WI, 1975–83)	56	3,123	1,771	87	5/22	3.40	35.8	2	1
4	20.50	B.A.W. Mendis (SL, 2008–14)	70	3,359	2,481	121	6/13	4.43	27.7	6	3
5	20.82	D.K. Lillee (Aus, 1972–83)	63	3,593	2,145	103	5/34	3.58	34.8	5	1

DEADLIEST BOWLER-BATSMAN COMBINATION: TOP 5

Bowler	Batsman	Span	Mat	Wkts	Ave	Ducks
Waqar Younis (Pak)	S.T. Jayasuriya (SL)	1989–2002	45	13	12.76	2
Wasim Akram (Pak)	D.L. Haynes (WI)	1985–93	41	12	16.91	1
S.M. Pollock (ICC/SA)	A.C. Gilchrist (Aus)	1997–2007	43	12	19.41	2
W.P.U.J.C. Vaas (Asia/SL)	S.P. Fleming (ICC/NZ)	1994–2007	29	11	10.09	4
W.P.U.J.C. Vaas (SL)	Saeed Anwar (Pak)	1994–2002	38	11	24.63	0

A poor day at the office

Australia's Mick Lewis had a day to forget as South Africa chased down a victory target of 435 to win by one wicket at Johannesburg on 12 March 2006. The fast-medium bowler went for 113 runs off his 10 overs – the most ever conceded by a bowler to bowl his full allocation of overs in an ODI.

Wasim provides glimpse into a glorious future

Playing in only his fourth one-day international for Pakistan (against Australia at Melbourne on 24 February 1989), **Wasim Akram** gave notice of the talent that would see him become the most successful fast bowler in ODI history. The left-arm paceman took 5 for 21 to become, aged 18 years 66 days, the youngest player to take five wickets in an innings in ODI history. Waqar Younis (18 years 164 days) broke the record (6 for 26 v Sri Lanka) on 29 April 1990.

Magic Malinga carves through South Africa

There have been 34 hat-tricks in the history of one-day international cricket, but there has been only one case of a bowler taking four wickets in four balls: **Lasith Malinga** dismissed Shaun Pollock (bowled), Andrew Hall (caught), Jacques Kallis (caught) and Makhaya Ntini (bowled) in successive deliveries during Sri Lanka's World Cup Super Eight match against South Africa at Providence, Guyana, on 28 March 2007, but still saw his side lose by one run.

Age no barrier for Dhaniram

Sunil Dhaniram created a slice of history during Canada's match against Bermuda at Ontario on 29 June 2008. The Canadian slow left-armer, playing in his 26th one-day international, took 5 for 32 to become, aged 39 years 256 days, the oldest player in history to take five wickets in an innings in a 50-over international. Sadly for Dhaniram, his record-breaking effort did not turn out to be a match-winning one: Bermuda went on to win the rain-affected match by 11 runs.

Breaking the mould

With his late reverse swing that was as likely to crash into the base of the stumps as it was to cannon into a batsman's foot, **Waqar Younis** set a new trend for fast bowlers. He was mightily effective in all formats of the game, but his record in one-day international cricket was truly exceptional: in 262 matches for Pakistan between 1989 and 2003 he took 416 wickets and broke the records for the most five-wicket hauls (13) and the most of four wickets plus (27). He is also the only bowler in one-day international cricket history to take three successive five-wicket hauls.

Most wickets taken...

Bowled: 176 – Wasim Akram (Pakistan, 1984–2003)

Caught: 290 – Muttiah Muralitharan (Sri Lanka, 1993–2011)

Caught and bowled: 35 – Muttiah Muralitharan (Sri Lanka, 1993–2011)

Caught by a fielder: 246 – Muttiah Muralitharan (Sri Lanka, 1993–2011)

Caught by a wicketkeeper: 93 – Wasim Akram (Pakistan, 1984–2003)

LBW: 92 – Wasim Akram (Pakistan, 1984–2003)

Stumped: 56 – Muttiah Muralitharan (Sri Lanka, 1993–2011)

Hit wicket: 3 – Courtney Walsh (West Indies, 1985–2000); and Wasim Akram (Pakistan, 1984–2003)

Most balls bowled in an ODI career

No bowler has bowled more deliveries in one-day international cricket than Muttiah Muralitharan, who bowled 18,811 balls for Sri Lanka in 350 matches between 1993 and 2011. The Sri Lankan spin maestro also holds the record for conceding the most runs in a career (12,326).

Leading from the front

Here's another in the long list of Waqar Younis' ODI records: as Pakistan captain against England at Headingley on 17 June 2001, he took 7 for 36 – the best bowling figures by a captain in ODI history – to lead his side to victory.

Lee makes his mark

One of the quickest bowlers on the international circuit since he made his debut in January 2000, Australia's Brett Lee, mainly as a result of a catalogue of serious injuries, never quite lived up to the hype his searing pace generated. However, he has been a very effective performer in all forms of cricket, particularly One Day Internationals. The New South Wales paceman reached both the 300 and 350-wicket milestones in fewer matches than any other player, in 171 and 202 matches, respectively.

Best bowler-fielder combination

The most successful bowler-fielder combination in one-day international cricket history is that between South Africa's Makhaya Ntini and Mark Boucher. The pair combined for 75 dismissals in 164 matches between 1998 and 2009.

FASTEST TO...

Wkts	Player	Matches
50	**B.A.W. Mendis** (SL)	19
100	Saqlain Mushtaq (Pak)	53
150	Saqlain Mushtaq (Pak)	78
200	Saqlain Mushtaq (Pak)	104
250	Saqlain Mushtaq (Pak)	138
300	B. Lee (Aus)	171
350	B. Lee (Aus)	202
400	Waqar Younis (Pak)	252
450	M. Muralitharan (Asia/ICC/SL)	295
500	M. Muralitharan (Asia/ICC/SL)	324

OTHER RECORDS

MOST CATCHES IN A CAREER: TOP 5

Pos	Ct	Player	Mat	Inns
1	202	D.P.M.D. Jayawardene (Asia/SL, 1998–2014)	412	407
2	160	R.T. Ponting (Aus/ICC, 1995–2012)	375	372
3	156	M. Azharuddin (Ind, 1985–2000)	334	332
4	140	S.R. Tendulkar (Ind, 1989–2012)	463	456
5	133	S.P. Fleming (ICC/NZ, 1994–2007)	280	276

A day to forget behind the stumps for Ashraf Ali

Forced to play second fiddle to Wasim Bari for most of his career, Ashraf Ali eventually played 16 one-day internationals for Pakistan between 1980 and 1985 but got his international career off to the worst possible start. In his debut match, against the West Indies at Sialkot on 5 December 1980, he conceded 20 byes – the most by any wicketkeeper in an innings in one-day international cricket – in a game the West Indies went on to win by seven wickets.

Electric Rhodes is the greatest fielder of them all

South Africa's Jonty Rhodes in full flight in the field was as majestic a sight as a bowler or batsman at the very top of his game: in short, he was the greatest fielder to play the game, and a record-breaking one, too. In South Africa's match against the West Indies at Mumbai on 14 November 1993 he took five catches – the most catches in an innings by a fielder in one-day international cricket history.

Most dismissals in a career for Gilchrist

The player who perhaps contributed more than any other to Australia's three successive World Cup triumphs between 1999 and 2007, **Adam Gilchrist** was as colossal behind the stumps as he was destructive at the top of the batting order. In 287 one-day internationals for his country between 1996 and 2008, he claimed a record 472 dismissals, with 417 catches and 55 stumpings.

Captaincy records

Australia's most capped player, Ricky Ponting led his country in a record 230 one-day internationals between 2002 and 2012. He is also the most successful captain in one-day international cricket history, recording 165 wins (a win percentage of 76.14). The record for most consecutive matches as captain is held by South Africa's **Hansie Cronje**: 130 between 6 December 1994 and 27 March 2000.

HIGHEST PARTNERSHIP BY WICKET

Wkt	Runs	Partners	Team	Opposition	Venue	Date
1st	286	W.U. Tharanga/S.T. Jayasuriya	Sri Lanka	England	Leeds	1 Jul 2006
2nd	331	S.R. Tendulkar/R. Dravid	India	New Zealand	Hyderabad	8 Nov 1999
3rd	238	H.M. Amla/A.B. de Villiers	SA	Pakistan	Johannesburg	17 Mar 2013
4th	275*	M. Azharuddin/A. Jadeja	India	Zimbabwe	Cuttack	9 Apr 1998
5th	226	E.J.G. Morgan/R.S. Bopara	England	Ireland	Dublin	3 Sep 2013
6th	218	D.P.M.D. Jayawardene/M.S. Dhoni	Asia XI	Africa XI	Chennai	10 Jun 2007
7th	130	A. Flower/H.H. Streak	Zimbabwe	England	Harare	7 Oct 2001
8th	138*	J.M. Kemp/A.J. Hall	South Africa	India	Cape Town	26 Nov 2006
9th	132	A.D. Mathews/S.L. Malinga	Sri Lanka	Australia	Melbourne	3 Nov 2010
10th	106*	I.V.A. Richards/M.A. Holding	West Indies	England	Manchester	31 May 1984

Most matches as an umpire

One of the most respected umpires in the modern game, South Africa's **Rudi Koertzen** has officiated in more one-day internationals than any other umpire. The former bank clerk, famed for his slow finger raise, stood in the middle on 209 occasions between 1992 and 2010.

The Little Master's other records

The leading run-scorer in one-day international cricket, **Sachin Tendulkar** also holds the record for the most consecutive matches played in the 50-over format of the game. The Little Master appeared in 185 consecutive games for India between 25 April 1990 and 24 April 1998. Tendulkar also holds the record for the most man of the match awards, with 62.

Perfect partners

The most productive partnership in the history of one-day international cricket is that between India's Sachin Tendulkar and Sourav Ganguly. The pair combined to score 8,227 runs in 176 innings for their country between 1992 and 2007, with 26 century stands at an average of 47.55 runs per partnership.

Master blaster Richards shows his all-round skills

Revered throughout world cricket for his power displays with the bat, Viv Richards was also a handy and effective contributor with the ball, particularly in one-day cricket. On 18 March 1987, playing for the West Indies against New Zealand at Dunedin, he hit 119 with the bat and then took 5 for 41 with the ball to become the first player in one-day international cricket history to hit a century and take four or more wickets in a match. The feat has since been repeated on ten occasions.

Tendulkar and Dravid steal the show

Sachin Tendulkar (186 not out) and Rahul Dravid (153) combined to stunning and record-breaking effect as India thrashed New Zealand by 174 runs in the second one-day international of the five-match series between the two countries at Hyderabad on 8 November 1999. The pair added 331 for the second wicket – the highest partnership in one-day international cricket history.

ICC TROPHY

First contested in 1979, the ICC Trophy is a one-day match tournament for non-Test-playing nations. In recent years it has gained extra significance: it serves as a qualifying tournament for the ICC World Cup – the 2009 edition of the tournament saw Ireland, Canada, Netherlands and Kenya qualify for the 2011 World Cup. Scotland won the trophy for the second time in 2013–14 in New Zealand.

ICC TROPHY WINNERS

Year	Winners	Host
1979	Sri Lanka	England
1982	Zimbabwe	England
1986	Zimbabwe	England
1990	Zimbabwe	Netherlands
1994	United Arab Emirates	Kenya
1997	Bangladesh	Malaysia
2001	Netherlands	Canada
2005	Scotland	Ireland
2009	**Ireland**	South Africa
2013–14	**Scotland**	New Zealand

Fun in the sun for MacLeod

Calum MacLeod was in supreme form with the bat as Scotland crushed Canada by 170 runs in the two countries' ICC Trophy clash at Christchurch, New Zealand, on 23 January 2014. The opener smashed 175 off 141 balls (with 14 fours and five sixes) as Scotland, batting first, compiled an imposing 341 for 9. MacLeod's knock is the best in ICC Trophy history.

Schiferli shines in SA

The Netherlands' march to third place at the 2009 ICC Trophy tournament in South Africa had much to do with the form of Edgar Schiferli. The right-arm medium-fast bowler took a tournament record 24 wickets in ten matches, with a best of 4 for 23 against Kenya at Potchefstroom on 19 April 2009.

Netherlands power past East and Central Africa

It took just 20.5 overs for the Netherlands to dismiss the challenge of East and Central Africa in the two sides' match at the 1997 ICC Trophy in Kuala Lumpur. After winning the toss and electing to bowl, the Netherlands dismissed East and Central Africa for a paltry 26 all out in 15.2 overs – the lowest team total in the tournament's history. The Netherlands reached the minimal victory target in 5.3 overs for the loss of two wickets.

Tau Ao hit to all parts of the ground

Papua New Guinea's Tau Ao bore the brunt of Canada's onslaught during the two sides' Group 2 encounter at Walsall in the 1986 ICC Trophy. As Canada reached an imposing 356 for 5, the Papua New Guinea opening bowler went for 116 off his 12-over allocation – the most runs conceded in an innings by a bowler in the tournament's history.

Longevity the key for Lefebvre

A player who performed with distinction in county cricket for a number of years (he played for Somerset and Glamorgan between 1990 and 1995), **Roland Lefebvre** put his skills to good use in the ICC Trophy for the Netherlands between 1986 and 2001. He holds the record for the most wickets in the tournament's history (71) and also for the most matches played (43).

Largest margin of victory

By runs: by 369 runs – Papua New Guinea v Gibraltar at Cannock on 18 June 1986.

By wickets: by ten wickets on 13 occasions.

By balls remaining: 337 balls remaining – Canada v Gibraltar at Swindon on 20 June 1986.

Smallest margin of victory

By runs: by two run – Bangladesh v Malaysia at Kidderminster on 28 June 1982; and PNG v Uganda at Dublin on 11 July 2005.

By wickets: by one wicket on eight occasions.

By balls remaining: off the last ball of the match on three occasions.

Kenya pay heavy price for indiscipline in the field

Perhaps the principal reason for Kenya's surprise 37-run loss to Papua New Guinea at The Hague in the two sides' 1990 ICC Trophy encounter was their record-breaking indiscipline in the field. During Papua New Guinea's innings (230 all out), the Kenyans conceded a massive 54 extras (16 leg-byes, 35 wides and three no-balls) – the most in the tournament's history. In reply, the Kenyans slipped to 193 all out.

Khurram Khan finds his form for the UAE

Khurram Khan's form with the bat at the 2013–14 ICC Trophy in New Zealand was a major factor behind the United Arab Emirates' best showing at the tournament since they lifted the trophy in 1994. The left-hander struck a competition record 581 runs in eight matches, with a best of 138 against Papua New Guinea on 26 January 2014.

Off to a flying start

Rene Schoonheim (117) and R.E. Lifmann (155 not out) provided the perfect platform for the Netherlands during their 125-run victory over Malaysia in the two sides' Group 2 encounter at Redditch in the 1982 ICC Trophy. The pair put on 257 runs for the opening wicket – the highest partnership in the tournament's history.

PNG hit the heights

Papua New Guinea were simply too strong for Gibraltar when the two sides met at Cannock in the 1986 ICC Trophy. Batting first, Papua New Guinea amassed a colossal 455 for 9 (off 60 overs), with B. Harry top-scoring with 127. In reply, Gibraltar wilted to a sorry 86 all out to lose the match by 369 runs.

Good things come to those who wait

A star performer for Barbados against the England tourists in 1973–74 (a match in which he hit an imperious 158), **Nolan Clarke** may not have reached the dizzy heights that many at the time predicted he would, but he did go on to enjoy a lengthy and successful career with the Netherlands. In 18 ICC Trophy matches for them between 1990 and 1994 he scored 1,040 runs (with a highest score of 154 against Israel at Amstelveen on 4 June 1990) at an average of 74.28 – the highest by any batsman to have scored 1,000 runs or more in ICC Trophy history. He also holds the tournament record for the most hundreds scored (five).

Khan records best single-innings bowling figures

Asim Khan was the main destroyer when East and Central Africa slipped to a record-breaking low of 26 all out against the Netherlands at Kuala Lumpur in the 1997 ICC Trophy. The Dutch paceman produced figures of 7 for 9 off 7.2 overs – the best in the tournament's history.

Mortensen makes waves with the ball

A burly seam bowler who performed with great success in county cricket with Derbyshire for over a decade, Ole Mortensen was an outstanding performer in the ICC Trophy for Denmark: in 26 matches in the tournament between 1979 and 1994 he set the all-time records for the best average (10.41), the most four-wicket-plus hauls (seven) and the best strike-rate (taking a wicket every 25.4 deliveries).

MOST RUNS: TOP 5

Pos	Runs	Player	Mat	Inns	NO	HS	Ave	100	50	0
1	1,369	Khurram Khan (UAE, 2001–14)	35	33	7	138	52.65	2	10	3
2	1,173	M.O. Odumbe (Kenya, 1990–97)	25	24	7	158*	69.00	3	6	1
3	1,048	S.O. Tikolo (Kenya, 1994–2014)	35	32	7	147	41.92	1	7	2
4	1,040	N.E. Clarke (Neth, 1990–94)	18	18	4	154	74.28	5	3	1
5	897	B. Zuiderent (Neth, 1997–2009)	24	22	9	119	69.00	3	5	0

MOST WICKETS: TOP 5

Pos	Wkts	Player	Mat	Overs	Mdns	Runs	BBI	Ave	Econ	SR	4	5
1	71	R.P. Lefebvre (Neth, 1986–2001)	43	334.4	72	827	5/16	11.64	2.47	28.2	1	1
2	63	O.H. Mortensen (Den, 1979–94)	26	267.4	52	656	7/19	10.41	2.45	25.4	6	1
3	50	J.A.R. Blain (Scotland, 1997–2009)	27	227.3	22	997	5/45	19.94	4.38	27.3	2	1
4	48	A.Y. Karim (Kenya, 1986–97)	30	261.1	41	798	5/20	16.62	3.05	32.6	2	1
5	44	A. Edwards (Berm, 1986–94)	23	218.2	28	764	6/38	17.36	3.49	29.7	0	2

ODI CRICKET RECORDS: BY TEAM

One-day international cricket is played more in some parts of the world than in others. For example: Kevin Pietersen (England) and M.S. Dhoni (India) both made their one-day international debuts in 2003 and have been regulars ever since; as of April 2013, however, Pietersen had appeared in 134 ODIs compared to Dhoni's 240. As such, the relative chances of a player featuring among the list of one-day international cricket's all-time cumulative record-holders depend on which country he plays for. To be one's country's all-time ODI leading performer, however, is an altogether different matter and is always a coveted honour.

Special moment: Sri Lanka paceman **Chaminda Vaas,** who recorded the best-ever one-day international bowling figures – 8/19 against Zimbabwe in 2001 – retired after taking his 400th wicket in 50-over cricket.

AUSTRALIA

Australia are the most successful team in the history of one-day international cricket: they have won the most matches (509), have won the ICC World Cup more times than any other country (in 1987, 1999, 2003 and 2007) and are one of only two teams (India being the other) to have won the ICC Champions Trophy on two occasions (emerging victorious in 2006 and 2009).

RESULT SUMMARY

Opposition	Span	Mat	Won	Lost	Tied	NR	W/L%
Afghanistan	2012	1	1	0	0	0	100.00
Bangladesh	1990–2011	19	18	1	0	0	94.73
Canada	1979–2011	2	2	0	0	0	100.00
England	1971–2014	127	73	49	2	3	59.67
ICC World XI	2005	3	3	0	0	0	100.00
India	1980–2013	115	66	40	0	9	62.26
Ireland	2007–2012	3	2	0	0	1	100.00
Kenya	1996–2011	5	5	0	0	0	100.00
Namibia	2003	1	1	0	0	0	100.00
Netherlands	2003–2007	2	2	0	0	0	100.00
New Zealand	1974–2013	125	85	34	0	6	71.42
Pakistan	1975–2012	89	54	31	1	3	63.37
Scotland	1999–2013	4	4	0	0	0	100.00
South Africa	1992–2011	80	41	36	3	0	53.12
Sri Lanka	1975–2013	90	55	31	0	4	63.95
USA	2004	1	1	0	0	0	100.00
West Indies	1975–2013	135	70	59	3	3	54.16
Zimbabwe	1983–2011	28	26	1	0	1	96.29

Australia's ODI batting master

Despite never really hitting the heights in the Test arena (in which his vulnerability to the short ball meant he only appeared in 18 Tests in the mid-1990s), Michael Bevan suffered no such problems in the 50-over format of the game and went on to form an integral part of Australia's one-day side for a decade, during which he gained a reputation as being one of the best finishers in the business. Relying on exquisite placement and speed between the wickets rather than powerful strokeplay, he amassed an impressive 6,912 runs in 232 one-day internationals between 1994 and 2004 at an average of 53.58 – the best by any Australia batsman in history.

Lillee tops bowling averages

More renowned for his performances in the Test arena, in which he took 355 wickets in 70 Tests, Dennis Lillee was also extremely effective in the one-day game. In 63 matches for Australia between 1972 and 1983 he took 103 wickets at an average of 20.82 – the best by any Australian bowler in history to have bowled 2,000 balls or more in one-day international cricket.

More than six of the best as Watson shines in Dhaka

Australia's victory target of 230 to beat Bangladesh in the second one-day international at Dhaka on 11 April 2011 may not have been too imposing, but Shane Watson's performance with the bat made sure they reached it in imperious fashion. The Queensland opener smashed 15 four and an all-time record 15 sixes in his 96-ball unbeaten 185 – the highest score by an Australian batsman in one-day international history – as Australia coasted across the winning line for the loss of just one wicket and with 144 balls to spare.

A true legend of the game

A true rock upon which Australia have built their considerable success in one-day international cricket in recent years, **Ricky Ponting** will go down in history as one of cricket's greatest players, and his record in one-day international cricket is among the best of all time. He holds Australia's all-time records for: most runs (13,589), centuries (29 – with a highest of 164 against South Africa at Johannesburg on 12 March 2006), catches (159) and matches (374). He is also the most successful one-day captain in Australia's history, notching up 164 wins in 229 matches as captain between 2002 and 2012.

Highest and lowest

Highest score: 434 for 4 against South Africa at Johannesburg on 12 March 2006.

Lowest score: 70 all out, against New Zealand at Adelaide on 27 January 1986; and against England at Edgbaston on 4 June 1977.

Biggest victories

By runs: by 256 runs against Namibia at Potchefstroom on 27 February 2003.

By wickets: by ten wickets on four occasions.

By balls remaining (in the second innings): with 253 balls remaining against the United States at Southampton on 13 September 2004.

Smallest victories

By runs: by one run on five occasions.

By wickets: by one wicket on four occasions.

By balls remaining (in the second innings): off the final ball of the match on four occasions.

Watson and Ponting put England to the sword

Shane Watson (136 not out) and Ricky Ponting (111 not out) dashed any hopes England may have had of defending a modest total of 257 in the semi-final of the 2009 ICC Champions Trophy at Centurion on 2 October 2009. Coming together with the score on 6 for 1 in the second over, the pair added an unbeaten 252 runs to see Australia over the winning line with 8.1 overs to spare. It was the highest partnership for Australia in one-day international cricket history.

Magic McGrath leads the way

The most successful one-day bowler in Australia's history (with 380 wickets in 249 matches), **Glenn McGrath** also holds the record for the best figures ever recorded by an Australian bowler in one-day international cricket, with 7 for 15 against Namibia at Potchefstroom in the 2003 World Cup (also a World Cup best).

Most four-wicket-plus innings hauls

One of only three Australian bowlers to have taken a hat-trick in one-day international cricket – the others being Bruce Reid (against New Zealand at Sydney in January 1986) and Anthony Stuart (against Pakistan at Melbourne in January 1997) – Brett Lee has recorded more four-wicket-plus hauls than any other Australian bowler in one-day international cricket history (23 in 221 matches between 2000 and 2012).

Glorious Gilchrist prospers for Australia

Adam Gilchrist will be remembered as the best wicketkeeper-batsman ever to have played the game. In 286 matches for Australia he hit 9,595 runs at a strike-rate of 96.89 runs per 100 balls faced (the best by any Australian in history to have completed 50-plus innings) and also excelled behind the stumps, claiming 470 dismissals (416 catches and 54 stumpings) – another all-time Australian record.

MOST RUNS: TOP 5

Pos	Runs	Player	Mat	Inns	NO	HS	Ave	100	50	0
1	13,589	R.T. Ponting (1995–2012)	374	364	39	164	41.81	29	82	20
2	9,595	A.C. Gilchrist (1996–2008)	286	278	11	172	35.93	16	55	19
3	8,500	M.E. Waugh (1988–2002)	244	236	20	173	39.35	18	50	16
4	7,683	M.J. Clarke (2003–14)	236	215	43	130	44.66	8	55	10
5	7,569	S.R. Waugh (1986–2002)	325	288	58	120*	32.90	3	45	15

MOST WICKETS: TOP 5

Pos	Wkts	Player	Mat	Balls	Runs	BBI	Ave	Econ	SR	4	5
1	380	G.D. McGrath (1993–2007)	249	12,928	8,354	7/15	21.98	3.87	34.0	9	7
=	380	B. Lee (2000–12)	221	11,185	8,877	5/22	23.36	4.76	29.4	14	9
3	291	S.K. Warne (1993–2003)	193	10,600	7,514	5/33	25.82	4.25	36.4	12	1
4	208	M.G. Johnson (2005–14)	136	6,647	5,384	6/31	25.88	4.85	31.9	8	3
5	203	C.J. McDermott (1985–96)	138	7,461	5,018	5/44	24.71	4.03	36.7	4	1

ENGLAND

Although they have been runners-up three times in the ICC World Cup (in 1979, 1987 and 1992), England have always struggled to hit the heights in one-day international cricket. In 616 matches played since their opening one-day international against Australia in 1971 they have notched up 299 victories – of all the current Test-playing nations, only Bangladesh, New Zealand and Zimbabwe have recorded fewer.

Best career strike-rate

A hard-hitting middle-order batsman and slow left-arm bowler, Samit Patel has been in and out of England's one-day set-up since he made his debut against Scotland in 2008. A player who struggles with his fitness levels, when selected, he has scored 482 runs in 22 innings at an average of 32.13. Hardly spectacular numbers until one sees his strike-rate: it is 93.23 runs per 100 balls – the best by any England player in ODI history.

Smith puts on a show at Edgbaston

Australia eventually won the match (and with it the series) against England at Edgbaston on 21 May 1993, but not before they had encountered one of the most destructive one-day innings ever seen on English soil. **Robin Smith** powered his way to a 163-ball unbeaten 167 – the highest score by an England player in one-day international cricket history – as the home side reached 277 for 5. Australia reached the target for the loss of four wickets with nine balls to spare.

RESULT SUMMARY

Opposition	Span	Mat	Won	Lost	Tied	NR	%
Australia	1971–2014	127	49	73	2	3	40.32
Bangladesh	2000–2011	15	13	2	0	0	86.66
Canada	1979–2007	2	2	0	0	0	100.00
East Africa	1975	1	1	0	0	0	100.00
India	1974–2013	87	35	47	2	3	42.85
Ireland	2006–2013	6	5	1	0	0	83.33
Kenya	1999–2007	2	2	0	0	0	100.00
Namibia	2003	1	1	0	0	0	100.00
Netherlands	1996–2011	3	3	0	0	0	100.00
New Zealand	1973–2013	77	33	38	2	4	46.57
Pakistan	1974–2012	72	42	28	0	2	60.00
Scotland	2008–2010	2	1	0	0	1	100.00
South Africa	1992–2013	51	22	25	1	3	46.87
Sri Lanka	1982–2013	51	26	25	0	0	50.98
UAE	1996–1996	1	1	0	0	0	100.00
West Indies	1973–2014	88	42	42	0	4	50.00
Zimbabwe	1992–2004	30	21	8	0	1	72.41

Stewart proves an effective performer behind the stumps

An opening batsman who was forced behind the stumps by the England selectors' desire to find balance in the team, Alec Stewart developed into a top-class wicketkeeper. In 170 one-day internationals between 1989 and 2003 he took an all-time English record 163 dismissals (with 148 catches and 15 stumpings).

England's Mr Dependable

Jonathan Trott's ODI career for England may not have got off to the best of starts – he was dismissed for a five-ball duck on debut against Ireland in Dublin – but, as has become his trademark, the Warwickshire right-hander got his head down, nailed down a place in the England line-up and did what he does best ... score runs, and plenty of them. He posted his first century (of three) against Bangladesh in his sixth innings, became the fastest player (alongside Viv Richards and Kevin Pietersen) to reach 1,000 one-day international runs (in 21 innings), starred for England at the 2011 ICC World Cup and, to date, has scored 2,819 runs in 65 innings at an average of 51.25 – the highest average by any England batsman in history.

MOST RUNS: TOP 5

Pos	Runs	Player	Mat	Inns	NO	HS	Ave	100	50	0
1	5,092	P.D. Collingwood (2001–11)	197	181	37	120*	35.36	5	26	7
2	4,677	A.J. Stewart (1989–2003)	170	162	14	116	31.60	4	28	13
3	4,635	I.R. Bell (2004–14)	140	136	11	126*	37.08	3	29	5
4	4,422	K.P. Pietersen (2005–13)	134	123	16	130	41.32	9	25	7
5	4,335	M.E. Trescothick (2000–06)	123	122	6	137	37.37	12	21	13

MOST WICKETS: TOP 5

Pos	Wkts	Player	Mat	Balls	Runs	BBI	Ave	Econ	SR	4	5
1	245	J.M. Anderson (2002–13)	174	8,609	7,132	5/23	29.11	4.97	35.1	10	2
2	234	D. Gough (1994–2006)	158	8,422	6,154	5/44	26.29	4.38	35.9	10	2
3	168	A. Flintoff (1999–2009)	138	5,496	3,968	5/19	23.61	4.33	32.7	6	2
=	168	S.C.J. Broad (2006–14)	108	5,472	4,767	5/23	28.37	5.22	32.5	9	1
5	145	I.T. Botham (1976–92)	116	6,271	4,139	4/31	28.54	3.96	43.2	3	0

The ultimate professional

Paul Collingwood is the perfect example of just how far hard work and professionalism can take you. Widely admired as a gritty, determined performer in the Test arena, he initially cemented his reputation in one-day international cricket, a format in which he has gone on to set numerous all-time records for his country: he is the most capped one-day international cricketer in England's history (winning 197 caps between 2001 and 2011); has taken the most catches (108); and, surprisingly, holds the record for the best bowling figures ever recorded by an England player in a one-day international – 6 for 31 against Bangladesh at Trent Bridge on 21 June 2005 (he also scored a century in the match to become the first player in one-day international cricket history to record a century and take six wickets in a match).

Top performer with the ball

Arguably a finer performer with the ball than with the bat, **Andrew Flintoff** was England's go-to bowler. In 138 one-day internationals between 1999 and 2009 he took 168 wickets for 3,968 runs at an average of 23.61 runs per wicket – the best by any England player to have bowled 2,000 balls or more in one-day international cricket history.

Most successful captain

He may not have performed at his best with the bat in the 50-over format of the game, but Michael Vaughan was the most successful English captain of all time in one-day international cricket, recording 32 wins in 60 matches between 2003 and 2007 – a win percentage of 58.92.

Highest and lowest

Highest score: 391 for 4 against Bangladesh at Trent Bridge on 21 June 2005.

Lowest score: 86 all out against Australia at Old Trafford on 14 June 2001.

Biggest victories

By runs: by 202 runs against India at Lord's on 7 June 1975.

By wickets: by ten wickets on four occasions.

By balls remaining (in the second innings): with 277 balls remaining against Canada at Old Trafford on 13 June 1979.

Smallest victories

By runs: by one run on two occasions: against India at Cuttack on 27 December 1984; and against West Indies at Providence, Guyana, on 20 March 2009.

By wickets: by one wicket on six occasions.

By balls remaining (in the second innings): off the last ball of the match on three occasions.

Anderson heads England wicket-takers' list

England's best exponent of swing bowling since Ian Botham, no Englishman has taken more wickets for his country James Anderson in all forms of the game. He has enjoyed much success in ODI cricket: his haul of 245 wickets in 174 matches between 2002 and 2013 is an all-time record for an England player.

INDIA

Cricket-mad India has developed a taste for the one-day game like no other country on earth, playing more matches (853) than any other cricketing nation. And they have enjoyed considerable success, too: sensationally they won the ICC World Cup in 1983, repeated the feat in front of an adoring home crowd in 2011 and have notched up 425 victories – only Australia (509) and Pakistan (437) have more.

RESULT SUMMARY

Opposition	Span	Mat	Won	Lost	Tied	NR	%
Afghanistan	2014	1	1	0	0	0	100.00
Australia	1980–2013	115	40	66	0	9	37.73
Bangladesh	1988–2014	25	22	3	0	0	88.00
Bermuda	2007	1	1	0	0	0	100.00
East Africa	1975	1	1	0	0	0	100.00
England	1974–2013	87	47	35	2	3	57.14
Hong Kong	2008	1	1	0	0	0	100.00
Ireland	2007–2011	2	2	0	0	0	100.00
Kenya	1996–2004	13	11	2	0	0	84.61
Namibia	2003	1	1	0	0	0	100.00
Netherlands	2003–2011	2	2	0	0	0	100.00
New Zealand	1975–2014	93	46	41	1	5	52.84
Pakistan	1978–2014	126	50	72	0	4	40.98
Scotland	2007	1	1	0	0	0	100.00
South Africa	1991–2013	70	25	42	0	3	37.31
Sri Lanka	1979–2014	144	78	54	1	11	59.02
UAE	1994–2004	2	2	0	0	0	100.00
West Indies	1979–2013	112	50	59	1	2	45.90
Zimbabwe	1983–2013	56	44	10	2	0	80.35

Dashing Dhoni leads averages list

Mahendra Singh Dhoni, who has been a steady performer behind the stumps for India since making his debut against South Africa in December 2004, has more dismissals to his name – 298 (221 catches, 77 stumpings) – than any other wicketkeeper in one-day international history, and has been captain of the side since September 2007. It is Dhoni's swashbuckling performances with the bat, however, that have marked him out as an all-round player of the highest calibre. In 240 one-day internationals he has scored 7,872 runs (with a highest score of 183 not out against Sri Lanka at Jaipur on 31 October 2005) at an average of 52.83 – it is the highest average by any Indian batsman to have completed 25 innings or more in one-day international cricket history.

Superb Sehwag's demolition job

India's **Virender Sehwag** is among the most destructive top-order batsmen in the game's history, going after bowlers from the first ball. And he was at his very best in the fourth one-day international against the West Indies at Indore on 8 December 2011. Leading the side in the absence of Mahendra Singh Dhoni, he reached 50 off 41 balls, 100 off 69, 150 off 112 and 200 off 140 before finally falling for 219 – the highest individual score in one-day international history. India posted 418 for 5 (their highest-ever total) and went on to win the match by 153 runs.

Tendulkar and Dravid combine to devastating effect

Sachin Tendulkar (186 not out) and Rahul Dravid (153) produced a headline-grabbing performance as India beat New Zealand by 174 runs at Hyderabad on 8 November 1999. The pair added 331 runs for the second wicket – an all-time record in one-day international cricket.

Tendulkar's march to cricket greatness

The most complete batsman of his generation, possessing a game without any apparent weaknesses, **Sachin Tendulkar** has become a serial record-breaker in one-day international cricket. In 463 matches for India between 1989 and 2012 (no one in history has played in more) he has set all-time records for the most runs (18,426) and the most centuries (49), and was the fastest to reach every target from 10,000 to 18,000 runs. On 24 February 2010, against South Africa at Gwalior, he smashed 200 not out to become the first player to hit a double-century in ODI cricket.

Haryana Express races into the record books

A legend in Indian cricket both for his all-round brilliance that led India to ICC World Cup success in 1983 and for doggedly chasing down Richard Hadlee's overall aggregate record of Test wickets, **Kapil Dev** – nicknamed the "Haryana Express" by doting cricket fans – was also an exemplary performer in one-day cricket. In 225 matches for his country between 1978 and 1994 he took 253 wickets at an average of 27.45 – the best by any Indian player to have bowled 2,000 balls or more in one-day international cricket history.

Agarkar posts most four-wicket-plus hauls

Tipped as Kapil Dev's natural successor when he first broke into the India set-up in 1998, Ajit Agarkar may not have lived up to the hype in the Test arena (appearing in only 26 Tests between 1998 and 2006), but he more than made his mark in one-day international cricket. In 191 matches between 1998 and 2007, he took 288 wickets – with a best return of 6 for 42 against Australia at Melbourne on 9 January 2004 – including an Indian all-time record 12 four-wicket-plus hauls.

Highest and lowest

Highest score: 418 for 5 against West Indies at Indore on 8 December 2011.

Lowest score: 54 all out against Sri Lanka at Sharjah on 29 October 2000.

Biggest victories

By runs: by 257 runs against Bermuda at Port of Spain, Trinidad, on 19 March 2007.

By wickets: by ten wickets on five occasions.

By balls remaining (in the second innings): with 231 balls remaining against Kenya at Bloemfontein on 12 October 2001.

Smallest victories

By runs: by one run on four occasions.

By wickets: by one wicket, on three occasions, against New Zealand at Auckland on 11 January 2003; against West Indies at Cuttack on 29 November 2011; and against Sri Lanka at Port of Spain on 11 July 2013.

By balls remaining (in the second innings): with one ball remaining on seven occasions.

Most successful captain

Mohammad Azharuddin was the most successful Indian captain in one-day international cricket history, recording 90 wins in 174 matches as captain between 1990 and 1999. He also holds the all-time Indian record for the most catches, taking 156 in 334 matches between 1985 and 2000, when his career was brought to a sudden halt by match-fixing allegations.

MOST RUNS: TOP 5

Pos	Runs	Player	Mat	Inns	NO	HS	Ave	100	50	0
1	18,426	S.R. Tendulkar (1989–2012)	463	452	41	200*	44.83	49	96	20
2	11,221	S.C. Ganguly (1992–2007)	308	297	23	183	40.95	22	71	16
3	10,768	R. Dravid (1996–2011)	340	314	39	153	39.15	12	82	13
4	9,378	M. Azharuddin (1985–2000)	334	308	54	153*	36.92	7	58	9
5	8,237	Yuvraj Singh (2000–13)	290	265	38	139	36.28	13	51	18

MOST WICKETS: TOP 5

Pos	Wkts	Player	Mat	Balls	Runs	BBI	Ave	Econ	SR	4	5
1	334	**A. Kumble** (1990–2007)	269	14,376	10,300	6/12	30.83	4.29	43.0	8	2
2	315	J. Srinath (1991–2003)	229	11,935	8,847	5/23	28.08	4.44	37.8	7	3
3	288	A.B. Agarkar (1998–2007)	191	9,484	8,021	6/42	27.85	5.07	32.9	10	2
4	269	Z. Khan (2000–12)	194	9,815	8,102	5/42	30.11	4.95	36.4	7	1
5	255	Harbhajan Singh (1998–2011)	227	11,939	8,550	5/31	33.52	4.29	46.8	2	3

NEW ZEALAND

From the moment they played their first-ever one-day international in 1973, New Zealand, five-time semi-finalists in the ICC World Cup, have provided dogged opposition in the shortened format of the game and have evolved into one of the most consistent sides on the one-day circuit; the Black Caps are capable of beating anyone on their day.

Most centuries

There is a strong case for regarding the free-scoring **Nathan Astle** as the finest one-day player New Zealand has ever produced. In 223 one-day internationals for his country between 1995 and 2007 he scored 7,090 runs at an average of 34.92 and hit 16 centuries – the most by any New Zealand batsman in one-day international cricket – with a highest score of 145 not out against the United States at The Oval on 10 September 2004.

RESULT SUMMARY

Opposition	Span	Mat	Won	Lost	Tied	NR	%
Australia	1974–2013	125	34	85	0	6	28.57
Bangladesh	1990–2013	24	16	8	0	0	66.66
Canada	2003–11	3	3	0	0	0	100.00
East Africa	1975	1	1	0	0	0	100.00
England	1973–2013	77	38	33	2	4	53.42
India	1975–2014	93	41	46	1	5	47.15
Ireland	2007–2008	2	2	0	0	0	100.00
Kenya	2007–2011	2	2	0	0	0	100.00
Netherlands	1996	1	1	0	0	0	100.00
Pakistan	1973–2011	89	35	51	1	2	40.80
Scotland	1999–2008	2	2	0	0	0	100.00
South Africa	1992–2013	58	20	34	0	4	37.03
Sri Lanka	1979–2013	82	37	38	1	6	49.34
UAE	1996	1	1	0	0	0	100.00
USA	2004	1	1	0	0	0	100.00
West Indies	1975–2014	60	23	30	0	7	43.39
Zimbabwe	1987–2012	35	25	8	1	1	75.00

Terrific Turner tops averages list

An uncompromising, straight-playing opening batsman who ensured he wrung every ounce of talent out of his game, Glenn Turner was as successful in one-day cricket for New Zealand as he was in the Test arena. In 41 one-day internationals for his country between 1973 and 1983, he scored 1,598 runs (with a highest score of 171 not out against East Africa in the 1975 ICC World Cup) at an average of 47.00 – the highest by any New Zealand batsman to have completed 20 innings or more in one-day international cricket history.

One of the best in the business

Although his career was blighted by a succession of injuries – many of which kept him out of the game for lengthy periods – **Shane Bond** proved, when fit, that he was one of the finest fast bowlers of his generation. He holds several all-time records for New Zealand in one-day international cricket: for the best bowling in an innings (6 for 19 against India at Bulawayo on 26 August 2005); the best career average (20.88); the most four-wicket-plus hauls (11 in 82 matches between 2002 and 2010); and the best strike-rate (29.2).

Guptill stars for NZ

Martin Guptill scored a century on his ODI debut (122 against the West Indies on 10 January 2009), but although the runs continued to flow, he reached three figures again only once in his next 66 innings. Then came England in 2013: he hit an unbeaten 103 at Lord's (on 31 May) and, two days later, 189 not out at Southampton – the latter is a national record.

MOST RUNS: TOP 5

Pos	Runs	Player	Mat	Inns	NO	HS	Ave	100	50	0
1	8,007	S.P. Fleming (1994–2007)	279	268	21	134*	32.41	8	49	17
2	7,090	N.J. Astle (1995–2007)	223	217	14	145*	34.92	16	41	19
3	5,172	B.B. McCullum (2002–14)	229	199	28	166	30.24	4	26	17
4	4,881	C.L. Cairns (1991–2006)	214	192	25	115	29.22	4	25	9
5	4,707	C.D. McMillan (1997–2007)	197	183	16	117	28.18	3	28	9

MOST WICKETS: TOP 5

Pos	Wkts	Player	Mat	Balls	Runs	BBI	Ave	Econ	SR	4	5
1	274	D.L. Vettori (1997–2011)	268	12,663	8,701	5/7	31.75	4.12	46.2	6	2
2	235	K.D. Mills (2001–14)	165	7,977	6,284	5/25	26.74	4.72	33.9	8	1
3	203	C.Z. Harris (1990–2004)	250	10,667	7,613	5/42	37.50	4.28	52.5	2	1
4	200	C.L. Cairns (1991–2006)	214	8,132	6,557	5/42	32.78	4.83	40.6	3	1
5	173	J.P.D. Oram (2001–12)	160	6,911	5,047	5/26	29.17	4.38	39.9	3	2

Cairns Senior powers his way into the record books

Now more famous for being the father of Chris Cairns (who would go on to play in 62 Tests and 215 one-day internationals for New Zealand between 1989 and 2006), **Lance Cairns** was an uncomplicated bully of a cricketer whose performances with the bat in particular often brought crowds to their feet. In 78 one-day internationals for New Zealand between 1974 and 1985 he scored 987 runs from 941 deliveries at a strike-rate of 104.88 runs per 100 balls faced – the best by any New Zealand batsman to have faced 500 balls or more in one-day international cricket history.

The Marshall and McCullum show destroys Ireland

Hamish Marshall (161) and Brendon McCullum (166) produced a rampant performance with the bat at the top of the order to propel New Zealand to a crushing 290-run victory – the highest winning margin in one-day international cricket history – over hapless Ireland at Aberdeen on 1 July 2008. The pair put on 274 runs for the opening wicket – the best part-nership of all time for New Zealand in one-day international cricket.

McCullum bags Kiwi record for the most dismissals

First drafted into the New Zealand one-day side as a batsman (against Australia at Sydney in January 2002) following an outstanding career in international youth cricket, **Brendon McCullum** has gone on to become an established and consistent performer behind the stumps. In 229 matches between 2002 and 2014 he has claimed 242 dismissals (with 227 catches and 15 stumpings) – an all-time record for New Zealand in the 50-over format of the game.

Highest and lowest

Highest score: 402 for 2 against Ireland at Aberdeen on 1 July 2008.

Lowest score: 64 all out against Pakistan at Sharjah on 15 April 1986.

Biggest victories

By runs: by 290 runs against Ireland at Aberdeen on 1 July 2008.

By wickets: by ten wickets on six occasions.

By balls remaining (in the second innings): with 264 balls remaining against Bangladesh at Queenstown on 31 December 2007.

Smallest victories

By runs: by one run on four occasions.

By wickets: by one wicket on seven occasions.

By balls remaining (in the second innings): off the last ball of the match on five occasions.

Serial record-breaker

Stephen Fleming was a prolific run-scorer for New Zealand in one-day international cricket over a 13-year career stretching from 1994 to 2007 (his 8,007 career runs is the most by any New Zealand batsman in history in one-day international cricket), and the most successful captain his country has ever produced (notching up 98 wins in 218 matches as captain between 1997 and 2007). Fleming also holds the all-time New Zealand records for the most one-day international matches played (279) and for the most catches taken (132).

PAKISTAN

There is no team in world cricket quite like Pakistan, a frustrating blend of sparkling brilliance and overt ordinariness. Their ability to hit heady heights one day and almost laughable lows the next is reflected in their ODI performances. In 1992 their star shone brightly when they won the ICC World Cup; in 2007, however, they failed to progress beyond the group stages.

RESULT SUMMARY

Opposition	Span	Mat	Won	Lost	Tied	NR	%
Afghanistan	2012–14	2	2	0	0	0	100.00
Australia	1975–2012	89	31	54	1	3	36.62
Bangladesh	1986–2014	32	31	1	0	0	96.87
Canada	1979–2011	2	2	0	0	0	100.00
England	1974–2012	72	28	42	0	2	40.00
Hong Kong	2004–08	2	2	0	0	0	100.00
India	1978–2014	126	72	50	0	4	59.01
Ireland	2007–13	5	3	1	0	1	70.00
Kenya	1996–2011	6	6	0	0	0	100.00
Namibia	2003	1	1	0	0	0	100.00
Netherlands	1996–2003	3	3	0	0	0	100.00
New Zealand	1973–2011	89	51	35	1	2	59.19
Scotland	1999–2013	3	3	0	0	0	100.00
South Africa	1992–2013	71	23	47	0	1	32.85
Sri Lanka	1975–2014	139	80	54	1	4	59.62
UAE	1994–96	2	2	0	0	0	100.00
West Indies	1975–2013	126	55	68	3	0	44.84
Zimbabwe	1992–2013	47	42	3	1	1	92.39

Perfect partners

Aamer Sohail (134) and Inzamam-ul-Haq (137 not out) produced a record-breaking and ultimately match-winning performance against New Zealand at Sharjah on 20 April 1994. The pair put on 263 runs for the second wicket – an all-time record partnership for Pakistan in one-day international cricket – to lead their team to a comfortable 62-run victory.

All-time high strike-rate for "Boom Boom" Afridi

When he is on his game, nobody can demolish an opponent's bowling attack with as much devastating brutality as **Shahid "Boom Boom" Afridi**. In 373 matches for Pakistan (excluding his five matches for the ICC World XI and the Asia XI) between 1996 and 2014 the flamboyant all-rounder has scored 7,582 runs at an average of 23.69 and at a strike-rate of 115.54 runs per 100 balls faced – an all-time record in one-day international cricket for any batsman to have faced 500 deliveries or more.

The master opener

A sweet timer of the ball and a graceful stroke-maker, Saeed Anwar stood tall at the top of the Pakistan batting order in all forms of the game for over a decade, but some of his performances in one-day international cricket (he played in 247 matches between 1989 and 2003) were particularly eye-catching. On 21 May 1997, against India at Chennai, he smashed an imperious 194 off 146 balls to break Viv Richards's record for the highest-ever individual score in a one-day international. It was one of 20 one-day centuries compiled in his career – an all-time record for a Pakistan batsman.

The Asian Bradman

Dubbed the "Asian Bradman" in his prime for the single-minded consistency with which he accumulated runs, **Zaheer Abbas** was a refined stroke-player who compiled big scores with an array of shots all around the wicket. In 62 one-day internationals for his country between 1974 and 1985, he scored 2,572 runs (with a highest score 123 against Sri Lanka at Lahore on 29 March 1982) at an average of 47.62 – the highest by any Pakistan player to have completed 20 innings or more in one-day international cricket history.

Highest and lowest

Highest score: 385 for 7 against Bangladesh at Dambulla on 21 June 2010.

Lowest score: 43 all out against the West Indies at Cape Town on 25 February 1993.

Biggest victories

By runs: by 233 runs against Bangladesh at Dhaka on 2 June 2000.

By wickets: by ten wickets on four occasions.

By balls remaining (in the second innings): with 206 balls remaining against New Zealand at Sharjah on 1 May 1990.

Smallest victories

By runs: by one run on two occasions: against the West Indies at Sharjah on 21 October 1991; and against South Africa at Port Elizabeth on 27 November 2013.

By wickets: by one wicket on seven occasions.

By balls remaining (in the second innings): off the last ball of the match on five occasions.

Most successful captain

As the finest cricketer Pakistan has ever produced, it seemed highly appropriate that **Imran Khan** should be the man to lead the side to the finest moment in its country's history, winning the ICC World Cup in 1992, in the final match of his career. He will be remembered as the greatest captain his country has ever had: leading his side to 75 wins in 139 one-day internationals as captain between 1982 and 1992.

Afridi finds new role with the ball

A young **Shahid Afridi** burst onto the international cricket scene as a swashbuckling batsman, but as he approaches the latter part of his career, his leg-break bowling has become his major asset. Still a regular in Pakistan's one-day international and T20 teams 18 years after his debut, he has taken 376 wickets in 373 ODI matches for his country with a best of 7 for 12 against the West Indies at Providence, Guyana, on 14 July 2013 (a national record for Pakistan).

Most dismissals

He may have spent most of his career vying with Rashid Latif for the wicketkeeper's berth in the Pakistan line-up but, when he played, Moin Khan proved he was an admirable performer behind the stumps. In 219 one-day international matches for Pakistan between 1990 and 2004, the Rawalpindi keeper claimed 287 dismissals (214 catches and 73 stumpings) – a record for Pakistan in the 50-over format of the game.

Inzamam's inspirational 16-year ODI career

A colossus for his country in 378 ODIs between 1991 and 2007 – a record number of matches for a Pakistan player – Inzamam-ul-Haq leads his country's all-time list for the most runs scored (11,701 – putting him fifth on the all-time list) – with a top score of 137 not out against New Zealand at Sharjah on 20 April 1994) and, surprisingly given his reputation for slovenliness in the field, is third for the most catches (113, behind Younis Khan, 126, and Shahid Afridi, 119).

MOST RUNS: TOP 5

Pos	Runs	Player	Mat	Inns	NO	HS	Ave	100	50	0
1	11,701	Inzamam-ul-Haq (1991–2007)	375	348	52	137*	39.53	10	83	20
2	9,554	Mohammad Yousuf (1998–2010)	281	267	40	141*	42.08	15	62	15
3	8,824	Saeed Anwar (1989–2003)	247	244	19	194	39.21	20	43	15
4	7,582	Shahid Afridi (1996–2014)	373	345	25	124	23.69	6	36	28
5	7,381	Javed Miandad (1975–96)	233	218	41	119*	41.70	8	50	8

MOST WICKETS: TOP 5

Pos	Wkts	Player	Mat	Balls	Runs	BBI	Ave	Econ	SR	4	5
1	502	**Wasim Akram** (1984–2003)	356	18,186	11,812	5/15	23.52	3.89	36.2	17	6
2	416	Waqar Younis (1989–2003)	262	12,698	9,919	7/36	23.84	4.68	30.5	14	13
3	376	Shahid Afridi (1996–2014)	373	16,539	12,753	7/12	33.91	4.62	43.9	4	9
4	288	Saqlain Mushtaq (1995–2003)	169	8,770	6,275	5/20	21.78	4.29	30.4	11	6
5	268	Abdul Razzaq (1996–2011)	261	10,851	8,452	6/35	31.53	4.67	40.4	8	3

SOUTH AFRICA

Ever since their return to the international cricket fold after 21 years in the wilderness – their first match back was an ODI against India at Kolkata on 10 November 1991 – South Africa have proved they are a considerable force in the 50-over game. Of the current Test-playing nations only Australia (64.18) have a higher winning percentage than South Africa's 63.87 percent.

Amla's electric arrival on the international scene

His international career is still in its relatively early stages but, after establishing himself in the South Africa team, Hashim Amla – the first player of Indian descent to play for the country – has shown himself to be a player of the highest quality. With his trademark wristy flicks and limitless concentration, he has compiled 4,054 runs in 85 one-day internationals at an average of 53.34 – the highest by any South African batsman to complete 20 innings or more in one-day internationals.

Best career strike-rate

Tipped from an early age to develop into a world-class all-rounder, Albie Morkel may not have lived up to such hype, but he has become a consistent and effective performer in the shorter formats of the game. In 56 one-day internationals for South Africa between 2004 and 2012 he has hit 790 runs from 750 balls faced at a strike-rate of 101.33 runs per 100 balls – the best by any South Africa batsman to have faced 500 balls or more in one-day international cricket.

RESULT SUMMARY

Opposition	Span	Mat	Won	Lost	Tied	NR	%
Australia	1992–2011	80	36	41	3	0	46.87
Bangladesh	2002–11	14	13	1	0	0	92.85
Canada	2003	1	1	0	0	0	100.00
England	1992–2013	51	25	22	1	3	53.12
India	1991–2013	70	42	25	0	3	62.68
Ireland	2007–11	3	3	0	0	0	100.00
Kenya	1996–2008	10	10	0	0	0	100.00
Netherlands	1996–2013	4	4	0	0	0	100.00
New Zealand	1992–2013	58	34	20	0	4	62.96
Pakistan	1992–2013	71	47	23	0	1	67.14
Scotland	2007	1	1	0	0	0	100.00
Sri Lanka	1992–2013	56	26	28	1	1	48.18
UAE	1996	1	1	0	0	0	100.00
West Indies	1992–2013	52	38	12	1	1	75.49
Zimbabwe	1992–2010	32	29	2	0	1	93.54

Amla and de Villiers rescue SA

South Africa were in a spot of bother when AB de Villiers joined Hashim Amla at the crease with his side on 42 for 2 in the 14th over of the Third One-Day International against Pakistan at Johannesburg on 17 March 2013. But with Amla scoring 122 and de Villiers 128, the pair combined in match-winning fashion, putting on 238 (a national record) to lead South Africa to 343 for 5 and an eventual 34-run victory.

Kirsten runs riot at Rawalpindi

The opposition may not have been the strongest, but **Gary Kirsten** made a mockery of pre-match predictions that the wicket for South Africa's 1996 ICC World Cup Group B encounter against the United Arab Emirates at Rawalpindi would be a bowler-friendly surface. The left-handed opener batted through the innings to compile a 159-ball unbeaten 188 – the highest score in the tournament's history and the highest-ever score by a South Africa batsman in one-day international cricket.

Glorious Gibbs heads centuries list

One of the most electric stroke players in the modern game – at times it appears no shot is beyond him – **Herschelle Gibbs** has hit more one-day international centuries than any other South African player in history (21). The highlight of his glittering career came when he smashed a 111-ball 175 against Australia at Johannesburg on 12 March 2006 to help his side chase down a seemingly unattainable 435-run victory target.

Deadly Donald delivers the goods

Allan Donald got his international career off to a blistering and eye-catching start – taking 5 for 29 in South Africa's first match back in the international fold, against India at Kolkata on 10 November 1991 – and went on to cement a reputation as the finest bowler his country has ever produced. In 164 one-day internationals between 1991 and 2003 he took 272 wickets – with best figures of 6 for 23 against Kenya at Nairobi on 3 October 1996 – at an average of 21.78, the best by any South African to have bowled 2,000 balls or more in one-day international cricket.

Magic Makhaya sends Australia packing

A devastating spell of bowling from Makhaya Ntini helped South Africa to their biggest-ever victory over Australia at Cape Town on 3 March 2006. Making the most of the seamer-friendly conditions under the Newlands lights, the Mdingi-born paceman took 6 for 22 – the best bowling figures by a South African in one-day international cricket history – to reduce Australia to 93 all out and set up South Africa's crushing 196-run win.

Pollock: South Africa's precision record-breaker

A bowler who relied on metronomic accuracy rather than express pace, **Shaun Pollock**, who made 294 appearances for South Africa between 1996 and 2008 – second only to Jacques Kallis) has taken more four-wicket-plus hauls for his country (17) and more wickets (387) than any other player in his country's history. His best performance came when he took 6 for 35 against the West Indies at East London on 24 January 1999.

Highest and lowest

Highest score: 438 for 9 against Australia at Johannesburg on 12 March 2006.

Lowest score: 69 all out against Australia at Sydney on 14 December 1993.

Biggest victories

By runs: by 272 runs against Zimbabwe at Benoni on 22 October 2010.

By wickets: by ten wickets on six occasions.

By balls remaining (in the second innings): with 228 balls remaining against Bangladesh at Bloemfontein on 22 February 2003.

Smallest victories

By runs: by one run on four occasions.

By wickets: by one wicket on four occasions.

By balls remaining (in the second innings): off the last ball of the match on seven occasions.

Most successful captain

History will remember him as the man at the centre of the most damaging scandal in the game's history – he was banned for life after admitting to his role in several match-fixing episodes – but no one led South Africa with greater success in one-day international cricket than Hansie Cronje. The Free State batsman led his side to 99 wins in 138 matches as captain between 1994 and 2000.

MOST RUNS: TOP 5

Pos	Runs	Player	Mat	Inns	NO	HS	Ave	100	50	0
1	11,545	J.H. Kallis (1996–2013)	320	306	53	139	45.63	17	86	16
2	8,094	H.H. Gibbs (1996–2010)	248	240	16	175	36.13	21	37	22
3	6,989	G.C. Smith (2002–13)	196	193	10	141	38.19	10	47	7
4	6,798	G. Kirsten (1993–2003)	185	185	19	188*	40.95	13	45	11
5	6,181	A.B. de Villiers (2005–13)	154	148	25	146	50.25	16	35	6

MOST WICKETS: TOP 5

Pos	Wkts	Player	Mat	Overs	Runs	BBI	Ave	Econ	SR	4	5
1	387	S.M. Pollock (1996–2008)	294	2,571.4	9,409	6/35	24.31	3.65	39.8	12	5
2	272	A.A. Donald (1991–2003)	164	1,426.5	5,926	6/23	21.78	4.15	31.4	11	2
3	269	J.H. Kallis (1996–2013)	320	1,773.0	8,568	5/30	31.85	4.83	39.5	2	2
4	265	M. Ntini (1998–2009)	172	1,440.5	6,501	6/22	24.53	4.51	32.6	8	4
5	192	L. Klusener (1996–2004)	171	1,222.4	5,751	6/49	29.95	4.70	38.2	1	6

SRI LANKA

Following their elevation to Test status in 1982, for many years Sri Lanka were considered to be the minnows of world cricket, but they used the one-day international arena to propel themselves into the world's elite. In 1996, spectacularly, they shocked Australia in the final to capture the ICC World Cup and have been treated with the greatest respect ever since.

RESULT SUMMARY

Opposition	Span	Mat	Won	Lost	Tied	NR	%
Afghanistan	2014	1	1	0	0	0	100.00
Australia	1975–2013	90	31	55	0	3	36.04
Bangladesh	1986–2014	37	32	4	0	1	88.88
Bermuda	2007	1	1	0	0	0	100.00
Canada	2003–11	2	2	0	0	0	100.00
England	1982–2013	51	25	26	0	0	49.01
India	1979–2014	144	54	78	1	11	40.97
Ireland	2007	1	1	0	0	0	100.00
Kenya	1996–2011	6	5	1	0	0	83.33
Netherlands	2002–06	3	3	0	0	0	100.00
New Zealand	1979–2013	82	38	37	1	6	50.65
Pakistan	1975–2014	139	54	80	1	4	40.37
Scotland	2011	1	1	0	0	0	100.00
South Africa	1992–2013	56	28	26	1	1	51.81
UAE	2004–08	2	2	0	0	0	100.00
West Indies	1975–2013	51	21	27	0	3	43.75
Zimbabwe	1992–2011	47	39	7	0	1	84.78

Jayawardene's all-round contributions

Not only a prolific performer with the bat (he has scored 11,243 runs in 407 ODIs for Sri Lanka between 1998 and 2014), **Mahela Jayawardene** has also made a huge contribution in the field for Sri Lanka over the years. He holds the national record for the most catches in the 50-over game with 196.

Spectacular for more than 20 years

Behind Sachin Tendulkar the second-most capped ODI player of all time (appearing in a staggering 441 matches between 1989 and 2011), **Sanath Jayasuriya** started the trend of modern pinch-hitters at the top of the batting order and did much to help Sri Lanka towards the most glorious moment of their cricket history – winning the ICC World Cup in 1996. Over a decade and a half later he is still one of the most destructive hitters in the modern game, and has set numerous all-time records for his country: he has scored the most runs (13,364), holds the record for the highest score (189 against India at Sharjah on 29 October 2000) and has hit the most centuries (28). He also took a very handy 320 wickets for his country.

Highest partnership

A spectacular performance by Upal Tharanga (109) and Sanath Jayasuriya (152) at the top of the order at Headingley on 1 July 2006 laid the foundations for Sri Lanka overhauling England's mighty total of 321 with a staggering 75 balls to spare. The pair put on 286 runs for the opening wicket – the highest partnership for any wicket for Sri Lanka in one-day international history.

Slick Sangakkara heads dismissals list

A highly influential performer for his country from the moment he made his debut against Pakistan at Galle in July 2000, **Kumar Sangakkara** is one of the best wicketkeeper-batsmen in world cricket. In 362 matches for Sri Lanka he has scored 12,241 runs (with a highest score of 169 against South Africa at Colombo on 20 July 2013) at an average of 40.39 – a Sri Lanka record – and also holds the national ODI wicketkeeping record of 424 dismissals behind the stumps (with 339 catches and 85 stumpings).

Highest and lowest

Highest score: 443 for 9 against the Netherlands at Amstelveen on 4 July 2006.

Lowest score: 43 all out against South Africa at Paarl on 11 January 2012.

Biggest victories

By runs: by 245 runs against India at Sharjah on 29 October 2000.

By wickets: by ten wickets on five occasions.

By balls remaining (in the second innings): with 274 balls remaining against Zimbabwe at Colombo on 8 December 2001.

Smallest victories

By runs: by one run against Australia at Dambulla on 22 February 2004.

By wickets: by one wicket on two occasions; against England at Adelaide on 23 January 1999; and against Australia at Melbourne on 3 November 2010.

By balls remaining (in the second innings): with one ball remaining on three occasions.

Vaas tears into Zimbabwe

Chaminda Vaas ripped through Zimbabwe's batting line-up at Colombo on 8 December 2001 and stormed into the record books as the first bowler in one-day international cricket history to take eight wickets in an innings. The left-arm pace bowler finished with figures of 8 for 19 as Zimbabwe slumped to a miserable 38 all out.

Murali silenced his detractors in record-breaking fashion

The first and only Tamil of Indian origin to play for Sri Lanka, **Muttiah Muralitharan** brushed aside the repeated controversies regarding his action that have remained throughout his career (the ICC has investigated the mechanics of his action twice) – by taking wicket after wicket. An integral part of Sri Lanka's 1996 ICC World Cup-winning outfit, the history-making spin bowler set numerous all-time records for his country. In 343 matches between 1993 and 2011 he took the most wickets (523) and had the most four-wicket-plus innings hauls (25, with a best return of 7 for 30 against India at Sharjah on 27 October 2000).

Four in a row for lethal Malinga

Lasith Malinga secured his reputation as one of the deadliest death bowlers in the business at Sri Lanka's Super Eight Match against South Africa in Guyana at the 2007 ICC World Cup. With two balls left in the 45th over, South Africa, needing 210 for victory, were cruising to the target on 206 for 5: Malinga dismissed Shaun Pollock (bowled) and Andrew Hall (caught) ... 206 for 7. He started his following over (the 47th) by dismissing Jacques Kallis (caught) to complete his hat-trick and then bowled Makhaya Ntini to make it four wickets in four balls – the only time this has happened in ODI history ... South Africa were 206 for 9. Unfortunately for Malinga and Sri Lanka, South Africa limped to the target to win by one wicket.

Ranatunga leads from the front

An innovative, forceful captain who led Sri Lanka to the greatest triumph in their history with victory in the 1996 ICC World Cup, Arjuna Ranatunga is the most successful leader in one-day international matches for Sri Lanka, having collected 89 wins in 193 matches as captain between 1988 and 1999.

MOST RUNS: TOP 5

Pos	Runs	Player	Mat	Inns	NO	HS	Ave	100	50	0
1	13,364	S.T. Jayasuriya (1989–2009)	441	429	18	189	32.51	28	68	34
2	12,241	K.C. Sangakkara (2000–14)	362	339	36	169	40.39	18	82	14
3	11,243	D.P.M.D. Jayawardene (1998–2014)	407	380	37	144	32.77	15	69	27
4	9,284	P.A. de Silva (1984–2003)	308	296	30	145	34.90	11	64	17
5	8,529	M.S. Atapattu (1990–2007)	268	259	32	132*	37.57	11	59	13

MOST WICKETS: TOP 5

Pos	Wkts	Player	Mat	Overs	Runs	BBI	Ave	Econ	SR	4	5
1	523	M. Muralitharan (1993–2011)	343	3,072.1	12,066	7/30	23.07	3.92	35.2	15	10
2	399	W.P.U.J.C. Vaas (1994–2008)	321	2,620.1	10,955	8/19	27.45	4.18	39.4	9	4
3	320	S.T. Jayasuriya (1989–2011)	441	2,456.0	11,737	6/29	36.67	4.77	46.0	8	4
4	256	S.L. Malinga (2004–14)	166	1,333.1	6,879	6/38	26.87	5.15	31.2	8	7
5	183	C.R.D. Fernando (2001–12)	146	1,074.3	5,612	6/27	30.66	5.22	35.2	2	1

WEST INDIES

They were the kings of Test and one-day cricket in the 1970s and early '80s, years which saw them rule the roost in the five-day game and appear in three successive ICC World Cup finals (winning two of them). Since then the cricket gods have been less kind to the West Indies in the Test arena, but the men from the Caribbean have more than held their own in one-day cricket.

Russell makes his mark

A useful seam bowler and lower-order batsman, Andre Russell made a name for himself with his exploits for West Indies A against Ireland in June 2010, smashing 61 off 34 balls and then taking 6 for 34. After making his senior ODI debut against Ireland in March 2011, the Jamaican has been a mainstay of the West Indies ODI side, with his 35 matches to date bringing him 666 runs (with a highest score of 92 not out off 64 balls against India in June 2011) at an impressive strike-rate of 119.78 – the highest by any West Indian batsman in ODI history.

The meanest sight in modern cricket

An ability to propel the ball with searing pace from a 6ft 7in frame made Curtly Ambrose the most feared sight for batsmen for over a decade. He was a magnificent performer both in Test matches (where he took 405 wickets in 98 matches) and in one-day internationals, with 225 wickets in 176 matches between 1988 and 2000, including ten four-wicket-plus hauls – a West Indies record – and a best return of 5 for 17 against Australia at Melbourne on 15 December 1988.

Gayle forces his way into the record books

When **Chris Gayle** is on his A game, there are few finer sights in world cricket. A bully at the crease in the Viv Richards mould, he has the ability to destroy the opposition's attack, off both the front foot and the back. In 252 one-day internationals for the West Indies between 1999 and 2013 he has scored 8,688 runs (at an average of 37.77) including a West Indies record 21 centuries (with a highest score of 153 not out, against Zimbabwe at Bulawayo on 22 November 2003).

RESULT SUMMARY

Opposition	Span	Mat	Won	Lost	Tied	NR	%
Australia	1975–2013	135	59	70	3	3	45.83
Bangladesh	1999–2012	25	16	7	0	2	69.56
Bermuda	2008	1	1	0	0	0	100.00
Canada	2003–10	4	4	0	0	0	100.00
England	1973–2014	88	42	42	0	4	50.00
India	1979–2013	112	59	50	1	2	54.09
Ireland	2007–14	5	4	0	0	1	100.00
Kenya	1996–2003	6	5	1	0	0	83.33
Netherlands	2007–11	2	2	0	0	0	100.00
New Zealand	1975–2014	60	30	23	0	7	56.60
Pakistan	1975–2013	126	68	55	3	0	55.15
Scotland	1999–2007	2	2	0	0	0	100.00
South Africa	1992–2013	52	12	38	1	1	24.50
Sri Lanka	1975–2013	51	27	21	0	3	56.25
Zimbabwe	1983–2013	44	34	9	0	1	79.06

Davis demolishes Australia

Winston Davis produced a devastating spell of fast bowling on an unpredictable Headingley pitch to catapult the West Indies to a 101-run victory over Australia in the two sides' 1983 ICC World Cup Group B encounter. The St Vincent-born paceman took 7 for 51 – the best bowling figures by a West Indies player in one-day international cricket.

Born to play one-day cricket

Viv Richards was perhaps the most destructive batsman ever to play one-day international cricket. Displaying an ability to bully bowling attacks from the moment he made his debut against Sri Lanka at Old Trafford in June 1975, he became the fastest player in history to reach 1,000 one-day international runs (in 21 matches, a record since equalled by England's Kevin Pietersen and Jonathan Trott) and went on to set numerous West Indian all-time records in the one-day game: he recorded the highest score (189 not out against England at Old Trafford on 31 May 1984); holds the record for the best average (47.00); and, despite never lifting the ICC World Cup (unlike Clive Lloyd, who lifted it twice), was the most successful West Indian captain in one-day history, leading his side to 67 wins in 125 matches as captain between 1980 and 1991).

MOST RUNS: TOP 5

Pos	Runs	Player	Mat	Inns	NO	HS	Ave	100	50	0
1	10,348	B.C. Lara (1990–2007)	295	285	32	169	40.90	19	62	14
2	8,778	S. Chanderpaul (1994–2011)	268	251	40	150	41.60	11	59	6
3	8,688	C.H. Gayle (1999–2013)	252	247	17	153*	37.77	21	44	21
4	8,648	D.L. Haynes (1978–94)	238	237	28	152*	41.37	17	57	13
5	6,721	I.V.A. Richards (1975–91)	187	167	24	189*	47.00	11	45	7

MOST WICKETS: TOP 5

Pos	Wkts	Player	Mat	Balls	Runs	BBI	Ave	Econ	SR	4	5
1	227	C.A. Walsh (1985–2000)	205	10,822	6,918	5/1	30.47	3.83	47.6	6	1
2	225	C.E.L. Ambrose (1988–2000)	176	9,353	5,429	5/17	24.12	3.48	41.5	6	4
3	193	C.L. Hooper (1987–2003)	227	9,573	6,958	4/34	36.05	4.36	49.6	3	0
4	191	D.J. Bravo (2004–14)	158	6,319	5,680	6/43	29.73	5.39	33.0	5	1
5	157	M.D. Marshall (1980–92)	136	7,175	4,233	4/18	26.96	3.53	45.7	6	0
=	157	C.H. Gayle (1999–2013)	252	6,985	5,498	5/46	35.01	4.72	44.4	3	1

Most dismissals

Jeff Dujon is the most successful wicketkeeper in one-day international cricket. The Jamaican gloveman snared 204 victims (183 catches and 21 stumpings) in 169 matches between 1981 and 1991.

Most catches

No West Indian player has taken more catches in one-day international cricket than Carl Hooper. The Guyana-born batsman was no slouch in the field, taking 120 catches in 227 matches between 1987 and 2003.

Big Bird swoops into record books

A shoo-in for any all-time one-day international XI, Joel Garner has the best bowling average in the shortened format of the game of any player to have bowled 2,000 balls or more in one-day international cricket. The giant, 6ft 8in fast bowler, nicknamed "Big Bird", took 146 wickets in 98 matches between 1977 and 1987 at an average of 18.84.

Chanderpaul and Hooper's rescue act

Shavnarine Chanderpaul (150) and Carl Hooper (108) produced a remarkable two-man show to drag the West Indies to a 43-run victory over South Africa at East London on 24 January 1999. The only two batsmen in their team to reach double figures, the pair added 226 runs for the fourth wicket – the best partnership by a West Indian pair in one-day international cricket – to haul their side to 292 for 9. South Africa were 249 all out in reply.

Highest and lowest

Highest score: 363 for 4 against New Zealand at Hamilton on 8 January 2014.

Lowest score: 54 all out against South Africa at Cape Town on 25 January 2004.

Biggest victories

By runs: by 215 runs against Netherlands at Delhi on 28 February 2011.

By wickets: by ten wickets on ten occasions.

By balls remaining (in the second innings): with 239 balls remaining against Scotland at Leicester on 27 May 1999.

Smallest victories

By runs: by one run on three occasions.

By wickets: by one wicket on ten occasions.

By balls remaining (in the second innings): off the last ball of the match on six occasions.

Most matches

Brian Lara has played in more one-day internationals than any other West Indies player. The West Indies' all-time leading run-scorer (he scored 10,348 runs at an average of 40.90) played in 295 one-day internationals between 1990 and 2007.

BANGLADESH

Considered the best of the rest following their victory in the ICC Trophy in Malaysia in 1997, Bangladesh were granted Test status in 2000 and soon found life with cricket's big boys a harsher proposition in all formats of the game. Having won just 80 of 283 one-day internationals, Bangladesh have the worst record of any of the current Test-playing nations.

OVERALL ONE-DAY INTERNATIONAL RECORD

Opposition	Span	Mat	Won	Lost	Tied	NR	%
All opponents	1986–2014	283	80	200	0	3	28.27

Highest and lowest

Highest score: 326 for 3 against Pakistan at Dhaka on 4 March 2014.

Lowest score: 58 all out against West Indies at Dhaka on 4 March 2011.

Biggest victories

By runs: by 160 runs against West Indies at Khulna on 2 December 2012.

By wickets: by nine wickets on two occasions: against Kenya at Khulna on 20 March 2006; and against Zimbabwe at Khulna on 30 November 2006.

By balls remaining (in the second innings): with 229 balls remaining against Zimbabwe at Chittagong on 3 November 2009.

Smallest victories

By runs: by three runs against New Zealand at Dhaka on 17 October 2010.

By wickets: by one wicket on two occasions: against Zimbabwe at Harare on 10 February 2007; and against Zimbabwe at Chittagong on 5 November 2009.

By balls remaining (in the second innings): with four balls remaining on three occasions.

Tamim Iqbal secures unlikely victory

Having watched Charles Coventry compile a world record 194 not out to lead Zimbabwe to a massive total of 312 for 8 in the fourth one-day international at Bulawayo on 16 August 2009, Bangladesh could easily have slid to a despondent defeat. To their great credit, however, they chased down the total with relish. **Tamim Iqbal's** 154 off 138 balls – the highest-ever score by a Bangladesh player in a one-day international – was the foundation as Bangladesh reached the victory target with four wickets and 3.1 overs to spare.

A bright light for Bangladesh

One of Bangladesh's most impressive performers in all formats of the game in recent times, Shakib Al Hasan made his one-day international debut against Zimbabwe aged 19 in August 2006 and scored an unbeaten 30 to help his side to a comfortable eight-wicket victory. It was a sign of things to come: in 133 one-day internationals to date, the classy left-hander has scored 3,779 runs at an average of 34.99 with five centuries, a record for a Bangladesh player in one-day international cricket.

Razzak defies doubters to set the pace

A left-arm spinner who has fallen foul of referees for a suspect action – ICC tests subsequently found his bowling arm was bent up to 28 degrees (13 more than the permissible amount), **Abdur Razzak** has endured a stop-start international career. When he has played, however, he has been effective, taking 206 wickets in 150 matches – a record haul for a Bangladesh player in the 50-over format of the game.

Magic Mortaza too good for Kenya

Mashrafe Mortaza was the chief architect of Bangladesh's six-wicket victory over Kenya at the Gymkhana Club Ground in Nairobi on 15 August 2006 – Bangladesh's 20th victory in one-day international cricket. The medium-fast bowler ripped the heart out of the home side's batting line-up, taking 6 for 26 – the best figures by a Bangladesh bowler in one-day international history – to reduce Kenya to 118 all out. Bangladesh reached the victory target for the loss of four wickets with 138 balls to spare.

Highest partnership

Rajin Saleh (108 not out) and captain Habibul Bashar (64 not out) combined to great effect against Kenya at Fatullah on 25 March 2006, putting on an unbroken stand of 175 for the fourth wicket – a national record in ODI cricket – to secure a seven-wicket victory.

IRELAND

Granted one-day international status in 2005, Ireland have gone on to earn a reputation as the giant-killers of world cricket. At the 2007 ICC World Cup they produced some headline-grabbing results – a tie with Zimbabwe and a sensational three-wicket victory over Pakistan – to reach the Super Eights. And they did it again at the 2011 ICC World Cup when they beat England.

OVERALL ONE-DAY INTERNATIONAL RECORD

Opposition	Span	Mat	Won	Lost	Tied	NR	%
All opponents	2006–14	82	37	38	3	4	49.35

Most four-wicket-plus hauls

Six players have taken a record two four-wicket-plus hauls for Ireland in ODI cricket: Trent Johnston (59 matches, 2006–12); Andre Botha (42 matches, 2006–11); Kyle McCallan (39 matches, 2006–09); John Mooney (43 matches, 2006–12); George Dockrell (38 matches, 2010–14; and Kevin O'Brien (76 matches, 2006–14.

Mr Consistency

Ed Joyce enjoyed mixed fortunes in his 17 ODIs for England, scoring one century (107 against Australia at Sydney on 2 February 2007), but he has been an unquestionable success since he re-qualified for Ireland in 2011. The Dublin-born left-hander has scored 806 runs in 23 matches at an average of 40.30 – the best by any Ireland batsman in ODI history.

Highest and lowest

Highest score: 329 for 7 against England at Bangalore on 2 March 2011.

Lowest score: 77 all out against Sri Lanka at St George's, Grenada, on 18 April 2007.

Biggest victories

By runs: by 133 runs against Canada at Dublin on 19 September 2011.

By wickets: by nine wickets on two occasions.

By balls remaining (in the second innings): with 177 balls remaining against the Netherlands at Dublin on 18 August 2010.

Smallest victories

By runs: by one run against the Netherlands at Belfast on 11 July 2007.

By wickets: by one wicket against Scotland in Belfast on 6 September 2013.

By balls remaining (in the second innings): with one ball remaining against Scotland at Belfast on 6 September 2013.

Records fall in losing cause

Kevin O'Brien, with 142 – the second-highest individual score by an Ireland player in a one-day international – and William Porterfield, with 104 not out, produced the best partnership in Ireland's history (227) to haul their side to a challenging 284 for 4 against Kenya in the two sides' ICC World Cricket League encounter at Nairobi on 2 February 2007. But their record-breaking performances were not enough to win Ireland the game; Kenya just reached their target with one wicket and six balls in hand.

O'Brien guns down England

Ireland's match against England at the 2011 ICC World Cup seemed to be heading to the pre-game script: England had posted 327 for 8 and Ireland, in reply, were floundering on 111 for 5 in the 25th over and heading for defeat. But Kevin O'Brien had other ideas: he smashed a 63-ball 113, hitting six sixes and reaching his century off a mere 50 balls to help Ireland to a three-wicket victory.

Age no barrier for Johnston

An Australian by birth, whose career developed at New South Wales alongside the likes of Brett Lee, Mark Taylor and Michael Slater before he switched his allegiance to Ireland, **Trent Johnston** has been a mainstay of his country's bowling attack in ODI cricket despite his advancing years. On 19 April 2009 (10 days before his 35th birthday), he enjoyed his best moments in the international arena, taking an Irish record 5 for 14 against Canada at Centurion. He is also Ireland's leading wicket-taker (with 63).

KENYA

Kenya caused one of the greatest shocks in ODI cricket history when they reached the semi-finals of the 2003 ICC World Cup, but that performance remains the exception in the Africans' encounters at the top table of international cricket. They remain very much among the second tier of world cricket.

OVERALL ONE-DAY INTERNATIONAL RECORD

Opposition	Span	Mat	Won	Lost	Tied	NR	%
All opponents	1996–2014	154	42	107	0	5	28.18

Highest and lowest

Highest score: 347 for 3 against Bangladesh at Nairobi on 10 October 1997.

Lowest score: 69 all out against New Zealand at Chennai on 20 February 2011.

Biggest victories

By runs: by 190 runs against Scotland at Mombasa on 17 January 2007.

By wickets: by ten wickets against Bermuda at Nairobi on 29 January 2007.

By balls remaining (in the second innings): with 191 balls remaining against Bermuda on 29 January 2007.

Smallest victories

By runs: by six runs against Scotland at Mombasa on 21 January 2007.

By wickets: by one wicket on two occasions: against Ireland at Nairobi on 2 February 2007; and against Bermuda at Nairobi on 28 October 2007.

By balls remaining (in the second innings): with six balls remaining against Ireland at Nairobi on 2 February 2007.

Kenya's finest

Steve Tikolo is regarded as the finest player in history to emerge from the non-Test-playing nations. He holds numerous all-time records for Kenya in one-day international cricket: he has played in the most matches (131 between 1996 and 2014); he has scored the most runs (3,369 at the respectable average of 29.55); and he has recorded the most centuries (three – with a highest score of 111 against Bermuda at Mombasa on 14 November 2006).

All-round asset

Thomas Odoyo's wholehearted all-round performances have made him a key member of Kenya's side from the moment he made his debut as a 17-year-old at the 1996 ICC World Cup. The first non-Test player to achieve the 1,500-run, 100-wicket double in one-day international cricket, he has scored 2,366 runs with the bat (with a highest score of 111 not out against Canada at Nairobi on 18 October 2007) in 131 matches, but it is his performances with the ball that are more noteworthy: he holds his country's all-time records for the most wickets (141) and for the most four-wicket-plus hauls (five – with a best of 4 for 25 against Bermuda at Mombasa on 12 November 2006).

Obuya heroics with the ball cause a stir

It was one of the finest days in Kenya's cricket history, and a sensational spell of bowling from Collins Obuya lay at the heart of it. The leg-spin bowler took 5 for 24 – the best-ever figures by a Kenyan bowler in a one-day international – to help his side to a headline-grabbing 53-run victory over Sri Lanka in the two countries' Pool B encounter at Nairobi in the 2003 ICC World Cup.

Kenya shock Bangladesh with record-breaking display

Dipak Chudasama (122) and Kennedy Otieno (144 – the highest-ever score by a Kenyan batsman in one-day cricket) recorded not only the highest partnership in their country's history but also the highest opening partnership in all 1,239 one-day internationals (their 225 surpassed Australian pair Geoff Marsh and David Boon's 212 in Jaipur in 1986–87) as Kenya cantered to a comfortable 150-run win over Bangladesh at Nairobi on 1 March 1997 – this was the first match for both countries after being granted one-day international status.

NETHERLANDS

Winners of the ICC Trophy in 2001, the Netherlands have never been able to make the transition from second-tier standouts to minor members of world cricket's elite. Regular qualifiers for the ICC World Cup (they appeared in 1996, 2003, 2007 and 2011), they have won one one-day international match against a Test-playing nation – against Bangladesh in 2010 – in 23 attempts.

OVERALL ONE-DAY INTERNATIONAL RECORD

Opposition	Span	Mat	Won	Lost	Tied	NR	%
All opponents	1996–2014	76	28	44	1	3	39.04

A serious talent

The Netherlands' big-name player – and fast developing a reputation as being the best player outside the Test game – South African-born, but of Dutch descent, **Ryan ten Doeschate** has produced some outstanding performances for his country with both bat and ball since making his debut in July 2006. In 33 one-day internationals he has set Netherlands records for the most runs scored (1,541, at a hefty average of 67.00), for the most centuries (five, with a highest score of 119 against England at Nagpur on 22 February 2011), and stands second on his country's all-time wicket-taking list with 55.

Breaking the World Cup duck

Revelling in the chance to play against opponents of whom they had the measure on the one-day game's greatest stage, Feiko Kloppenburg (121) and Klaas-Jan von Noortwijk (134 not out) produced a performance of the highest class to propel their side to a first-ever victory in the ICC World Cup. The pair put on a record 228 for the second wicket to lead the Netherlands' charge to 314 for 4 against Namibia at Bloemfontein on 3 March 2003; they then bowled out Namibia for 250 to win the match by 64 runs.

Most successful captain

A steady performer behind the stumps, and an inspirational figure in the Netherlands squad, **Jeroen Smits** is the most successful Netherlands captain in one-day international cricket, leading his side to 11 wins in 17 matches as captain between 2007 and 2009.

Bukhari becomes the go-to man

Consistency has been the key to Mudassar Bukhani's 46-match career with the Netherlands since he made his ODI debut against Canada in Toronto on 3 July 2007 and, without destroying sides has become a performer his captain can rely upon. The medium-fast bowler's haul of 57 wickets for his country (with a best of 3 for 17 against Kenya at Nairobi on 18 February 2010) is an all-time national record.

Barresi shines in defeat

It did not turn out to be the day to remember Wesley Barresi might have imagined after he had hit his first century in ODI cricket and his country's highest-ever score. For although the right-hander's 137 not out led his side to 265 for 6 against Kenya at Lincoln, New Zealand, on 23 January 2014, the Kenyans reached the target with 14.2 overs and four wickets to spare.

Highest and lowest

Highest score: 315 for 8 against Bermuda at Rotterdam on 18 August 2007.

Lowest score: 80 all out against the West Indies at Dublin on 10 July 2007.

Biggest victories

By runs: by 172 runs against Bermuda at Rotterdam on 18 August 2007.

By wickets: by nine wickets on two occasions.

By balls remaining (in the second innings): with 183 balls remaining against Canada at King City, Canada, on 29 August 2013.

Smallest victories

By runs: by six runs against Ireland at Nairobi on 5 February 2007.

By wickets: by one wicket against Canada at Benoni on 1 December 2006.

By balls remaining (in the second innings): with two balls remaining against Canada at Benoni on 1 December 2006.

SCOTLAND

Scotland have been a standout team in world cricket's second tier in recent years, but have failed to find the ingredients required to move to the next level. ICC Trophy winners for the first time in 2005 and again in 2013–14, they have qualified for two of the last three ICC World Cups, but have still to record their first victory in the tournament and have never beaten a Test-status side in a one-day international.

OVERALL ONE-DAY INTERNATIONAL RECORD

Opposition	Span	Mat	Won	Lost	Tied	NR	%
All opponents	1999–2014	66	24	39	0	3	38.09

Highest and lowest

Highest score: 341 for 9 against Canada at Christchurch on 23 January 2014.

Lowest score: 68 all out against the West Indies at Leicester on 27 May 1999.

Biggest victories

By runs: by 170 runs against Canada at Christchurch on 23 January 2014.

By wickets: by six wickets on two occasions: against the Netherlands at Dublin on 29 July 2008; and against Afghanistan at Ayr on 17 August 2010.

By balls remaining (in the second innings): with 166 balls remaining against the Netherlands at Dublin on 29 July 2008.

Smallest victories

By runs: by two runs against the Netherlands at Nairobi on 2 February 2007.

By wickets: by one wicket against the Netherlands at Amstelveen oin 1 July 2010.

By balls remaining (in the second innings): off the last ball of the match against Ireland at Nairobi on 30 January 2007.

Most centuries

The Scotland record for the most career centuries in one-day internationals is two, a feat achieved by two players: **Neil McCallum** (in 41 matches between 2006 and 2010, with a highest score of 121 not out against Ireland at Benoni on 1 April 2009); and Gavin Hamilton (in 38 matches between 1999 and 2011, with a highest score of 119 against Canada at Aberdeen on 7 July 2009).

Majid provides measure of calm

Majid Haq's right-arm off-spin has been a steadying presence in the Scotland bowling attack from the moment he made his debut against Bangladesh at Dhaka on 17 December 2006. Economic rather than destructive (he has a career economy rate of 4.38), he has gone on to play 43 times for his country and has taken a national record 51 wickets, with a best of 4 for 28 against the West Indies at Dublin on 12 July 2007.

Second time lucky

Gavin Hamilton put the disappointment of a solitary, non-run-scoring, non-wicket-taking Test appearance for England (against South Africa at Johannesburg in November 1999) behind him to forge a long and successful career with Scotland. The West Lothian-born all-rounder has appeared in 38 ODIs for his country since 1999 and has scored a Scottish record 1,231 runs.

Majestic MacLeod

A standout performance with the bat from Calum MacLeod saw Scotland crush Canada by 170 runs in the two countries' ICC Trophy match at Hagley Oval, Christchurch, New Zealand, on 23 January 2013. The Glasgow-born opener smashed the highest score in his country's one-day international history – 175 off 141 balls (with five sixes and 14 fours) as Scotland amassed an imposing 341 for 9. Canada were all out for 171 in reply.

Record tumbles in a losing cause

Gavin Hamilton (119) and Fraser Watts (101) put on a record-breaking display against Canada at Aberdeen on 7 July 2009, but Scotland's day still ended in disappointment. The pair added 203 for the opening wicket – a record partnership for Scotland in one-day internationals – to lead their side to a seemingly formidable 286 for 4; Canada, however, reached the target with six wickets in hand and eight balls to spare.

ZIMBABWE

Zimbabwe was a cricket nation on the up. They appeared in nine successive ICC World Cups between 1983 and 2007, causing several upsets along the way, and by the turn of the 21st century could call upon a core of players of real international class. But as the country crumbled politically, so did its cricket team and, once again, Zimbabwe stands among the second tier of world cricket.

OVERALL ONE-DAY INTERNATIONAL RECORD

Opposition	Span	Mat	Won	Lost	Tied	NR	%
All opponents	1983–2013	421	110	297	5	9	27.30

Leader of the bowling pack

The finest fast bowler Zimbabwe has produced, lion-hearted Heath Streak shone in both Test cricket (the first and only Zimbabwe bowler to take 100 Test wickets, he ended up with 216 scalps in a 65-Test career) and in one-day international cricket (in 187 matches between 1993 and 2005 he took 237 wickets, with a Zimbabwe record eight four-wicket-plus hauls and a best bowling performance of 5 for 32 against India at Bulawayo on 15 February 1997).

Olonga outclasses England

Henry Olonga produced the best bowling figures by a Zimbabwe bowler in a one-day international at Cape Town on 28 January 2000 – and the best by any bowler on African soil – to send England crashing to their sixth defeat in eight meetings against Zimbabwe. The paceman took 6 for 19 to send England (chasing 212) tumbling to 107 all out and a 104-run defeat.

Heroics by Coventry but defeat for Zimbabwe

It says much for the current state of Zimbabwe cricket that a match in which one of their players produced a world record-equalling performance in ODI cricket could end in defeat. Charles Coventry smashed an unbeaten 194 against Bangladesh at Bulawayo on 16 August 2009 – equalling Saeed Anwar's record in 50-over matches (but since broken by Sachin Tendulkar) – to lead Zimbabwe to 312 for 8; yet Bangladesh eased to the target with four wickets in hand and 2.1 overs to spare.

Highest and lowest

Highest score: 351 for 7 against Kenya at Mombasa on 29 January 2009.

Lowest score: 35 all out against Sri Lanka at Harare on 25 April 2004.

Biggest victories

By runs: by 202 runs against Kenya at Dhaka on 27 March 1999.

By wickets: by nine wickets against Kenya at Bulawayo on 15 December 2002.

By balls remaining (in the second innings): with 204 balls remaining against Kenya at Bulawayo on 15 December 2002.

Smallest victories

By runs: by one run against New Zealand at Christchurch on 4 March 1998.

By wickets: by one wicket on four occasions.

By balls remaining (in the second innings): off the last ball of the match on three occasions.

Most matches

A top-order batsman capable of churning out big scores and a slow left-arm bowler with wicket-taking capabilities, Grant Flower has played in more one-day internationals for Zimbabwe than any other player: 221 between 1992 and 2011.

Highest partnership

While those around them crumbled, Stuart Carlisle and Sean Ervine produced a determined performance to take Zimbabwe to within a whisker of pulling off a memorable victory over India at Adelaide on 24 January 2004. Chasing 281 for victory, the pair came together at 46 for 3 and added 202 runs in 34.2 overs – a record for Zimbabwe in one-day international cricket – before Ervine fell for 100. Carlisle was out for 109 just 12 balls later, and Zimbabwe finished their innings an agonizing three runs short.

OTHER TEAMS

The ICC's decision in recent years to allocate one-day international status to matches between world cricket's second-tier nations has led to a surge in the number of matches: in 1990, 61 one-day internationals were played throughout the world; by 2009, that number had risen to 150. Here are some of the outstanding performances from the best of the rest.

OVERALL RESULTS SUMMARY (AGAINST ALL OPPONENTS)

Opposition	Span	Mat	Won	Lost	Tied	NR	%
Afghanistan	2009–14	31	17	14	0	0	54.83
Africa XI	2005–07	6	1	4	0	1	16.67
Asia XI	2005–07	7	4	2	0	1	57.14
Bermuda	2006–09	35	7	28	0	0	20.00
Canada	1979–2014	77	17	58	0	2	22.66
East Africa	1975	3	0	3	0	0	0.00
Hong Kong	2004–08	4	0	4	0	0	0.00
ICC World XI	2005	4	1	3	0	0	25.00
Namibia	2003	6	0	6	0	0	0.00
UAE	1994–2014	12	1	11	0	0	8.33
USA	2004	2	0	2	0	0	0.00

[Hong Kong, Israel, Wales and others appeared in 1970s/80s World Cups or qualifiers]

Crowd-pleasing performance

In a match hastily arranged to raise funds for victims of the 2004 Boxing Day tsunami, the ICC World XI put on a blistering batting display against an Asia XI at Melbourne on 10 January 2005. Propelled by a 102-ball 115 from Ricky Ponting and a belligerent 47-ball 69 from Chris Cairns, they reached 344 for 8 off their 50 overs. The Asia XI slipped to 232 all out in reply to lose the match by 112 runs.

Canada put in their place

Having recorded a shock 60-run victory over Bangladesh in their first-ever ICC World Cup match in 2003, Canada had their hopes dented when they lost to Kenya by four wickets and then came crashing down to earth with a humiliating thump as Sri Lanka outclassed them in devastating fashion. Inserted on a lively pitch at Paarl, Canada were reduced to 36 all out in 18.4 overs – the lowest score in World Cup history. Sri Lanka then eased to the target in just 4.4 overs for the loss of one wicket.

Bagai the pick of the batsmen

Alongside the Netherlands' Ryan ten Doeschate, Canada's **Ashish Bagai** is the only player from one of cricket's minor nations to have scored 1,000 runs in ODIs. The Delhi-born wicketkeeper-batsman has scored 1,964 runs in 62 matches between 2003 and 2013, with a highest score of 137 not out against Scotland at Nairobi on 31 January 2007.

LEADING BATSMEN (BY TEAM)

Team	Player	Mat	Inns	NO	Runs	HS	Ave	100	50	0
Afghanistan	Mohammad Shahzad (2009–14)	29	29	1	884	118	31.57	3	3	1
Africa XI	S.M. Pollock (2005–07)	6	6	2	298	130	74.50	1	1	0
Asia XI	D.P.M.D. Jayawardene (2005–07)	5	5	1	269	107	67.25	1	2	0
Bermuda	I.H. Romaine (2006–09)	35	34	3	783	101	25.25	1	4	5
Canada	A. Bagai (2003–13)	62	60	8	1,964	137*	37.76	2	16	2
East Africa	Frasat Ali (1975)	3	3	0	57	45	19.00	0	0	1
Hong Kong	Tabarak Dar (2004–08)	4	4	0	101	36	25.25	0	0	0
ICC World XI	K.C. Sangakkara (2005)	3	3	0	138	64	46.00	0	2	0
Namibia	A.J. Burger (2003)	6	6	0	199	85	33.16	0	1	0
UAE	Mazhar Hussain (1994–96)	7	7	0	179	70	25.57	0	1	0
USA	C.B. Lambert (2004)	1	1	0	39	39	39.00	0	0	0

LEADING BOWLERS (BY TEAM)

Team	Player	Mat	Overs	Runs	Wkts	BBI	Ave	Econ	SR	4	5
Afghanistan	Samiulla Shenwari (2009–14)	31	222.5	967	36	4/31	26.86	4.33	37.1	1	0
Africa XI	M. Morkel (2007)	3	30.0	166	8	3/50	20.75	5.53	22.5	0	0
Asia XI	Z. Khan (2005–07)	6	47.0	199	13	3/21	15.30	4.23	21.6	0	0
Bermuda	R.D.M. Leverock (2006–09)	32	280.4	1,123	34	5/53	33.02	4.00	49.5	0	1
Canada	H. Osinde (2006–13)	42	282.0	1,389	45	4/26	30.86	4.92	37.6	2	0
East Africa	Zulfiqar Ali (1975)	3	35.0	166	4	3/63	41.50	4.74	52.5	0	0
Hong Kong	Ilyas Gull (2004)	2	19.0	113	4	3/46	28.25	5.94	28.5	0	0
ICC World XI	D.L. Vettori (2005)	4	40.0	179	8	4/33	22.37	4.47	30.0	1	0
Namibia	R.J. van Vuuren (2003)	5	50.0	298	8	5/43	37.25	5.96	37.5	0	1
UAE	Khurram Khan (2004–14)	5	50.0	259	8	4/32	32.37	5.18	37.5	1	0
USA	R.W. Staple (2007)	2	10.0	76	2	2/76	38.00	7.60	30.0	0	0

Out of his depth

Weighing in at approximately 20 stones, Bermuda's **Dwayne Leverock** (the leading wicket-taker for Bermuda in one-day internationals) was probably the armchair fan's favourite player during the 2007 ICC World Cup, but he found himself on the wrong end of a good old-fashioned pummelling when Bermuda met India in a Group B encounter at Port of Spain, Trinidad, on 19 March 2007. The slow left-armer went for 96 runs off his ten overs, although he did take the wicket of Yuvraj Singh) – the second most expensive spell of bowling in World Cup history. India scored for 413 for 5 and went on to win the match by 257 runs – the largest margin of victory in one-day international cricket history.

Notable partnership

Mahendra Singh Dhoni (139 not out) and Mahela Jayawardene (107) proved the difference between the two sides as the Asia XI completed a 3–0 series sweep over the Africa XI at Chennai on 10 June 2007. Coming together in the 17th over with their side struggling on 72 for 5, the pair added 218 for the sixth wicket to lead the Asia XI to a mighty 331 for 8. In a spirited reply, the Africa XI were all out for 318.

Dhaniram enjoys second career with Canada

Having endured a brief and relatively unsuccessful first-class career as a lower-middle-order batsman with Guyana, the country of his birth, in the early 1990s, **Sunil Dhaniram** moved to Canada, added slow left-arm bowling to his armoury and revitalized his career as a solid all-rounder in the second tier of international cricket. In 44 one-day internationals for Canada between 2006 and 2010 he took a notable 41 wickets, with best figures of 5 for 32 against Bermuda at Ontario on 29 June 2008.

Codrington makes history for Canada

Canada's first-ever ICC World Cup campaign got off to a headline-grabbing start when they beat Bangladesh by 60 runs at Durban on 11 February 2003 to become the first "minor" cricket nation to record a victory over a Test-playing nation. The star of the show was Austin Codrington, a 27-year-old, Jamaican-born apprentice plumber who took 5 for 27 with his medium-pace bowling to help reduce Bangladesh (chasing 181) to 120 all out.

First forfeit of ODI

Canada forfeited their one-day international at Mombasa on 20 January 2007 owing to player illness; Kenya thus won the match without a ball being bowled – the only instance of such a case in the history of one-day international cricket.

PART III:
TWENTY20 CRICKET

Given the staggering manner in which Twenty20 cricket has been received by fans around the world, it seems strange to think the first Twenty20 international was staged as recently as 17 February 2005 and that it was taken less than seriously, with New Zealand players adorned with retro 1970s wigs and moustaches. It took a hastily arranged World Cup in South Africa in 2007 to change all that.

The 2007 ICC World Twenty20 was a spectacular success. When India faced off against Pakistan in the final, the match was beamed across 100 countries worldwide and became the tenth most-watched sports event of the year. India's five-run victory, and the ecstatic manner in which it was received, led to the subsequent establishment of the Indian Premier League and assured Twenty20 cricket's status on the domestic scene. The success of the five ICC World Twenty20 tournaments held to date has ensured international Twenty20 cricket is here to stay. For now, it may have been sidelined by existing television contracts committed to showing one-day internationals, but do not be too surprised if the 20-over game starts to form an increasing part of the cricket calendar in the years to come.

Sri Lanka became the fifth different winner of the ICC World Twenty20 when they took the crown in 2013–14.

ICC WORLD TWENTY20

It took some time, but the ICC finally realised that Twenty20 cricket not only provided great entertainment, but could was a considerable money-spinner. The first five ICC World Twenty20s, held in South Africa, England, the West Indies, Sri Lanka and Bangladesh, respectively, have all been a spectacular success. The tournament looks set to become a permanent fixture on the international cricket calendar.

Smallest victory (by wickets)

The smallest margin of victory (by wickets) in ICC World Twenty20 competition is a win by two wickets, which has occurred three times: when New Zealand beat Sri Lanka at Providence, Guyana, on 30 April 2010; when Pakistan beat South Africa at Colombo, Sri Lanka, on 28 September 2012; and when Hong Kong beat Bangladesh by two wickets at Chittagong on 20 March 2014.

Indiscipline with ball costs West Indies

When the West Indies looked back to see how they failed to defend a target of 205 against South Africa in the opening match of the 2007 ICC World Twenty20 at Johannesburg, they would have looked no further than the extras column. The men from the Caribbean delivered an astonishing 23 wides (a tournament record) as South Africa cruised to an eight-wicket victory with 14 balls to spare.

ICC WORLD TWENTY20 WINNERS

2007	India	(South Africa)
2009	Pakistan	(England)
2010	England	(West Indies)
2012	West Indies	(Sri Lanka)
2014	Sri Lanka	(Bangladesh)

Minnow-bashing at its best

Sri Lanka pulverized Kenya in the two sides' Group C meeting at Johannesburg in the 2007 ICC World Twenty20. Batting first, they blitzed the Kenyan bowling attack to all parts of the ground in amassing a gargantuan 260 for 6 off their 20 overs – the highest score by any team in any Twenty20 match – with **Sanath Jayasuriya** top-scoring with 88. Overwhelmed, Kenya crept to 88 for 9. Sri Lanka's 172-run margin of victory is the highest (by runs) in international Twenty20 history.

Australia cruise into final four

With both sides needing to win to progress to the semi-finals of the 2007 ICC World Twenty20, the match between Australia and Sri Lanka at Cape Town on 20 September 2007 was billed as a high-stakes, winner-takes-all encounter. It certainly wasn't a nail-biting one, however. Australia dismissed Sri Lanka for 101 and reached 102 without losing a wicket – **Matthew Hayden** (58 not out) and Adam Gilchrist (31 not out) in 10.2 overs. South Africa (94/0) recorded the second ten-wicket victory in the World Twenty20 against Zimbabwe (93/8) at Hambantota on 20 September 2012.

The Netherlands crumble

After qualifying for the main draw of the 2014 ICC World Twenty20, things could not have got off to a worse start for the Netherlands in their opening group game against Sri Lanka at Chittagong. After losing the toss, they were skittled for a paltry 39 in just 10.3 overs. Sri Lanka needed just five overs to knock off the runs to record the biggest victory by balls remaining (90) in the tournament's history. Things did get better for the Netherlands: a week later they beat England by 45 runs.

Most defeats

Bangladesh have suffered the most defeats in ICC World Twenty20 matches, 15 in 18 matches. England, champions in 2010, stand second on the list with 14 defeats in 26 matches.

Most victories

Sri Lanka, the 2013–14 winners, hold the record for the most victories in ICC World Twenty20 matches (with 21 in 31 matches played). Pakistan, the 2009 champions, stand second on the list with 18 victories in 30 matches.

ICC WORLD TWENTY20 LEAGUE TABLE (RANKED BY WIN PERCENTAGE)

Pos	Team (Span)	Mat	Won	Lost	Tied	NR	%
1	Sri Lanka (2007–14)	31	21	9	1	0	69.35
2	Nepal (2014)	3	2	1	0	0	66.66
3	India (2007–14)	28	17	9	1	1	64.81
4	Pakistan (2007–14)	30	18	11	1	0	61.66
5	South Africa (2007–14)	26	16	10	0	0	61.53
6	Australia (2007–14)	25	14	11	0	0	56.00
7	West Indies (2007–14)	25	12	11	1	1	52.08
8	New Zealand (2007–14)	25	11	12	2	0	48.00
9	Netherlands (2009–14)	9	4	5	0	0	44.44
10	England (2007–14)	26	11	14	0	1	44.00
11	Zimbabwe (2007–14)	9	3	6	0	0	33.33
=	Hong Kong (2014)	3	1	2	0	0	33.33
13	Ireland (2009–14)	12	3	7	0	2	30.00
14	Bangladesh (2007–14)	18	3	15	0	0	16.66
15	Afghanistan (2010–14)	7	1	6	0	0	14.28
16	Scotland (2007–09)	4	0	3	0	1	0.00
=	United Arab Emirates (2014)	3	0	3	0	0	0.00
=	Kenya (2007)	2	0	2	0	0	0.00

BELOW: *South Africa celebrate their slender one-run victory over New Zealand in their Group D encounter at the 2009 ICC World Twenty20 at Lord's.*

Last-ball successes

The Netherlands shocked hosts England at the home of cricket, Lord's, in the two sides' opening Group B encounter at the 2009 ICC World Twenty20. Chasing 163 for victory, they squeaked over the winning line off the last ball of the match to record a memorable four-wicket victory. There have been four other last-ball success in ICC World Twenty20 history: Sri Lanka beat India at Gros Inlet on 11 May 2010; India beat South Africa at Colombo on 2 October 2012; Ireland beat Zimbabwe at Sylhet on 17 March 2014; and Zimbabwe beat the Netherlands at Sylhet on 19 March 2009.

ABOVE: *The Netherlands celebrate their unlikely last-ball victory over England at Lord's at the 2009 ICC World Twenty20.*

Fine line between victory and defeat

New Zealand have made a habit of being involved in ICC World Twenty20 games that have been resolved by the slenderest of margins. In their Group D encounter against South Africa at Lord's in 2009, they fell to defeat by one run; eleven months later, against Pakistan at Bridgetown, Barbados, they won by one run. The tournament's other one-run victory occurred when India beat South Africa at Colombo on 2 October 2012.

Runs galore at Durban

India and England's Group E encounter at Durban in the 2007 ICC World Twenty20 captured the very essence of all that is good about the shortest format of the game – hard hitting and plenty of runs. India, boosted by six sixes in a Stuart Broad over from **Yuvraj Singh** – reached 218 for 4. England reached a spirited 200 for 6 in reply to lose the match by 18 runs. The match aggregate of 418 runs is the highest in the tournament's history.

BATTING RECORDS

MOST RUNS: TOP 10

Pos	Runs	Player	Mat	Inns	NO	HS	Ave	100	50	0
1	1,016	D.P.M.D. Jayawardene (SL, 2007–14)	31	31	5	100	39.07	1	5	1
2	807	C.H. Gayle (WI, 2007–14)	23	22	2	117	40.35	1	7	1
3	764	T.M. Dilshan (SL, 2007–14)	31	30	4	96*	29.38	0	5	5
4	661	K.C. Sangakkara (SL, 2007–14)	31	30	4	68	25.42	0	4	2
5	637	B.B. McCullum (NZ, 2007–14)	25	25	3	123	28.95	1	2	2
6	607	A.B. de Villiers (SA, 2007–14)	26	25	4	79*	28.90	0	4	0
7	585	R.G. Sharma (Ind, 2007–14)	23	20	8	79*	48.75	0	6	0
8	580	K.P. Pietersen (Eng, 2007–10)	15	15	2	79	44.61	0	4	0
9	541	Yuvraj Singh (Ind, 2007–14)	27	24	3	70	25.76	0	4	0
10	524	G. Gambhir (Ind, 2007–12)	21	20	0	75	26.20	0	4	2

Most ducks

It seems to be "boom boom" or bust for Shahid Afridi with the bat at the ICC World Twenty20. The hard-hitting Pakistan player may stand third on the tournament's all-time career strike-rate list (hitting 149.50 runs per every 100 balls faced) but he also tops the list of batsmen who have recorded the most ducks (with five).

On-song Samuels is a big hit for Windies

When Sri Lanka dismissed danger man Chris Gayle for a mere three (off 16 balls) to reduce the West Indies to 14 for 2 after 5.5 overs of the 2012–13 ICC World Twenty20 final, they must have thought they already had one hand on the trophy. But Marlon Samuels had other ideas: the Jamaican right-hander held the West Indies together, hitting six sixes en route to a 56-ball 76 – the highest individual score ever recorded in an ICC World Twenty20 final – to lead his side to a respectable 137 for 6. Samuels' man of the match-winning efforts proved too much for Sri Lanka, who slipped to 101 all out in reply.

Getting off to a record-breaking start

The 2007 ICC World Twenty20 got off to an explosive start from the moment the West Indies started their innings against hosts South Africa at Johannesburg on 11 September 2007. **Chris Gayle**, playing at his destructive best, smashed a sensational 57-ball 117 – the first century in international Twenty20 cricket. The left-hander blazed 88 of his runs in boundaries (a staggering 75.2 per cent), with a tournament record ten sixes and seven fours, to lead his side to 205 for 6. The fireworks did not end there. South Africa, inspired by an unbeaten 90 from Herschelle Gibbs, reached the victory target for the loss of two wickets with 14 balls to spare. Gayle may have experienced disappointment on that occasion, but his hard-hitting exploits did not end there: he holds two all-time ICC World Twenty20 records: the most career sixes (49); and the most scores of 50 or over (eight).

Kohli shines for India

Following the conclusion of the 2014 ICC World Twenty20, few could doubt Virat Kohli's claim as being the most in-form batsman on the planet. For the Delhi-born right-handed stroke-player was in scintillating form throughout the tournament, hitting an all-time high 319 runs, with four half-centuries, including an unbeaten, match-winning 72 against South Africa in the semi-final and 77 (off 58 balls) in the final against Sri Lanka. Not that his performance was enough to land India the title: Sri Lanka reached India's total of 130 for 4 with six wickets and 13 balls to spare.

HIGHEST SCORES BY BATTING POSITION

Pos	Score	Player	For	Against	Venue	Date
1/2	117	C.H. Gayle	West Indies	SA	Johannesburg	11 Sep 2007
1/2	116*	A.D. Hales	England	SL	Chittagong	27 Mar 2014
3	123	**B.B. McCullum**	New Zealand	Bang	Pallekelle	21 Sep 2012
4	94	Umar Akmal	Pakistan	Aus	Dhaka	23 Mar 2014
5	86*	J.P. Duminy	South Africa	NZ	Chittagong	24 Mar 2014
6	85*	C.L. White	Australia	SL	Bridgetown	9 May 2010
7	60*	M.E.K. Hussey	Australia	Pak	Gros Inlet	14 May 2010
8	44	Gulbodin Naib	Afghanistan	Eng	Colombo	21 Sep 2012
9	34	G.P. Swann	England	SL	Pallekelle	1 Oct 2012
10	22	Hamid Hassan	Afghanistan	SA	Bridgetown	5 May 2010
11	13*	J.D. Nel	Scotland	Pak	Durban	12 Sep 2007

Six sixes in an over

Yuvraj Singh is rightly regarded as one of the cleanest and most destructive strikers of the ball in world cricket, as Stuart Broad found out. In the 18th over of India's Group E match against England at Durban on 19 September 2007, the left-hander smashed the hapless English bowler for six consecutive sixes to become the first player in Twenty20 cricket (and the fourth in senior cricket) to achieve the feat.

Smith's end-of-innings blitz

Dwayne Smith provided some late-order fireworks to haul the West Indies to a respectable total of 164 for 8 in their must-win Group A encounter with Bangladesh at Johannesburg in the 2007 ICC World Twenty20. Batting at No. 7, the Barbados all-rounder smashed 29 off seven balls – his innings strike-rate of 414.28 runs scored per 100 balls is the highest in the tournament's history (for a batsman who has scored more than 20 runs). Not that it was a match-winning performance: Bangladesh reached the target for the loss of four wickets with two overs to spare to send the West Indies crashing out of the tournament.

Kohli's coming of age for India

An ICC Under-19 World Cup-winning captain in 2008 and part of the India side that won the ICC World Cup on home soil three years later, **Virat Kohli** is starting to fulfil the promise that led many to predict he would be the leading batsman of India's post-Tendulkar era. After overcoming a difficult start to his international career, perhaps overcome by the weight of expectation that any bright young star attracts in India, he has matured into a truly modern player; one who paces his innings at a high tempo and who possesses shots all round the ground. He has shone at the ICC World Twenty20, scoring 185 runs in his debut tournament in 2012 and a record 319 in 2014. His overall average in the competition (72.00) is comfortably the best of any player to have played in the event and some way ahead of the second-placed player on the list, Australia's Mike Hussey (with 54.62).

McCullum's new record

Any hopes Bangladesh might have had of restricting New Zealand to a low score in the ICC World Twenty20 at Pallekele on 21 September 2012 disappeared as soon as Brendon McCullum strode to the crease. He was in electric form, passing 50 in 29 balls and reaching his century off just 51 balls before finally falling for a tournament-record 123. His innings propelled New Zealand to an imposing 191 for 3 and an easy 59-run victory.

Mahela's magic touch

Mahela Jayawardene excels in all forms of cricket. Sri Lanka's best Test batsman (his total of 11,319 runs is sixth all-time), he has been outstanding in the 20-over game, particularly at the ICC World Twenty20. He is the tournament's all-time leading run-scorer, with 1,016 runs in 31 matches (209 more than second-placed Chris Gayle), is one of only six players to score a World Twenty20 century (100 against Zimbabwe at Providence on 3 May 2010). He also holds the tournament record for the most balls faced (754).

BOWLING RECORDS

MOST WICKETS: TOP 10

Pos	Wkts	Player	Mat	O	M	R	BBI	Ave	Econ	SR	4	5
1	38	S.L. Malinga (SL, 2007–14)	31	102.4	0	763	5/31	20.07	7.43	16.2	0	1
2	36	Saeed Ajmal (Pak, 2009–14)	23	89.2	1	607	4/19	16.86	6.79	14.8	3	0
3	35	B.A.W. Mendis (SL, 2009–14)	21	78.3	3	526	6/8	15.02	6.70	13.4	1	1
=	35	Shahid Afridi (Pak, 2007–14)	30	119.0	1	788	4/11	22.51	6.62	20.1	2	0
=	35	Umar Gul (Pak, 2007–14)	24	82.4	0	604	5/6	17.25	7.30	14.1	1	1
6	30	S.C.J. Broad (Eng, 2007–14)	26	86.5	2	671	3/17	22.36	7.72	17.3	0	0
7	29	D.W. Steyn (SA, 2009–14)	21	77.1	1	511	4/17	17.62	6.62	15.9	1	0
8	24	M. Morkel (SA, 2007–14)	17	62.4	0	452	4/17	18.83	7.21	15.6	2	0
9	22	G.P. Swann (Eng, 2009–12)	16	55.0	2	358	3/24	16.27	6.50	15.0	0	0
10	20	M.G. Johnson (Aus, 2007–10)	14	52.1	0	351	3/15	17.55	6.72	15.6	0	0
=	20	D.L. Vettori (NZ, 2007–12)	17	67.1	0	392	4/20	19.60	5.83	20.1	1	0
=	20	N.L. McCullum (NZ, 2007–14)	20	62.1	0	378	3/15	18.90	6.08	18.6	0	0
=	20	Shakin Al Hasan (Bang, 2007–14)	18	65.1	0	420	4/34	21.00	6.44	19.5	1	0

Malinga tops the charts

No fast bowler has struck more fear into the hearts of opposition batsmen in Twenty20 cricket than **Lasith Malinga** (right) Armed with pinpoint-accurate yorkers, the Sri Lankan paceman has excelled in the game's shortest format, and in particular at the ICC World Twenty20, at which he has taken an all-time record 38 wickets in 31 matches (with a best of 5 for 31 against England at Pallekele on 1 October 2012).

Narine bounces back in style

Adversity can sometimes bring out the best in everyone. Just ask Sunil Narine. For when the Trinidad off-spinner's action was questioned in 2011 and he was forced to re-model his action, it could have signalled the beginning of the end of his career; instead, he came back better than ever. He has been a sensation at the ICC World Twenty20, taking 15 wickets in two tournaments (2012 and 2014) with an economy rate of 5.17 runs per over – the best of any bowler in the competition's history.

Most maidens bowled

Given the nature of the game, a maiden over is a particularly rare feat in international Twenty20 cricket. The record for the most career maidens bowled in ICC World Twenty20 matches is four, set by Harbhajan Singh. The Indian off-spinner has achieved the feat in 18 overs between 2007 and 2012.

Mendis bounces back in style

Anyone who thought that **Ajantha Mendis** (above) had lost his way in international cricket was forced to eat their words following his performances at the 2012 ICC World Twenty20. The Sri Lankan spin magician was back to his very best, bamboozling batsmen throughout the tournament and setting numerous records along the way: for the most wickets in a single tournament (15); for the best figures in an innings (6 for 8 against Zimbabwe at Hambantota on 18 September 2012). He was part of the Sri Lankan side that won the title in 2013–14 and holds the all-time tournament records for the best average (13.40) and for the best strike-rate (15.02).

MOST WICKETS TAKEN (BY TEAM): TOP 5

Pos	Wkts	Team (Span)	Mat	Won	Lost	Tied	NR	W/L	Ave	RPO
1	212	Pakistan (2007–14)	30	18	11	1	0	1.63	20.64	7.41
2	201	Sri Lanka (2007–14)	31	21	9	0	0	2.33	19.38	7.17
3	189	India (2007–14)	28	17	9	1	1	1.88	20.68	7.53
4	183	South Africa (2007–14)	26	16	10	0	0	1.60	20.18	7.48
5	166	Australia (2007–14)	25	14	11	0	0	1.27	22.62	7.79

Gul hits new heights

A mainstay of Pakistan's bowling attack since making his international debut as a 19-year-old in 2003 (having made just nine prior first-class appearances), Umar Gul is the perfect death bowler, capable of bowling high-speed reverse-swinging yorkers in the closing overs of an innings. The leading wicket-taker in both the 2007 and 2009 tournaments, he was in particularly devastating form in the latter and was at his very best in Pakistan's match against New Zealand at The Oval on 13 June 2009. In that match he took an incredible 5 for 6 to become the first bowler in the tournament's history to take five wickets in an innings. Sri Lanka's Lasith Malinga, Ajantha Mendis, and Rangana Herath and the Netherlands Ashan Malik have since equalled his feat.

Ajmal is a late bloomer

Saeed Ajmal was a late starter to international cricket (playing his first Test aged 32), but the off-spinner has become an integral part of Pakistan's attack in all forms of the game and has enjoyed considerable success at the ICC World Twenty20. He was the second-highest wicket-taker at both the 2009 and 2010 tournaments and has the most four-wicket-plus hauls in an innings, with three – the best of which came when he took 4 for 19 against Ireland at The Oval on 15 June 2009.

LEADING WICKET-TAKER BY TOURNAMENT

Year (hosts)	Player (country)	Wickets
2007 (South Africa)	Umar Gul (Pakistan)	13
2009 (England)	Umar Gul (Pakistan)	13
2010 (West Indies)	Dirk Nannes (Australia)	14
2012 (Sri Lanka)	Ajantha Mendis (Sri Lanka)	15
2014 (Bangladesh)	Imran Tahir (South Africa)	12
	Ashan Malik (Netherlands)	12

Afridi's records with the ball

Shahid Afridi's exploits with the bat may have grabbed him more headlines over the years, but it is his exploits with the ball that have earned him a place among the ICC World Twenty20's record-breakers. The Pakistani leg-spinner has bowled more overs (119.0) and conceded more runs (788) than any other bowler in the tournament's history.

Most runs conceded in an innings

The ICC World Twenty20 record for the most runs conceded by a bowler in an innings is 64. Sri Lanka's **Sanath Jayasuriya** recorded figures of 4.0-0-64-0 against Pakistan at Johannesburg on 17 September 2007. Pakistan went on to win the match by 33 runs.

OTHER RECORDS

HIGHEST PARTNERSHIPS: TOP 10

Pos	Runs	Partners	Wkt	Team	Against	Venue	Date
1	166	D.P.M.D. Jayawardene, K.C. Sangakkara	2nd	Sri Lanka	WI	Bridgetown	7 May 2010
2	152	A.D. Hales, E.J.G. Morgan	3rd	England	SL	Chittagong	27 Mar 2014
3	145	C.H. Gayle, D.S. Smith	1st	West Indies	SA	Johannesburg	1 May 2010
4	145	T.M. Dilshan, D.P.M.D. Jayawardene	2nd	Sri Lanka	Eng	Chittagong	27 Mar 2014
5	142	Kamran Akmal, Salman Butt	1st	Pakistan	Bang	Gros Islet	1 May 2010
6	136	G. Gambhir, V. Sehwag	1st	India	Eng	Durban	19 Sep 2007
7	133	C.H. Gayle, A.D.S. Fletcher	1st	West Indies	Aus	The Oval	6 Jun 2009
=	133	S.R. Watson, D.A. Warner	1st	Australia	Ind	Colombo	28 Sep 2012
9	124	T.M. Dilshan, S.T. Jayasuriya	1st	Sri Lanka	WI	Nottingham	10 Jun 2009
=	124	Mohammez Hafeez, Imran Nazir	1st	Pakistan	Bang	Pallekelle	25 Sep 2012

Sri Lankan stars put West Indies to the sword

Two sublime innings from the team's two best batsmen helped Sri Lanka ease to a comfortable victory over hosts West Indies in the two sides' Super Eight encounter at Bridgetown, Barbados, on 7 May 2010. Mahela Jayawardene (98 not out) and Kumar Sangakkara (68) added 166 runs off 16.3 overs for the second wicket – the highest partnership in the tournament's history – to lead Sri Lanka to an imposing 195 for 3. In response, the West Indies slipped to 138 for 8 and defeat by 57 runs.

Most wicketkeeping dismissals

Kamran Akmal's wayward performances behind the stumps may have cost him his place in the Pakistan Test team since 2010, but, principally as a result of his hard-hitting batting, he has retained his place in his country's limited-overs teams and has enjoyed particular success at the ICC World Twenty20. He holds the all-time tournament record for the most dismissals with 30 – 12 catches and 18 stumpings – in 30 games between 2007 and 2014.

Most catches in an innings by a fielder

The record for the most catches in an innings by a fielder is four, by Darren Sammy, for the West Indies against Ireland at Providence, Guyana, on 30 April 2010.

De Villiers leads the way in the field

South Africa's **A.B. de Villiers** is fast developing a reputation as the best fielder in world cricket. Positioned for the most part at backward point or short midwicket – regular spots for many of the 20-over game's best fielders – he has taken more catches in ICC World Twenty20 matches than any other player (21 in 26 matches between 2007 and 2014).

HIGHEST PARTNERSHIPS: BY WICKET

Wkt	Runs	Partners	Team	Against	Venue	Date
1st	145	C.H. Gayle, D.S. Smith	West Indies	SA	Johannesburg	11 Sep 2007
2nd	166	D.P.M.D. Jayawardene, K.C. Sangakkara	Sri Lanka	WI	Bridgetown	7 May 2007
3rd	152	A.D. Hales, E.J.G. Morgan	England	SL	Chittagong	27 Mar 2014
4th	107	A.D. Hales, E.J.G. Morgan	England	WI	Pallekelle	27 Sep 2012
5th	119*	Shoaib Malik, Misbah-ul-Haq	Pakistan	Aus	Johannesburg	18 Sep 2007
6th	101*	C.L. White, M.E.K. Hussey	Australia	SL	Bridgetown	9 May 2010
7th	74	M.E.K. Hussey, S.P.D. Smith	Australia	Ban	Bridgetown	5 May 2010
8th	53	M.E.K. Hussey, M.G. Johnson	Australia	Pak	Gros Inlet	14 May 2010
9th	44	Gulbodin Naib, Shapoor Zadran	Afghanistan	Eng	Colombo	21 Sep 2012
10th	20	N.O. Miller, S.J. Benn	West Indies	Aus	Gros Inlet	11 May 2010
=	20	S.T. Finn, J.W. Dernbach	England	Ind	Colombo	23 Sep 2012

Most catches in a tournament

The record for the most catches in a single tournament is eight, a feat achieved by two players: Mike Hussey and Dave Warner, both for Australia at the 2010 ICC World Twenty20.

Most successful captain

Tournament success may may have eluded him in 2013–14, but **Mahendra Singh Dhoni** is the most successful captain in ICC World Twenty20 history, leading India to 17 wins in 28 matches between 2007 and 2014.

Most wicketkeeping dismissals in an innings

Seven wicketkeepers have recorded a competition-best four dismissals in an innings in ICC World Twenty20: Adam Gilchrist (Australia) against Zimbabwe on 12 September 2007 (4ct); Matt Prior (England) against South Africa on 16 September 2007 (4ct); Kamran Akmal (Pakistan) against the Netherlands on 9 June 2009 (4st); Niall O'Brien (Ireland) against Sri Lanka on 14 June 2009 (3ct, 1st); **M.S. Dhoni** (India) against Afghanistan on 1 May 2010 (4ct) and against Pakistan 30 September 2012 (4ct); AB de Villiers (South Africa) against Zimbabwe on 20 September 2012 (4ct); and Denesh Ramdin (West Indies) against Pakistan on 1 April 2014.

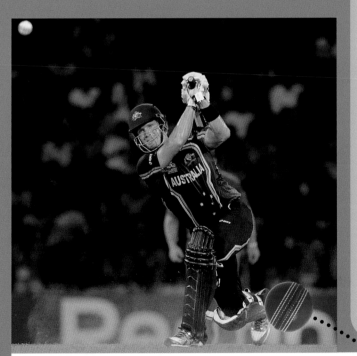

ICC WORLD TWENTY20 PLAYER OF THE TOURNAMENT WINNERS

2007	Shahid Afridi (Pakistan)
2009	Tillakaratne Dilshan (Sri Lanka)
2010	Kevin Pietersen (England)
2012	**Shane Watson** (Australia)
2014	Virat Kohli (India)

INTERNATIONAL TWENTY20

It took a comprehensive 100-run victory for England over Australia at the Rose Bowl in June 2005 before international Twenty20 cricket was taken seriously. Since then, as the ICC has tried to work out how best to integrate the new format into the international cricket calendar, matches – apart from the ICC World Twenty20 tournaments – have been few and far between, although they are becoming more regular.

RESULT SUMMARY

Team	Span	Mat	Won	Lost	Tied	NR	%
Afghanistan	2010–14	25	12	13	0	0	48.00
Australia	2005–14	73	37	33	2	1	52.77
Bangladesh	2006–14	40	11	29	0	0	27.50
Bermuda	2008	3	0	3	0	0	0.00
Canada	2008–13	19	4	14	1	0	23.68
England	2005–14	72	33	35	0	4	48.52
Hong Kong	2014	3	1	2	0	0	33.33
India	2006–14	52	30	20	1	1	59.80
Ireland	2008–14	37	20	14	0	3	58.82
Kenya	2007–13	29	10	19	0	0	34.48
Nepal	2014	3	2	1	0	0	66.66
Netherlands	2008–14	29	15	13	0	1	53.57
New Zealand	2005–14	75	34	34	5	2	50.00
Pakistan	2006–14	82	49	31	2	0	60.97
Scotland	2007–13	25	8	16	0	0	33.33
South Africa	2005–14	70	42	27	0	1	60.86
Sri Lanka	2006–14	66	41	23	1	1	63.84
United Arab Emirates	2014	3	0	3	0	0	0.00
West Indies	2006–14	63	29	30	3	1	49.19
Zimbabwe	2006–14	31	6	24	1	0	20.96

Highest and lowest

Highest score: 260 for 6 – Sri Lanka v Kenya at Johannesburg on 14 September 2007.

Lowest score: 39 all out – Netherlands v Sri Lanka at Chittagong on 24 March 2014.

Biggest victories

By runs: by 172 runs – Sri Lanka v Kenya at Johannesburg on 14 September 2007.

By wickets: by ten wickets on 11 occasions.

By balls remaining: with 90 balls remaining – Sri Lanka v Netherlands at Chittagong on 24 March 2013.

Smallest victories

By runs: by one run – on eight occasions.

By wickets: by one wicket – on two occasions.

By balls remaining: off the last ball of the match on 13 occasions.

Levi blasts his way into record books

Chasing 174 for victory and already 1–0 down in the three-match series, South Africa had it all to do in their Twenty20 international match against New Zealand at Hamilton on 19 February 2012. Their hero was an unlikely one: Richard Levi, in only his second match, was in scintillating form, smashing an incredible 51-ball unbeaten 117 (his century came off just 45 balls – the fastest in international T20 history) to lead them to a dominant eight-wicket victory with four overs to spare.

Finch puts England to the sword

Aaron Finch endured a faltering start to his international career with Australia since his debut in January 2011, but he showed he belonged at the game's highest level with a scintillating performance against England at Southampton on 29 August 2013. He smashed his way into the record books, hitting a sparkling 63-ball 156 (the highest score in international T20 history), including a world record 14 sixes. Finch's heroics helped Australia to a mighty 248 for 6 off their 20 overs; England never looked like reaching the target and eventually came up 39 runs short.

McCullum a big hit in Twenty20

There have been many examples of Twenty20 cricket enhancing a player's reputation, but perhaps the best is that of New Zealand's wicketkeeper-batsman **Brendon McCullum**. He ensured the Indian Premier League got off to a blistering start when he smashed 158 not out in the tournament's first-ever game – still the highest score in a Twenty20 match. He carried that form into international matches: he was the first batsman (of seven) to pass both 1,000 and 2,000 runs in Twenty20 internationals (1,814 runs, in 60 matches) and is the only batsman to have scored two centuries in Twenty20 international matches.

MOST RUNS: TOP 5

Pos	Runs	Player	M	I	NO	HS	Ave	BF	SR	100	50	0	4s	6s
1	2,044	B.B. McCullum (NZ, 2005–14)	68	67	10	123	35.85	1,505	135.81	2	13	3	192	85
2	1,493	D.P.M.D. Jayawardene (SL, 2006–14)	55	55	8	100	31.76	1,121	133.18	1	9	4	173	33
3	1,452	T.M. Dilshan (SL, 2006–14)	61	60	10	104*	29.04	1,217	119.30	1	9	8	168	27
4	1,391	D.A. Warner (Aus, 2009–14)	51	51	2	90*	28.38	1,001	138.96	0	10	5	133	63
5	1,382	K.C. Sangakkara (SL, 2006–14)	56	53	9	78	31.40	1,156	119.55	0	8	2	139	20

MOST WICKETS: TOP 5

Pos	Wkts	Player	Mat	Overs	Mdns	Runs	BBI	Ave	Econ	SR	4w	5w
1	85	Saeed Ajmal (Pak, 2009–14)	63	235.0	2	1,491	4/19	17.54	6.34	16.5	4	0
2	80	Umar Gul (Pak, 2007–14)	56	188.3	2	1,340	5/6	16.75	7.10	14.1	4	2
3	77	Shahid Afridi (Pak, 2006–14)	74	268.2	3	1,741	4/11	22.61	6.48	20.9	3	0
4	66	B.A.W. Mendis (SL, 2008–14)	39	147.3	5	952	6/8	14.42	6.45	13.4	3	2
5	65	S.C.J. Broad (Eng, 2006–14)	56	195.3	2	1,491	4/24	22.93	7.62	18.0	1	0
=	65	S.L. Malinga (SL, 2006–14)	56	193.5	0	1,407	5/31	21.64	7.25	17.8	0	1

Saeed Ajmal makes his mark

If proof were needed that a spin bowler takes time to learn his art, look no further than Saeed Ajmal. The off-spin bowler was a late newcomer to international cricket, making his debut in July 2008 aged 30, but when he arrived at the highest level of the game he did so as a master of his craft: his variation, control and wicket-taking abilities have seen him become an automatic selection for Pakistan. He has enjoyed particular success in international Twenty20 matches, taking a record 85 wickets in 63 matches with four four-wicket hauls and a best performance of 4 for 19 against Ireland at The Oval on 15 June 2009.

Safe pair of hands

The record for the most catches by a fielder in Twenty20 international matches is 36, a feat achieved by Ross Taylor (in 59 matches for New Zealand between 2006 and 2012).

Off to a galloping start

A forthright opening stand from Graeme Smith (88) and Loots Bosman (94) placed South Africa in a match-winning position in their international Twenty20 match against England at Centurion on 15 November 2009. The pair added 170 runs for the opening wicket – a record partnership in international Twenty20 cricket – to lead South Africa to an impressive 241 for 6. England wilted to a distant 157 for 8 in reply.

Hat-tricks

There have been three hat-tricks in international Twenty20 cricket: by Australia's Brett Lee, against Bangladesh at Cape Town on 16 September 2007 – Shakib Al Hasan (caught), Mashrafe Mortaza (bowled) and Alok Kapali (lbw); by New Zealand's Jacob Oram, against Sri Lanka at Colombo on 2 September 2009 – Angelo Mathews (caught and bowled), Malinga Bandara (caught) and Nuwan Kulasekara (caught); and by New Zealand's **Tim Southee**, against Pakistan at Auckland on 26 December 2010 – Younis Khan (caught), Mohammad Hafeez (caught) and Umar Akmal (lbw).

INDIAN PREMIER LEAGUE

First contested in 2008, principally off the back of the surge of enthusiasm in India for the new format of the game following the country's 2007 ICC World Twenty20 triumph, the Indian Premier League (IPL), featuring eight franchises, has been a huge success, attracting vast crowds and the best players from around the world.

INDIAN PREMIER LEAGUE WINNERS

2008	Rajasthan Royals
2009	Deccan Chargers
2010	Chennai Super Kings
2011	Chennai Super Kings
2012	**Kolkata Knight Riders**
2013	Mumbai Indians

RESULT SUMMARY

Team (Span)	Mat	Won	Lost	Tied	NR	%
Chennai Super Kings (2008–13)	99	59	38	1	1	60.71
Mumbai Indians (2008–13)	95	56	39	0	0	58.94
Sunrisers Hyderabad (2013)	17	9	7	1	0	55.88
Rajasthan Royals (2008–13)	90	48	41	1	0	53.88
Royal Challengers Bangalore (2008–13)	94	47	44	2	1	51.61
Kings XI Punjab (2008–13)	89	43	45	1	0	48.87
Kolkata Knight Riders (2008–13)	88	42	45	1	0	48.29
Delhi Daredevils (2008–13)	91	42	47	1	1	47.22
Kochi Tuskers Kerala (2011)	14	6	8	0	0	42.85
Deccan Chargers (2008–12)	75	29	46	0	0	38.66
Pune Warriors (2011–13)	46	12	33	0	1	26.66

Mumbai win IPL crown

Mumbai Indians underperformed in the first five editions of the Indian Premier League. That all changed in 2013: they won 11 of 16 matches in the round-robin phase and then recovered from a 48-run defeat to Chennai in the playoffs to beat Rajasthan (by 4 wickets) and Chennai (by 23 runs) in the final to win the trophy for the first time.

Glorious Gayle smashes his way into the records books

Ask any bowler in world cricket which batsman they would least like to bowl at when they are in full flow and the majority of them would say Chris Gayle. For when the former West Indies captain hits his straps, he can be virtually unstoppable: just ask the Pune Warriors bowling attack after Gayle, playing for Royal Challengers Bangalore, had dismantled them at the M. Chinnaswamy Stadium in Bangalore on 23 April 2013. Pune's nightmare started the moment they won the toss and elected to field. Gayle's onslaught started when he took 20 off the second over (which was interrupted for an hour by rain) and did not stop there: he took 24 off the fourth over (reaching his 50 off 17 balls), 17 off the fifth over, 28 off the sixth over (with four sixes) and reached his century off a mere 30 balls (to record the fastest hundred in Twenty20 history). By the time the 20-over innings was complete, Gayle was unbeaten on 175 (off 66 balls) – the highest-ever score in Twenty20 cricket, had struck a record 17 sixes and had helped Royal Challengers Bangalore to a massive 263 for 5 – the highest team total in Twenty20 history. Not surprisingly, the Challengers went on to win the game by 130 runs.

MOST RUNS: TOP 10

Pos	Runs	Player	Mat	Inns	NO	HS	Ave	BF	SR	100	50	0	4s	6s
1	2,802	S.K. Raina (2008–13)	99	95	15	100*	35.02	1,982	141.37	1	18	6	239	115
2	2,513	R.G. Sharma (2008–13)	97	93	16	109*	32.63	1,938	129.66	1	18	5	202	110
3	2,512	C.H. Gayle (2009–13)	59	58	10	175*	52.33	1,568	160.20	4	16	3	204	180
4	2,471	G. Gambhir (2008–13)	88	87	9	93	31.67	1,945	127.04	0	20	7	291	37
5	2,334	S.R. Tendulkar (2008–13)	78	78	11	100*	34.83	1,948	119.81	1	13	4	295	29
6	2,276	J.H. Kallis (2008–13)	90	89	10	89*	28.81	2,093	108.74	0	16	8	242	40
7	2,273	V. Kohli (2008–13)	93	85	13	99	31.56	1,831	124.13	0	14	1	218	71
8	2,243	M.S. Dhoni (2008–13)	96	84	25	70*	38.01	1,589	141.15	0	13	2	169	89
9	2,174	V. Sehwag (2008–13)	79	79	5	119	29.37	1,356	160.32	1	15	6	266	85
10	2,174	R. Dravid (2008–13)	89	82	5	75*	28.23	1,882	115.51	0	11	3	268	28

Star of the Show

Chris Gayle is, arguably, the most destructive batsman in world cricket. The former West Indian captain missed the inaugural IPL season, but has more than made up for it since. Playing for the Kolkata Knight Riders and Royal Challengers Bangalore, Gayle already is the all-time leader in centuries (four), sixes (180) and batting average (52.33).

Most scores of 50 or over

Gautham Gambhir has been one of the most consistent performers in the Indian Premier League's six-year history. The classy left-handed opener has racked up 20 scores of 50-plus in 88 matches for the Delhi Daredevils and Kolkata Knight Riders – an IPL record he shares with the prolific West Indian Chris Gayle.

Largest victories

By runs: by 140 runs – Kolkata v Bangalore at Bangalore on 18 April 2008.

By wickets: by ten wickets on six occasions.

By balls remaining: with 87 balls remaining – Mumbai v Kolkata at Mumbai on 16 May 2008.

Smallest victories

By runs: by one run on four occasions.

By wickets: by two wickets on two occasions – Bangalore v Chennai at Durban on 14 May 2009; Mumbai v Chennai at Mumbai on 6 May 2012.

By balls remaining: off the last ball of the match on 15 occasions.

Gayle hits new heights

Chris Gayle had a memorable IPL season for Bangalore in 2012. The hard-hitting opener compiled a single-season record 733 runs at an average of 61.08 with a strike-rate of 160.74 runs per 100 deliveries.

HIGHEST INDIVIDUAL SCORE: TOP 10

Pos	Runs	Player	Balls	4s	6s	SR	Team	Opposition	Ground	Date
1	175*	C.H. Gayle	66	13	17	265.15	Bangalore	Pune	Bangalore	23 Apr 2013
2	158*	B.B. McCullum	73	10	13	216.43	Kolkata	Bangalore	Bangalore	18 Apr 2008
3	128*	C.H. Gayle	62	7	13	206.45	Bangalore	Delhi	Delhi	17 May 2012
4	127	M. Vijay	56	8	11	226.78	Chennai	Rajasthan	Chennai	3 Apr 2010
5	120*	P.C. Valthaty	63	19	2	190.47	Punjab	Chennai	Mohali	13 Apr 2011
6	119	V. Sehwag	56	13	6	212.50	Delhi	Deccan	Hyderabad	5 May 2011
7	117*	A. Symonds	53	11	7	220.75	Deccan	Rajasthan	Hyderabad	24 Apr 2008
8	116*	M.E.K. Hussey	54	8	9	214.81	Chennai	Punjab	Mohali	19 Apr 2008
9	115	S.E. Marsh	69	11	7	166.66	Punjab	Rajasthan	Mohali	28 May 2008
10	114*	S.T. Jayasuriya	48	9	11	237.50	Mumbai	Chennai	Mumbai	14 May 2008
=	114*	M.K. Pandey	73	10	4	156.16	Bangalore	Deccan	Centurion	21 May 2009

MOST WICKETS: TOP 10

Pos	Wkts	Player	Mat	Inns	Overs	Mdns	Runs	BBI	Ave	Econ	SR	4	5
1	103	**S.L. Malinga** (2009–13)	73	73	282.2	5	1,849	5/13	17.95	6.54	16.4	2	1
2	95	A. Mishra (2008–13)	76	76	277.2	4	1,924	5/17	20.25	6.93	17.5	2	1
3	87	R.P. Singh (2008–13)	78	78	283.5	2	2,227	4/22	25.59	7.84	19.5	2	0
4	85	P.P. Ojha (2008–13)	79	77	268.3	0	1,929	3/11	22.69	7.18	18.9	0	0
5	84	R. Vinay Kumar (2008–13)	77	76	262.1	0	2,157	4/40	25.67	8.22	18.7	1	0
=	84	P.P. Chawla (2008–13)	87	87	297.2	2	2,237	4/17	26.63	7.52	21.2	1	0
7	79	D.J. Bravo (2008–13)	73	72	227.5	1	1,835	4/42	23.22	8.05	17.3	1	0
8	78	D.W. Steyn (2008–13)	69	69	266.0	7	1,688	3/8	21.64	6.34	20.4	0	0
=	78	Harbhajan Singh (2008–13)	82	80	284.3	3	1,925	5/18	24.67	6.76	21.8	1	1
10	76	I.K. Pathan (2008–13)	88	87	306.5	10	2,357	3/24	31.01	7.68	24.2	0	0
=	76	J.A. Morkel (2008–13)	78	75	254.1	3	2,058	4/32	27.07	8.09	20.0	1	0

Faulkner impresses with the ball

He may have come to the wider public's attention with some swashbuckling performances with the bat, notably a matchwinning 47-ball 69 for Australia against England in the second ODI at Brisbane in January 2014, but James Faulkner is fast developing a reputation as a highly promising all-rounder. And it is his performances with the ball that have earned him a place in the Indian Premier League's record books: he has taken 31 wickets in 19 matches in the competition at a record strike-rate of one wicket every 13.7 deliveries.

Terrific Tanvir tames the Super Kings

A scintillating spell of bowling from Sohail Tanvir saw Rajasthan cruise to victory over the Chennai Super Kings at Jaipur on 4 May 2008. The left-arm Pakistan paceman, who cost the Royals US$100,000 at auction, took 6 for 14 off his four-over stint – the best bowling figures in Twenty20 history (and the competition's only six-wicket haul) – to send Chennai spinning to 109 all out. Rajasthan cantered to victory for the loss of two wickets with 34 balls to spare.

Kolkata's Narine – the economy rate king

Sunil Narine has enjoyed a spectacular start to his Indian Premier League career with the Kolkata Knight Riders. The Trinidad-born, former West Indies Under-19 off-spinner made his IPL debut in 2012 and has gone on to take 46 wickets in 31 matches (with a best of 5 for 19) at the miserly economy rate of 5.47 runs per over – the best in the competition's history.

Highest partnership

Kings XI Punjab's Australian duo of Adam Gilchrist (106 off 55 balls) and Shaun Marsh (79 off 49 balls) put Bangalore's bowlers to the sword in an Indian Premier League group match at Dharamsala on 17 May 2011. The pair put on 206 runs for the second wicket – the highest partnership in the tournament's history – to lead their side to a mighty total of 232 for 2 off their 20-over allocation and an eventual 111-run victory.

Most dismissals

Not merely a belligerent performer with the bat (only ten players have scored more runs in the IPL), **Adam Gilchrist** has also shone behind the stumps for the Deccan Chargers: he has claimed 67 dismissals (51 catches, 16 stumpings) in 80 matches – an all-time tournament record.

Bravo hits his stride

How the West Indies have missed Dwayne Bravo's all-round talent in their Test side in recent years. After prioritizing Twenty20 cricket over the longest format of the game (he still plays one-day internationals for his country, currently as captain), the Trinidad star has played only 40 Tests (of the 81 for which he was available for selection) with his last appearance in the longest form of the game coming in 2010. But the West Indies' loss was Chennai Super Kings' gain during the 2013 edition of the Indian Premier League: Bravo took 32 wickets in 18 matches – a record for a single IPL season.

Keeping it tight

Wickets are not the be all and end all in Twenty20 cricket; a four-over stint that goes for anything less than six runs per over is a success. Two bowlers have done far better than that, each going for a miserly, tournament-record six runs off his four-over allocation (an economy rate of 1.50): Fidel Edwards (4.0-1-6-0 for Deccan against Kolkata at Cape Town on 19 April 2009); and **Ashish Nehra** (4.0-1-6-1 for Delhi against Punjab at Bloemfontein on 15 May 2009).

Most successful captain

A revelation for India since he took over the captaincy from Rahul Dravid in all forms of the game after leading his side to the ICC World Twenty20 crown in South Africa in 2007, **Mahendra Singh Dhoni** has proved equally inspirational for the Chennai Super Kings. He has guided his side to 58 wins in 96 matches – the most by any captain in the tournament's history – and led his side (the most expensive franchise in the competition) to the IPL crown in 2010 and 2011.

Regal Raina

Suresh Raina has made quite an impact on the Indian Premier League. The Chennai Super Kings left-hander has scored more runs than any other batsman in the competition's history (2,802 in 99 matches at an average of 35.02), has taken 52 catches (the most in Indian Premier League history) and has also made his mark with the ball: his spell of 2 for 0 off 0.3 overs against Rajasthan Royals at Jaipur on 9 May 2011 set the Indian Premier League record for the best strike-rate in an innings – one wicket every 1.5 deliveries.

Most matches as umpire

No one has officiated in more Indian Premier League matches than Simon Taufel. The Australian, who has stood in 74 Test matches (since 2000) and 174 one-day internationals (since 1999) has umpired 55 matches in the competition between 2009 and 2013.

HIGHEST PARTNERSHIP BY WICKET

Wkt	Runs	Partners	Team	Opposition	Venue	Date
1st	167	C.H. Gayle, T.M. Dilshan	Bangalore	Pune	Bangalore	23 Apr 2013
2nd	206	A.C. Gilchrist, S.E. Marsh	Punjab	Bangalore	Dhuramsala	17 May 2011
3rd	157	C.L. White, K.C. Sangakkara	Deccan	Pune	Cuttack	1 May 2012
4th	131	C.H. Gayle, A.B. de Villiers	Bangalore	Punjab	Mohali	20 April 2012
5th	130*	O.A. Shah, A.D. Mathews	Kolkata	Deccan	Mumbai	12 Mar 2010
	130*	D.A. Miller, R. Sathish	Punjab	Bangalore	Mohali	6 May 2013
6th	122*	A.T. Rayudu, K.A. Pollard	Mumbai	Bangalore	Bangalore	14 May 20012
7th	65	K.A. Pollard, Harbhajan Singh	Mumbai	Chennai	Chennai	6 Apr 2013
8th	53*	R. McLaren, Harbhajan Singh	Mumbai	Deccan	Mumbai	28 Mar 2010
9th	41	M.S. Dhoni, R. Ashwin	Chennai	Mumbai	Kolkata	26 May 2013
10th	29*	S.K. Trivedi, M.M. Patel	Rajasthan	Delhi	Bloemfontein	17 May 2009

INDEX

CREDITS

The publishers would like to thank the following sources for their kind permission to reproduce the pictures in this book. The page numbers for each of the photographs are listed below, giving the page on which they appear in the book.

Location indicator: (T-top, B-bottom, L-left, R-right).

ABOUT THE AUTHOR

Chris Hawkes is a former youth international cricketer who spent three seasons as a full-time professional with Leicestershire CCC (1990–92). Since retiring as a player, he has worked as a sports writer and editor as well as making several appearances on radio and television as a cricket analyst. He has written several books, including *Cricket World Cup Guide 2007*, The *Official ITV Sport Rugby World Cup Guide 2007*, The *IRB Rugby World Cup Guide 2011*, *Twenty20 Cricket Guide 2009*, *World Rugby Records* and *Winter Sports Records*. He lives in London.